AN ESSENTIAL COURSE IN
MODERN PORTUGUESE

AN ESSENTIAL COURSE
IN
MODERN PORTUGUESE

BY

R. CLIVE WILLIS, M.A., Ph.D.
Senior Lecturer in Portuguese at the University of Manchester

REVISED EDITION

Nelson

Thomas Nelson and Sons Ltd
Nelson House   Mayfield Road
Walton-on-Thames   Surrey KT12 5PL

51 York Place   Edinburgh EH1 3JD

Thomas Nelson (Hong Kong) Ltd
Toppan Building 10/F   22A Westlands Road
Quarry Bay   Hong Kong

Distributed in Australia by

Thomas Nelson Australia
480 La Trobe Street
Melbourne   Victoria 3000
and in Sydney, Brisbane, Adelaide and Perth

ISBN 0-17-445046-X
NPN 04

Printed in Hong Kong

PREFACE

This book was written to answer a long-standing demand: the need for an adult, reasonably detailed and up-to-date teaching grammar of the Portuguese language. As such, it is intended primarily for first-year university students with no previous knowledge of the language. Its aims are therefore the same as those of the work to which it may be regarded as a companion volume, namely *An Essential Course in Modern Spanish* (Harrap, 1959) by my colleague and friend, Professor Herbert Ramsden. Indeed, it is a companion volume in the fullest sense of the term in that, where possible, the above work has been used as a paradigm for many grammatical notes and exercises, and I readily acknowledge my considerable indebtedness to Professor Ramsden for allowing me to use his work as a model.

Because of the somewhat complex phonetic structure of Portuguese, I decided that the problems of pronunciation could only be presented in a scientific manner, and for this reason I have resorted to the alphabet of the International Phonetic Association both in the Introduction and in the body of the lessons. The Introduction presents the principal features of Portuguese pronunciation, while the more difficult or exceptional problems in this field are gradually and progressively presented alongside the grammar in Lessons VII–XXV. In order to offer a comprehensive phonetic pattern it has been found necessary to include the occasional rare word as the only available or suitable example of a particular phenomenon. This need not, however, discourage the student.

Owing to the fact that Portuguese poses rather more syntactical problems than does Spanish, and also owing to the lack of suitable Portuguese reference grammars, it was found necessary to give the language rather fuller treatment than is given to Spanish by Professor Ramsden in his book. Whereas the Ramsden grammar has twenty-five lessons, eight review and development sections

5

and a partial key to the exercises, the present course was expanded to forty lessons, but for reasons of space is without either review and development sections or key. A supplementary section of exercises has been supplied, however, and is aimed at testing each consecutive group of five lessons. Because of the fuller treatment offered, the student is also given an opportunity for practice in continuous passages for translation and prose composition in the exercises of Lessons XXXI–XL.

In drawing up grammatical rules I have based myself solely on an examination of modern texts. On the somewhat vexed question of the collocation of the weak object pronoun, however, I have limited myself in the main to a conservative and traditionalist *exposé* of the problem, bearing in mind that modern departures from the more accepted norms are largely a matter of style or euphony. In the field of accidence and morphology I have sought to give a fairly comprehensive treatment, although no attempt is made to give an exhaustive survey either of the irregular forms of the absolute superlative, or of the irregular nouns and adjectives ending in *-ão*; moreover, I have not discussed ordinal numerals beyond *décimo*. The student will find that any queries that might arise in these respects can readily be answered by intelligent use of a good Portuguese dictionary. On the issue of orthography and the written accent I have referred exclusively to the fourteenth edition of the *Prontuário de Ortografia* of António da Costa Leão (Lisbon, 1955), and in the field of pronunciation I have been guided in the main by the ever useful *Exposição da Pronúncia Normal Portuguesa* of Aniceto dos Reis Gonçalves Vianna (Lisbon, 1892). Conscious of the new momentum in the field of Latin-American Studies, I have also included an appendix on educated Brazilian usage.

My list of acknowledgments is a long one, but I would like to express especial gratitude to Mr Norman J. Lamb of Liverpool University (who originally conceived the idea for this work) and to Professor Ramsden, who have at all stages been a constant source of encouragement and scholarly advice. My sincere thanks for reading, checking, criticizing and correcting the typescript are due to these and also to Sra. Dídia Marques Reckert, formerly of Cardiff University, Dr S. George West of the British Council and Dr Luís de Sousa Rebelo of King's College, London. My thanks are also due to my colleague Dr Giovanni Pontiero and to Dr Raul Moreira Léllis of the Casa do Brasil for advice on the Brazilian Appendix. For various suggestions, words of encouragement and help in so many ways I am also grateful to Dr Hermilo Branco Ramalhete of the Instituto de Alta Cultura, Dr António Duarte of the Instituto Britânico in Lisbon, Mrs Selma Pousão Smith, formerly of Leeds University, Sr. António dos Santos Tavares of Liverpool University, and Dr Heinz Kroell of the University of Mainz. I am further indebted to Mrs Nancy Stålhammar for help with the typescript and to my colleagues Dr Gerald B. Gybbon-Monypenny and Mr Derek H. Gagen, who kindly agreed to assist me in the task of reading the proofs. Finally, and very especially, I have to express my gratitude to my friends of the Luso-Brazilian Council at Canning House and to the Calouste Gulbenkian Foundation respectively for arranging and making a most welcome grant towards the publication of this book.

R.C.W.

PREFACE TO THE SECOND EDITION

This second edition takes account of the many helpful suggestions of teachers and reviewers, has sought to simplify the phonetics of Portuguese on a more phonemic basis and includes the norms of the *Acordo Ortográfico* signed in Brasília in April 1971.   R.C.W.

CONTENTS

9

*The Portuguese Alphabet, Phonetics, Pronuncia-
tion, Liaison and Elision, Word Stress, the
Written Accent, Proclitics and Enclitics*

INTRODUCTION

*(The student should read this introduction and ensure that he under-
stands it before tackling Lesson I. Owing to the complexities of
Portuguese pronunciation, however, he should not attempt at this
stage to assimilate everything in it.)*

1. THE PORTUGUESE ALPHABET. This comprises the following
twenty-three letters:

Letter	Name	Letter	Name	Letter	Name
a	á	i	i	r	ęrre
b	bê	j	jǫta	s	ęsse
c	cê	l	ęle	t	tê
d	dê	m	ęme	u	u
e	é	n	ęne	v	vê
f	ęfe	o	ó	x	xis
g	gê	p	pê	z	zê
h	agá	q	quê		

NOTES. 1. All the letters are *masculine* in gender.

2. The letters **k** (capa), **w** (vê duplo) and **y** (ípsilǫn) are not found
in native Portuguese words, except in abbreviations for weights,
measures and chemical elements.

3. The digraphs **ch** (cê agá), **lh** (ęle agá) and **nh** (ęne agá) should
properly be regarded as individual signs in the alphabet, since they
denote simple sounds. A simple sound is also represented by **ç**
(**c** with a cedilla, *Portuguese* cê cedilhado).

13

2. TABLES OF PHONETIC SYMBOLS.   The symbols employed are those of the International Phonetic Association (IPA) and except in this paragraph will always appear between square brackets.

(a) Oral Vowels

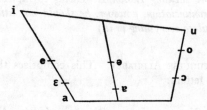

The sequence a, ε, e, i consists of *front* vowels (*i.e.*, pronounced at the front of the mouth) which are in series from the most *open* (a) to the most *closed* (i).   The terms *open* and *closed* refer to the position of the lips.   The sequence ɔ, o, u consists of *back* vowels (*i.e.*, pronounced at the back of the mouth), which are in series from the most *open* (ɔ) to the most *closed* (u). ɐ and ə are mixed or neutral vowels.

(b) Nasal Vowels

There are five nasal vowels: ẽ, ẽ, ĩ, õ, ũ.   They are the nasal counterparts of five of the oral vowels given above.

(c) Consonants

	Bi-labials		Labio-dentals		Dentals		Alveo-lars		Palatals		Velars	
Plosives	p	b			t	d					k	g
Fricatives			f	v		đ				j		w
Laterals								l		ʎ		
Nasals		m						n		ɲ		ŋ
Vibrants							r, rr					ɹ
Sibilants					s	z			ʃ	ʒ		

NOTES. 1. The alternate vertical columns indicate unvoiced and voiced consonants in that order.

2. j and w represent semi-consonants and semi-vowels.

3. EXAMPLES OF PHONETIC SYMBOLS.[1]

[a] a very open vowel between the *a* of Standard English *cat* and *father* (cf. the *a* of Northern English *cat, mat*): **lado** [ˈlaɖu].

[ɛ] a very open vowel like *e* in Northern English *jet* or *sell*: **ęla**[2] [ˈɛlɐ].

[e] a closed vowel, like *ey* in *they*, but without the English final [j] glide: **dęvo**[2] [ˈdevu].

[i] a closed vowel like *ee* in *seen*, but shorter and sharper: **mínimo** [ˈminimu].

[ɔ] an open vowel like *o* in *jolly*: **gǫsta** [ˈgɔʃtɐ].

---

[1] These symbols will from now on appear in square brackets. The stressed syllable is indicated by a preceding vertical stroke (ˈ).

[2] Throughout this work when a hook appears below a Portuguese vowel it indicates that the vowel is open (**ąparte, ęla, ǫlhos**); a dot below a vowel indicates that it is closed (**pąra, ęle, ǫlho**). These subscripts are included for didactic purposes only.

[o] a closed vowel like *o* in *note*, but without the English final [w] glide: **boca** [ˈbokɐ].

[u] a closed vowel like *oo* in *root*: **cru** [kru].

[ɐ] a neutral vowel between the *a* of Standard English *bad* and *idea*: **cama** [ˈkɐmɐ].

[ə] a neutral vowel like the second *e* in *general*: **pedir** [pəˈdir].

[ɐ̃], [ẽ], [ĩ], [õ], [ũ] indicate the nasal vowels that correspond to the oral vowels described above.

[p] unvoiced bilabial plosive like *p* in *petrol*: **pata** [ˈpatɐ].

[b] voiced bilabial plosive like *b* in *bad*: **bago** [ˈbagu].

[t] unvoiced dental plosive like *t* in *tug*, but less aspirate and with tongue against top front teeth: **tarifa** [tɐˈrifɐ].

[d] voiced dental plosive like *d* in *dog*, but less aspirate and with tongue against top front teeth: **dava** [ˈdavɐ].

[k] unvoiced velar plosive like *c* in *cat*: **caso** [ˈkazu].

[g] voiced velar plosive like *g* in *good*: **gato** [ˈgatu].

[f] unvoiced labiodental fricative like *f* in *fat*: **fala** [ˈfalɐ].

[v] voiced labiodental fricative like *v* in *vase*: **vinho** [ˈviɲu].

[đ] voiced dental fricative midway between *d* in *dog* and like *th* in *this*: **sęda** [ˈseđɐ].

[j] voiced palatal fricative semi-vowel like *y* in *play*: **vai** [vaj].

[w] voiced velar fricative
   { semi-consonant like *w* in *wet*: **qual** [kwal].
   { semi-vowel like *w* in *mower*: **pau** [paw].

[l] voiced alveolar lateral like *l* in *let*: **lua** [ˈluɐ].

[ʎ] voiced palatal lateral like the *lli* in *million*, but with the *l* and *y* sounds more closely associated: **filho** [ˈfiʎu].

[m] voiced bilabial nasal like *m* in *mat*: **mapa** [ˈmapɐ].

[n] voiced alveolar nasal like *n* in *net*: **nata** [ˈnatɐ].

[ɲ] voiced palatal nasal like *ni* in *onion*, but with the *n* and *y* sounds more closely associated: **ninho** [ˈniɲu].

[ŋ] voiced velar nasal like the *n* in *bank* or *sing*: **cinco** [ˈsĩŋku].

[r] voiced alveolar vibrant like the trilled *r* of Scots *bread*: **cara** [ˈkarɐ].

[rr] voiced alveolar vibrant like the foregoing but with a multiple trill: **carro** [ˈkarru].

[ɹɹ] voiced velar vibrant like [rr] but pronounced at the back of
      the mouth. It is a variant of [rr], found mainly in Lisbon
      and Setúbal and throughout Brazil: **carro** [ˈkaɹɹu].

[s]   unvoiced dental sibilant like *s* in *sat*: **saco** [ˈsaku].

[z]   voiced dental sibilant like *z* in *zebra*: **zẹlo** [ˈzelu].

[ʃ]   unvoiced palatal sibilant like *sh* in *shout*: **chuva** [ˈʃuvɐ].

[ʒ]   voiced palatal sibilant like *s* in *measure*: **jọgo** [ˈʒogu].

[j]   and [w̃] indicate the nasalized semi-vowels that correspon
      to [j] and [w] above.

4. PRONUNCIATION OF VOWELS IN PORTUGUESE. Owing to the
complexity of the Portuguese vocalic system, only the broad out-
lines are given here. Amplification will be found in later paragraphs throughout the course of the book. For didactic purposes, where the information given in this Introduction is in-
sufficient, a dot will be placed beneath a vowel to indicate that it
is closed, and a hook to indicate that it is open. Where it is not
possible to clarify the pronunciation by this method, a phonetic
transcription of all or part of the word will be supplied. These
aids to pronunciation will *not*, however, appear in the exercises.

In considering the pronunciation of the vowels in Portuguese,
it is of paramount importance to understand the function of *stress*.
For example, in the following English words, the stressed vowel
is written in italics: f*a*mily, fam*i*liar, famili*a*rity. Nearly all
Portuguese words have a stressed vowel or syllable. The only
exceptions are a number of atonic (*i.e.*, unstressed) monosyllables
and disyllables of a proclitic or enclitic nature [see § 9].

(a) Oral Vowels

Stressed **a.** Normally [a]: **casa** [ˈkazɐ], **parte** [ˈpartə];
                   before **m, n, nh** (all followed by another vowel) it
                   has the value [ɐ]: **cama** [ˈkɐmɐ], **ano** [ˈɐnu], **banho**
                   [ˈbɐɲu].

Unstressed **a.** Normally [ɐ]: **sabẹr** [sɐˈber], **tẹrra** [ˈtɛrrɐ].

Stressed **e.** Normally either [e]: **mesa** [ˈmezɐ], **ele** [ˈelə]; or [ɛ]: **pedra** [ˈpɛdrɐ], **ela** [ˈɛlɐ].

Unstressed **e.** Normally [ə]: **pedir** [pəˈdir], **arte** [ˈartə]. At the end of a word it is very faint indeed.

Stressed **i.** Always [i]: **vida** [ˈvidɐ], **triste** [ˈtriʃtə].

Unstressed **i.** Normally [i]: **dizer** [diˈzer], **igual** [iˈgwal].

Stressed **o.** Always either [o]: **todo** [ˈtodu], **boca** [ˈbokɐ]; or [ɔ]: **nove** [ˈnɔvə], **bola** [ˈbɔlɐ].

Unstressed **o.** Normally [u]: **dormir** [durˈmir], **puro** [ˈpuru]. At the end of a word it is rather faint and is usually reduced to a mere pursing of the lips.

Stressed **u.** Always [u]: **nu** [nu], **durmo** [ˈdurmu].

Unstressed **u.** Normally [u]: **mulher** [muˈʎɛr], **unir** [uˈnir].

(b) Oral Diphthongs

An oral diphthong is a combination of an oral vowel with a following **i** or **u** or with a preceding **gu** or **qu** in those cases where the **u** is uttered:

mais [majʃ], **maior** [mɐjˈɔr], **seu** [sew], **oito** [ˈojtu], **igual** [iˈgwal], **qual** [kwal].

The oral digraph **ou** is not a true diphthong in the standard pronunciation, since it has the phonetic value [o] in stressed *and* unstressed positions.

(c) Nasal Vowels and Nasal Diphthongs

Vowels and diphthongs in Portuguese are nasalized in the following circumstances:

(i) when a **til** (˜) is placed over a vowel;
(ii) when a word ends in **-m** or **-ns;**
(iii) when a vowel is followed by **m** + consonant;
(iv) when a vowel is followed by **n** + consonant, other than the digraph **nh,** and other than **-ns** at the end of a word [see above (ii)].

NOTE: Considerations of stress are unimportant in the pronunciation of nasals.

Letter	Phonetic Symbol	Circumstances
a	[ẽ]	-ã, a (+m+consonant), a (+n+consonant): lã [lẽ], campo ['kẽmpu], bando ['bẽndu].
	[ɐw̃]	-ão and -am: são [sɐw̃], falam ['falɐw̃].
	[ɐj]	-ãe and ãi: mãe [mɐj], cãibra ['kɐjmbrɐ].
e	[ẽ]	e (+m+consonant), e (+n+consonant): tempo ['tẽmpu], vender [vẽn'der].
	[ɐj]	-em and -ens: virgem ['virʒɐj], tens [tɐjʃ].
i	[ĩ]	i (+m+consonant), i (+n+consonant), -im and -ins: limpo ['lĩmpu], hindu [ĩn'du], fim [fĩ], patins [pɐ'tĩʃ].
o	[õ]	o (+m+consonant), o (+n+consonant), -om and -ons: pombo ['põmbu], pondo ['põndu], bom [bõ], bons [bõʃ].
	[oj]	-õe: põe [poj], nações [nɐ'sojʃ].
u	[ũ]	u (+m+consonant), u (+n+consonant), -um and -uns: chumbo ['ʃũmbu], fundo ['fũndu], um [ũ], comuns [ku'mũʃ].

NOTES. 1. põem ['pojɐj], têm ['tɐjɐj] mui [muj], muito ['mujntu].

2. In [ɐw̃], [ɐj], [oj], [uj] the *nasal resonance* is almost totally on the *second* half of the diphthong. It should be most carefully noted, however, that the actual *stress* falls on the *first* half of these four nasal diphthongs. The pronunciation of the following words should, however, be noted:

Bombaim [bõmbɐ'ĩ], Caim [kɐ'ĩ], ruim [rru'ĩ] [see § 7 (h)].

5. PRONUNCIATION OF CONSONANTS IN PORTUGUESE.

Letter or Digraph	Phonetic Symbol	When used
b	[b]	always: bastante [bɐʃ'tẽntɐ], ambos ['ẽmbuʃ] caber [kɐ'ber], sobre ['sobrɐ], sob [sob].
c	[s]	followed by e or i, or written with a cedilla before other vowels: certo ['sɛrtu], cinco

Letter or Digraph	Phonetic Symbol	When used
		['sĩŋku], **começar** [kumə'sar], **aço** ['asu], **açude** [ɐ'suđə].
	[k]	elsewhere: **ficar** [fi'kar], **comęr** [ku'mer], **custar** [kuʃ'tar], **claro** ['klaru], **cręr** [krer]. But before **t** or soft **c** [s] it is generally silent. For a full account of this see § 87.
ch	[ʃ]	always: **achar** [ɐ'ʃar], **chovęr** [ʃu'ver].
d	[d]	at the beginning of a word, or after a nasal consonant, or after **l: dou** [do], **anda** ['ĕndɐ], **mǫlde** ['mɔldə].
	[đ]	elsewhere: **sęda** ['seđɐ], **adro** ['ađru].
f	[f]	always: **fǫme** ['fɔmə], **defęsa** [də'fezɐ].
g	[ʒ]	followed by **e** or **i: gente** ['ʒĕntə], **surgir** [sur'ʒir].
	[g]	elsewhere: **grande** ['grĕndə], **ganga** ['gĕŋgɐ], **paga** ['pagɐ], **magro** ['magru]. In the groups **gue** and **gui**, the **u** is not normally pronounced. For a full account of this see § 99.
h	nil	This letter has no sound and no phonetic value except in the digraphs **ch** [ʃ], **lh** [ʎ], **nh** [ɲ]. Other than in the exclamations **ah!, eh!** and **oh!** it is always initial: **havęr** [ɐ'ver], **mal-humorado** [mal umu'rađu].
j	[ʒ]	always: **ajudar** [ɐʒu'đar], **janęla** [ʒɐ'nɛlɐ].
l	[l]	always: **luz** [luʃ], **cavalo** [kɐ'valu], **claro** ['klaru], **sal** [sal], **ręlva** ['rrɛlvɐ].
lh	[ʎ]	always: **ilha** ['iʎɐ], **ǫlho** ['oʎu].
m	[m]	at the beginning of a word, or between two vowels, or after a consonant, or before **b** or **p: męl** [mɛl], **cama** ['kɐmɐ], **calma** ['kalmɐ], **arma** ['armɐ], **sombra** ['sõmbrɐ], **sempre** ['sĕmprə]. Note that when before **b** or **p, m** also indicates a nasal resonance on the preceding vowel.

Letter or Digraph	Phonetic Symbol	When used
	nil	final: no consonantal value, but merely indicates a nasal resonance on the preceding vowel. Note that **-am** is [ɐw̃] and **-em** is [ɐj̃]. See § 4 (c).
n	[n]	at the beginning or end of a word, or between two vowels, or after a consonant, or before **d** or **t**: **novo** [ˈnovu], **hífen** [ˈifen], **ano** [ˈɐnu], **digno** [ˈdignu], **asno** [ˈaʒnu], **onde** [ˈõndə], **dente** [ˈdẽntə]. Note that when before **d** or **t**, **n** also indicates a nasal resonance on the preceding vowel.
	[ŋ]	before [k] or [g]: **branco** [ˈbrẽŋku], **bengala** [bẽŋˈgalɐ], **tango** [ˈtẽŋgu], **arenque** [ɐˈrẽŋkə]. Note that when before [k] or [g], **n** also indicates a nasal resonance on the preceding vowel.
	nil	before any other consonant: no consonantal value, but merely indicates a nasal resonance on the preceding vowel: **presença** [prəˈzẽsɐ], **ancho** [ˈẽʃu], **arranjar** [ɐrrẽˈʒar], **conflito** [kõˈflitu], **tenro** [ˈtẽrru], **senso** [ˈsẽsu], **convite** [kõˈvitə], **bons** [bõʃ]. See § 4 (c).
nh	[ɲ]	always: **vinho** [ˈviɲu], **banho** [ˈbɐɲu].
p	[p]	always: **mapa** [ˈmapɐ], **passar** [pɐˈsar]. But before **t** or soft **c** [s] it is often silent. For a full account of this see § 82.
q	[k]	always: **quando** [ˈkwẽndu], **quatro** [ˈkwatru]. It is always followed by **u**. In the groups **que** and **qui** the **u** is not normally pronounced. For a full account of this see § 99.
r	[r]	between two vowels, or before or after a consonant (except after **l, n, s**), or in the final position: **cara** [ˈkarɐ], **branco** [ˈbrẽŋku], **parte** [ˈpartə], **largo** [ˈlargu], **comprar** [kõmˈprar].

Letter or Digraph	Phonetic Symbol	When used
	[rr]	at the beginning of a word, or when written double, or when preceded by **l**, or **n**, or **s**: **rua** [ˈrruɐ], **carro** [ˈkarru], **melro** [ˈmɛlrru], **honra** [ˈõrrɐ], **Israel** [ˌiʒrrɐˈɛl].

NOTE: for [ɹɹ] see p. 17.

s	[s]	at the beginning of a word, or after a consonant (normally), or when written double: **sentir** [sẽnˈtir], **pulso** [ˈpulsu], **passo** [ˈpasu].
	[z]	when between two vowels: **caso** [ˈkazu], **mesa** [ˈmezɐ].
	[ʃ]	before an unvoiced consonant, or when final: **fresco** [ˈfreʃku], **nascer** [nɐʃˈser], **asfalto** [ɐʃˈfaltu], **cuspir** [kuʃˈpir], **busque** [ˈbuʃkə], **gostar** [guʃˈtar], **porcos** [ˈpɔrkuʃ].
	[ʒ]	before a voiced consonant: **asbesto** [ɐʒˈbɛʃtu], **desde** [ˈdeʒdə], **rasgar** [rrɐʒˈgar], **jugoslavo** [ʒuguʒˈlavu], **mesmo** [ˈmeʒmu], **asno** [ˈaʒnu], **Israel** [ˌiʒrrɐˈɛl], **transverso** [trẽʒˈvɛrsu].
t	[t]	always: **tudo** [ˈtuðu], **sete** [ˈsɛtə].
v	[v]	always: **vida** [ˈviðɐ], **livro** [ˈlivru].
x		see § 60.
z	[z]	at the beginning of a word, or between vowels: **zelo** [ˈzelu], **fazer** [fɐˈzer].
	[ʃ]	when final: **voz** [vɔʃ], **faz** [faʃ].

6. LIAISON AND ELISION IN WORD-GROUPS. The observations in §§ 4 and 5 are concerned with the pronunciation of the individual word. But Portuguese is characterized by the running together in pronunciation of words linked closely within a given sentence, unlike educated English where a momentary pause or glottal stop may be introduced to prevent the fusion of words (*an/awful/accident* as opposed to *a—nawfu—laccident*).

(a) Vowels with vowels

The final vowel of a word normally forms a smooth liaison with the initial vowel of a following word. If the two vowels are *phonetically* identical, a single vowel-sound results, slightly lengthened in quality, *e.g.*, **filho humilde** ['fiʎu] plus [u'mildə] becomes ['fiʎ-u'mildə] with lengthening of the [u]. The following cases should, however, be carefully noted:

Two **a**'s (open or closed) produce [a]: **minha amada** ['miɲa'madɐ]; **minha arte** ['miɲ-'artə].

If there is nasalization present, they produce [ã][1]: **via ambos** ['vi-'ãmbuʃ].

Final [ɐ] drops before stressed **e** and may do before stressed **o**: **ela era** ['ɛl-'ɛrɐ]; **nova obra** ['nɔv-'ɔɓrɐ] or ['nɔvɐ 'ɔɓrɐ].

Final [ɐ] joins with unstressed **o** to form [ɔ]: **nova ocasião** ['nɔv-ɔkɐ'ziɐ̃w̃].

Final [ə] drops before an unstressed vowel: **deve haver** ['dɛv-ɐ'ver].

Final [ə] either drops or becomes [i] before a stressed vowel: **nove horas** ['nɔvi-'ɔrɐʃ].

NOTE: The final -**e** of the words **que, porque, quase, treze, se** (*the conjunction only*) is always [i] before a word beginning with a vowel, be that vowel stressed or unstressed: **tenho que ouvir** ['tɐɲu ki-o'vir]; **diz que era** ['diʃ ki-'ɛrɐ]; **treze escudos** ['trezi-əʃ'kuðuʃ].

(b) Vowels or **r** with **d**

When the preceding word ends in an *oral* vowel or **r**, initial [d] becomes [ð]:

    quando dobrado ['kwɐ̃ndu-ðuɓ'raðu], **favor dado** [fɐ'vor-'ðaðu].

---

[1] These are the only circumstances in which [ã] is found in Portuguese.

(c) Sibilants with vowels and consonants

Final [ʃ] becomes [z] before a vowel: **meus olhos** [ˈmewz-ˈɔʎuʃ], **faz isso** [ˈfaz-ˈisu].

Final [ʃ] becomes [ʒ] before a voiced consonant other than [rr], [ʀ], [z], [ʒ]: **estas boas meninas** [ˈɛʃtɐʒ-ˈboɐʒ-məˈninɐʃ], **duas velhas duquesas** [ˈduɐʒ-ˈvɛʎɐʒ-đuˈkezɐʃ], **faz gritar** [ˈfaʒ-griˈtar].

Final [ʃ] tends with most speakers to drop from pronunciation before [rr], [ʀ], [z], [ʒ], [ʃ]: **dez rosas** [ˈdɛ-ˈrrozɐʃ], **duas zonas** [ˈduɐ-ˈzonɐʃ], **dois generais** [ˈdoj-ʒənəˈrajʃ], **dois jogos** [ˈdoj-ˈʒɔɠuʃ], **duas charruas** [ˈduɐ-ʃɐˈrruɐʃ].

7. Stress. *(a)* Words ending in **-a, -as; -e, es; -o, -os; -am; -em, -ens,** are stressed on the *syllable next to the last* (or *penult*):

mesa, mesas; lente, lentes; livro, livros; compram; virgem, virgens.

(b) The penult may be an immediately preceding **i** or **u** which is accordingly stressed:

filosofia, continuas; pronuncie, pronuncies; gentio, navios; constituam; pronunciem, continuem.

(c) If in a word with one of the above endings the penult contains one of the diphthongs **ai, ei, oi; au, eu, ou; iu, ui,** the *first* vowel of the diphthong is stressed. Note the standard pronunciation of **ou** [o]; it is, however, pronounced [ow] in certain regions; **ei** is usually pronounced [ɐj]; in a limited number of words ending in **-eia** and all those in **-eico** it is [ɛj].

paira, leite [ˈlɐjtə], **ideia** [iˈdɛjɐ], **toiro; pausa, deusa, outro; ruivo.**

(d) If, however, a vowel-group as in *(c)* is followed by **mb; nd, nf, nh, nt; rd, rm; u,** the *second* of the vowels is stressed:

Coimbra; ainda, triunfo, moinho, transeunte; sairdes, sairmos; saiu.

(e) If in a word with one of the endings as in (a), the two preceding syllables consist of one of the vowel-groups **ia, ię, iǫ, iǫ;
oa, oę, oę; ua, uę**, the *second* vowel of the group is stressed:

**Diana, diabo, dięta, miǫlo, miǫlos; Joana, poęma,
moęda; continuava, suęco.**

(f) Words ending in one of the diphthongs **-ai, -ei** [ɐj]; **-au,
-ęu, -ou; -ui, -iu; -ão, -ãe, -õe**, whether followed by **s** or not,
are stressed on the *first* vowel of the diphthong:

**recai, finais, comprei, vendeis; grau, degraus, judęu,
atęus, falou; fui, pauis, saiu; irmão, irmãos, compõe,
nações.**

(g) If, however, a vowel-group as in (f) is followed by final **l,
r**, or **z**, the stress falls on the *second* vowel of the group: **paul,
cair, juiz.**

(h) Words ending in **-i, -is** [except as in (f)]; **-u, -us** [except as
in (f)]; **-im, -ins; -um, -uns; -om, -ons; -ã, -ãs; -b, -c, -d, -l,
-n, -r, -x, -z**, are stressed on the *last* syllable:

**aqui, partis; hindu, compus; jardim, jardins; comum,
comuns; bombom, bombons; irmã, irmãs; Jacǫb, David,
animal, falar, rapaz.**

8. WRITTEN ACCENTS. Words not stressed according to the
principles of § 7 must bear a written accent on the stressed vowel.
There are three written accents in Portuguese, the *acute* (´), the
circumflex (^) and the *grave* (`). The last of these is limited in
use, and will be discussed in § 166. As stressed **i** and stressed **u**
do not vary in quality, only the acute accent is used on them.
But as stressed **a, e** and **o** have two distinct qualities each, the
acute accent is used when they are *open*, and the *circumf*lex when
they are *closed*. Exceptional are the stressed endings **-ém** [ɐj]
and **-éns** [ɐjʃ], where an acute accent is used on a *closed* nasal
diphthong.

(a) *Examples of words not stressed according to* § 7 (a):

comprará, venderás, maré, inglês, avó, avós, avôs, ninguém, armazéns.

(b) *Examples contrary to* § 7 (b):

importância, pronúncia, tragédia, literário, mútuo, água.

(c) *Examples contrary to* § 7 (c):

saída, caía, deísta, roído, saúde, amiúde, ciúme, miúdo, viúvo, juízes, ruído.

(d) *Examples contrary to* § 7 (e):

Lusíadas, Calíope, medíocre, período.

(e) *Examples contrary to* § 7 (f):

compráveis, úteis, bênção; aí, país, baú.

(f) *Examples contrary to* § 7 (h):

táxi [-ks-]**, vírus, órfã, órfãs, cônsul, hífẹn, açúcạr, clímạx** [-ks].

(g) Words stressed on the third from the last syllable (*antepenult*) must also bear a written accent:

pântano, cenáculo, pêssego, décuplo, aprendêssemos, déssemos, física, cômoro, cómico, único.

(h) The acute and circumflex accents are required in some words where they are not necessary for indicating stress, though indeed they *are* used on the stressed syllable:

(i) The acute accent is required on **e** and **o** in the stressed open diphthongs **ẹi, ọi** and **ẹu** in order to distinguish them from the stressed closed diphthongs **ei** [ɐj]**, oi** and **ẹu**:

papéis, sóis, céu; *contrast* **vendeis, sọis, sẹu.**

Note, however, that *no* acute accent is written on **combọio, dezọito,** or words ending in **-ẹia** or **-ẹico,** *e.g.*, **idẹia, platẹia, ọnomatopẹico.** This practice is due to regional varieties of pronunciation, where the vowel may be closed.

(ii) The acute or circumflex accents are required (according as the vowel is *open* or *closed*) on stressed monosyllables ending in -a, -as; -e, -es; -o, -os:

má, pás; sé, sê, dê, dês, mês, três; pó, pós, pôs.

(iii) The acute accent is also required on the following words:
the noun-forms: **péla, pélas; pólo, pólos.**
the verb-forms: **pélo, pélas, péla; pára; -ámos** [-ˈamuʃ].

(iv) The circumflex accent is also required on the following words:

the noun-forms: **Pêro, Pêra, Côa; pêlo, pêlos; pôlo, pôlos; pêra; pêro.**

the verb-forms: **côas, côa; pôde; dêmos, dêem; lêem; crêem; vêem; pôr; têm, contêm, mantêm,** etc. **vêm, convêm, intervêm,** etc.

NOTES. 1. The accents in (iii) and (iv) are to avoid confusion with certain words otherwise orthographically identical.
2. See also §§ 210–219.

9. PROCLITIC AND ENCLITIC WORDS.   The following words carry no stress and cannot stand alone.   They must precede (*proclitic*) or follow (*enclitic*) some other word to which they are closely syntactically linked.   For this reason their vowels are in the main pronounced according to the rules for unstressed vowels:

o [u], **a** [ɐ], **os** [uʃ], **as** [ɐʃ];
me [mə], **te** [tə], **se** [sə], **nos** [nuʃ], **vos,** [vuʃ], **lhe** [ʎə], **lhes** [ʎəʃ];
que [kə], **porque** [purkə], **se** [sə];
em [ɐ̃j], **a** [ɐ], **de** [də], **por** [pur], **pạra** [p(ɐ)rɐ];
e [i], **mạs** [mɐʃ];
cạda [kɐdɐ].

Pronunciation, the Noun, the Definite and Indefinite Articles, the Three Verb Conjugations (Present Indicative), Contraction of A, DE *and* EM *with the Definite Article, Contraction of* DE *and* EM *with the Indefinite Article*

LESSON I

10. PRONUNCIATION. Read and study §§ 4–6. Read also the words listed in the vocabulary at the end of the lesson.

11. THE NOUN. Nouns in Portuguese are either masculine (**livro**, *book*; **rapaz**, *boy*) or feminine (**caneta**, *pen*; **mulher**, *woman*). The plural form of nouns ending in a vowel (other than **-ão**) is obtained by adding **-s** to the singular (**livros**, *books*; **canetas**, *pens*); **-es** when it ends in **-r** or **-z** (**rapazes**, *boys*; **mulheres**, *women*).

12. THE DEFINITE ARTICLE. This has various forms in Portuguese: it is **o** [u] before a masculine singular noun, **os** [uʃ] before a masculine plural noun, **a** [ɐ] before a feminine singular noun, and **as** [ɐʃ] before a feminine plural noun.

o livro, the book	**os livros**, the books
o rapaz, the boy	**os rapazes**, the boys
a caneta, the pen	**as canetas**, the pens
a mulher, the woman	**as mulheres**, the women

13. THE INDEFINITE ARTICLE. **Um** is used before a masculine singular noun; **uma** before a feminine singular noun.

um livro, a book	**livros**, books
um rapaz, a boy	**rapazes**, boys
uma caneta, a pen	**canetas**, pens
uma mulher, a woman	**mulheres**, women

NOTE: There is no Portuguese equivalent of the French partitive article: **vinho**, *wine* (Fr. *du vin*), **casas**, *houses* (Fr. *des maisons*).

29

14. VERBS: THE THREE CONJUGATIONS. There are three classes (or conjugations) of verbs in Portuguese: those whose infinitive (English *to* —) ends in **-ar** belong to the first conjugation (**comprar**, *to buy*; **passar**, *to pass*), those ending in **-er** belong to the second conjugation (**vender**, *to sell*; **aprender**, *to learn*) and those in **-ir** belong to the third conjugation (**partir**, *to depart*; **unir**, *to unite*).

15. VERBS: THE PRESENT INDICATIVE. The present indicative tense is formed by adding to the stem (the infinitive minus **-ar**, **-er** or **-ir**) certain personal endings:

  I. **-ar** verbs take **-o, -as, -a, -amos, -ais, -am.**

  II. **-er** verbs take **-o, -es, -e, -emos, -eis**[1]**, -em.**

  III. **-ir** verbs take **-o, -es, -e, -imos, -is, -em.**

I. *infinitive*: **comprar** (to buy) *stem*: **compr-**

Singular

first person:	**compro**	I buy, do buy, am buying
second person:	**compras** **você compra** **o senhor compra** **a senhora compra**	you buy, do buy, are buying
third person:	**compra**	he (she, it) buys, does buy, is buying

Plural

first person:	**compramos**	we buy, do buy, are buying
second person:	**comprais** **vocês compram** **os senhores compram** **as senhoras compram**	you buy, do buy, are buying
third person:	**compram**	they buy, do buy, are buying

[1] [-ɐjʃ].

30

II. *infinitive:* **vendẹr** (to sell)   *stem:* **vend-**
Singular

first person:	**vendo**	I sell, do sell, am selling
second person:	**vendes** **vọcê vende** **o senhọr vende** **a senhọra vende** }	you sell, do sell, are selling
third person:	**vende**	he, (she, it) sells, does sell, is selling

Plural

first person:	**vendẹmos**	we sell, do sell, are selling
second person:	**vendeis** [-ɐjʃ] **vọcês vendem** **os senhọres vendem** **as senhọras vendem** }	you sell, do sell, are selling
third person:	**vendem**	they sell, do sell, are selling

III. *infinitive:* **partir** (to depart)   *stem:* **part-**
Singular

first person:	**parto**	I depart, do depart, am departing
second person:	**partes** **vọcê parte** **o senhọr parte** **a senhọra parte** }	you depart, do depart, are departing
third person:	**parte**	he (she, it) departs, does de-depart, is departing

31

Plural

first person: **partimos** we depart, do depart, are departing

second person: $\begin{cases} \textbf{partis} \\ \textbf{vocês partem} \\ \textbf{os senhores partem} \\ \textbf{as senhoras partem} \end{cases}$ you depart, do depart, are departing

third person: **partem** they depart, do depart, are departing

NOTES. 1. The pronoun subject is not usually expressed in Portuguese but is indicated in the verb ending.

Compro uma casa. I buy (do buy, am buying) a house.
Vendemos o livro. We sell the book.
Partem para Londres. They depart for London.

It is usual, however, to express the subjects **você, o senhor, a senhora** (*you*, sing.) and **vocês, os senhores** and **as senhoras** (*you*, pl.).

2. There are many ways of rendering the second person in Portuguese; only the most common are dealt with here. Such forms as **compras, vendes** and **partes** are used in very familiar speech, as between husband and wife, from parent to child or between very intimate friends, and to animals (such as horses, dogs, etc.). They are also used in poetry and in prayers to the Deity. The **você** forms are used between friends, or to a subordinate. The forms **o senhor** (masculine) and **a senhora** (feminine) are those used in normal polite conversation. In the plural, such forms as **comprais, vendeis** and **partis** are nowadays rare, and are confined to public speeches, sermons, etc., and in prayers to the Deity, particularly in the Roman Catholic Church.[1] The **vocês** forms are employed *both* as the plural of the **você** forms, *and* as the plural of such forms as **compras, vendes** and **partes**. The **os senhores** forms (masculine, or masculine with feminine), and the **as senhoras** forms (feminine) are, like their singular counterparts, employed in normal polite conversation.

3. **Você, vocês, o senhor, a senhora, os senhores** and **as senhoras** always take the same verb endings as the third person.

---

[1] These forms will be referred to as the *restricted* form of address.

4. **O senhor,** etc., may be abbreviated in writing to **o Sr., a Sra., os Srs., as Sras.** The pronunciation is not affected.

5. The pretonic vowel of **você** and **vocês** is open [ɔ].

6. Remember that such forms as **compram, vendem** and **partem** are stressed on the penultimate syllable, *not* on the final syllable.

16. A, de AND **em** WITH THE DEFINITE ARTICLE. The forms of the definite article combine with the prepositions **a** (*to*), **de** (*of, from, about*), **em** (*in, at*) as follows:

a+o:ao [aw]	**a+os:aos** [awʃ]
a+a:à [a]	**a+as:às** [aʃ]
de+o:do [du]	**de+os:dos** [duʃ]
de+a:da [dɐ]	**de+as:das** [dɐʃ]
em+o:no [nu]	**em+os:nos** [nuʃ]
em+a:na [nɐ]	**em+as:nas** [nɐʃ]

NOTE: Some writers prefer to write **no,** etc., in full: **em o,** etc. Nevertheless they must be pronounced as though contraction had taken place.

17. De AND **em** WITH THE INDEFINITE ARTICLE. The forms of the indefinite article combine with the prepositions **de** and **em** as follows:

de+um:dum	**de+uma:duma**
em+um:num	**em+uma:numa**

NOTES. 1. Some writers prefer to write the above in full: **de um, em um,** etc. Nevertheless they must normally be pronounced as though contraction had taken place.

2. **De um,** etc., is, however, sometimes emphatic:

De um [di-ũ] **destes homens só posso dizer que é um patife.** With regard to *one* of these men I can only say he's a scoundrel.

18. USE OF **de.** The English *'s* and *s'* are translated into Portuguese by means of the preposition **de** with inversion of the word order: **a casa de Pedro,** *Peter's house* (*lit., the house of Peter*); **o amigo dos rapazes,** *the boys' friend* (*lit., the friend of the boys*).

VOCABULARY

(Each Portuguese noun is listed with its definite article, though the English article is omitted. To facilitate the learning of the gender, it is recommended that a noun be memorized always with its article expressed.)

a [ɐ]	to	**Londres**	London
o amigo	friend	**Maria**	Mary
aprender	to learn	**o marido**	husband
a caneta	pen	**morar**	to live, reside
a carta	letter	**a mulher**	woman, wife
a casa	house	**partir**	to depart, leave;
comprar	to buy		to break
de [də]	of, from, about	**passar**	to pass, spend
e [i]	and	**Pedro**	Peter
em [ɐj]	in, at, on	**a rapariga**	girl
enviar	to send	**o rapaz**	boy
estudar	to study	**a semana**	week
a fábrica	factory	**trabalhar**	to work
falar	to talk, speak	**unir**	to unite
a laranja	orange	**vender**	to sell
o livro	book		

EXERCISES

I. (a) *Pronounce the following words and supply phonetic transcriptions:* cabo, lado, mandar, balde, grande, pagar, zangado, íman, branco, baú, ratazana, caro, carro, fábrica, carne, armar, Carlos, sapo, caso, senso, gazua, faz.

(b) *Put into the plural:* uma carta, a mulher, o livro, um rapaz, a rapariga, um marido, uma fábrica.

(c) *Put into the singular:* os amigos, casas, as cartas, livros, mulheres, os rapazes, as laranjas.

(d) *Read aloud and translate into English:* compro, compram, o senhor compra, envias, envia, enviais, vende, vendem, as senhoras vendem, uno, unimos, unis, partimos, partis, parte, você parte, vocês partem.

(e) *Translate into Portuguese:* she sends, they are sending, you (*singular very familiar*) do send, you (*singular fairly familiar*) work, you (*plural polite*) are studying, you (*pl. fam.*) are working, we learn, you (*sing. pol.*) do learn, they learn, you (*pl. fam.*) are speaking, you (*sermon*) are learning, she spends, you (*pl. pol.*) are departing, he does unite, I talk, you (*pl. fam.*) unite, you (*sing. pol.*) are buying, we reside, we are breaking.

II. (*a*) *Study and translate:* 1. Os senhores compram livros e canetas. 2. Trabalhamos na fábrica. 3. Você vende laranjas. 4. Envio uma carta ao rapaz. 5. Moramos numa casa em Londres. 6. O amigo da rapariga passa uma semana em Londres. 7. O senhor envia livros às raparigas. 8. O rapaz vende um livro ao marido de Maria. 9. As mulheres trabalham numa fábrica. 10. Os rapazes estudam os livros.

(*b*) *Translate:* 1. The boys are sending oranges to the girl's friend. 2. You (*sing. pol.*) sell the book to a girl. 3. The girls are talking to Mary's husband. 4. The boy sends a book to the girl. 5. We are studying. 6. The boy's friend works in a factory in London. 7. The women are selling oranges. 8. The husband sends a letter to the woman's friend. 9. The boys are studying and the girls are talking. 10. You (*pl. pol.*) are spending a week in the factory.

III. (*a*) *Study and translate:* 1. Você estuda o livro. 2. Trabalham numa fábrica. 3. A mulher compra uma caneta. 4. Vocês enviam cartas aos rapazes. 5. O marido e a mulher passam uma semana em Londres. 6. A mulher envia canetas e livros ao amigo da rapariga. 7. Vendo um livro a uma rapariga. 8. As mulheres estudam os livros. 9. O marido vende laranjas a um rapaz. 10. A mulher fala aos rapazes.

(*b*) *Translate:* 1. You (*pl. pol.*) buy the books. 2. A boy works in the house. 3. We send a letter to the husband. 4. You (*pl. fam.*) are buying oranges. 5. A boy is selling pens. 6. The woman buys a book. 7. We are sending the letters to a friend. 8. They work in a factory. 9. She sells the books to the girls. 10. You (*sing. very fam.*) are departing from London.

The Indirect Object, MORAR *and* VIVER, *Negation, Interrogation, Interrogatives, Relatives and Conjunctions,* DAR, LER, VER *and* IR, *Plural of Nouns in* -M, *Pronunciation*

LESSON II

19. A WITH THE INDIRECT OBJECT. In English the preposition *to* introducing the indirect object is frequently omitted and the order *direct object—indirect object* inverted (*i.e.*, instead of saying *He sends a book to the boy* we say *He sends the boy a book*). This is not possible in Portuguese; the preposition **a** must always appear before a noun used as indirect object (**Envia um livro ao rapaz**).

20. Morar AND **vivẹr. Morar** means only *to live* in the sense of *to reside.* **Vivẹr** means *to live* in the sense of *to be alive.* It *may* also be used in the sense of *to reside,* but **morar** is to be preferred for this meaning.

21. NEGATION. The negative in Portuguese is formed by placing the particle **não** immediately before the corresponding verb form.

Não compramos a casa.	We do not buy the house.
O senhọr não vende canẹtas.	You do not sell pens.
O rapaz não mọra em Paris.	The boy does not live in Paris.

22. INTERROGATION. A question is expressed in Portuguese by inversion of the order *subject—verb* (where a *subject* appears) if, and normally only if, there is an interrogative word present. It is in other circumstances indicated only by a rising intonation in speech.

Onde trabalha o senhọr?	Where do you work?
Vọcê fala de Londres?	Are you talking about London?
Não vende a casa a Pẹdro?	Is he not selling the house to Peter?
Porque bẹbe vinho?	Why does he drink wine?

23. INTERROGATIVES, RELATIVES AND CONJUNCTIONS. Interrogative words in Portuguese (cf. English *who? which? where?*, etc.) have corresponding forms used as relatives or conjunctions.

Interrogatives		*Relatives and Conjunctions*	
que ...? [kə]	what? which?	**que**	who, whom, which, that
o que ...?	what?	**o que**	what, that which
quem?	who? whom?	**quem**	who, whom
onde? (*at rest*)	where?	**onde**	where
aonde? (*motion*)	where (... to)?	**aonde**	(to) where, to which
quando?	when?	**quando**	when
como? [1]	how?	**como** [1]	as
porque ...? [2] [purkə]	why?	**porque**	because

Que ⎱ **compra o amigo de Pedro?** What is Peter's friend
O que ⎰ buying?
o livro que compro, the book (which) I buy
Que livros lê o senhor? Which books do you study (*i.e.*, read)?
a mulher que vende laranjas, the woman who sells oranges
Quem envia a carta? Who is sending the letter?
o rapaz a quem envio a carta, the boy to whom I send the letter
Onde trabalhas? Where do you work?
a fábrica onde trabalho, the factory where I work
Quando partem os senhores? When are you departing?
Lê livros quando não trabalha. He studies (reads) books when he is not working.
Porque não falas? Why don't you speak?
Não estudam porque trabalham na fábrica. They aren't studying because they are working at the factory.

---

[1] Some speakers pronounce this word with an open **o: como**.
[2] Also written **por que ...?**, especially by Brazilians.

NOTES. 1. The interrogatives **que, o que** and **porque** are written with a circumflex accent and pronounced accordingly when they stand alone or when they end a sentence, clause or phrase:

Quê?	What?
O quê?	What?
Porquê?	Why?
Não sabe porquê.	He doesn't know why.
Não tem de quê.	Don't mention it. (You are welcome.)

2. It is important to distinguish between the relative pronouns **que** and **quem.** **Que** refers to things:

a caneta que escreve, the pen that writes
a caneta que compro, the pen that I buy
a caneta com que escreve, the pen with which he writes

It also denotes persons, except after a preposition, when **quem** is used:

o amigo que trabalha, the friend who works
o amigo que tenho [ˈtɐɲu], the friend that I have

but

o amigo com quem trabalho, the friend with whom I work
os amigos com quem estudo, the friends with whom I study

3. In English a relative pronoun or the conjunction *that* may often be omitted. This is not possible in Portuguese: *the letter he writes* must be translated as **a carta que escreve,** *I believe he is not going* as **Acredito que não vai.**

4. In English a preposition is frequently separated from the interrogative or relative to which it belongs, and placed after the verb (often with omission of the relative as in Note 3). In Portuguese the preposition must be placed immediately before the word to which it refers.

Com quem trabalha você? Who(m) do you work with?
Em que fábrica trabalha? Which factory does he work in?
o amigo com quem trabalho, the friend I work with
a caneta com que escreve, the pen that he writes with

5. The words **que** and **quem** are invariable (*i.e.,* the same in singular and plural). It should be noted that, when used as the

subject of a clause, **quem** *must* take a singular verb. This does not apply when it is the *complement* of the verb **ser**, *to be*.

> **Que canętas vende vǫcê?** What pens do you sell?
> **as canętas que vende,** the pens he sells
> **Quem compra livros?** Who buy(s) books?
> **os amigos com quem trabalho,** the friends I work with
> **Quem são os senhǫres?** Who are you?

24. FOUR IRREGULAR VERBS: **dar, lęr, vęr** and **ir.**

	dar, *to give*		**lęr,** *to read*	
(1)	dou	damos	leio [ˈlɐju]	lęmos
(2)	dás	dais	lês	lędes
	vǫcê dá	vǫcês dão	vǫcê lê	vǫcês lêem
	o senhǫr	os senhǫres	o senhǫr	os senhǫres
	dá	dão	lê	lêem
	a senhǫra	as senhǫras	a senhǫra	as senhǫras
	dá	dão	lê	lêem
(3)	dá	dão	lê	lêem

	vęr, *to see*		**ir,** *to go*	
(1)	vejo [ˈvɐʒu]	vęmos	vou	vamos
(2)	vês	vędes	vais	ides
	vǫcê vê	vǫcês vêem	vǫcê vai	vǫcês vão
	o senhǫr	os senhǫres	o senhǫr	os senhǫres
	vê	vêem	vai	vão
	a senhǫra	as senhǫras	a senhǫra	as senhǫras
	vê	vêem	vai	vão
(3)	vê	vêem	vai	vão

NOTE: **Ir** is used with an infinitive to translate the English *to go to +* verb, *to go and* + verb. Like its English counterpart, **ir** in this construction may indicate future action as well as movement.

Vai comprar uma .maçã. He goes and buys an apple. (Also: He is going to buy an apple.)

Vamos lęr o livro. We are going to read the book.

25. PLURAL OF NOUNS (cont.). Nouns ending in the letter **m** form their plural by dropping **m** and substituting **ns**:

o homem,	the man	os homens,	the men
a viagem,	the journey	as viagens,	the journeys
a estalagem,	the inn	as estalagens,	the inns

26. PRONUNCIATION. Study the pronunciation of the Portuguese letters **c, d, g, r, s, z,** and read aloud the words listed in the vocabulary below.

VOCABULARY

a água	water	a maçã	apple
a bibliotéca	library	a mãe	mother; you[1]
a cidade	town, city	Miguel	Michael
com	with	não	no, not
o copo	tumbler, glass	o pai	father; you[1]
dar	to give	Paris	Paris
a estalagem	inn	a revista	magazine
há	there is, there are	a rua	road, street
o homem	man	tenho [ˈtɐɲu]	I have (got)
ir	to go	a tia	aunt
João	John	o tio	uncle
ler	to read	ver	to see
a lição	lesson	a viagem	journey
a livraria	bookshop	o vinho	wine
o livreiro	bookseller	viver	to live
[liˈvrɐjru]			

See also the words listed in § 23.

EXERCISES

I. (a) *Pronounce the following words and supply phonetic transcriptions:* coar, aço, cento, fitar, fio, fiar, ligadura, mal, malva, bom, bem, tempo, quarto, quê, que, quente, usual.

(b) *Put into the plural:* a um rapaz, ao amigo, à cidade, a uma tia, a um livreiro, ao tio, do homem, da fábrica, dum pai, duma mãe, do vinho, da viagem.

---

[1] Mode of address from child to parent; plural **os pais.**

(c) *Put into the singular:* aos homens, a mulheres, às cidades, aos livros, a cidades, dos vinhos, de revistas, das mães, dos copos, às estalagens.

(d) *Translate:* Não enviam. Trabalhas? Você não envia? Onde trabalha a senhora? Não partimos. Partes? Dão. Não vou. O senhor vai? Vocês vão. Não dais? Aonde vai? A tia de João. Do amigo do livreiro. Ao pai dos rapazes. Moramos em Paris.

(e) *Translate:* I do not learn. Does he study? He doesn't work. Don't they read? What are they learning? Where do you (*sing. pol.*) work? They don't send. I am not working. Do you (*pl. fam.*) work? She gives. Does he go? They don't give. I am going. What are you (*pl. pol.*) giving? They aren't going. From the girls' mother. Don't mention it.

II. (a) *Study and translate:* 1. Envio a carta ao pai do rapaz. 2. Aonde vão vocês com o pai de João? 3. Como não tenho livros, vou à livraria. 4. Miguel estuda na biblioteca. 5. O que lê quando não trabalha? 6. A que revista envias a carta? 7. Quando vão os senhores comprar a fábrica onde trabalho? 8. Há um homem que vende maçãs. 9. De que livros fala o rapaz? 10. O livreiro vende livros à biblioteca.

(b) *Translate:* 1. What do the women sell? 2. Who is he sending the letter to? 3. He gives the boy a pen. 4. Don't you (*pl. pol.*) sell books to John's uncle? 5. Why do you (*pl. fam.*) not read the magazines? 6. Michael's father doesn't read the books he buys. 7. Where are you (*sing. pol.*) going? 8. There's a man who sells pens to the boys. 9. He's not studying the lesson. Why? 10. I sell apples and oranges in the street.

III. (a) *Study and translate:* 1. Dou a revista ao marido. 2. Vou passar uma semana em Paris. 3. Vendemos os livros ao tio. 4. Quando vai enviar as revistas à biblioteca? 5. O homem dá um copo de vinho à mulher. 6. Vende livros, revistas e canetas. 7. Quando vais aprender a lição? 8. Vamos à livraria com a mulher de João. 9. O senhor não trabalha na fábrica do tio de Miguel? 10. A senhora dá uma laranja ao rapaz.

(b) *Translate:* 1. Why is he sending a letter to John's father? 2. The boys buy books because they're going to study. 3. Where does the man sell the apples? 4. We're going with John to the bookshop. 5. When are you (*sing. fam.*) going to talk to Peter's mother? 6. Mary's mother doesn't speak to John's father. 7. He talks about the house where the bookseller lives. 8. Who do you (*pl. pol.*) give the magazines to? 9. They send the boy a book. 10. The woman sells the girls apples and oranges.

LESSON III

27. PLURAL OF NOUNS (cont.): NOUNS ENDING IN **-s, -ão** AND **-l**.

(*a*) The plural of nouns ending in **-s** is formed by adding **-es,** if the stress is on the *final* syllable.

o dẹus [dewʃ], the god	**os dẹuses** [ˈdewzəʃ], the gods
o mês, the month	**os mẹses,** the months
o país, the country	**os países,** the countries

If the stress does not fall on the final syllable, no change is made.

o lápis, the pencil	**os lápis,** the pencils
o pires, the saucer	**os pires,** the saucers
o vírus, the virus, germ	**os vírus,** the viruses, germs

NOTE: This second group includes the nouns **o arrais,** *the bosun,* and **o cais,** *the quay, the (railway) platform,* despite the fact that the stress falls on their last syllable.

(*b*) The plural of nouns ending in **-ão** is generally formed by dropping **-ão** and substituting **-ões.**

a estação, the station	**as estações,** the stations
a lição, the lesson	**as lições,** the lessons
o Verão, the summer	**os Verões,** the summers

NOTES. 1. A number of nouns substitute **-ães.** The most common are: **o cão,** *the dog,* **o capitão,** *the captain,* and **o pão,** *the bread, the loaf.*

2. A number simply add **-s.** The most common are: **o grão,** *the grain,* **o irmão,** *the brother,* and **a mão,** *the hand.* This group includes all those which do not carry the stress on the final syllable, *e.g.,* **o órfão,** *the orphan.* Os Verãos is occasionally found for **os Verões.**

43

(c) The plural of nouns ending in **-l** is generally formed by dropping **-l** and substituting **-is.**

(i) **-al** (*always stressed*) becomes **-ais.**

o **hǫspital,** the hospital os **hǫspitais,** the hospitals
o **jornal,** the newspaper os **jornais,** the newspapers

EXCEPTIONS: o **mal,** *the evil,* plural os **males,** *the evils;*
    o **real** [rri'al], *the real* (old Portuguese coin),
      plural os **réis,** *the reals*

(ii) **-ęl** (*stressed*) becomes **-éis.**

o **hǫtęl,** the hotel os **hǫtéis,** the hotels
o **papęl,** the paper os **papéis,** the papers

NOTE: **-ęl** (*unstressed*) becomes **-eis** [-ɐjʃ].

o **móvęl,** the piece of furniture os **móveis,** the furniture

(iii) **-il** (*stressed*) becomes **-is.**

o **barril,** the barrel os **barris,** the barrels
o **covil,** the den os **covis,** the dens

NOTE: **-il** (*unstressed*) becomes **-eis** [-ɐjʃ].

o **fóssil,** the fossil os **fósseis,** the fossils
o **têxtil** ['teʃtil], the textile os **têxteis,** the textiles

(iv) **-ǫl** (*always stressed*)[1] becomes **-óis.**

o **lençǫl,** the sheet os **lençóis,** the sheets
o **Sǫl,** the sun os **sóis,** the suns

(v) **-ul** (*stressed*) becomes **-uis.**

o **paul,** the marsh os **pauis,** the marshes

NOTE: **-ul** (*unstressed*) becomes **-ules.**

o **cônsul,** the consul os **cônsules,** the consuls

[1] Except: o **álcoǫl,** *alcohol;* plural os **álcoǫis.**

28. Use of **a** and **para** [p(ɐ)rɐ]. Both **a** and **para** can translate the English *to*. **A** implies that there is only a brief stop at the point (to be) reached; **para** implies a stay of some length, its use in this sense being generally of broader acceptance than its Spanish equivalent. Its functions also embrace those of the Spanish word **hacia,** *towards*.

Vai à pọrta.	He goes to the door.
Vou pạra Paris.	I'm going to Paris.
Vamos pạra casa.	We are going home.
Vou pạra a cama.	I'm going to bed.
Avançam pạra a pọrta.	They advance towards the door.
João vai pạra a cidade.	John is going into town.

Note: In normal speech **para** contracts with **o, a, os** and **as,** although this is not reflected in the written language.

    para o: [prɔ] or [praw]; **para a**: [pra]; **para os**: [prɔʃ] or [prawʃ]; **para as**: [praʃ].

29. Cardinal Numbers 1–20.

um, uma	one	**onze**	eleven
dọis, duas	two	**dọze**	twelve
três	three	**trẹze**	thirteen
quatro	four	**catọrze**	fourteen
cinco	five	**quinze**	fifteen
seis [sɐjʃ]	six	**dezasseis** [-ɐjʃ]	sixteen
sẹte	seven	**dezassẹte**	seventeen
ọito	eight	**dezọito**	eighteen
nọve	nine	**dezanọve**	nineteen
dẹz	ten	**vinte**	twenty

O professọr lê um capítulo. The teacher reads one (*or* a) chapter.

O pai lê dọis capítulos e o filho um. The father reads two chapters and the son one.

Miguẹl tem uma canẹta; ẹu também tenho uma. Michael has one (*or* a) pen; I also have one.

NOTES. 1. Apart from **uma** and **duas,** all these numerals have the same form for masculine and feminine.

2. The final **-e** of **treze** must always be clearly enunciated, even when the next word begins with a vowel, in order to distinguish from **três.**

30. AN IRREGULAR VERB: **ter,** *to have, have got.*

(1)	**tenho**	**temos**
	tens	**tendes**
(2)	**você tem**	**vocês têm** [ˈtɐjɐj]
	o Sr. tem	**os Srs. têm**
	a Sra. tem	**as Sras. têm**
(3)	**tem**	**têm**

NOTE: **Ter de** or **ter que** with a following infinitive means *to have (got) to*; the latter variety is more common in Brazilian Portuguese.

Tenho de trabalhar na fábrica. I have to work in the factory.
Têm de ir comprar batatas. They've got to go and buy potatoes.

31. PRONUNCIATION. Study the Portuguese pronunciation of the nasal vowels and nasal diphthongs. Study the principles for the use of the written accents (§§ 7-8).

VOCABULARY

a batata	potato	**gostar de**	to like
a cama	bed	**a irmã**	sister
o capítulo	chapter	**Lisboa**	Lisbon
o comboio	train	**a luz**	light
conservar	to keep, pre-serve	**Madrid**	Madrid
		a mesa	table
fabricar	to manufacture	**a mostarda**	mustard
a filha	daughter	**os móveis**	furniture
o filho	son	**para**	to, towards, for

46

a pimenta	pepper	o Sǫl	sun
a pǫrta	door	tęr	to have (got)
Portugal	Portugal	a tinta	ink
o professǫr	teacher	o Verão	summer
o sal	salt	viajar	to travel
sǫbre	on		

Study also the nouns listed in § 27 and the numbers listed in § 29.

NOTE: The nouns Sǫl (in the singular only) and Verão (sing. and pl.) are written with capital initial letter.

EXERCISES

I. (a) *Pronounce the following and explain any written accents:*
bons, irmã, irmãos, órfãos, órgãos, bênçãos, nações, fins, cães, mãe, a minha ânsia, tens, seu, céu, útil, sois, sóis, aí, baú, comédia, filosofia.

(b) *Put into the plural:* um cônsul, um real, o mal, o arrais, uma mão, o pão, um pires, o sal, um hotel, um lençol, o órfão, uma irmã, a luz, o barril, um pão, o Verão, a porta.

(c) *Put into the singular:* os lápis, as estações, os pauis, os pães, as mães, cais, capitães, têxteis, móveis, os hotéis, os hospitais, cônsules, os sais, dois lençóis, duas mãos, os males, covis, os vírus.

(d) *Translate:* Três capitães e sete arrais. Um pão. Que mulheres? Dezasseis hotéis. Vinte hospitais. Nove rapazes. Quatro ruas. Sete filhos e sete filhas. Livros, revistas e jornais. Lápis, canetas, papel e tinta. A luz do Sol. Grãos de pimenta sobre a mesa. Viajar para Lisboa. Estudar livros na biblioteca. Seis portas. Dois capítulos. O capítulo três. Dezoito professores. Quatro pires. Vinte réis. Há dois lençóis na cama. Três lições. Mostarda, pimenta e sal. Em Lisboa e em Paris.

47

(*e*) *Translate:* The gods. Portugal is (é) a country. Twenty oranges and fourteen apples. In Lisbon there are hotels, hospitals, libraries and factories. The dogs in the street. Peter's father sells pens and pencils in Madrid. What is John reading in the bookshop? Why is Peter studying the fossils? Who is selling apples? Mary is giving an apple to the teacher. The boy I study with is going to Madrid. When are you (*sing. very fam.*) going to learn the lesson? What is (é) a virus?

II. (*a*) *Study and translate:* 1. Sobre a mesa há pimenta, vinho e copos de água. 2. Temos de ir para Lisboa. 3. O livreiro vende livros, revistas, jornais, lápis, canetas, papel e tinta. 4. As mulheres vão comprar laranjas, maçãs e batatas. 5. Os rapazes têm que viajar para Lisboa, em Portugal. 6. Gostamos de Lisboa. 7. João e Maria têm de ir para a cidade. 8. O arrais não vai gostar do capitão. 9. Fabricam têxteis numa fábrica. 10. Pedro e Miguel vão para casa. 11. O marido de Maria vai para a cama. 12. Vejo que não gostais de viajar.

(*b*) *Translate:* 1. There are three newspapers on the table. 2. The train is going to depart. 3. The boys are travelling to Paris with John's uncle. 4. They are going to spend six months in London. 5. We keep the apples in barrels. 6. You (*pl. fam.*) have got to speak with the consul. 7. We are going to spend the summer in Lisbon. 8. There are four weeks in a month. 9. The orphans are going to like the dog. 10. There are sheets on the beds. 11. Peter and Mary have three daughters and one son. 12. We have got to go to the hospital.

III. (*a*) *Study and translate:* 1. Vamos para Londres porque temos de falar com o cônsul. 2. Vejo que o comboio vai partir para Londres. 3. O arrais lê um jornal sobre o cais. 4. Envio revistas aos hospitais. 5. Quando vão os Srs. passar uma semana num dos hotéis de Lisboa? 6. Para onde vão as mulheres? 7. Gostamos dos móveis da casa de Pedro e Maria. 8. Vês os grãos de pimenta sobre a mesa? 9. João lê um livro na biblioteca porque tem que estudar. 10. Como vamos viajar para Madrid?

(b) *Translate:* 1. We've got to go and see John's aunt. 2. The husband works in a factory in Paris. 3. We like apples and oranges. 4. When does the train depart for Lisbon? 5. Who are we going to sell the potatoes to? 6. We are going to buy a pen for the boy and two pencils for the girl. 7. John's two sisters are studying the lesson in the library. 8. Mary's brother is going to the station. 9. Michael's uncle is spending three weeks in Lisbon. 10. You (*sing. fam.*) are going to live in a hotel.

LESSON IV

32. ENDINGS AND AGREEMENT OF ADJECTIVES. An adjective in
Portuguese, like the definite article, agrees in number (*i.e.*, singular or plural) and gender (*i.e.*, masculine or feminine) with the
noun it qualifies. From the masculine singular, quoted in dictionaries and vocabularies, we can deduce the remaining forms:

(1) *Adjectives which have a masculine singular ending in* -o,
though NOT -ão (**barato,** *cheap*; **amarẹlo,** *yellow*). The feminine
singular is formed by changing the -o to -a (**barata, amarẹla**).
The plural is obtained by adding -s to the singular (masc. pl.
baratos, amarẹlos; fem. pl. **baratas, amarẹlas**).

um livro barato, livros baratos, a cheap book, cheap books
a canẹta barata, as canẹtas baratas, the cheap pen, the cheap
   pens

Notice that the adjective is placed after the noun.

(2) *Adjectives which have a masculine singular ending in* -ọr *or*
-ês (**faladọr,** *talkative*; **inglês,** *English*). The feminine singular
is formed by adding -a to the masculine singular (**faladọra,
inglẹsa**). The plural is obtained by adding -es for the masculine
(**faladọres, inglẹses**) and -as for the feminine (**faladọras,
inglẹsas**).

um jornal inglês, jornais inglẹses, an English paper, English papers
uma mulhẹr faladọra, mulhẹres faladọras, a talkative
   woman, talkative women.

NOTE: Adjectives of nationality or regional origin are written in
Portuguese with a small initial letter, as also the corresponding
name of the inhabitants and of the language: **o francês,** *the French-
man, French*; **o inglês,** *the Englishman, English*; **um inglês,** *an
Englishman.* For the use of the capital letter, see Lesson XVII,
Vocabulary Note.

(3) *Adjectives which have a masculine singular ending in* -u (**cru,** *raw*; **nu,** *naked*; **hindu,** *Hindu*). The feminine singular is formed by adding **-a** to the masculine singular (**crua, nua, hindua**[1]). The plural is obtained by adding **-s** to the singular (masc. pl. **crus, nus, hindus;** fem. pl. **cruas, nuas, hinduas**[1]).

um tomate cru, tomates crus, a raw tomato, raw tomatoes
uma batata crua, batatas cruas, a raw potato, raw potatoes

(4) *Adjectives which have a masculine singular ending in* -eu (**europeu,** *European*; **ateu,** *atheistic*). The feminine singular is formed by changing **-eu** to **-eia** (**europeia, ateia**). For the omission of the written accent on the ending **-eia,** see § 54 (*c*). Two adjectives, **judeu,** *Jewish,* and the rare **sandeu,** *stupid,* change **-eu** to **-ia.** The plural is formed in all instances by adding **-s** to the singular (masc. pl. **europeus, ateus; sandeus, judeus;** fem. pl. **europeias, ateias; sandias, judias**).

um país europeu, países europeus, a European country, European countries
uma família europeia, famílias europeias, a European family, European families
um costume judeu, costumes judeus, a Jewish custom, Jewish customs
uma prática judia, práticas judias, a Jewish practice, Jewish practices

(5) *Adjectives which have a masculine singular ending in* -ão (**brincalhão,** *playful*; **sabichão,** *priggish*). The feminine singular is formed by changing **-ão** to **-ona** (**brincalhona, sabichona**). The masculine plural is obtained by changing **-ão** to **-ões** (**brincalhões, sabichões**). The feminine plural is obtained by adding **-s** to the feminine singular (**brincalhonas, sabichonas**).

um rapaz brincalhão, rapazes brincalhões, a playful boy, playful boys
uma rapariga brincalhona, raparigas brincalhonas, a playful girl, playful girls

---

[1] Alternative feminine forms (**hindu, hindus**) are also to be found for this adjective.

NOTES. 1. A number of adjectives in -ão have feminine singular in -ã, masculine plural in -ães, and feminine plural in -ãs. Such are **alemão**, *German*, and **catalão**, *Catalan*.

2. A number have feminine singular in -ã, masculine plural in -ãos, and feminine plural in -ãs. Such are **são**, *sound*, **vão**, *vain*, and **cristão**, *Christian*.

3. The adjective **beirão**, *of (the province of) Beira*, has feminine singular in -ǫa, or -ã, masculine plural in -ões, and feminine plural in -ǫas or -ãs.

(6) *Other adjectives.* The feminine forms, both singular and plural, of other adjectives are the same as the masculine. Their plurals are analogous to the plural of nouns with similar endings.

(*a*) *Those ending in any other vowel:* **vęrde**, *green*, plural **vęrdes**; **pęrsa**, *Persian*, pl. **pęrsas**; **só**, *alone*, pl. **sós**.

(*b*) *Those ending in* -ar: **suplementar**, *additional*, pl. **suplementares**.

(*c*) *Those ending in* -z: **feliz**, *happy*, pl. **felizes**.

(*d*) *Those ending in* -m: **comum**, *common*, pl. **comuns**.

(*e*) *Those ending in* -l:

banal,	*banal*,	pl. **banais**
crueḷ,	*cruel*,	pl. **cruéis**
terrívęl,	*terrible*,	pl. **terríveis**
civil,	*civil*,	pl. **civis**
fácil,	*easy*,	pl. **fáceis**
azul,	*blue*,	pl. **azuis**.

NOTES. 1. Contrary to (2), the adjectives **cortês**, *polite*, **descortês**, *rude*, and **pedrês**, *piebald*, fall within this group (6):

masculine and feminine singular: **cortês, pedrês**;
masculine and feminine plural: **cortęses, pedręses.**

2. Also contrary to (2), there fall within this group (6) the following adjectives in -ǫr:

multicǫr, *many-coloured*, **multicolǫr**, *many-coloured*, **incolǫr**, *colourless*, **bicolǫr**, *two-tone*, **tricolǫr**, *three-tone*; **bimotǫr**, *twin-engined*, and all those in -motǫr (but note **a fǫrça motriz**, *driving-force*); **indolọr**, *painless*; **superiọr**, *upper*; *superior*; **inferiọr**, *lower*; *inferior*; **exteriọr**, *outer, exterior*; **interiọr**, *inner*; *interior*; **ulteriọr**, *ulterior*; **posteriọr**, *posterior*; **anteriọr**, *prior, previous*.

masculine and feminine singular: **bicolọr, superiọr**, etc.,
masculine and feminine plural: **bicolọres, superiọres**, etc.

3. The comparative adjectives in **-ọr** fall within this group (6): **maiọr**, *bigger*,[1] **menọr**, *smaller*,[1] **melhọr**, *better*, **piọr**, *worse*.

masculine and feminine singular: **maiọr, menọr, melhọr, piọr**;
masculine and feminine plural: **maiọres, menọres, melhọres, piọres**.[2]

(7) *Unclassifiable Adjectives.* The following adjectives are irregular or unclassifiable: **bom**, *good*, **mau**, *bad*; **espanhọl** [əʃpɐˈɲɔl], *Spanish*, **andaluz**, *Andalusian*; **simples**, *simple*, **prẹstes**, *ready*, **rẹles**, *worthless*.

masc. sing.	fem. sing.	masc. plural	fem. plural
bom	bọa	bons	bọas
mau	má	maus	más
espanhọl	espanhọla	espanhóis	espanhọlas
andaluz	andaluza	andaluzes	andaluzas
simples	simples	simples	simples
prẹstes	prẹstes	prẹstes	prẹstes
rẹles	rẹles	rẹles	rẹles

33. MORE ABOUT AGREEMENT. If the adjective qualifies more than one noun, the following applies:

(1) If the nouns are all masculine, the adjective is used in the masculine plural:

um cọpo e um prato partidos, a broken glass and plate

---

[1] **Mais grande** is occasionally to be found, but should be regarded as ungrammatical; **mais pequẹno** is, however, a perfectly acceptable alternative to **menọr**.
[2] Similarly the rather rare adjectives **júniọr**, *junior*, and **séniọr**, *senior*.

(2) If the nouns are all feminine, the adjective takes the feminine plural form:

uma mulhẹr e uma rapariga portuguẹsas, a Portuguese woman and girl

(3) If the nouns are of different gender, the adjective is generally in the masculine plural:

o rapaz e a rapariga espanhóis, the Spanish boy and girl

Notice the repetition of the articles: this is the *normal* practice and the student is urged to adopt it.

34. POSITION OF ADJECTIVES. Adjectives in Portuguese are usually placed after the noun. But used more frequently before than after it are certain common adjectives such as **bom** (*good*), **mau** (*bad*), **lindo** (*beautiful*), **pequẹno** (*small, little*), **vẹlho** (*old*) and **único** (*sole, only*); ordinal numbers **primeiro** [pri'mɐjru] (*first*) **segundo** (*second*), etc.; **próximo** ['prɔsimu] (*next*) and **último** (*last*).

um pequẹno dicionário, um dicionário pequẹno, a small dictionary

um vẹlho senhọr, um senhọr vẹlho, an old gentleman

a primeira vẹz, a vẹz primeira, the first time

NOTE: An adjective which is used frequently before the noun nevertheless comes after it when the adjective is itself modified by an adverb.

 um livro muito ['mujntu] **bom,** a very good book
 uma casa bastante vẹlha, rather an old house
 uma rapariga mais vẹlha, an older (*lit.*, more old) girl

More will be said about the position of adjectives in § 38.

35. AN IRREGULAR VERB: sẹr, *to be.*

(1)	**sou**	**sọmos**
	és	**sọis**
(2)	**vọcê é**	**vọcês são**
	o Sr. é	**os Srs. são**
	a Sra. é	**as Sras. são**
(3)	**é**	**são**

O Sr. é inglês?   Are you English?
A rapariga é espanhọla.   The girl is Spanish (a Spaniard).
As maçãs são bọas.   The apples are good.

36. PRONUNCIATION. Study the Portuguese pronunciation of
the letters **b, f, h, j, l, p, q, t, v** and of the digraphs **ch, lh, nh.**
Revise the pronunciation of the letters **m, n, r, s, z.**

VOCABULARY

bastante	rather, fairly, quite	**militar**	military
bonito	nice, pretty	**muito** [ˈmujntu]	very; much
o carro	car	**nọvo**	new; young
a chávena	(tea)cup	**partido**	broken
a cọisa	thing	**portuense**	(of) Oporto (adj.)
o costume	custom	**português**	Portuguese
difícil	difficult, hard	**a prática**	practice
do que	than	**o prato**	plate, dish
a família	family	**quarto**	fourth
francês	French	**o senhọr**	gentleman; you
a língua	language, tongue	**sẹr**	to be
lisboẹta	(of) Lisbon (adj.)	**terceiro** [-ɐjru]	third
a lọja	shop, store	**o tomate**	tomato
mais	more, most	**vermelho** [-ɐʎu]	red
mạs	but	**a vẹz**	time (occasion)

Study also the adjectives listed in §§ 32 and 34.

EXERCISES

I. (a) *Pronounce the following and supply phonetic transcriptions:*
fato, haver, mal-humorado, asfalto, chuva, choramingar,
palha, canalha, patrulha, banho, moinho, rainha, tenro,
genro, com, capim, falam, as boas meninas, zonas e regiões,
dois jornais.

(b) *Put into the plural:* uma coisa barata, o lápis amarelo, a mulher mais faladora, um senhor inglês, um costume judeu, uma rapariga cortês, a família europeia, uma batata crua, o tomate cru, um homem sabichão, uma rapariga brincalhona, um amigo alemão, uma prática cristã, o homem cruel, uma mulher comum, a lição difícil, a flor azul, o rapaz andaluz, uma loja portuguesa, uma lição simples, o primeiro capítulo, um livreiro muito velho, um carro bicolor, uma mulher sabichona, a porta exterior, uma chávena partida, a única casa, a linda rapariga, o alemão e o inglês, um livreiro espanhol, uma prática militar, um velho costume militar.

(c) *Put into the singular:* os carros vermelhos, as flores azuis, países europeus, os costumes judeus, as raparigas catalãs, vinhos alemães, as línguas mais fáceis, senhores ingleses, dos jornais franceses, chávenas verdes, nas fábricas espanholas, as mulheres cruéis, práticas alemãs, lindos hotéis, velhas mulheres judias, costumes europeus, os senhores sabichões, duas raparigas simples, rapazes andaluzes, velhos fósseis, cônsules portugueses, dois réis, pratos partidos, que livros?, línguas difíceis, práticas civis, os velhos costumes persas.

(d) *Put into the feminine:* alemão, europeu, bom, sabichão, inglês, judeu, falador, multicolor, ulterior, melhor, hindu, verde, persa, só, simples, andaluz, francês, cortês, catalães, cristãos, brincalhões, sãos, vãos, ateus, azuis, cruéis, banais, corteses, portugueses, bons, maus, espanhóis, exteriores, faladores, felizes, nus, judeus, bonitos, únicos, sós, menores, tricolores, multicores, sabichões, beirões, interiores, piores, anteriores, multicolores, prestes, portuenses.

(e) *Put into the masculine:* judias, cruas, ateias, amarelas, faladoras, portuguesas, sabichonas, vãs, cristã, nua, alemã, boa, má, espanhola, inglesa, prestes, azul, fácil, cortês, portuguesa, andaluza, pedrês, terríveis, partida, sã, catalãs, maior, posteriores, europeia, pequena, persas, difíceis, fácil, más, cristãs, brincalhona, só, lisboeta.

II. (a) *Study and translate:* 1. Há três flores vermelhas sobre a mesa. 2. Os senhores catalães vão morar numa casa bastante velha. 3. A rapariga espanhola é muito sabichona. 4. Enviamos flores aos hospitais de Lisboa 5. Que livros tem você na mão? 6. João estuda a terceira lição, mas Maria estuda a quarta. 7. As flores azuis são muito bonitas. 8. O tio de João tem uma velha casa em Paris. 9. Vamos com a mãe de Maria ao novo hospital. 10. João é bom, mas as irmãs de Miguel são más. 11. O senhor judeu vai comprar um carro vermelho. 12. A mulher vende as flores amarelas à tia de Pedro, mas vai vender flores azuis ao pai de Maria. 13. São as únicas revistas alemãs que tenho na loja. 14. Portugal é um país europeu. 15. João e Pedro estudam costumes portuenses. 16. Na biblioteca há livros verdes, azuis, amarelos, vermelhos, e multicolores. 17. Maria lê livros alemães na livraria. 18. O velho hindu viaja para Paris. 19. O tio de Maria vai passar três semanas em Londres. 20 Vai gostar dos hotéis de Lisboa, porque são muito bonitos.

(b) *Translate:* 1. We like the Portuguese hotels, but we don't like the Portuguese inns. 2. The old Catalan gentleman is selling cheap pens and pencils in the street. 3. I am going to buy (news)papers and magazines for John. 4. Mary works in an old hospital in Lisbon. 5. What are the two Portuguese girls selling? 6. John has got a new two-tone car. 7. Who are we going to sell the blue flowers to? 8. When are you (*pol. pl.*) going to buy the old Jew's bookshop? 9. There is pepper, salt and mustard on the table. 10. Why is Mary's aunt giving John a broken cup and plate? 11. The Catalan's going to work in a factory in Paris, but isn't going to like the French customs and practices. 12. We sell very nice pens and pencils. 13. They are studying two difficult lessons and one easier lesson. 14. The houses of Madrid are bigger but the Andalusian houses are nicer. 15. Who are you (*sing. pol.*) studying the fourth lesson with? 16. I am going to spend seven weeks in Lisbon with John's family. 17. They have a small house in London. 18. When is Michael's father going to buy a new car? 19. Portugal is a fairly small country. 20. Paris is smaller than London but bigger than Madrid.

III. (a) *Study and translate:* 1. Você vai vender o novo carro vermelho? 2. A tia de Pedro é muito faladora. 3. Vou comprar uma caneta e um lápis amarelos. 4. Lisboa, Paris e Madrid são cidades europeias. 5. É muito pior ser sabichão do que ser descortês. 6. João e Maria são muito felizes. 7. Duas raparigas lisboetas lêem jornais alemães na biblioteca. 8. Onde trabalha o velho senhor portuense? 9. O marido de Maria é inglês. 10. Sobre a mesa há copos de vinho e de água, pratos, chávenas e pires. 11. A velha mulher catalã vende batatas, tomates, maçãs e laranjas na rua. 12. O tio de Miguel fala espanhol, português e francês. 13. Vamos à biblioteca no carro de Pedro. 14. É melhor do que o velho carro do tio de João. 15. A loja de João é muito pequena, mas é maior do que a livraria do velho senhor judeu. 16. Os capitães e os arrais vão passar uma semana em Lisboa. 17. Os amigos de Pedro aprendem português na biblioteca. 18. Tens de enviar cartas à mulher do velho livreiro. 19. Quando vamos partir para Londres? 20. Os órfãos não vão gostar de trabalhar na fábrica.

(b) *Translate:* 1. The flowers we have are blue and yellow. 2. Who are you (*fam. pl.*) buying the easier books for? 3. John's father's house is very small. 4. The only things we have are raw potatoes and green tomatoes! 5. There are four shops and nineteen houses in the street. 6. Mary's brother is studying the second lesson. 7. The Andalusians are selling cheap pens to the English gentlemen. 8. We sell English, French and German newspapers, and Spanish and Portuguese books and magazines. 9. Peter's mother is Portuguese and speaks English and Portuguese. 10. Michael's father is English; he speaks English but does not speak Portuguese. 11. Mary is bigger than John but smaller than Peter. 12. The Spanish hotels aren't superior to the Portuguese hotels.   13. The Oporto girls are going to Madrid in Michael's new car.   14. Mary's daughter is very priggish; she is worse than Peter.   15. John's got to go to bed because he is a bad boy.   16. The boys' new teacher is French.   17. I've got to go to the hospital three times.   18. The last house is the biggest.   19. Peter's father's very cruel and very rude.   20. The fourth lesson is very difficult.

LESSON V

37. NOUNS AND THEIR GENDER. Nouns in Portuguese are either masculine or feminine and each noun should be memorized with its gender. There are, however, certain guides to the gender of a given noun: (1) in the meaning of the word and (2) in its ending.

(1) Nouns denoting male beings are masculine and those denoting female beings are feminine:

o homem	man	**a mulher**	woman
o senhor	gentleman	**a senhora**	lady
o pai	father	**a mãe**	mother
o filho	son	**a filha**	daughter
o irmão	brother	**a irmã**	sister
o rapaz	boy	**a rapariga**	girl
o tio	uncle	**a tia**	aunt
o avô	grandfather	**a avó**	grandmother
o rei [rrej]	king	**a rainha**	queen
o touro	bull	**a vaca**	cow
		a esposa ⎫	
o marido	husband	**a mulher** ⎬ wife	
		a senhora ⎭	

NOTES. 1. A masculine plural may *often* refer to persons of both sexes.

os pais, the parents
os filhos, the son(s) and daughter(s), children
os irmãos, brothers and sisters
os tios de João, John's aunt and uncle
os Reis Católicos, the Catholic Monarchs

2. Notice the following:
os avôs, the grandfathers
as avós, the grandmothers

os avós, the grandparents; the ancestors, forebears (also os antepassados)

(2) (i) Nouns ending in -o (though not necessarily those in -ão or -ó) are masculine:

o livro	book	o ano	year
o capítulo	chapter	o copo	glass, tumbler
o rio	river	o vinho	wine

Exceptions: a rádio (wireless),[1] a foto (photo, snap), a tribo (tribe).

(ii) Nouns ending in -me are masculine:

o nome	name	o volume	volume, tome

Exception: a fome (hunger).

(iii) Nouns ending in -a are feminine:

a hora	hour	a casa	house
a data	date	a idéia	idea
a fábrica	factory	a pêra	pear

Exceptions: 1. Words from the Greek ending in -ma: o drama (drama), o telegrama (telegram), o programa (programme), etc.
2. Words denoting male beings: o guia (guide), o cura (priest), o papa (pope), o lojista (shopkeeper), etc.; but a sentinela (sentry).
3. O dia (day), o mapa (map), o planeta (planet), o cometa (comet), o guia (guidebook).

(iv) Nouns ending in -gem, -ie, -dade, -tude are feminine:

a coragem	courage	a universidade	university
a viagem	journey	a liberdade	freedom
a espécie	sort, kind	a virtude	virtue
a superfície	surface	a juventude	youth

Exception: The noun personagem (character, personage) is occasionally masculine when it refers to a male character.

(v) Nouns ending in -ção, -são, -stão, -gião, are feminine

---

[1] But o rádio (wireless set, radio).

where these endings correspond respectively to the English endings -tion, -sion, -stion, -gion.

a nação	nation	**a combustão**	combustion
a posição	position	**a congestão**	congestion
a confusão	confusion	**a região**	region
a ilusão	illusion	**a religião**	religion

38. MORE ON THE POSITION OF ADJECTIVES. (1) *Always placed before the noun* are adjectives which limit rather than describe: cardinal numbers used as such (**uma lição,** *one lesson*; **duas lições,** *two lessons*); adjectives of quantity such as **muito** (*much, a lot of*; pl. *many, a lot of*), **pouco** (*little, not much*; pl. *few, not many*), **bastante** (*enough*), **tanto** (*so much*; pl. *so many*), **demasiado** (*too much*; pl. *too many*), **vários** (*several*), **quanto?** (*how much? pl. how many?*) **algum** (*some, any*), **nenhum** (*no, not any*); and the invariable interrogative adjective **que ...?** (*which ...? what ...?*).

Quantas cartas vai ler?	How many letters is he going to read?
Tenho muitos irmãos.	I have a lot of (many) brothers.
Lêem poucos jornais.	They don't read many papers.
Que livros compra você?	Which books are you buying?
Temos demasiado pão.	We've got too much bread.

(2) Cardinal numbers may also be used with ordinal sense and are then placed after the noun: **na página vinte** (*on page twenty*) as opposed to the purely cardinal use in **O livro tem vinte páginas** (*The book has twenty pages*). The cardinal does not normally agree in gender with a feminine noun when used in this way, *e.g.*, **a lição dois** [1] (*lesson two*). Notice that the definite article *must* be retained (except in titles or headings).

---

[1] *i.e.*, a lição (número) dois.

(3) *Used before and after the noun* but with a different meaning are:

	before the noun	after the noun
grande	great	big
męsmo	same, very (*adj.*)	himself, herself, themselves, myself, etc.
pǫbre	poor (to be pitied)	poor (impecunious)
vários	several	various, miscellaneous

(4) The final word *one* is not to be translated into Portuguese in such expressions as *a green one*, *one green one*, *the green one(s)*, etc.:

João tem um carro azul, mąs Pędro tem um vęrde.
John's got a blue car, but Peter's got a green one.

João tem dǫis carros azuis e Pędro tem um vęrde.
John's got two blue cars and Peter's got one green one.

Gostamos dos azuis, mąs não gostamos do vęrde.
We like the blue ones, but we don't like the green one.

39. Ąlgum AND nenhum. (1) **Ąlgum** (*feminine singular* **ąlguma**, *masculine plural* **ąlguns**, *feminine plural* **ąlgumas**) is used in affirmative sentences.

Os Srs. fazem ąlguma mudança? Are you making any change?

Fazęmos ąlguma. We are making the odd one (*lit.*, some one).

(2) **Nenhum** (*feminine singular* **nenhuma**) is used only in negations. Note the double negative.

Vǫcê tem ąlguma ǫbjęcção [obʒɛˈsɐ̃ŵ]? Have you any objection?

Não tenho nenhuma ǫbjęcção. I haven't any objection.
Não leio nenhum jornal. I don't read any paper(s).
Não leio nenhum. I don't read any.

It is hardly ever used in the plural.

Não leio nenhum livro. I don't read any books *or* I read no books.

(*Contrast:* **Leio ąlguns livros.** I read some books.)

(3) **Algum** may sometimes replace **nenhum** in negations; but in this instance it *must* follow the noun. Its use is more emphatic.

Não tenho nenhum livro (*or* **livro nenhum**). I haven't got any books.

Não tenho livro algum. I haven't got any books whatsoever.

(4) **Algum** and **nenhum** are frequently omitted in Portuguese where English *some* and *any* appear.

> **Ele compra pão.** He buys some bread.
> **Tens amigos aqui?** Have you any friends here?
> **Não tenho amigos.** I haven't got any friends.

(5) The indefinite article has plural forms **uns** and **umas** meaning *some* (**uns livros interessantes,** *some interesting books*), though the English *some* may frequently be left unexpressed in Portuguese or be rendered by **alguns.** Uns and umas also translate *some* (=*approximately*) before a numeral.

40. AN IRREGULAR VERB: **fazer,** *to do, to make.*

(1)	**faço**	**fazemos**
(2)	**fazes**	**fazeis** (-ɐjʃ)
	você faz	**vocês fazem**
	o Sr. faz	**os Srs. fazem**
	a Sra. faz	**as Sras. fazem**
(3)	**faz**	**fazem**

41. PRONUNCIATION. Study the pronunciation of the words listed in § 9.

VOCABULARY

algum	some; any	**interessante**	interesting
alto	tall, high	**a mudança**	change
aqui	here	**nenhum**	no, not any,
Coimbra	Coimbra		none
como	how, as, like	**a objecção**	objection
fazer	to do, to make	[obʒɛ'sɐw̃]	
inteligente	intelligent, clever	**a página**	page

possívęl	possible	**a sala**	room (*living*
o quarto	room (*bedroom,*		*room*)
	bathroom)	**sǫbre**	on; about
que ...!	what a ...!	**tão**	as, so
	how ...!	**o touro** *or*	
de quem?	whose?	**tǫiro**	bull

tão ... cǫmo ...   as ... as ...; so ... as ...

See also the nouns listed in § 37 and the adjectives listed in § 38.

EXERCISES

I. (*a*) *Pronounce the following and supply phonetic transcriptions:*
dez homens, dois homens, dos homens, aos touros, por
minha causa, manda-nos, fá-lo-ão, que boa ideia, Dom
Carlos, Dom Pedro, Dom António, São Tomás, para as
mulheres, grão-turco, grão-duque, grã-duquesa, cem copos
de vinho, guarda-mor [mɔr].

(*b*) *Translate:* O rapaz é inteligente. A porta é verde. De
quem é o lápis azul? Catorze flores azuis e duas amarelas.
Nove lápis. Os pais de Miguel e João. Onde é a biblioteca? Coimbra é uma grande cidade portuguesa. Uma
loja muito boa. Umas ideias bastante interessantes. Um
grande amigo de Pedro. Muitas cidades inglesas.

(*c*) *Translate:* Where is the shop? It is here. They (*fem.*)
are beautiful. He is very clever. The lady is English. It
isn't possible. Six and eight are fourteen. Three English
gentlemen and a Spanish boy. What is John doing in the
shop? Is he reading or (**ou**) working? Do you (*pol. pl.*) see
Mary's grandmother? The kings and queens of Portugal.

II. (*a*) *Study and translate:* 1. Fazem duas vezes a mesma
coisa. 2. Os vinhos portugueses são muito bons. 3.
Quantas vezes vai você ter de ir ao mesmo hospital? 4.
Portugal tem poucas cidades grandes. 5. Os livros de
Pedro não são maus, mas tenho uns muito mais interessantes.
6. De quem são os livros? 7. É a primeira vez que via-
jamos para Madrid. 8. Não há muitos rios em Portugal.

9. Vamos enviar um telegrama para os tios de João. 10. Os dramas de Shakespeare têm muitas personagens.

(b) *Translate:* 1. Why do you (*fam. pl.*) buy so many apples? 2. A gentleman who sells cars in the city sends the shopkeeper a telegram. 3. What are the two German girls studying at the university? 4. We have a very nice house in Coimbra. 5. John's ideas are very interesting, because he is so intelligent. 6. Peter's not as big as Michael. 7. Mr Gonçalves has got two big dogs. 8. But it isn't possible to travel from Lisbon to Paris in two hours! 9. How many pages are there in the magazine? 10. Mary has no objection.

III. (a) *Study and translate:* 1. Na sala do Sr. Gonçalves há três mesas. 2. Quantos quartos tem a casa de Pedro? 3. O lojista vai fazer mudanças na loja. 4. Há quatro universidades em Portugal. 5. O pai de Miguel vai vender três vacas e um toiro. 6. Um dia vou comprar uma casa grande em Londres. 7. Os tios de Maria lêem um guia sobre Portugal. 8. Que altas são as irmãs do senhor lisboeta! 9. Não é possível estudar uma lição tão difícil. 10. A rapariga catalã é mais alta do que muitas inglesas.

(b) *Translate:* 1. The yellow flowers are more beautiful than the blue ones. 2. Where's John's father's shop? 3. The houses are very interesting. 4. Peter's sister is taller than Mary. 5. A Spanish boy is going to live with Mary's mother and sister. 6. Which friend do they send flowers to? 7. I have to buy several things for the Jewish shopkeeper. 8. The letters he sends to Michael's mother are very interesting ones. 9. Has he any friends in London? No, he hasn't any. 10. The French boy's aunt and uncle don't read any books whatsoever.

*Plurals of Nouns and Adjectives, the Three
Verb Conjugations (Present Indicative),* SER DE,
Demonstrative Adjectives and Pronouns, MUITO,
Pronunciation

LESSON VI

42. PLURALS OF NOUNS AND ADJECTIVES (SUMMARY). Revise the
rules for the formation of the plurals of nouns (§§ 11, 25, 27) and
for the formation of the feminines and plurals of adjectives (§ 32).
For the formation of *all* plural forms the following norms should
be observed.

(*a*) The plurals of all nouns and adjectival forms which end in
a vowel are formed by adding **-s.** Exceptional are the larger
groups of nouns and masculine singular adjectives ending in **-ão**
and making their plurals in **-ões (nação, nações; sabichão,
sabichões),** and the smaller group of nouns and masculine
singular adjectives ending in **-ão** and making their plurals in
-ães (cão, cães; alemão, alemães).

(*b*) The plurals of all nouns and adjectival forms which end in
-m are formed by substituting **-ns.**

(*c*) The plurals of all nouns and adjectival forms which end in
-r or **-z** are formed by adding **-es.**

(*d*) The plurals of all nouns and adjectival forms which end in
-s are formed by adding **-es** if the last syllable is stressed, and
remain the same if the last syllable is unstressed. Exceptional
are the nouns **cais** and **arrais** which are the same in the singular
and the plural.

(*e*) The plurals of all nouns and adjectival forms which end in
-l are formed in principle by substituting **-is.** Forms ending in
-ol and stressed **-el** require an acute accent on **o** and **e** respectively. Special attention, however, should be paid to forms ending in stressed **-il (barril, barris; civil, civis),** in unstressed **-il
(fóssil, fósseis; fácil, fáceis)** and in unstressed **-ul (cônsul,
cônsules).** Exceptional are the nouns **mal** (pl. **males**) and
real (pl. **réis**).

43. VERBS: PRESENT INDICATIVE. Revise § 15. As the verb forms of **você(s)**, **o(s) senhor(es)**, etc., are always the same as the corresponding third-person forms, from this juncture they will not be listed separately.

44. USES OF **ser de.**[1]

(1) *Place of origin:*

Sou de Paris. I come (am) from Paris.
São de Portugal. They come (are) from Portugal.

(2) *Ownership:*

A casa é de Miguel. The house belongs to Michael.
De quem é a loja? Who does the shop belong to?

(3) *Material:*

A casa é de madeira [mɐˈdɐjrɐ]. The house is made of wood.
O hotel é de pedra. The hotel is built in stone.

45. DEMONSTRATIVES. (*a*) The English *this* is translated by the Portuguese **este** or its related forms. *That* may be translated by **esse** or **aquele**: **esse** indicates something near to or associated with the person addressed, **aquele** something more remote. Like other adjectives the demonstratives agree in number and gender with the noun they qualify. They precede the noun. The forms are:

	Singular		*Plural*	
	masculine	feminine	masculine	feminine
this	este	esta	estes	estas
that (near you)	esse	essa	esses	essas
that (over there)	aquele	aquela	aqueles	aquelas

**este homem, esta mulher, estes homens, estas mulheres
esse jornal, essa caneta, esses jornais, essas canetas
aquele francês, aquela cidade, aqueles franceses, aquelas cidades**

---

[1] The expressions **vir de** (*to come from*), **pertencer a** (*to belong to*) and **ser feito de** (*to be made of*) are also available.

NOTE: Like the definite and indefinite articles (§ 32) a demonstrative cannot generally be expressed before one noun and understood (but unexpressed) before another. It must usually be repeated.

ęstes hǫmens e ęstas mulhęres, these men and women

(b) The demonstratives are used as pronouns as well as adjectives, and translate the English *this (one)*, *that (one)*, *that (one)*.

Que revista tens? Which magazine have you got?
Tenho ęsta, ęssa, aquęla. I have this one, that one, that one.
Que casas compra o espanhǫl? Which houses does the Spaniard buy?
Compra ęstas, ęssas, aquęlas. He buys these, those, those.

NOTES. 1. The English *one* is contained in the Portuguese pronoun (cf. § 37, 4).
2. Ęste and its related forms also translate English *the latter* and **aquęle** *the former*.

Tenho uma irmã e um irmão. Ęste trabalha mạs aquęla não. I have a sister and a brother. The latter works but the former doesn't.

(c) There are forms of the demonstrative pronoun not listed above: the neuter singular forms **isto, isso, aquilo.** Neuter demonstrative pronouns refer to something indeterminate or collective, unlike the masculine and feminine accented forms which refer to specific nouns.

isto, this   **isso,** that (near you)   **aquilo,** that (yonder)

Compreendes tudo isto? Do you understand all this?
Isso é impossívęl. That's impossible.
O que fọi aquilo? What was that?

46. THE USES OF **muito.** (a) As an adjective: in the singular, it means *much, a lot of*; in the plural, *many, a lot of*. (b) As a

pronoun: in the singular, *much, a lot*; in the plural, *many, a lot*.
(c) As an adverb; three meanings: *much*; *very*; *too*.

Tęmos muito pão.	We've got a lot of bread.
Compro muitos livros.	I buy many books.
Pędro não compra muitos.	Peter doesn't buy many.
Isso é muito melhǫr.	That's much better.
Ęste carro é muito nǫvo.	This car is very new.
É muito grande pạra mim.	It's too big for me.

47. PRONUNCIATION. Revise §§ 1–9.

VOCABULARY

o baú	trunk	o quarto (de	
bem	well	dormir)	bedroom
a casa de		a sala de es-	
banho	bathroom	tar	lounge
o cinęma	cinema	a sala de	
a comédia	play, comedy	jantar	dining-room
a cozinha	kitchen	a sala de	
as divisões	rooms (*of an en-*	visitas	drawing-room
	tire house)	sǫbretudo	especially
o filme	film	também	also, as well, too
hǫje	today	o teatro	theatre
o jardim	garden	tomar banho	to have a bath
a lei [lɐj]	law	tomar café	to have coffee
a madeira	wood (*sub-*	tomar o café	to have break-
[mɐˈdɐjrɐ]	*stance*)		fast
mal	badly	tomạr chá	to have tea
a pędra	stone		
o quarto de			
banho	bathroom		

See also the adjectives and pronouns listed in §45, and revise
the vocabulary of lessons 1–5.

EXERCISES

I. (a) *Pronounce the following and supply phonetic transcriptions:*
vendeis, enviais, estudamos, porque, estalagens, livreiro,
tenho, tendes, lápis, fósseis, estações, têxtil, civis,

difícil, exteriores, melhor, vermelho, inteligente, portuenses.

(b) *In the following words the stressed vowel is italicized but no accents have been written in.* *Read each word aloud and write in the accents where necessary:* rapido, raizes, imagens, franceses, policia, ideia, bau, ali, ai, juiz, continua, tombola, necessario, bem, tambem, comprais, juizo, paul, sairem, cairdes, bainha, pauis, espanhois, papeis, dezoito, Raul, Luis.

(c) *Translate:* Tomamos café. Somos de Lisboa. Esta loja é dum judeu. Vamos ao cinema. Dezasseis divisões. Esta velha senhora. Vemos o filme hoje. Gostamos da casa, sobretudo da sala de visitas. Vou tomar banho. Tomamos café na sala de jantar. Quantos tios tem você? Vão tomar o café.

(d) *Translate:* those small houses, these Oporto friends, this old man, nineteen cups, too many laws, large theatres and cinemas, some very big hospitals, some good boys, no small houses.

II. (a) *Study and translate:* 1. Quem vai vender aqueles móveis? O velho lojista francês. 2. Essa lição é muito difícil para as raparigas alemãs. 3. Há um bom filme no cinema. 4. Quantos filhos tem o Sr. Gonçalves? 5. Aquela casa de banho é muito bonita. 6. Sobre a mesa da sala de jantar há flores azuis, amarelas e vermelhas. 7. Os tios do rapaz inglês lêem o terceiro capítulo do novo livro. 8. Vamos ao teatro muitas vezes porque gostamos de dramas e comédias, e sobretudo dos dramas de Shakespeare. 9. Há muitos baús no comboio porque vai para Paris. 10. A casa do senhor inglês é de pedra, mas a velha casa da senhora francesa é de madeira.

(b) *Translate:* 1. We're going to have tea in the lounge. 2. Mary's working in the kitchen. 3. This house is very big; it has fourteen rooms. 4. Peter is reading a book in the garden. 5. Who does that old house belong to? 6. Are

71

you (*sing. very fam.*) going into town today? 7. Do you (*pol. pl.*) depart today? 8. John's going to have a bath. 9. The French girls read very badly, but the German boys read fairly well. 10. This country has too many laws!

III. (*a*) *Study and translate:* 1. O velho livreiro lisboeta não tem amigo algum. 2. Na cozinha temos sal, pimenta, mostarda, tomates, batatas, vinho, chávenas, pires e pratos. 3. Também temos café e chá. 4. Vamos tomar café na cozinha, mas Pedro vai tomar banho. 5. As raparigas vão para a cama. 6. Quando parte este comboio para Lisboa? 7. Essa casa é muito grande, com cozinha, sala de jantar, sala de estar, sala de visitas, casa de banho e cinco quartos de dormir. 8. As raparigas andaluzas vendem lápis e canetas aos senhores ingleses na rua. 9. Hoje ides estudar a quarta lição. 10. Porque não ledes o capítulo nove?

(*b*) *Translate:* 1. The third lesson isn't too difficult for the Catalan boy. It isn't so difficult as lesson four. 2. We like Michael's new car—it's so beautiful! 3. The girl's father hasn't got many friends. 4. There's a very good film on at the new cinema. 5. We don't like the old house because it's built of stone. 6. Mary and the French girl come from Paris. 7. Who does that beautiful new car belong to? 8. The Portuguese boy's got to send a letter to John's grandparents. 9. Is the captain reading a telegram? Why? 10. How pretty the flowers are!

LESSON VII

48. One of the principal difficulties of Portuguese is that of distinguishing between the verbs **sęr** and **estar,** both of which translate the English *to be*.

sęr, *to be*		estar, *to be*	
sou	sǫmos	estou	estamos
és	sǫis	estás	estais
é	são	está	estão

49. ENGLISH *to be* + *adjective*. (*a*) **Sęr** indicates an inherent or essential characteristic, with no suggestion of change from any other state; **estar,** on the other hand, denotes an accidental quality, the result of change from, or liability to change into, a different state.

sęr:

Ęsta lição é difícil.   This lesson is difficult.

Aquęlas casas são grandes.   Those houses are big.

A mulhęr é espanhǫla.   The woman is Spanish.

Isto não é possívęl.   This is not possible.

Ęste amigo é muito inteligente.   This friend is very intelligent.

Ęssas flǫres são amaręlas.   Those flowers are yellow.

estar:

Estamos muito contentes.   We are very pleased.

Hǫje estou um pouco triste.   I'm a little sad today.

Ęsta pêra não está madura.   This pear is not ripe.

As pǫrtas estão abęrtas.   The doors are open.

A janęla está partida.   The window is broken.

A mãe não está $\begin{Bmatrix} \text{bǫa} \\ \text{bem} \end{Bmatrix}$.   The mother's not well.

73

(b) Most adjectives can be used with both **ser** and **estar**. Not, however, indiscriminately. The distinction established above still applies.

A rapariga é pálida. The girl is pale (*of naturally pale complexion*).

A rapariga está pálida. The girl is pale (*because of illness, shock, etc.*).

Êste senhor é muito alegre. This gentleman is very cheerful (*of a cheerful disposition*).

Êste senhor está muito alegre. This gentleman is very cheerful (*in a cheerful mood*).

O gêlo é frio. Ice is cold (*inherent characteristic*).

Êste café está frio. This coffee is cold (*accidental quality: it has gone cold*).

O pai é (um) doente. The father is ill (*a chronic invalid*).

A mãe está $\begin{Bmatrix} \text{doente} \\ \text{mal} \end{Bmatrix}$. The mother is ill (*with influenza, etc.*).

(c) Some adjectives have a different meaning according to whether they are used with **ser** or **estar**.

ser bom	to be good
estar $\begin{Bmatrix} \text{bom} \\ \text{bem} \end{Bmatrix}$	to be well
ser mau	to be bad, evil
estar mau	to be naughty
ser pronto	to be prompt
estar pronto	to be ready

Êste senhor é muito pronto. This gentleman is very prompt.
Estamos prontos a partir. We are ready to leave.

NOTE: Either the adjective **bom** or the adverb **bem** may be used with **estar** to translate *well*; either the adjective **doente** or the adverb **mal** may be used with **estar** to translate *ill*. **Mal** implies a very serious illness. **Estar bom** is somewhat colloquial.

(d) *A General Aid.* In deciding whether to use **sẹr** or **estar** in a given case the following will prove useful: if *in a* (+adj.) *state* can be substituted for the adjective alone without change of meaning, use **estar;** otherwise (*i.e.*, if *a* (+adj.+noun) would be a more appropriate substitution) use **sẹr.**

I am pleased (*i.e.*, in a pleased state).
> **Estou contente.**

The pear is ripe (*i.e.*, in a ripe state).
> **A pêra está madura.**

The house is big (*not* in a big state *but* a big house).
> **A casa é grande.**

The bookseller is English (*not* in an English state *but* an English person).
> **O livreiro é inglês.**

John's father is rich (*not* in a rich state *but* a rich man).
> **O pai de João é rico.**

In a case like *He is cheerful* both substitutions are equally possible: *He is in a cheerful state* and *He is a cheerful person.* But which is meant? If it is the first one, **estar** is used; if the second, **sẹr.**

50. ENGLISH *to be*+ *an element other than an adjective.* **Estar** is used to indicate temporary position, **sẹr** to indicate permanent position; **sẹr** alone is used in all other cases.

estar (*temporary position*):
> **Onde estás? Estou aqui.**   Where are you?   I'm here.
> **Está atrás da pọrta.**   He is behind the door.
> **Estamos em Londres agọra.**   We are now in London.

sẹr (*permanent position*):
> **Onde é a bibliotẹca?**   Where is the library?
> **Lisbọa é em Portugal.**   Lisbon is in Portugal.
> **O correio é na Praça dos Restauradọres.**   The post-office is in the Praça dos Restauradores.

ser (*other cases*):

O que é isso? What is that?

Qual é o hotel? É um grande. É o mesmo. Which hotel is it? It is a big one. It is the same one.

Morar em Lisboa não é conhecer Portugal. To live in Lisbon is not to know Portugal.

Três e quatro são sete. Three and four are seven.

De quem é este livro? É de João. É do senhor. Whose book is this? It's John's. It's yours.

Donde é? É de Faro. É um bom rapaz. Where's he from? He comes from Faro. He's a good lad.

NOTES. 1. **Estar** is hardly ever followed by a noun complement: **Este é** (*never* **está**) **o tio de Miguel** (*This is Michael's uncle*).

2. The uses of **ser, estar** and **ficar** with past participles are discussed in §§ 220–222.

3. The uses of **ser, estar** and **ficar** with regard to *position* are amplified in §§ 79–80.

51. POSSESSIVE ADJECTIVES AND PRONOUNS.

	Thing(s) possessed			
	Singular		*Plural*	
	Masculine	Feminine	Masculine	Feminine
my, mine	**meu**	**minha**	**meus**	**minhas**
your(s) (*sing.*)	**teu**	**tua**	**teus**	**tuas**
his, her(s), its	**seu**	**sua**	**seus**	**suas**
our(s)	**nosso**	**nossa**	**nossos**	**nossas**
your(s) (*pl.*)	**vosso**	**vossa**	**vossos**	**vossas**
their(s)	**seu**	**sua**	**seus**	**suas**

NOTES. 1. Except in cases which will be explained later (see § 158), the possessives when used *before* a noun must be preceded by the definite article.

o meu livro, my book
a nossa casa, our house
as suas irmãs, her sisters

2. Generally speaking, only when the noun is preceded by the indefinite article may the possessive adjective follow the noun. In these cases, it has the meaning *of mine, of yours,* etc.

um amigo meu, a friend of mine (*also* **um meu amigo**)

3. *Your(s),* when referring to people addressed as **você, vocês, o Sr., a Sra., os Srs., as Sras.,** is rendered by the third person forms **seu, sua, seus, suas,** just as those words govern the *third* person of verb-forms, *e.g.,* **Tem o seu livro?** (*Have you got your book?*)   This is the most frequent function of **seu, sua,** etc.

4. The forms **teu, tua, teus, tuas** correspond to the *very familiar* forms of address; **vosso, vossa, vossos, vossas** to the *restricted* form of address [see § 15, 2].   Colloquially, however, **vosso,** etc., are used as the possessive forms of **vocês.**

5. When the possessive adjective stands alone (*i.e.,* not preceding or following a noun), it is only preceded by the definite article when emphatic distinction of ownership or possession is indicated.

Este livro é meu.   This book is mine.

but **Este livro é o meu, mas esse é o teu.**   This book is mine, but that's yours.

52. THE ADJECTIVES **novo** AND **jovem.**   The meaning of **jovem** is exclusively *young;* **novo** may mean either *new or young,* and is normally the word to be used in the comparison of people's ages.

João é muito $\left\{ \begin{matrix} \textbf{jovem} \\ \textbf{novo} \end{matrix} \right\}$.   John is very young.

Este é o chapéu novo.   This is the new hat.
O seu pai é mais novo do que o meu.   Your father is younger than mine.

NOTES. 1. Both these adjectives may either precede or follow the noun.

2. *Elder* (*older*) is translated by **mais velho.** Occasionally **maior (de idade)** and **menor (de idade)** are to be found for *elder* (*older*) and *younger* respectively.

77

53. THE IRREGULAR VERBS **vir** AND **pôr** (second conjugation, Old Portuguese *pôer* or *poer*).

vir, *to come*		**pôr**, *to put, place*	
venho [ˈvɐɲu]	vimos	ponho	pomos
vens	vindes	pões	pondes
vem	vêm	põe	põem [ˈpojɐj]

54. PRONUNCIATION: THE DIPHTHONG **ei**. (*a*) This diphthong is ordinarily pronounced [ɐj]:

cheio, *full*; **os fósseis**, *fossils*; **vendeis**, *you sell* (restricted form).

(*b*) When carrying an acute accent (**éi**), it is pronounced [ɛj]:

papéis, *papers, pieces of paper*; **hotéis**, *hotels*.

(*c*) In a number of words, **ei** is pronounced [ɛj], although carrying no accent, *i.e.*, contrary to the rule established in § 8 (*h*) (i).

This group comprises all the feminine flections of adjectives with masculine singular in **-eu**,[1] many nouns ending in **-eia**, and all the flections of adjectives with masculine singular in **-eico**:

europeia, europeias; ateia, ateias; a ideia, as ideias; onomatopeico, onomatopeica, onomatopeicos, onomatopeicas.

VOCABULARY

aberto	open	o correio	post-office
agora	now	doente	ill
alegre	cheerful, gay	donde[2]	{where . . . from / whence
atrás de	behind (*prep.*)		
cansado	tired	frio	cold
cansativo	tiresome	o gelo	ice
o chapéu	hat	jovem	young
contente	pleased, happy	maduro	ripe

[1] Except **judeu** and **sandeu** [§ 32 (4)].

[2] Do not confuse this with Spanish *dónde* or *donde*. Also used is **de onde** [di-ˈõndə].

pálido	pale, pallid	quente	hot
pôr	to put, place	rico	rich
pôr a mẹsa	to lay the table	Setúbạl	Setúbal
pronto	prompt; ready	triste	sad, gloomy

Study also the possessive adjectives listed in § 51, and the words discussed in §§ 52–54.

EXERCISES

I. (a) *Pronounce the following and explain written accents:* hotéis, vendeis, ideias, ateia, onomatopeicas, comédia, polícia, contemporâneo, chapéu, objecção, congestão, ruim.

(b) *Translate:* Está cansada. Somos alegres. São espanhóis. Estamos em Portugal. A porta é verde. A porta está partida. Sou muito pronta. Está pronto agora. Onde está Miguel? O seu irmão. Os meus amigos. A nossa casa e os nossos jardins. Catorze flores azuis. Nove lápis velhos.

(c) *Translate:* Where are you (*sing. pol.*)? She is here. They (*fem.*) are beautiful. He is very clever. The lady is English. This is not possible. The doors are open. We are ill. You (*fem. sing. pol.*) are tired. I am well. This pen is very bad. Those oranges are not ripe. Our mothers and sisters.

II. (a) *Study and translate:* 1. A tua mãe não vai para a cidade porque está muito cansada. 2. Estes rapazes portuenses falam bastante bem o inglês. 3. — Onde estão vocês? — Estamos aqui no quarto de dormir. 4. Os meus lápis são amarelos. 5. Esta caneta está partida. 6. Porque estão os meus irmãos aqui? 7. — De quem são aquelas casas tão bonitas? — São dum senhor de Setúbal. 8. Vocês têm muitas flores no jardim? 9. Não é difícil fazer isto. 10. Aquela rapariga alemã é mais alta do que muitas inglesas.

79

(b) *Translate:* 1. My hat is behind the door. 2. The new cinema is behind the post-office. 3. We are going to read the first chapter of the new book. 4. They are sad because they aren't going in my father's car. 5. This coffee isn't hot! 6. The pencils are much cheaper than the pens. 7. It's not possible to buy cheap wine here. 8. He's a very intelligent boy but he's ill. 9. I am very pleased because the apples are ripe. 10. "Whose idea is this?" (=Whose is this idea?) "It's Peter's."

III. (a) *Study and translate:* 1. Está triste e pálida porque não vai para Portugal. 2. Esse vinho é do velho lojista. 3. Donde é aquele senhor rico? 4. Vamos pôr a mesa na sala de jantar. 5. A minha irmã é muito jovem. 6. Que alegre estás hoje! 7. Que altas são as irmãs do senhor inglês! 8. De quem são esses livros que tens? 9. Pedro é muito cansativo. 10. O gelo é muito frio.

(b) *Translate:* 1. The yellow flowers are much more beautiful than the blue ones. 2. They're tired because they study a lot. 3. Our houses are very interesting. 4. She is in the shop with my mother. 5. This house has rather a small garden with not many flowers. 6. "Where are you from?" "I'm from Setúbal." 7. Is it possible to do this today? 8. Your sister is taller than my mother. 9. Peter is much younger than Michael. 10. They are very cheerful today because the gardens are open.

LESSON VIII

55. THE IMPERFECT INDICATIVE (English *I was buying, used to buy, bought*).

I. **-ar** verbs: stem plus endings **-ava, -avas, -ava, -ávamos, -áveis, -avam.**

II. **-er** verbs: stem plus endings **-ia, -ias, -ia, -íamos, -íeis, -iam.**

III. **-ir** verbs: stem plus endings **-ia, -ias, -ia, -íamos, -íeis, -iam.**

I. **comprar,** *to buy*	II. **vender,** *to sell*	III. **partir,** *to depart*
comprava	vendia	partia
compravas	vendias	partias
comprava	vendia	partia
comprávamos	vendíamos	partíamos
compráveis	vendíeis	partíeis
compravam	vendiam	partiam

Antes morávamos em Lisbọa. Formerly we lived in Lisbon.

O sẹu irmão vendia jornais. His brother used to sell newspapers.

O que comprava vọcê? What were you buying?

A minha mãe estava doente. My mother was ill.

Recebiam muitas cartas. They used to get a lot of letters.

56. IRREGULAR IMPERFECTS.[1] There are only four irregular imperfects:

sẹr, *to be*

ẹra	éramos
ẹras	éreis
ẹra	ẹram

[1] Students of Spanish should note that the imperfects of **ir** and **vẹr** are regular in Portuguese, *i.e.,* **ia,** etc., **via,** etc., respectively.

tęr, *to have (got)*

tinha	tínhamos
tinhas	tínheis
tinha	tinham

vir, *to come*	pôr, *to put, place*
vinha	punha
vinhas	punhas
vinha	punha
vínhamos	púnhamos
vínheis	púnheis
vinham	punham

57. THE INTERROGATIVES **que** AND **qual**. These words are used in both direct and indirect questions.

(*a*) **Que** is both pronoun and adjective. When used as a pronoun it is often preceded by **o**.

Que
O que } **faz vǫcê?** What are you doing?

Que livros vais comprar? What (*or* Which) books are you going to buy?

(*b*) **Qual** (plural **quais**) is, strictly speaking, a pronoun and indicates a more limited range of selection than the adjective **que**.

Quais dos livros vais enviar a João? Which (of the) books are you going to send to John?
Qual dos irmãos está aqui? Which brother is here?

(*c*) The English *which* and *what* before part of the verb *to be* is usually translated by **qual (quais)**. **Que** is used only when a definition is asked for.

Qual é o melhǫr livro? Which is the best book?
Quais são as suas ǫbjęcções? What are your objections?
Qual é a sua matéria predilęcta? What's your favourite subject?

but Que
O que } **é isto?** What's this?

Que
O que } **é um arrais?** What is a boatswain?

(*d*) There is a colloquial tendency, often deprecated by purists, to use **qual** (**quais**) as an interrogative adjective in place of **que.**

Quais livros vais comprar?   Which books are you going to buy?

Quais livros vais enviar a João?   Which books are you going to send to John?

Qual irmão está aqui?   Which brother is here?

Qual livro é o melhọr?   Which is the best book?

58. SUBJECT PRONOUNS, FORMS AND USES. It has been stated [§ 15, note 1] that the subject pronoun is not usually expressed in Portuguese, but is indicated in the verb ending. Nevertheless, subject pronouns *are* used when there is emphasis on the corresponding English pronoun, or when it is necessary to indicate the author(s) of an action in greater detail than the verb endings allow. They have the following forms:

Singular	*Plural*
ẹu, I	**nós,** we
tu, you (*very fam.*)	**vós,** you (*restricted*)
vọcê, you (*fairly fam.*)	**vọcês,** you (*fam.*)
o Sr., you (*pol. masc.*)	**os Srs.,** you (*pol. masc. or masc. and fem.*)
a Sra., you (*pol. fem.*)	**as Sras.,** you (*pol. fem.*)
ẹle, he, it (*masc.*)	**ẹles,** they (*masc. or masc. and fem.*)
ẹla, she, it (*fem.*)	**ẹlas,** they (*fem.*)

Nós trabalhávamos até às seis, mạs ẹles terminavam às cinco.   *We* used to work until six o'clock, but *they* would finish at five.

Ẹu ia ao cinẹma e ẹles (iam) ao teatro.   *I* used to go to the pictures, but *they* went to the theatre.

Tu e ẹu vamos ạmanhã.   You and I are going tomorrow.

NOTES. 1. In a few cases the use of the subject pronoun may serve to avoid confusion, to indicate, for instance, which of the various meanings of **vendia** (*I* [*he, she, you*] *used to sell*) is intended. Usually, however, the context alone will make it clear and no subject pronoun is therefore expressed. The English-speaking student tends to over-use the Portuguese subject pronoun.

2. The subject pronouns **vǫcê, vǫcês, o Sr., a Sra., os Srs., as Sras.** are more generally expressed even where there is no stress on the English pronoun and no possibility of confusion.

3. In colloquial usage the subject pronoun **nós** is frequently replaced by **a gente.** The student should avoid this usage.

59. FURTHER CONTRACTIONS—DEMONSTRATIVES. (*a*) Contraction is necessary where the prepositions **de** and **em** would precede the demonstratives **ęste, ęsse, aquęle,** together with their flexions and neuter forms:

de: **dęste, dęsta, dęstes, dęstas, disto; dęsse, dęssa, dęsses, dęssas, disso; daquęle, daquęla, daquęles, daquęlas, daquilo.**

em: **nęste, nęsta, nęstes, nęstas, nisto; nęsse, nęssa, nęsses, nęssas, nisso; naquęle, naquęla, naquęles, naquęlas, naquilo.**

NOTE: Some writers prefer to write **nęste, nęsse, naquęle,** etc., in full: **em ęste, em ęsse, em aquęle,** etc. Nevertheless they must be pronounced as though contraction had taken place.

(*b*) Contraction is necessary where the preposition **a** would precede the demonstrative **aquęle,** etc.:

àquęle, àquęla, àquęles, àquęlas, àquilo. (The **à**=[a].)

60. PRONUNCIATION: THE CONSONANT **x.** (*a*) In the initial position, it has the value [ʃ]: **a xícara,** *coffee-cup.*

(*b*) Before an unvoiced consonant, it has the value [ʃ]: **o êxtase,** *ecstasy.*

(*c*) It is never found before a voiced consonant in the same word.

(*d*) In the intervocalic position, it has four values:

   (i) in the prefix **ex-** before a following vowel, it has the value [z]: **o êxito,** *success;*

   (ii) in words of popular derivation, it has the value [ʃ]: **deixar,** *to leave, let;* **a caixa,** *box;* **o luxo,** *luxury;* **Alexandre,** *Alexander;* **o México,** *Mexico;*

(iii) in words of learned derivation, it has the value [ks]:
fixar, *to fix*; **o reflęxo**, *reflex*;

(iv) in the following words, and words derived therefrom or
related thereto, it has the value [s]: **ąuxiliar**, *auxiliary*;
próximo, *next*; **a máxima**, *maxim*; **a sintaxe**, *syntax*;
trouxe (part of the verb **trazęr**, *to bring*).

(*e*) In the final position, it has the value [ks]: **o ónix**, *onyx*;
o tórąx, *thorax*.

NOTES. 1. The following are exceptional: **o flux** [fluʃ], *flux*; **a
fénix** [ˈfɛniʃ], *phoenix*; **o cálix** [ˈkaliʃ], *calyx*; *chalice*; **Félix** [ˈfɛliʃ],
Felix.

2. Nouns ending in **x** are usually identical in the plural form:
o clímąx, *climax*, pl. **os clímąx**. However, a number have
alternative singular forms on which the plural is based, notably:
o códęx *or* **o códice**, *codex*, pl. **os códices**; **o cálix** *or* **o cálice**,
calyx; wineglass, pl. **os cálices**; **o índęx** *or* **o índice**, *index*, pl.
os índices.

VOCABULARY

ali	there	**comęr**	to eat, have a
ąmanhã	tomorrow		meal
o ano	year	**demais**[1]	too (much)
antes	before, pre-	**depọis**	afterwards
	viously	**descansar**	to rest
bebęr	to drink	**dọce**	sweet
o cálice	wineglass (*for*	**durante**	during
	Port wine)	**enquanto**	while, whilst
o campo	country(side);	**escrevęr**	to write
	field	**havia**	there was, there
em casa	at home		were
pąra casa	(to) home	**mandar**	to send
cędo	early (*adverb*)	**a manhã**	morning

[1] This word is used *after* an adverb or adjective to translate *too*: **Ęste
chapéu é grande demais** (*This hat is too big*).   In literary language one
may also find occasionally **demasiado** and **demasiadamente** used in
the same sense, but placed *before* the adverb or adjective.

muitas vẹzes	often	sempre	always (*usu.*
ontem	yesterday		*follows verb*)
o país	country	a tarde	afternoon,
	(*political*)		evening
a pêra (pl.		terminar	to finish
as pẹras)	pear	tọdo	all, every
quase	almost, nearly	às vẹzes	} sometimes, at
recebẹr	to receive	por [pur]	times
		vẹzes	

em casa dos mẹus pais   at my parents' house
pạra casa dos mẹus pais   to my parents' house
tọdo o dia (ano)[1]   all day (year), the whole day (year)
tọda a manhã (tarde)[1]   all morning (afternoon, evening)
tọdos os dias (anos)   every day (year)
tọdas as manhãs (tardes)   every morning (afternoon, evening)

Study also the words listed in §§ 58 and 60.

EXERCISES

I. (*a*) *Pronounce the following and explain written accents:*
deixar, os nossos amigos, luxuoso, fixáramos, na próxima
semana, vendíeis, a xícara amarela, para ambos os homens,
uma caixa de fósforos.

(*b*) *Study and translate:* Nós comprávamos. Eles moravam.
Ele bebia demais. Ela comia mais. Todos iam. O que
dáveis? Elas liam muito. Onde trabalhavam os senhores?
Via. Nós púnhamos a mesa. Eu vinha todos os dias.
Quem era? Porque não comias? Àquele homem. Qual é
a melhor pêra? Qual é a sua religião? Escreviam cartas à
sua mãe. Onde estava ele? Ele fazia isto. Para onde
viajavam? Com que caneta escrevias? Eu lia pouco. Tu
tinhas de partir ontem. O chá estava quente. O vinho
estava muito frio.

[1] Also **o dia tọdo, a manhã tọda**, etc.

(c) *Translate* (*using a pronoun subject where possible*): He used to give. They were going. We ate. Which did you[1] use to buy? What were they (*fem.*) writing? She would send. They used to drink too much. I hadn't any idea. Which books were you receiving? What books did you send? I worked. Where did you use to live? We used to go. Where were you going? We used to work. He didn't use to study. Who was he? Where were you? They used to talk a lot. We used to receive a lot of letters. What was he selling? He hasn't any sisters. The tea was cold. The pears were not ripe. My father was reading a newspaper. What were you doing in that shop?

II. (a) *Study and translate:* 1. Íamos quase todos os dias ao campo. 2. Muitas vezes mandavam livros e jornais ingleses aos meus amigos espanhóis. 3. Em que dias ias àquele hospital? 4. Eu não via muito bem a loja aonde tínhamos de ir. 5. Às vezes, quando eu era pequeno, íamos para casa dos meus avós. 6. Enquanto ela viajava comia muitas laranjas e maçãs. 7. Esse chapéu é grande demais para o pai de Miguel. 8. Antes ele morava em Setúbal mas agora estuda em Coimbra. 9. Em casa dos meus tios havia muitos móveis. 10. Estas peras não são muito doces.

(b) *Translate:* 1. "Where were you?" "I was at my grand-parents." 2. The doors of this house were all yellow. 3. My mother and sister used to live in London. 4. I used to speak a lot of Portuguese with his German friends. 5. You used to work much harder (=much more) than he [did].[1] 6. Why did they all use to leave so early? 7. I used to live in this country in a very old house. 8. Where did

---

[1] Henceforth, no indication will be given of which second person is intended. A complete sentence will often provide sufficient context on which to base the choice. Otherwise, use the singular polite or, better still, give all possible forms for extra practice.

[2] Words in brackets [ ] are not to be translated; words in parentheses are explanations or recommended means of translation.

your brother use to work when he lived in Paris ? 9. We used to buy many French and Spanish newspapers. 10. What did you use to do when you went to your grandparents ?

III. (a) *Study and translate:* 1. Escrevíamos muitas cartas aos nossos amigos de Madrid. 2. Eles estudavam muito, mas nós estudávamos mais. 3. Porque não vamos para casa dos teus tios ? 4. Enquanto ela trabalhava naquele jardim, eu passava os dias com uns amigos que tinha ali. 5. Quando morávamos no campo, íamos quase todos os dias para casa do senhor Gonçalves. 6. Amanhã não vou proque tenho de trabalhar nesta loja. 7. O que fazias ontem? — Descansava em casa. 8. Todos os anos o meu pai passava um mês em Lisboa, onde tinha muitos amigos. 9. Todas as manhãs a rapariga punha a mesa para a minha mãe. 10. Madava cartas quase todos os dias para os meus pais.

(b) *Translate:* 1. Who were the women who were selling the apples and pears ? 2. Which country did he live in when he was younger ? 3. They would work all afternoon in this garden, but we used to rest in the house. 4. Peter always came to our house in the summer. 5. Sometimes he would spend three weeks at our house in the country. 6. Our teacher always finished the lesson early especially when he had to go to the theatre afterwards. 7. He was going to receive several letters yesterday. 8. My grandfather always drank too much. 9. I was ill this morning but I'm better now. 10. We would be very pleased when our parents came.

Uses of TER, ESTAR COM *and* FAZER, *the Gerund,*
the Progressive Tenses, other Modes of Address,
Initial Unstressed (H)E

LESSON IX

61. USES OF **tẹr** AND **estar com.** (*a*) Revise §§ 30 and 48.

(*b*) Note the following idiomatic uses of **tẹr**:

tẹr frio (*m.*)	to be cold (*of living beings*)
tẹr calọr (*m.*)	to be warm, hot (*of living beings*)
tẹr sẹde (*f.*)	to be thirsty[1]
tẹr fọme (*f.*)	to be hungry[1]
tẹr sọno (*m.*)	to be sleepy
tẹr sọrte (*f.*)	to be lucky
tẹr prẹssa (*f.*)	to be in a hurry
tẹr mẹdo (*m.*)	to be afraid
tẹr razão (*f.*)	to be right
não tẹr razão (*f.*)	to be wrong
tẹr { cuidado (*m.*) / cạutẹla (*f.*) }	to be careful
tẹr saudades [sɐu-] (*f.*) de	to miss, long for
tẹr vontade (*f.*) de	to be keen to, feel like

In all the above expressions, **estar com** is very often used in place of **tẹr.** In the following expressions, **tẹr** *only* is employed:

tẹr (que vẹr) com	to have to do with
tẹr { cọisas pạra / que } fazẹr	to have things to do
tẹr . . . anos (*m.*)	to be . . . years old

Que frio tínhamos! How cold we were!

Tenho vontade de ir pạra Portugal. I'm keen to go to
Portugal.

---

[1] Note also **passar sẹde,** *to experience thirst*; **passar fọme,** *to go hungry*; also found are **sentir frio, calọr, sẹde, fọme, sọno, saudades de, vontade de,** *to feel cold, hot,* etc.

Tinha que fazẹr em casa. He had jobs to do at home.

Tenho muitas cọisas que/pạra estudar. I've got a lot of things to study.

Isto não tem nada (que vẹr) com ẹle. This has got nothing to do with him.

Maria está com sọno. Mary's sleepy.

Tu estás com razão. *You're* right.

Quantos anos tens? *or* **Que idade tens?** How old are you?

A sua irmã tem trẹze anos. His sister is thirteen (years old).

NOTE: In cases where the Portuguese **tẹr, estar com** + *noun* correspond to the English *to be* + *adjective*, an English modifying adverb must be translated by the corresponding Portuguese adjective (*e.g.*, *I am very thirsty* becomes **Tenho muita sẹde,** lit., *I have much thirst*).

62. USES OF **fazẹr:** (*a*) Revise § 40.

(*b*) **Fazẹr** is used to indicate certain states of the weather.

Que tempo faz?	What is the weather like?
Faz calọr. Faz muito frio.	It is warm. It is very cold.
Fazia bom (mau) tempo.	It was fine (bad) weather.
Fazia bom dia.	It was a fine day.
Faz sọl. Faz escuro.	It's sunny. It's dark.
Faz um tempo péssimo.	The weather is shocking.
Faz vento.	It's windy.

NOTES. 1. **Faz escuro** and **faz frio** may be replaced by **está escuro** and **está frio.   Está calọr** is on the other hand somewhat colloquial. Observe also **Cọmo está o tempo? Que tempo está?** and **Está bom (mau) tempo.**

2. **Sọl** is not written with a capital initial letter when it means *sunshine* or *heat of the sun.*

63. THE GERUND. (*a*) The Portuguese gerund is formed by removing the final **-r** of the infinitive and substituting **-ndo;** thus **comprando, vendendo, partindo.** The gerund of **pôr** is

pondo. The gerund usually corresponds to the English present participle *-ing*, or to *by -ing*.

A mãe trabalhava na cozinha preparando o jantar.
The mother was working in the kitchen preparing dinner.

A gente pǫde tornar-se rica comprando e vendendo cǫisas.
People can get rich (by) buying and selling things.

Não é mortificando-se que se resǫlvem os problęmas dęsta vida.
It is not by mortifying oneself that one solves the problems of this life.

(*b*) It may translate other English verb parts when they express time or cause.

Estando em Portugal, falava português.
When he was in Portugal, he used to talk Portuguese.

Sendo jǫvens, trabalhavam mais.
When (*or* As) they were young, they worked harder.

(*c*) But a gerund does *not* translate the English *-ing* in the following cases:

(i) after a preposition: an infinitive is used.[1]

antes de recebęr a carta, before receiving the letter
depǫis de terminar a lição, after finishing the lesson
sem sabęr porquê, without knowing why
por ʃpur] estar mal, through being ill

Notice also the construction **ao** + *infinitive* (*on -ing*): **ao vęr a minha amiga,** *on seeing my friend* (f.); **ao chegar a casa,** *when I* (*he*, etc.) *arrive(d) home*.

(ii) when *-ing* fulfils the function of a noun: an infinitive is used; the infinitive is preceded by the masculine singular definite article when there is a definite article in English, and may also be

---

[1] For the special construction **em** + gerund see § 92 (*a*).

preceded by the article when it is the subject of a sentence or clause.

Gǫsto de lęr. I like reading (= I like to read).
o murmurar das fontes, the murmuring of the fountains.
o ir e vir de tanta gente, the coming and going of so many people
Estudar ⎱ **aproveita.** Studying is profitable (It is profitable to
O estudar ⎰ study).

(iii) when *-ing* fulfils an adjectival function: an adjective or adjectival clause is the usual solution.

um livro muito interessante, a very interesting book
pais tão compreensivos e amorǫsos, such understanding and loving parents
uma mala $\left\{\begin{array}{l}\text{que continha}\\\text{contendo}\end{array}\right\}$ **papéis,** a suitcase containing papers

GENERAL NOTE: The Portuguese gerund is essentially verbal and emphasizes the duration of the action it presents. The further the English present participle (*i.e.*, *-ing*) deviates from this function the less likely it is to be translated by the Portuguese gerund.

64. THE PROGRESSIVE TENSES. These are used less frequently than the corresponding English forms (*I am buying, he was selling*, etc.) for they imply longer duration or greater repetition of the verbal action. They may be formed either by the appropriate tense of **estar** followed by **a** + *infinitive*, or by the appropriate tense of **estar** together with the gerund of the verb in question, though some purists reject this latter construction as an intrusive Brazilianism.

Está sempre $\left\{\begin{array}{l}\text{a cantar}\\\text{cantando}\end{array}\right\}$. She's always singing.

Estávamos $\left\{\begin{array}{l}\text{a terminar}\\\text{terminando}\end{array}\right\}$ **a lição.** We were finishing the lesson.

65. OTHER MODES OF ADDRESS. Portuguese is very rich in modes of address (*i.e.*, ways of translating *you*). Other than those studied in § 15, there are several others in common use.

(a) **Vọssa Excelência** [ˈvɔs(ɐ) əʃsəˈlẽsjɐ] (in rapid speech [vɔˈsẽsjɐ]), is a mode of address implying a certain respect, although it is by no means always as exalted as the English *Your Excellency*. It is often abbreviated in writing as **V. Exª.**[1]

(b) **Vọssa Senhoria** [ˈvɔsɐ səɲuˈriɐ] is a similar mode to the above, but is normally limited to correspondence, particularly of a commercial nature. It is often abbreviated in writing as **V. Sa.**[1]

(c) **O menino** and **a menina** are employed for addressing boys and girls respectively. It should be noted that **a senhọra** is used for addressing both married women and maiden ladies. **A menina** is also used for addressing female servants.

(d) **O mẹu amigo** and **a minha amiga** are used as friendly modes of address, though not from one sex to another.

(e) **A senhọra Dọna** followed by a feminine Christian name is also often found. It is often abbreviated in writing as **a Sra. D.** All the above modes govern the third person of the verb, and are represented by third person possessives and object pronouns.

V. Exª. canta muito bem. You sing very well, sir (*e.g., the teacher*).
A menina tem vontade de partir? Do you want to leave, miss?
O mẹu amigo está muito alẹgre! You're very cheerful!
A senhọra Dọna Isabẹl tem razão. You're right, Mrs . . .

66. Pronunciation: Initial Unstressed (h)e. (a) When followed by **s**+consonant or **x**+consonant, it has the value: [ə]

    esperar, to wait; to hope;
    esgotar, to drain; to exhaust;
    explorar, to explore; to exploit.

---

[1] Adjectives remain in the masculine with **V. Exª.** and **V. Sª.** except when the person addressed is female.

(*b*) When followed by a nasal + consonant, it has the value [ẽ], except in slipshod pronunciation where it has the value [ĩ]:

> **enviar,** to send;
> **a empada,** pie;
> **Henrique,** Henry;
> **entreaberto,** half-open, ajar.

(*c*) When followed by 1 + consonant, or **rb** or **rv,** it has the value [ɛ]:

> **Elvira,** Elvira;
> **o herbívoro,** herbivore;
> **o ervanário,** herbalist;
> *but* **a ervilha** [irˈviʎɐ], pea.

(*d*) When followed by **r** + *any other* consonant its quality vacillates between a very closed [e] and a clipped [i]:

> **Herculano,** Herculano (*a surname*);
> **errar,** to err; to wander;
> **erguer,** to lift, raise.

(*e*) When followed by **ct** or **pt,** it has the value [ɛ]:

> **o ectoplasma,** ectoplasm;
> **o hectolitro,** hectolitre;
> **o heptágono,** heptagon.

(*f*) When followed by any other consonant, it has the value [i]:

> **o exame,** exam., examination;
> **hesitar,** to hesitate;
> **emaranhar,** to entangle;
> **eterno,** eternal.

(*g*) When followed by a vowel, it forms a normal diphthong:

> **Heitor** [ɐjˈtor], Hector;
> **a Europa** [ewˈrɔpɐ], Europe.

NOTES. 1. It has the value [ɐj] in the prefix **ex-**, when this forms a separate element meaning *former*, *e.g.*, **o ex-ministro** [ɐjʒ-mi'niʃtru].

2. Rule (*f*) is not altered by the addition of the negative prefix **in-**: **elástico**, *elastic*; **inelástico** [ini'laʃtiku], *inelastic*.

VOCABULARY

antes de	before (*prep.*)	**ou**	or
chegar	to arrive	**perto de**	near, close to
chegar a	to reach, arrive at, in	**a praça**	square
		o presente	present, gift
dar um		**principal**	main, principal
passeio	to go for a walk	**sem**	without
depois de	after (*prep.*)	**o tempo**	time; weather
o edifício	building	**a (*or* em)**	in time, on
importante	important	**tempo**	time
Isabel	Elizabeth, Isabella	**a visita**	visit; visitor (*m. and f.*]
levar	to take, carry	**visitar**	to visit
levar em conta	to bear in mind, take into account	**o vizinho**	neighbour

Study also the words and expressions listed in §§ 61, 62, 65 and 66.

EXERCISES

I. (*a*) *Pronounce the following:* esperávamos, as pirâmides do Egipto, a vida eterna, Henrique, Herculano, estavam a hesitar, a expulsão dos jesuítas, uma madeixa emaranhada, Heitor e Aquiles, a Europa e a África, três hectolitros, ecoavam.

(*b*) *Study and translate:* Recebendo. Mandando. Estando. Tendo. Sendo. Pondo. Levando em conta. Depois de chegar. Ao terminar a lição. Estávamos escrevendo.

Está a trabalhar. Ela tinha muita pressa. Estavas com sono. Quem tem medo? V. Ex.ª tem calor? Fazia muito calor. Faz escuro. Está frio. O tempo estava frio. Fazia mau tempo. Eu sentia vontade de partir. Está a partir.

(c) *Translate:* Doing. Buying. Living. Without resting. Before going. On drinking too much. He's having a meal. We were studying. You were drinking. I am finishing. They were writing to their uncle. I see my parents. They are visiting our friends. He always arrived in time. They were cold and I was hungry. She had to be careful. He was very warm. It was very warm. You were very sleepy. You're not right, Mary. The coffee was cold. How old is Elizabeth's mother?

II. (a) *Study and translate:* 1. Fazia muito frio porque todas as portas estavam abertas. 2. Durante o bom tempo íamos quase todos os dias ao campo. 3. Ela não levava em conta o frio que faz agora em Londres. 4. Por vezes, quando fazia muito calor ou quando estávamos com fome, íamos para casa dos meus avós. 5. A menina tem de ter muito cuidado. 6. Passávamos muitas horas falando dos países que íamos visitar. 7. Ia escrever a carta antes de visitar os seus amigos. 8. Mandava todos os filhos para Portugal, onde aprendiam a língua. 9. Muitos dos nossos vizinhos trabalhavam numa fábrica que era perto donde morávamos. 10. Visitávamos todos os senhores mais importantes da cidade.

(b) *Translate:* 1. Why were they all so afraid? 2. Who was right? You or I? 3. She was hungry and they were very thirsty. 4. I used to live in a country where the weather was always fine. 5. We used to take our friends to the station when the weather was bad. 6. It is better to spend the afternoon resting at home than to go for a walk with the heat as it is now. 7. The building he was talking about is very close to the main square. 8. When we read this we have to take into account that in Portugal it is much warmer than here. 9. My sister had a lot of friends but you hadn't any. 10. You were very gloomy yesterday, old boy!

III. (a) *Study and translate:* 1. Que pressa tinha! Aonde ia? 2. Fazia bastante calor em casa e ele não sentia vontade de estudar lições tão difíceis. 3. Fazia mau tempo e todos tínhamos muito frio. 4. Mas o que tinha que ver isso com a ideia que tinha o meu amigo ontem? 5. Amanhã não vou porque tenho muito que fazer em casa. 6. Eu tenho vontade de ir ao cinema mas a minha mulher vai passar a tarde em casa dos seus pais. 7. A minha amiga tinha muita sorte porque não tinha de ir ao hospital. 8. Quantos anos tinha o teu avô quando trabalhava naquela fábrica? 9. Todos tinham saudades do seu país e da sua família. 10. Passávamos as tardes estudando a língua, escrevendo cartas ou recebendo alguma visita dos nossos vizinhos.

(b) *Translate:* 1. When it is cold we eat much more than when it is warm. 2. He has to be very careful with the new car. 3. What luck to live in this country, where the weather is nearly always fine! 4. When he went home, he didn't take any present for his mother. 5. How old were you, sir, when you worked with our brother? 6. I always finish the first chapter before reading the second. 7. They are visiting some friends they have in this town. 8. He used to take my sisters to the station every morning. 9. She wasn't keen to go because she was rather ill. 10. They were buying presents for one of their friends who was going to Madrid.

LESSON X

67. CARDINAL NUMBERS. (*a*) Revise § 29.

(*b*)

21 vinte e um/uma	400 quątrocentos, -as
22 vinte e dǫis/duas	500 quinhentos, -as
23 vinte e três	600 seiscentos, -as
30 trinta	700 sętecentos, -as
31 trinta e um/uma	800 ǫitocentos, -as
32 trinta e dǫis/duas	900 nǫvecentos, -as
40 quarenta	1000 mil
50 cinquenta	1001 mil e um/uma
[sĩŋ'kwẽntɐ]	1099 mil e noventa e nǫve
60 sessenta	1100 mil e cem
70 setenta	1101 mil cento e um/uma
80 ǫitenta	1199 mil cento e noventa e
90 noventa	nǫve
100 cem	1200 mil e duzentos, -as
101 cento e um/uma	1566 mil quinhentos (-as) e
	sessenta e seis
102 cento e dǫis/duas	2000 dǫis/duas mil
120 cento e vinte	100,000 cem mil
200 duzentos, -as	200,000 duzentos (-as) mil
201 duzentos (-as) e	1,000,000 um milhão (de)
um(uma)	[mɪ'ʎɐw̃]
300 trezentos, -as	2,000,000 dǫis milhões (de)

NOTES. 1. Except for expressions involving the use of **um, dǫis** or the plural hundreds, cardinal numbers are invariable.

    quarenta e cinco canętas, forty-five pens
but **duas mil sętecentas e sessenta e uma casas,** 2761 houses

    2. **Cento** is only used when the link **e** follows, or as a noun, or in the expression **por cento** (*per cent*). Its use is different

from that of the Spanish **ciento,** in that it does *not* translate
100.

    cento e vinte e três, 123
    um cento de árvores (= **cem árvores**), one hundred trees
    cem por cento, one hundred per cent

3. When thousands are followed by any lower numeral from 1 to
100 inclusive, **e** is used as a link with what follows:

    três mil e cem, 3100
    duas mil e vinte e uma, 2021

4. When thousands are followed by any lower numeral from 101
to 199 inclusive, no link is used with what follows:

    cinco mil cento e quarenta e nọve, 5149

5. When thousands are followed by any lower numeral from 200
to 999 inclusive, **e** is used as a link with what follows only when
both the last two figures are noughts:

    quatro mil e trezentos, 4300
but **mil nọvecentos e vinte,** 1920

6. When hundreds are followed by any lower numeral, **e** is used
as a link with what follows:

    mil sẹtecentos e cinquenta e cinco, 1755

7. The English *a, one* is not translated before **cem, cento,** or **mil**
(except where it is necessary for the meaning: **trinta e uma mil
mulhẹres,** *thirty-one thousand women*). It *is* translated before
milhão which, being a noun, takes the preposition **de** before the
object numbered (though **de** is omitted when another numeral
follows). For **cento,** however, see note 2 above also.

    mil aviões e um milhão de sọldados, a thousand aircraft
       and a million men
    um milhão e um habitantes, a million and one inhabitants

8. Counting by hundreds does not go beyond the nine hundreds.
    mil e sessenta e seis, ten sixty-six
    os mil e nọvecentos, the nineteen hundreds

9. *Than* before a numeral is translated by **de.**

mais
menos } **de vinte árvores,** more
less } than twenty trees

Care should be taken not to confuse the above with the expression **não ... mais que,** *only*.

Não temos { **mais que**
senão } **dez.** We've only got ten.

68. ORDINAL NUMBERS.

primeiro, -a	first	**sexto, -a**	sixth
segundo, -a	second	**sétimo, -a**	seventh
terceiro, -a	third	**oitavo, -a**	eighth
quarto, -a	fourth	**nono, -a**	ninth
quinto, -a	fifth	**décimo, -a**	tenth

NOTE: The ordinals are rather rarely used in Portuguese beyond the tenth (though somewhat more frequently than in Spanish), being replaced by cardinals. Because of their relative rarity ordinals beyond the tenth are omitted here.

Isabel II (Isabel segunda), Isabella II, Elizabeth II
but **Afonso XIII (Afonso treze),** Alphonso XIII
o século V (o século quinto), the fifth century
but **o século XV (o século quinze),** the fifteenth century.

Notice that in titles and centuries ordinals and cardinals alike follow the noun. The English *the* that precedes the number in titles is not normally translated.

69. THE TIME. The time of day is indicated by means of the verb **ser.** The word **hora** (*hour*), or its plural **horas,** may be omitted, but is usually supplied when no fraction of the hour follows. When the expression of time is preceded by a preposition **hora** and **horas** are accompanied by or represented by the feminine definite article. With the first hour **ser** is used in the singular, with the rest it is used in the plural. The conjunction **e** indicates time *past* the hour, and **menos** time *to* the hour. *Half past* is rendered by **e meia,** *quarter past* by **e um quarto,** *quarter to* by **menos um quarto; minutos** (*minutes*) is usually added with the finer divisions of time (*i.e.*, within the five-minute division). *At* is rendered by **a**, a word normally meaning *to*.

Que horas são? **São duas horas.** What time is it? It's two o'clock.
É uma e cinco. It's five past one.
Era uma e nove minutos. It was nine minutes past one.
São cinco menos vinte. It's twenty to five.
Eram onze e um quarto. It was a quarter past eleven.
À uma e meia. At half past one.
Às onze menos um quarto. At a quarter to eleven.

NOTES. 1. In official time-tables the twenty-four hour clock system is often used; the words **hora(s)** and **minuto(s)** are usually omitted.

às seis e dez (*at* 6.10 *a.m.*); **às dezoito e quarenta e nove** (*at* 6.49 *p.m.*)
o comboio das dezasseis e trinta, e quinze, e quarenta e cinco (*the* 4.30, 4.15, 4.45 *p.m. train*)

2. Time *to* the hour may also be expressed by using the verb **faltar** (*to be lacking*): **faltam oito (minutos) para as sete** (*it's eight minutes to seven*); **falta um quarto para as três** (*it's a quarter to three*).

Note also: **às cinco para as duas** (*at five to two;* **são cinco para as duas** (*it's five to two*).

3. Observe the following, paying particular attention to the presence or absence of articles (note that it is extremely rare to refer to *twelve o'clock* as **doze horas**):

É meio-dia. It's noon, midday, twelve o'clock.
Ao meio-dia. At noon, twelve o'clock.
É meia-noite. It's midnight, twelve o'clock.
À meia-noite. At midnight, twelve o'clock.
Antes do meio-dia. Before midday, noon, twelve o'clock.
Depois da meia-noite. After midnight.
É meio-dia e meia (hora). It's half past twelve.
É meia-noite menos dez. It's ten to twelve, ten minutes to midnight.

4. The English *a.m.* (also *in the morning*) and *p.m.* (also *in the afternoon, in the evening, at night*) are rendered as follows *when preceded by a clock-time*:

da madrugada, in the morning (a.m. before sunrise)
da manhã, in the morning (a.m. after sunrise)
da tarde, in the afternoon, in the evening (p.m. until after nightfall)
da noite, at night (late p.m. and very early a.m.)

70. THE DAYS OF THE WEEK.

(a) The days of the week are:

o domingo	Sunday
a segunda-feira	Monday
a terça-feira	Tuesday
a quarta-feira	Wednesday
a quinta-feira	Thursday
a sexta-feira	Friday
o sábado	Saturday

The termination **-feira** is sometimes omitted.

(b) The definite article is normally omitted before the names of the days of the week except when they are preceded by the prepositions **em** and **a.**

Domingo é o primeiro dia da semana. Sunday is the first day of the week.

Hoje é quarta-feira. Today is Wednesday.

Amanhã, sexta-feira, vamos para a cidade. Tomorrow, Friday, we're going into town.

Vou terminar isto para sábado. I'm going to finish this by (for) Saturday.

o almoço de domingo, Sunday lunch

but **Vou partir na terça.** I'm going to leave on Tuesday.

(c) The preposition used to translate *on* is **em**; **a** is also found, particularly in timetables and to express habitual action. Occasionally the name of the day stands unaccompanied.

no sábado, na segunda (-feira), on Saturday, on Monday

O comboio vai à(s) segunda(s) e à(s) sexta(s). The train goes on Mondays and Fridays, on Monday and Friday in general.

Sábado à noite vamos ao cinema. We go/are going to the pictures on Saturday night.

71. THE DATE.

(*a*) The names of the months are: **Janeiro, Fevereiro, Março, Abril, Maio, Junho, Julho, Agosto, Setembro, Outubro, Novembro, Dezembro.**

(*b*) There exist two ways in Portuguese of indicating the day of the month:

(1) By using **estar a** (usually in the first person plural) followed by the appropriate *cardinal* number:

A quantos estamos? What's the date? *or* What date is it?

Estamos a catorze. It's the fourteenth.

Estávamos $\left\{ \begin{array}{l} \textbf{a} \\ \textbf{no dia} \end{array} \right\}$ **um de Maio.** $\left\{ \begin{array}{l} \text{It was the first of} \\ \text{May.} \end{array} \right.$

(2) By using **ser** and the appropriate *cardinal* number:

Quantos são hoje? Que data é hoje? What's the date?

Hoje $\left\{ \begin{array}{l} \textbf{é o dia} \\ \textbf{são} \end{array} \right\}$ **quinze.** Today is the fifteenth.

Era (o dia) um de Junho. It was the first of June.

(*c*) The preposition used to translate *on* is **a,** followed by the appropriate cardinal number (**no dia, em** and **aos** are also found).

　　a dois de Setembro, on the second of September

　　a vinte e um de Fevereiro, on the 21st of February

(*d*) The month is introduced, even after figures, by **de:** so also is the year.

　　a vinte de Janeiro de 1936, on the 20th (of) January, 1936

Note the following constructions also:

O dia 29 de Novembro de 1848 marca o fim de tanta angústia. The 29th November, 1848, marks the end of so much anguish.

em } 1950   in } 1950.
no ano de   in the year

antes de 3 de Maio, before May 3rd

a sua carta de 30 de Julho, your letter of July 30th

(e) The *first* day of the month is nowadays nearly always expressed by means of **(o dia) um,** except when there is any particular significance attachable to that day, in which case **o Primeiro** is used.

o Primeiro de Janeiro, New Year's Day

After **estar** or to render *on*, **o Primeiro** is preceded by **em:**

Estamos no Primeiro de Janeiro. It's New Year's Day.
No Primeiro de Janeiro. On New Year's Day.
but **Ęra o Primeiro de Janeiro.** It was New Year's Day.

72. THE SEASONS. The four seasons are: **o Invęrno** (*winter*), **a Primavęra** (*spring*), **o Verão** (*summer*), **o Outǫno** (*autumn*). They should always be preceded by the article except (usually) when preceded by the preposition **de** to form a phrase equivalent to an attributive adjective: **um dia de Verão** (*a summer day*); **de** is also used occasionally to translate *in*.

73. PRONUNCIATION: e AND i WITH PALATALS. (a) Unstressed e is extremely faint when in conjunction with [ʃ], [ʎ], [ɲ] or [ʒ].

Typical are the following words:

estar, to be; **esgotar,** to drain, to exhaust; **vendes,** you sell; **fechar,** to close, to shut; **chegar,** to arrive; **melhǫr,** better, best; **o talhe,** cut, shape, figure; **desenhar,** to draw, to design; **o champanhe,** champagne; **vegetal,** vegetable (*adj.*); **genuíno,** genuine; **protejamos,** let's protect; **hǫje,** today; **o mexilhão,** mussel; **o peixe,** fish.

(*b*) Stressed **e** before [ʃ], [ʎ], [ŋ] or [ʒ] has the value [ɐ] in Standard Portuguese:

fecho [ˈfɐʃu], I close, I shut; **o espelho** [ɪʃˈpɐʎu], mirror, looking-glass; **venho** [ˈvɐɲu], I come; **tenho** [ˈtɐɲu], I have; **vejo** [ˈvɐʒu], I see; **mexo** [ˈmɐʃu], I stir.

There exist a number of exceptions, *e.g.*, **vęlho** (*old*), **a invęja** (*envy*), **a gręlha** (*grill*), **o evangęlho** (*gospel*), **a gęlha** (*wrinkle*), **o escabęche** (*pickle*), **a sęge** (*chaise*).

(*c*) Unstressed **i** is extremely faint when in conjunction with [ʃ], [ʎ], [ɲ] or [ʒ]. Typical are the following:

a distância, distance; **Lisbǫa,** Lisbon; **o lápis,** pencil; **o pichęl,** tankard; **um milhão,** a million; **o vinhędo,** vineyard; **ligeiro,** light; **o gigante,** giant; **o tijǫlo,** brick; **a jibóia,** boa-constrictor; **o lixeiro,** dustman; **o xilofǫne,** xylophone.

VOCABULARY

a	at (*of time*)	**Filipe**	Philip
ainda [ɐˈĩndɐ]	still, yet	**o habitante**	inhabitant
até	until, as far as,	**mais**	more, most, plus
até a	(up) to	**meio, -a**	half
o avião	aeroplane	**męnos**	less, minus
Cąmões	Camoens	**o mercado**	market
o censo	census	**a nǫite**	night
dęsde	since, from	**pąra**	by (*of time*), for
dias feriados	Sundays and public holidays	**a pessǫa**	person, *pl.* people
dias úteis	weekdays	**em ponto**	just, exactly, "on the dot" (*of time*)
o escudo	escudo (*Portuguese money*; *approx.* 70 to the £)	**a população**	population
		o quarto	room; quarter, fourth
fazęr anos	to have one's birthday	**a sardinha**	sardine
		o século	century

segundo	according to	**à** ⎫	
só ⎫	only	**por** ⎬ **volta de** (at) about	
somente ⎭		[pur] ⎭	

Que horas são?	What time is it?
Está na hora ⎫ **de ir**, etc.	It's time to go, etc.
São horas ⎭	
A que horas . . . ?	At what time . . . ?
Hoje faço anos.	It's my birthday today.
Quando fazes anos?	When's your birthday?
para o ano	in a year's time, next year

Study also the numerals, names of the days of the week, months of the year and seasons listed in §§ 67–72, and the words listed in § 73.

EXERCISES

I. (a) *Pronounce the following:* compras batatas e ervilhas, a vida de Jesus, feche a porta, um prato de mexilhões, envelhecíamos, as legiões romanas, os vinhedos do Douro, três lápis azuis, o Evangelho segundo São Marcos, faz muito vento hoje.

(b) *Study and translate:* Cinquenta e seis capítulos. Trinta e duas páginas. Mais de mil aviões. A página quarenta e sete. Noventa e um lápis. Cem lojas boas. Cento e sessenta pessoas. Quinhentas e vinte e uma casas. Dois milhões e meio de habitantes. Mil novecentos e cinquenta e oito. Mil setecentos e setenta e sete. A página vinte e um. Isabel segunda. Filipe quinto. O século onze. Depois da uma. Às cinco em ponto da tarde. Até às quatro menos um quarto da madrugada. Desde antes das seis. Às seis e vinte e seis minutos. Por volta das duas e meia. São três horas. Eram nove horas da manhã. O comboio das sete e meia. Era um de Março. Que dia do mês é

hoje? Estamos a quinze. A dezoito de Abril fazes anos.
O comboio vai nos dias úteis. Para o ano.

(c) *Translate:* Twenty-two women. Five hundred and
fifty-five houses. A hundred shops. Two thousand seven
hundred people. In seventeen ninety-seven. Nineteen
eighty-four. Three hundred and twenty-one buildings.
A hundred thousand inhabitants. More than a million
escudos. The seventh chapter. (The) page two hundred
and one. (The) lesson twenty-one. Peter the Second.
The nineteenth century. By half past five in the morning.
Before eleven p.m. Until after seven in the morning.
From five to six until ten past eight. At about ten to one at
night. It is Wednesday today. The first of June. On the
sixteenth of October. My birthday is on the twelfth of
November. Only on public holidays.

II. (a) *Study and translate:* 1. Agora, no século vinte, não é
difícil viajar para vários países. 2. Quinhentos e sessenta e
sete mais trezentos e trinta e um são oitocentos e noventa e
oito. 3. Ele trabalhava desde as oito da manhã até às cinco
da tarde. 4. — A que horas vai chegar o comboio de
Setúbal? — À volta das seis menos um quarto. 5. Às
segundas íamos para casa dos meus tios e aos sábados para
casa dos meus avós. 6. — Que dia do mês era? — Eram
catorze de Janeiro. 7. Eu não estudo tantas línguas como tu.
8. O meu pai ia para a fábrica no comboio das sete e trinta e
cinco. 9. Todos tínhamos que estudar até às quatro menos
cinco. 10. Às nove e meia a Sra. não estava em casa.

(b) *Translate:* 1. Camões still lived in Lisbon in the year
fifteen seventy-six. 2. Two hundred and fifty-three plus
seven hundred and eighty-nine are one thousand and forty-
two. 3. I'm going to finish this by three o'clock on
Wednesday. 4. I work every day from nine to five, but
she only used to work six hours. 5. He used to reach
Coimbra on the first of January and had to be in London
before the first of February. 6. Portugal has a population
of almost ten million inhabitants. 7. This train travels to

Paris on Mondays, Wednesdays and Fridays. 8. We have to be at the station before ten to eight because the train leaves at five to. 9. There are one hundred and twenty-one houses in this street. 10. He's going to arrive on the twenty-seventh of August at about six p.m.

III. (a) *Study and translate:* 1. Segundo o último censo Lisboa tem mais de oitocentos mil habitantes, mas Coimbra tem menos de cinquenta mil. 2. Amanhã às sete horas da manhã vamos partir para Paris. 3. Não iam no mesmo comboio que nós. 4. A que horas vamos chegar à estação? 5. A velha mulher vende sardinhas e mexilhões no mercado às quartas e quintas-feiras. 6. — A quantos estamos hoje? — Hoje são cinco. 7. Às terças estou sempre em casa. 8. — Que horas são? — São dez horas e sete minutos. 9. Vou terminar todas estas lições antes de trinta e um de Julho. 10. Só tínhamos bastante para cem pessoas.

(b) *Translate:* 1. They used to work every day from six in the evening until four in the morning. 2. I'm always at home from seven to eight. 3. We have to be at the station by half past five. 4. There are one hundred and thirty million people who speak Portuguese. 5. "What time is it?" "Seven o'clock exactly." 6. The lessons were all very difficult. 7. At what time did you use to arrive home? 8. Today is the fifteenth of April, nineteen fifty-seven. 9. Seven hundred and sixty-nine minus five hundred and fifty-two are two hundred and seventeen. 10. The Setúbal train used to arrive here at nine forty-three p.m.

Uses of SER, ESTAR, IR *and* DAR, *Interrogation,*
Negation, DIZER, *Unstressed* E *and* O *before* A,
E, O

LESSON XI

74. FURTHER USES OF **ser, estar, ir** AND **dar.** (*a*) **Ser.** Revise
§§ 48–50 (**ser** and **estar**), § 69 (time), § 71 (date) and note the
following:

Quem é? Sou eu. Who is it? It is I (*lit.*, I am).
És tu? (É o Sr? Sois vós? São vocês?) Is it you? (*lit.*,
Are you?)
Éramos nós. It was us [we] (*lit.*, We were).

NOTE: The subject pronoun in this construction is usually placed
after the verb, even when the sentence is affirmative.

(*b*) **Estar.** Revise §§ 48–50 (**ser** and **estar**), § 71 (date), § 64
(progressive tenses), and distinguish between the following uses
with preposition and infinitive:

estar em, to be inclined to
estar para, to be about to, be on the point of;[1] to be in a position
to
estar por [pur], to be yet to be + *past participle* (*i.e.*, in passive
sense only)

Estou em crer que ele não me compreende. I'm inclined
to believe he doesn't understand me.
O comboio estava para partir. The train was about to leave.
Já não estamos para fazer isso. We're no longer in a position
to do that.
O pão está por partir. The bread hasn't yet been broken, is
yet to be broken.

(*c*) **Ir.** Revise § 24 and study the following idiomatic uses of **ir**:

---

[1] Estar $\begin{Bmatrix} a \\ ao \end{Bmatrix}$ **ponto de** and **estar a** (less commonly) may also be used
for this.

(i) to form the progressive tenses (**ir** emphasizes more than **estar** the *gradual* progress in the verbal action).

A minha irmã estava muito doente, mas agora vai melhorando. My sister used to be very ill, but now she is (gradually) improving.

Como eu ia dizendo ... As I was saying ...

Note: The use of **ir a** + *infinitive* in this sense is dialectal only.

(ii) **Vamos!** Let's go! Come on! Come now!

Note also $\begin{Bmatrix} \textbf{Vamos andando!} \\ \textbf{Vamos lá!} \end{Bmatrix}$ Let's be going!

(iii) **Vamos** + *infinitive*, Let's ... (*besides* We are going to ...).

Vamos comprar um chapéu. Let's buy a hat.

(iv) **ir** (*or* **ficar**) **bem a alguém,** to suit someone

Este vestido vai (*or* **fica**) **bem à minha tia.** This dress suits my aunt very well.

(*d*) **Dar.** Besides translating *to give*, **dar** has the following idiomatic uses:

dar os bons dias a	to say, wish, good morning to
dar as boas tardes a	to say, wish, good afternoon to
dar as boas noites a	to say, wish, good evening/night to
dar as boas vindas a	to welcome
dar um passeio	to go for a walk
dar uma volta	to go for a walk (round) *or* a spin
dar a volta a alguma coisa	to go round something
dar de beber a[1]	to water (*animals*); to give to drink
dar de comer a[1]	to feed; to give to eat
dar corda a	to wind up (watches, clocks, etc.)
dar as horas	to strike the hour

----

[1] **Dar a beber** (**comer**) **a** is also found.

dar com   to come across, find, catch
dar para   to look (out) on to;[1] to have a flair for[2]
dar por [pur]   to notice

Damos a volta à Praça da República.   We're walking round
the Praça da República.
A nossa janela dá para o mar.   Our window overlooks the sea.
Dá a uma; davam as quatro.   It's striking one; it was striking
four.

NOTE: Like **ser** [§ 69], **dar** is used in the singular with the first
hour and in the plural with the rest.

75. INTERROGATION: USE OF é que. Very often in asking
questions the Portuguese resort to the use of **é que** (*is it that*) as
a means of adding emphasis to the question (cf. French *est-ce que*).

> **Onde é que está João?**   Where's John?
> **Quando é que vamos chegar?**   When *are* we going to
> arrive?

NOTE: This expression is used affirmatively to translate *The fact is
that . . .*, or *It is a fact that . . .*

76. NEGATION. (*a*) The simplest form of negation is that in
which **não** is placed immediately before the appropriate verb
[§ 21]. Other negative particles which may be similarly placed
are **nunca** (*never*), **jamais** (*never*), **nem** (*neither, nor*), **nem
(sequer)** (*not even*), **ninguém** (*no one, nobody*), **nada** (*nothing*)
and **nenhum, -a** (*none, no*). *Not either* is rendered by **também
não** or more rarely by **tão-pouco**.

Nunca tinha dinheiro.   He never had any money.
Nem estuda nem trabalha.   He neither studies nor works.
Nem (sequer) dá os bons dias.   He doesn't even say good
morning.

---

[1] **Deitar para** is also used for this meaning.
[2] Brazilianism.

Ninguém acompanha a minha mãe. No one is going with my mother.

Nada acontęce nęsta cidade. Nothing happens in this town.

Nenhum vendia canętas. None (of them) sold pens.

Nenhum português pronuncia assim. No Portuguese pronounces like that.

Também não ia o męu irmão. My brother wasn't going either.

(*b*) These same words may also be placed after the verb but **não** must then precede it.

Não vęmos nunca a nǫssa mãe. We never see our mother.

Não vendia nem livros nem jornais. He sold neither books nor papers.

Não vendia livros nem jornais. He didn't sell books or papers.

Não vendia nem (sequęr) jornais. He didn't even sell papers.

Não ia ninguém pạra Portugal. No one was going to Portugal.

Não sucęde nada. Nothing is happening.

Não ia nenhuma rapariga. No girls used to go.

NOTE: Contrast English usage in which the use of *not* with the verb makes the following adverb, pronoun or adjective affirmative (*i.e.*, *I never go* or *I don't ever go*).

(*c*) In the examples with **nada, ninguém** and **nenhum** listed above, these elements are the subjects of their respective verbs. They may also be the objects (direct, indirect or prepositional).

Não vejo nada. I don't see anything.

Não trabalha em nada. He isn't working on anything.

Não vejo ninguém. I see no one *or* I don't see anyone.

Não dou ęste livro a ninguém. I'm not giving this book to anyone.

Não discuto com ninguém. I'm not arguing with anyone.

Não escręvo com nenhuma facilidade. I don't write with any ease.

NOTE: See § 39 (4) and notice the following differences of emphasis:

Não compra livros.	He doesn't buy [any] books.
Não compra nenhum livro.	He doesn't buy *any* books.
Não compra nem um único livro.	He doesn't buy a single book.

(*d*) More than one of these elements of negation may be present in the same sentence. Usually one of them is placed before the verb as in (*a*) and the negative **não** is not used; if they are both (all) placed after the verb, **não** must precede the verb.

Ẹle nunca compreende nada.	⎫ He never understands
Ẹle não compreende nunca nada.	⎭ anything.
Ẹle nunca faz nada pạra ninguém.	⎫ He never does any-
Ẹle não faz nunca nada pạra ninguém.	⎭ thing for anyone.

(*e*) **Sem** (*without*) and **antes de** (*before*) take the same negative words as **não**, but **não** is not then expressed before the verb.

sem dizẹr nem uma palavra, without saying a (single) word
sem chegar nunca a tempo, without ever arriving in time
antes de falar com ninguém, before talking to anyone
antes de mais nada, before anything (*or* all) else

77. THE IRREGULAR VERB **dizẹr** (*to say, tell*).
    pres. indic.: **digo, dizes, diz, dizẹmos, dizeis, dizem**
    impf. indic.: **dizia,** etc. [see § 78 (*c*)]
    gerund: **dizendo**

Dizia ao professọr que não gostava de estudar. He would (= used to) tell the teacher that he didn't like studying.

78. PRONUNCIATION: UNSTRESSED **e** AND **o** BEFORE **a, e** OR **o**.

(*a*) Unstressed **e** when followed by **a, e** or **o** has the phonetic value [i]:

cear [si'ar], to have supper;
veemente [viə'mẽntə], vehement;
a geografia [ʒiugrɐ'fiɐ], geography.

(b) Unstressed o when followed by a, e or o has the phonetic value [u]:

voar [vu'ar], to fly;
o poęta [pu'ɛtɐ], poet;
o álcoọl ['alkuɔl], alcohol.

VOCABULARY

a (after verbs of motion)[1]	at; to	o leite,	milk
apanhar	to catch, seize	o monu-mento	monument
avançar	to advance	mostrar	to show
a casa de pasto	(cheap) restaurant	nacional	national
a casa vizinha	(the house) next door	nadar	to swim
devagar	slowly	ọbrigado, -a	thank you
devagarinho	very slowly	ọlhar (pạra)	to look (at)
dividir (em)	to divide (into)	pertinho (adv.) (de)	quite close (to)
a escọla	school	procurar	to look for
ao ⎫ estran- pạra o ⎭ geiro	abroad (motion towards)	quase nada	hardly anything
no estran-geiro	abroad (static)	o relógio	watch; clock
o estrangeiro	foreigner	o restaurante	restaurant
estrangeiro	foreign	se	if; whether
o gato	cat	a sé	cathedral
o grupo	group	sẹr verdade	to be true
a janẹla	window	sọzinho	(all) alone
já não	no longer	tẹr saudades de	to be homesick for, yearn for
jantar	to dine, have dinner	tọda a gente	everybody
o jantar	dinner	o turista	tourist
		o vestido	dress

[1] E.g., chegar a, to arrive at; ir comẹr a, to go and eat at, etc.; pạra is often used in the same way, but not, however, with chegar; chegar pạra means to be sufficient to or for.

114

bom dia[1]   good morning, good day
bọa tarde[1]   good afternoon, good evening
bọa nọite[1]   good night

não é verdade? **não é (assim)?** **não acha?**	isn't it? doesn't he? aren't they? etc. (cf. French **n'est-ce pas?**); the second form must be used in the appropriate tense, person and number, whenever apposite; the third form implies *don't you agree?*

Study also the words listed in §§ 74, 76, 77 and 78 and revise the vocabulary of Lessons VI–X.

EXERCISES

I. (a) *Pronounce the following:* voavam, três poesias, os poetas, o estudo da geografia, respostas veementes, os perigos do alcoolismo, tudo o que dizia, a Gália romana estava dividida em três partes, durante a noite, nós dividiríamos, as civilizações, a Imitação de Cristo, vivíeis.

(b) *Study and translate:* Sou eu. Éramos nós. Estou para partir. Ele estava para chegar. A minha janela dava para a rua. Ele dá para as línguas estrangeiras. Nunca líamos nada. Não vinha ninguém. É verdade, não é? Vivia. Vai dividir os turistas em três grupos. Estava para visitar os seus tios. Olhava para a sé velha. Dava sempre as boas noites a toda a gente. Estavam a dar as cinco da tarde. Vamos andando.

(c) *Translate:* They were about to leave. He was homesick for his house and family. They always welcomed the old man when he arrived at the school. Nobody sees the aeroplane. As he was saying. Is it you? They often gave the cat milk to drink. Before doing anything else. She wasn't selling anything. It was striking ten. Neither he nor I

---

[1] Less commonly **bons dias, bọas tardes, bọas nọites.**

were very cold. Without speaking to anybody. He sees nobody. We were looking for my brother. The fact is that he's looking for John.

II. (a) Study and translate: 1. Aquele vestido ficava muito bem à minha tia. 2. Porque não dava os bons dias? 3. Dava de beber aos filhos se estavam com muita sede. 4. Boa tarde, senhor, como está V. Exa? — Muito bem, obrigado. E você? 5. Na casa vizinha morava um senhor que trabalhava no mesmo hotel. 6. Depois de visitar a Sé Velha em Coimbra íamos comer a um restaurante que era pertinho. 7. Diz que nunca gostava de trabalhar sozinho. 8. Vamos lá porque são horas, rapazes! 9. O pobre homem ia avançando devagarinho para a porta. 10. Fechavam sempre as portas às cinco e meia da tarde, não era assim?

(b) Translate: 1. I always used to spend the whole day writing letters. 2. This is one of the friends I used to study with in Coimbra. 3. He is no longer in a position to do this. 4. On Sundays we used to go for a spin in my father's car. 5. I wind my watch up every night before going to bed. 6. The three old ladies were walking round the Praça da República. 7. This shopkeeper is very bad; he doesn't even sell fish. 8. I often saw my friends when I went for a walk. 9. On finishing work he would catch the 6.30 train. 10. This bookseller sells neither magazines nor newspapers.

III. (a) Study and translate: 1. O guia ia mostrando aos turistas os monumentos mais importantes da cidade. 2. A janela do meu quarto dava para a praça mais bonita de toda a cidade. 3. Vamos dar um passeio antes de ir jantar. 4. Quando estávamos no estrangeiro passávamos sempre a manhã a olhar para os monumentos. 5. Descansávamos porque fazia um calor terrível. 6. Nunca recebia tantas visitas como quando estava doente. 7. Não ia ninguém visitar os meus tios quando moravam em Portimão. 8. Esta-

vam procurando um amigo que ia chegar de Évora.
9. Lisboa tem muitos e lindos monumentos nacionais.
10. Não estás a comer quase nada, rapaz!

(b) *Translate:* 1. I often saw Michael on Wednesdays
because he didn't eat at home. 2. In general we would
dine at a small restaurant quite close to the Praça dos
Restauradores. 3. None of the girls liked swimming because they were afraid of the water. 4. We never go to our
grandparents' when the weather is so bad. 5. Let's go and
eat at that little restaurant near the post-office. 6. Why is
he eating nothing? 7. They would work all day without
eating anything. 8. I don't feel like dining at six o'clock.
It's too early in this country. 9. We're going for a spin in
the country. 10. Nobody ever tells anybody anything in
this town!

LESSON XII

79. THE VERBS **ser** AND **estar.** Revise §§ 44, 48, 50, 64, 69, 71, 74 (*a*) and (*b*).

By now the student will probably have experienced some difficulty in choosing the correct verb, **ser** or **estar,** in a given context. He will have understood by now that **ser** tells us *what* a thing is, **estar** *what condition* a thing is in.

— **Como é o Sr. Costa?** — **É muito alto.**
"What's Mr Costa like?" "He's very tall."

— **Como está o Sr. Costa?** — **Está doente.**
"How's Mr Costa?" "He's ill."

Nevertheless, he will have experienced, perhaps, that some instances seem very borderline or open to more than one possible interpretation. He should gain comfort from the fact that the situation is flexible and that in a good number of these instances different speakers of Portuguese will probably react in different ways. The problem may often be regarded as possessing a subjective solution. One person may view something as it inherently *is* (**ser**); another may gain only a fleeting impression of something and will only permit himself to use **estar**; another may be speaking ironically, and so on. The following notes will amplify the student's appreciation of the factors involved.

(1) **ser** *and* **estar** *with adjectives*

$$\left.\begin{array}{l} \textbf{É} \\ \textbf{Está} \end{array}\right\} \textbf{rico.} \quad \textit{He's rich.}$$

If we say **é rico,** we are thinking solely of the man and his wealth, without any overtones; he may not always have been wealthy; he may not always continue to be wealthy; but these considerations do not concern us. If we say **está rico,** we may imply that he is throwing his money about or making a display of it (we may not know whether he's normally rich or poor); if we know that he's normally poor, then our statement contains a ring of irony; or again, if a man has had a windfall, won a lottery or otherwise "struck it rich", and has changed his condition from poor to wealthy, we will say **está rico** if we have this in mind. Similar conditions will be observed in distinguishing between **é pǫbre** and **está pǫbre** (*he's poor*), between **é jǫvem** and **está jǫvem** (*he's young*), and between **é vęlho** and **está vęlho** (*he's old*).

Apre! que ęste embrulho $\begin{Bmatrix} \text{é} \\ \text{está} \end{Bmatrix}$ **pesado.** *Phew, this parcel's heavy!*

If in this example we use **sęr,** we imply simple recognition that the parcel is heavy by any standards; if we use **estar,** then the statement ceases to be objective; it implies that the parcel *seems* heavy to us (because we're weak, or tired, or ill, or perhaps because we're accustomed to lightweight parcels). Similarly:

O céu é azul.   The sky is blue.
O céu está azul.   The sky is blue [*i.e.*, for once; in this area it's nearly always cloudy].
O tempo está lindo hǫje.   The weather's fine today.
No Brasil o tempo é lindo.   In Brazil the weather [*i.e.*, the climate] is beautiful.

(2) **sęr** *and* **estar** *in impersonal expressions*

In impersonal expressions (*i.e.*, expressions beginning in English with a neuter *it is*, *this is* or *that is*) **sęr** is normally the correct choice:

É verdade, possívęl, provávęl.   It is true, possible, probable.

Isso é natural, lógico.   That is natural, logical.

In a number of cases, however,
  (a) **estar** is an alternative,
  (b) **estar** alone may be used.

(a) É
    Está } **claro (que ...)** It is clear (that ...); of course.

    É
    Está } **cẹrto (que ...)** It is correct, certain, true, (that ...)

(b) **Está** { **bem**
              bom } **(que ...)** (It's) all right (that ...);
                                       O.K., very well.

    Está visto (que ...) It is evident (that ...);
                              evidently; naturally.

    Está { **subentendido**
              compreendido } **(que ...)** It is taken for granted,
                                                understood (that ...)

    Está { **combinado**
              convencionado } **(que ...)** It is settled, agreed
                                                 (that ...)

    Está dito! Right you are (sir)!

    Está feito! Really! (*ironic, in inter-
                     ruption of a narrative*)

and a few more.

Note also the following expressions of the weather:

Está abafado.	It's sultry, stuffy.
Está carregado.	It's overcast.
Está escuro.	It's dark.
Está frio.	It's cold.
Está nublado.	It's cloudy.

NOTE: In coīloquial usage it is very common to find **Está calọr** (*It's hot*), **Está bom tempo** (*It's good weather*), etc., for **Faz calọr, Faz bom tempo,** etc. These have developed by analogy with **Está/Faz escuro, Está/Faz frio,** where *both* constructions are admissible.

(3) **sẹr** *and* **estar** *in expressions of position*

It has been seen that in expressions of position **sẹr** tends to be used for non-movables and **estar** for movables (**Onde está**

João? Onde é a bibliotẹca?)   In the case of non-movables
estar is, however, very occasionally to be found, particularly when
one wishes to pinpoint more precisely where a building, etc.,
stands (cf. Latin **stare**, *to stand*, whence Portuguese **estar**).   This
usage may also be regarded as a shortened form of **estar situado**
(*to be situated*).

Onde é Lisbọa? Lisbọa é em Portugal; $\left\{ \begin{array}{l} \text{é} \\ \text{está} \end{array} \right\}$ **na margem**
   direita do Tejo.   Where is Lisbon?   Lisbon is in Portugal;
   it is (*stands*) on the right bank of the Tagus.

Onde é o correio?   O correio é na Praça da República;
   $\left\{ \begin{array}{l} \text{é} \\ \text{está} \end{array} \right\}$ **na esquina.**   Where's the post-office?   The post-
   office is in the Praça da República; it is (*stands*) on the
   corner.

(4) **sẹr** *and* **estar** *with noun-complement*

   Normally only **sẹr** may introduce a noun-complement (**É um**
livro.   É o pai de Miguẹl.)   Occasionally, especially in familiar,
conversational language, **estar** may be used in certain limited
circumstances; it is usually elliptical for **estar feito** (*to have
become*; *to have turned out*) or the like.

Estás um họmem!   You're quite a grown man now, you know!
Ẹssa rapariga está họje uma belẹza.   That girl's turned out
   to be quite a beauty [*i.e.*, now, by now, nowadays].
Lọpes está nọivo!   Lopes has gone and got engaged!
Está um rico tempo!   Turned out nice again!
Está uma tarde muito fresca.   It's a very cool afternoon.

80. THE VERB ficar.   The verb **ficar** is a difficult verb to use in
Portuguese largely because it has a variety of meanings.   Basically its meanings are *to stay*; *to remain*; *to continue to be*; *to
become*; according to the context.   It has, however, a special
meaning in expressions of position.   With non-movables it
translates *to be situated* (sometimes rendered by **estar situado,**
cf. also **sẹr**).

O Pôrto fica no nôrte de Portugal.
Oporto is (situated) in the north of Portugal.

O mosteiro fica numa colina.
The monastery stands (*or* is situated) on a hill.

A parêde fronteira fica à (mão) direita.
The front wall is (situated) on the right(-hand side).

Onde fica essa rua?
Where's that road situated?

Fica a uma milha de distância.
It's a mile away.

A nossa casa fica a dois passos.
Our house is a couple of steps away.

81. EXPRESSIONS OF TIME (cont.).

de pela[1] } manhã	in (*i.e.*, during) the morning(s)
ontem de manhã	yesterday morning
esta manhã	this morning
amanhã de manhã	tomorrow morning
de pela[1] } tarde à	in the afternoon(s)
ontem à tarde	yesterday afternoon
esta tarde	this afternoon
amanhã à tarde	tomorrow afternoon
de pela[1] } noite à	at night(s)

[1] [p(ə)lɐ].

122

ontem à noite	last night, last evening
esta noite	tonight, this evening
amanhã à noite	tomorrow night

NOTES. 1. The expression **à manhã** is avoided owing to possible confusion with **amanhã**.

2. Also found are **hoje de manhã** (*this morning*), **hoje à tarde** (*this afternoon*), **hoje à noite** (*tonight*), **logo à noite** (*tonight*), all of which are normally used when the speaker is speaking during some *other* part of the day. In colloquial usage **da/na parte da manhã/tarde/noite** are also to be found.

3. **A tarde** lasts from noon to just before the evening meal, at which point **a noite** takes over. *Evening* may therefore be rendered by **tarde** or **noite** according to context.

Note the following for reference:

ao amanhecer   at daybreak

de madrugada }
de manhãzinha }   early in the morning

à tardinha }
ao entardecer }   at fall of evening, in the evening

à noitinha }
ao anoitecer }   at nightfall, in the evening

passar o serão em família, to spend the evening at home, with the family

o sarau   soirée, evening party

de dia e de noite }
noite e dia }   by day and by night, night and day

4. **Esta noite** is sometimes used to translate *last night* especially in comments made the morning following on what has happened during the night, *e.g.*, **Choveu** (*preterite tense*) **esta noite,** *It rained last night, It's rained during the night.* Cf. French **Il a plu cette nuit,** and Spanish **Ha llovido esta noche.**

82. PRONUNCIATION: **p** BEFORE **t** AND BEFORE SOFT **c**. There is much vacillation in Portuguese with regard to the pronunciation of **p** before **t** and soft **c**. Words containing such consonantal clusters may be divided into three groups:

(1) those in which **p** *must* be uttered;
(2) those in which the pronunciation of **p** is optional;
(3) those in which **p** *must not* be uttered.

For didactic and practical purposes groups (1) and (2) may be united as the student cannot err if he always pronounces the **p** in words of these groups. This leaves group (3) which comprises the following words:

o b**a**ptismo, *baptism*, o (ana)b**a**ptista, *(Ana)baptist*, b**a**ptizar, *to baptize*, b**a**ptismal, *baptismal*, o b**a**ptistério, *baptistery*; o c**e**ptro, *sceptre*; exc**e**pto, *except*, a exc**e**pção, *exception*, exc**e**pcional, *exceptional*, exc**e**ptuar, *to except*; ad**o**ptar, *to adopt*, a ad**o**pção, *adoption*, ad**o**ptivo, *adoptive*; a **ó**ptica, *optics*, **ó**ptico, *optical*; **ó**ptimo, *excellent*; *optimum*, o **o**ptimismo, *optimism*, (o) **o**ptimista, *optimist*; *optimistic*.

NOTE: In *all* words with these consonantal clusters the immediately preceding **a**, **e** or **o**, whether stressed or unstressed, is always *open*.

VOCABULARY

ab**e**rto	open, opened	a margem	bank, edge, margin
o **a**lgodão	cotton		
aplicado	hard-working	o pac**o**te	packet, parcel
bom	good, fine	a p**a**daria	bakery
a cadeira	chair	a par**e**de	wall
o café	coffee; café	o passo	step
o céu	sky, heaven	a poesia	poem; poetry
o cobert**o**r	blanket	a política	policy; politics
a diferença	difference	pr**e**to	black
(em) br**e**ve	soon	o primo	cousin (*m.*)
entre	between	a prima	cousin (*f.*)
a esquina	corner	a refeição	meal
explicar	to explain	o s**o**ldado	soldier
a f**e**sta	party	sujo	dirty
ficar n**o**ivo	to get (*or* be) engaged	t**e**r tempo de (*or* p**a**ra)	to have time to
a lã	wool	v**o**ltar p**a**ra	
limpo	clean	(*or* a) casa	to return home

Study also the words and phrases listed in §§ 79–82.

EXERCISES

I. (*a*) *Pronounce the following:* a pia baptismal, ideias optimistas, o grande ceptro, recepção, uma ilusão óptica, um pichel cheio de cerveja, dezasseis divisões, opta por partir, óptimo!

(*b*) *Study and translate:* Este café está muito doce. A cadeira estava partida. A refeição estava muito quente. A porta era verde. A sua mãe é andaluza. Sou eu. Que pálida está! As paredes estavam muito sujas. De quem é essa ideia? É do senhor Pereira. Está muito alegre hoje. Que triste é esta poesia! Eu estava muito triste. Essa política é muito má. O carro é preto. Onde é Londres? Onde é que estão os rapazes? É muito difícil explicar a diferença entre *ser* e *estar*. Amanhã de manhã. Muitas vezes ela dava com o filho na cozinha.

(*c*) *Translate:* My father is in Paris. Who is it? It is Mr Gonçalves. My wife is French but I am Spanish. He is a great friend. We are sad because they're going to leave soon. Where are these soldiers from? London stands on the banks of the Thames (**o Tamisa**). The bakery is on the corner. The four windows were open. Are you cold? It's very hot weather this summer. It's taken for granted that I've got to go. The water is very cold. It is very sultry here. Today is the twentieth. Turned out nice again! The shop is a couple of steps away. The weather's better today than last night.

II. (*a*) *Study and translate:* 1. É muito dinheiro para um rapaz como tu. 2. Ontem estávamos a vinte e três de Fevereiro. 3. O meu primo Miguel tem uma boa cama no quarto. 4. Os cobertores são de lã e os lençóis de algodão. 5. As portas estão limpas mas as janelas estão muito sujas. 6. Quando este soldado estava bom trabalhava muito. 7. Mas quando estava mal não gostava de trabalhar. 8. O teu amigo está muito rico hoje! 9. Em Portugal o tempo é lindo, sobretudo no Verão. 10. Isto era possível mas não era provável.

(b) *Translate:* 1. On Wednesdays we returned home at six o'clock. 2. The walls of my room were clean but now they are dirty. 3. It is very cold at night but these sheets and blankets are fairly warm. 4. He was very thirsty yesterday afternoon and wanted a glass of water. 5. The blankets are woollen (=made of wool) but they aren't clean. 6. My brother is not at home now, he is at our parents'. 7. We had two fine beds with clean sheets. 8. There used to be a lot of books in John's bedroom. 9. Mr Martins used to be very poor but he is now quite rich. 10. Mary's quite well, isn't she?

III. (a) *Study and translate:* 1. — Como é o Sr. Martins? — É bastante pequeno. 2. Estás muito cansado hoje, rapaz! 3. Jorge é mais novo três anos do que a sua prima Alice. 4. Este pacote está muito ligeiro. 5 Está claro que não temos tempo de fazer isso agora. 6. Está feito! Está visto que vocês não são muito aplicados! 7. Hoje está muito frio e o céu está carregado. 8. Mas é certo que o tempo está mais lindo do que ontem de manhã. 9. A loja do pai de Miguel é nesta rua. É na esquina. 10. A irmã de Miguel fica noiva.

(b) *Translate:* 1. "This sheet belongs on your bed, doesn't it?" "Of course." 2. O.K. Right you are. Let's visit your uncle tonight. 3. But where does he live? His house is situated in the Praça da República, isn't it? 4. My parents always used to spend the evening at home with the family. 5. Michael is never very optimistic; he never adopts that practice. 6. He used to work very hard, night and day! 7. On Thursday mornings (=On Thursdays in the morning) I used to go to the library. 8. We used to have parties on Friday evenings. 9. He never used to work neither by day nor by night. 10. That's understood of course; but how is it that he's got a lot of money?

LESSON XIII

83. THE PRETERITE TENSE (English *I bought, I did buy, I have bought*).

I. **-ar** verbs: stem plus endings **-ei, -aste, -ou, -ámos, -astes, -aram.**

II. **-er** verbs: stem plus endings **-i, -este, -eu, -emos, -estes, -eram.**

III. **-ir** verbs: stem plus endings **-i, -iste, -iu, -imos, -istes -iram.**

I. **comprar**	II. **vender**	III. **partir**
comprei	vendi	parti
compraste	vendeste	partiste
comprou	vendeu	partiu
comprámos	vendemos	partimos
comprastes	vendestes	partistes
compraram	venderam	partiram

NOTE: In the first person plural, **-er** and **-ir** verbs (but not **-ar** verbs) have the same forms as the present indicative: **vendemos, partimos.** The acute accent in the first person plural of **-ar** verbs indicates that the **a** is open [kŏmpˈramuʃ]; contrast present indicative **compramos** [kŏmpˈrɐmuʃ].

84. THE IMPERFECT AND THE PRETERITE. It is often difficult for the English-speaking student to distinguish between the use of the imperfect and the use of the preterite in Portuguese. The Portuguese imperfect translates the English *was —ing* and *used to —* (at times also *would —*) and in these cases there should be no confusion. The difficulty arises in the translation of the English *I —ed* and *I did —*, and a careful distinction must be made. The imperfect considers verbal action in its duration, *without indication of beginning or end* (a state of mind free of time limits, for instance, or an action repeated an indeterminate number of times); the preterite, on the other hand, usually presents verbal action in its completeness, ascribed to a particular moment or to a definite period of time; it is used to indicate past actions with a specific duration *or* a specific beginning *or* a specific end.

Imperfect

O que fazias? What were you doing?

Tọdos éramos muito felizes. We were all very happy.

Moravam em Coimbra. They lived (=used to live) in Coimbra.

Quando terminávamos o nọsso trabalho, íamos ao cinẹma. When we finished our work we would go to the pictures.

Preterite

Ao outro dia vi o mẹu pai. The next day I saw my father.

Passou duas họras com o professọr. He (has) spent two hours with the teacher.

Estive (§ 85) três anos em Portugal. I was in Portugal for three years.

V. Exª. partiu a tempo? Did you leave in time?

85. IRREGULAR PRETERITES

ir   fui, fọste, fọi, fọmos, fọstes, fọram

sẹr   fui, fọste, fọi, fọmos, fọstes, fọram

estar estive, estivẹste, estẹve, estivẹmos, estivẹstes, estivẹram

tẹr   tive, tivẹste, tẹve, tivẹmos, tivẹstes, tivẹram

fazẹr fiz, fizẹste, fẹz, fizẹmos, fizẹstes, fizẹram

pôr   pus, pusẹste, pôs, pusẹmos, pusẹstes, pusẹram

dizẹr disse, dissẹste, disse, dissẹmos, dissẹstes, dissẹram

vir   vim, viẹste, veio, viẹmos, viẹstes, viẹram

dar   dei, dẹste, dẹu, dẹmos, dẹstes, dẹram

Also irregular is **vẹr**, which takes the endings of the **-ir** conjugation: vi, viste, viu, vimos, vistes, viram.

NOTE: Extreme care should be taken not to confuse the verbs **vir** and **vẹr** both in the present indicative and in the preterite.

86. The Preposition **por** [pur] (*by, along, through*; see also § 226).

Por contracts with a following definite article:
    por + o: pelo [p(ə)lu]; **por + a: pela** [p(ə)lɐ];
    por + os: pelos [p(ə)luʃ]; **por + as: pelas** [p(ə)lɐʃ].

A carta fọi escrita por Miguẹl. The letter was written by
    Michael.
Viẹmos pelo parque. We came (have come) through the park.
O ladrão entrou pela janẹla. The thief got in by (through)
    the window.
Andava pela rua. She was walking along (down) the street.

87. Pronunciation: **c** before **t** and before soft **c**. Much vacillation exists in Portuguese as to whether or not **c** should be
uttered before **t** and *soft* **c**. In many words it is *never* uttered, in
others it is *always* uttered, and in yet others it is largely a matter of
personal choice. It is less easy to formulate rules in this respect
than in the case of **p** in similar circumstances. Generally speaking, the student will find the following pointers helpful, *i.e.*, he
should pronounce the **c** before **t** and *soft* **c** in the following
words only:

(*a*) In all words with **bact-, fact-, jact-, lact-, ect-, hect-,
ict-, fict-, pict-, oct-, noct-** (except **nọcturno,** nocturnal), and all
their derivatives in which **t** is converted into *soft* **c**:

a bạctéria, *bacterium,* **a bạcteriologia,** *bacteriology,* **o facto,**
fact, **a fạcção,** *faction,* **fạccioso,** *factious,* **o jacto,** *jet,* **jạctar-se,**
to boast, **a jạctância,** *boastfulness,* **a lạctọse,** *lactose,* **a Via
Láctea,** *Milky Way,* **o ẹctoplasma,** *ectoplasm,* **o hẹctolitro,**
hectolitre, **a ictiologia,** *ichthyology,* **fictício,** *ficticious,* **a ficção,**
fiction, **pictórico,** *pictorial,* **o ọctogenário,** *octogenarian,* **nọc-
tívago,** *nocturnal,* etc.

(*b*) In all words containing the syllables **-pact-, -fect-, -sect-,
-vict-,** and all their derivatives in which **t** is converted into *soft* **c**:

o pacto, *pact,* **compacto,** *compact,* **infẹcto,** *infected,* **a infẹcção,**
infection, **perfẹctívẹl,** *perfectible,* **o sẹctọr,** *sector,* **a sẹcção,**

section, **seccional**, *sectional*, **a intersecção**, *intersection*, **o convicto**, *convict*, **a convicção**, *conviction*, etc.

(c) In the following words and their derivatives:

a dicção, *diction* (but **o dicionário**, *dictionary*), **a fricção**, *friction*, **a sucção**, *suction*, **o factótum**, *factotum*, and all words ending in **-ectomia**, *e.g.*, **a cistectomia**, *cystectomy*.

NOTE: In all these words whether **c** is pronounced or not, the preceding **a**, **e** or **o** before the **c** are *open* in both stressed and unstressed position.

VOCABULARY

andar	to walk; to go	**ao longe**	in the distance, far away
antigo	ancient		
apenas	only	**o momento**	moment
o árabe	Arab	**a palavra**	word
a canção	song	**o parque**	park
a capital	capital (city)	**perguntar**	ask, inquire
cumpri-mentar	to greet, pay one's respects to	**um quarto de hora**	quarter of an hour
entrar	to enter, go in, come in	**saudar** [seu'ðar]	to greet, pay one's respects to
grego	Greek	**o templo**	temple
logo	then, next, presently	**a viagem**	journey, trip, voyage

ao outro dia
no dia seguinte ⎫ (on) the following day

na manhã seguinte (on) the following morning
fazer grandes frios to be extremely, bitterly cold

Study also the words listed in §§ 86 and 87.

EXERCISES

I. (a) *Pronounce the following:* activo, acção, acto, compacto, secção, contracção, nocturno, convicção.

(b) *Study and translate:* Bebeste. Morou. Recebi. Esteve. Demos. Fizeste. Tiveram. Vivi. Mandaste. Terminámos. Comeu. Foi. Pôs. Viemos. Vimos. Aonde foste? O que fez? Não deu. Com que escreveram V. Ex^{as}.? Não li nada. Vivia. Dava os bons dias. Estavam a dar as nove. A porta foi aberta por Félix. Olhou para a Sé Velha. Dei as boas noites. Andou pela rua.

(c) *Translate:* They received. I wrote. Did you see? When did he come? Have you given? He has seen the soldier today. They saw their teacher yesterday morning. She was laying the table. He has had a bath. We worked all day. He came across an old friend. We were looking for my brother. The following morning I visited my uncle. My cousin was ill [for] three days. We always come through the park. It was yesterday that I came. I saw the teacher in the distance. He walked towards the door.

II. (a) *Study and translate:* 1. Partiu de Lisboa a vinte de Abril, esteve uns dias em Setúbal, e chegou a Portimão no dia vinte e seis pela manhã. 2. Eram nove e meia em ponto quando partiram para a tua casa. 3. Deu de comer ao meu filho porque este tinha muita fome. 4. Naquele momento entrou um turista a perguntar onde ficava o Hotel Metrópole. 5. Chegámos a Évora na segunda pela tarde, e na manhã seguinte fomos ver o Templo de Diana. 6. — Bom dia. Como está a Sra.? — Muito bem, obrigada. E você? 7. Explicou a diferença entre as duas palavras. 8. Durante três dias fez um frio terrível e ninguém tinha vontade de partir. 9. Ficou feliz quando viu a tua mãe. 10. Os Árabes[1] viveram muitos séculos em Portugal.

[1] For use of capitals with nationalities see Lesson XVII, Vocabulary Note.

(b) *Translate:* 1. I spent the whole day reading magazines.
2. We lived two years in Santos and then went to live in São
Paulo. 3. Did you see my cousin when he passed through
here? 4. They were very pleased because our children
were arriving at four that afternoon. 5. This is one of the
friends I studied three years with in Coimbra. 6. At Sintra
we saw some very beautiful gardens, but it was so hot that
we returned home on the 5.30 train. 7. They used to live
here before going to live at Cascais. 8. You learnt a lot of
songs during your trip to Portugal, didn't you? 9. Quite
near to the Cathedral there is a very nice restaurant where
we used to go and eat. 10. The ninth chapter was too
difficult for my cousin, but he did the first one very well.

III. (a) *Study and translate:* 1. Disseram que eram vinte e um de
Outubro quando chegaram à capital. 2. O guia foi mostrando aos turistas o antigo templo grego. 3. Primeiro foi
a uma fábrica bastante grande e logo a uma muito pequena.
4. Chegámos às seis e um quarto no comboio de São Paulo
mas estivemos apenas duas horas. 5. A janela desta
divisão dava para a praça. 6. Fomos dar um passeio antes
de ir comer ao novo restaurante grego. 7. Ao outro dia
fomos visitar os nossos avós que moravam pertinho do novo
teatro. 8. Estava a dar a uma quando demos uma volta pela
cidade. 9. Passámos a manhã olhando para os monumentos, e à tarde fomos para casa duns amigos que moravam
bastante perto da praça principal. 10. Fazia grandes frios
quando estiveram em Bristol e quase não viram nada daquela
cidade.

(b) *Translate:* 1. I spent the whole day speaking English
with a tourist who said that he was living at the same hotel.
2. We were there for two hours but we didn't see anyone.
3. We were looking for my friend for a quarter of an hour.
4. On passing through Madrid I went to pay my respects to
John's parents. 5. They were about to have dinner when
your sister arrived with a present for my wife. 6. We have
read the whole of the (=all the) first chapter, but it was

rather difficult. 7. It was striking one when we reached the restaurant. 8. We were about to leave Coimbra when I came across my old friend who used to work in the same factory as my brother. 9. What did you write the letter with if you had neither pens nor pencils? 10. The third day we spent in Lisbon it was terribly hot and we only saw the cathedral.

LESSON XIV

88. WEAK OBJECT PRONOUNS (English: he visits *me*, he sends *it to me*, etc.).   Weak (*or* unstressed *or* conjunctive) object pronouns are those which in Portuguese cannot stand apart from the verb. They precede or follow the verb in accordance with rules given below (§§ 91–3).

Vê-me.   Não me vê.   Quem me vê? He sees me.   He does not see me.   Who sees me?

Porque não me manda vọcê o pacọte?   Why don't you send me the parcel?

NOTE: When the object pronoun follows the verb it is linked to it by a hyphen.

89. DIRECT AND INDIRECT OBJECT PRONOUNS.   Portuguese has two series of weak object pronouns: those indicating a direct object (English *me*, *him*, *her*, etc.) and those indicating an indirect object (English [*to*] *me*, [*to*] *him*, [*to*] *her*, etc.).   In certain persons the two forms coincide.

	Subject	*Object*	
		Direct	*Indirect*
(1)	ẹu	me	me
(2)	tu	te	te
	vọcê, etc.	o (*m*.), a (*f*.)	lhe
(3)	ẹle (*he, it*)	o	lhe
	ẹla (*she, it*)	a	lhe
(1)	nós	nos	nos
(2)	vós	vos	vos
	vọcês, etc.	os (*m*.), as (*f*.)	lhes
(3)	ẹles	os	lhes
	ẹlas	as	lhes

NOTES.   1. The forms o Sr., a Sra., etc., which are strictly speaking nouns, may also be used as the direct and indirect object.   This use is particularly to be recommended where otherwise confusion might arise with third person forms.

Vejo o Sr. I see you.
Dou o livro à Sra. I give you the book.

2. **o** is also used to represent the neutral, genderless *it* or *so*:
Quem o disse? Who said so?
Quando o fęz? When did he do it?

90. ORDER AND CONTRACTION OF WEAK OBJECT PRONOUNS. When a verb has two weak object pronouns, the indirect object precedes the direct. They form contracted combinations as follows:

me+o: **mo**	nos+o: **no-lo**
me+a: **ma**	nos+a: **no-la**
me+os: **mos**	nos+os: **no-los**
me+as: **mas**	nos+as: **no-las**
te+o: **to**	vos+o: **vo-lo**
te+a: **ta**	vos+a: **vo-la**
te+os: **tos**	vos+os: **vo-los**
te+as: **tas**	vos+as: **vo-las**
lhe+o: **lho**	lhes+o: **lho**
lhe+a: **lha**	lhes+a: **lha**
lhe+os: **lhos**	lhes+os: **lhos**
lhe+as: **lhas**	lhes+as: **lhas**

Ęle dá-mo.	He gives it to me.
Ęle dá-tos.	He gives them to you.
Ęle dá-no-las.	He gives them to us.
Ęle dá-vo-lo.	He gives it to you.
Ęle dá-lho.	He gives it to him, her, them *or* you.
etc.	etc.

NOTES. 1. PRONUNCIATION. The weak object pronouns are atonic when used either singly or in combination [see § 9].

2. It is not possible to form a combination of **me** or **nos** with **te** or **vos** or vice versa, or of any of these with **lhe** or **lhes**. In such instances the indirect object is rendered by using the strong or disjunctive object pronoun [see §§ 147 (*d*), 170 (*b*) (2)].

3. Both **lhe + o** and **lhes + o** become **lho,** etc.

4. For the use of personal **a** in these and other constructions see § 227.

91. Position of Weak Object Pronouns with Finite Parts of the Verb. (*a*) Normally the weak object pronoun follows the verb as in English, in which case it is linked to it by means of a hyphen:

Prefiro-o assim.   I prefer it like this.

(*b*) It precedes the verb, however, in negative and subordinate clauses:

Não o dei ao professor.   I didn't give (haven't given) it to the teacher.

Quando a vi, ęla disse que me procurava.   When I saw her, she said she was looking for me.

Conheço o sǫldado que a matou.   I know the soldier who killed her.

(*c*) It also precedes the verb in clauses introduced by

  (i) an interrogative or exclamatory particle;

  (ii) one of a few short adverbs such as **já,** *already,* **lǫgo,** *at once, then, presently,* **assim,** *like this, like that, thus,* **também,** *also, too, as well, etc.*[1]

  (iii) **tudo,** *everything,* and **tǫda a gente,** *everybody*;

  (iv) **tǫdos, -as,** *everybody, (they) all,* and **ambos, -as,** *(they) both.*

Quem nos chamava?   Who was calling us?

O que te disse o lojista?   What did the shopkeeper tell you?

Que bǫa idęia me dęste!   What a good idea you've given me!

Assim o vi sempre.   I have always seen it like that.

Tǫda a gente nos procurava.   Everybody was looking for us.

Ambos me viram.   Both of them saw me.

(*d*) It *may* precede the verb for various reasons of style, euphony and cadence, and in Brazilianisms. The student is advised not to copy these features but to observe them in the course of his general reading.

[1] Among others there are also **ainda** (*still*), **bem** (*well, quite*), **mal** (*hardly*) and **pouco** (*little*).

NOTE: The weak object pronoun should *never* be the first word of a sentence, clause or phrase.

92. POSITION WITH NON-FINITE PARTS OF THE VERB.

(a) *The Gerund*

The weak object pronoun follows the gerund (*i.e.*, forms in **-ndo**), except when this is negatived or preceded by the preposition **em** (=*if* or *whenever* + finite verb, with reference to habitual action). When the gerund is introduced by an auxiliary (*e.g.*, **estar, ir**) the weak object pronoun must combine with the auxiliary in accordance with rules (a) to (c) of § 91 above.

terminando-o, (by) finishing it
não te insultando, (by) not insulting you
Em me vendo, tirava o chapéu. If (*or* Whenever) he saw me, he used to take his hat off.
Está-o comendo. He's eating it.
Não o está comendo. He's not eating it.

(b) *The Infinitive*

The weak object pronoun follows the infinitive but may (and preferably does) precede it if the infinitive in its turn is preceded by a preposition. If, however, the preposition is **a** or **ao**, or if, in the case of the preposition **por,** the direct object pronoun is alone and in the third person, then the pronoun *must* follow the infinitive. The pronoun *must* precede a negatived infinitive.

Desejam ver-nos.
Têm vontade de ver-nos. } They wish to see us.
Têm vontade de nos ver.

Começam a detestar-nos. They're beginning to detest us.
Ao ver-me, saiu. On seeing me, he went out.
Acabaram por me escutar. } They finished up listening to
Acabaram por escutar-me. } me.
Acabaram por mo dar. } They ended up giving it to me.
Acabaram por dar-mo.
but **Acabaram por odiá-los.** They ended up by hating them.
Para não os ver. In order not to see them.

NOTES. 1. For an explanation of **odiá-los** (for **odiar + os**) in the last example see § 94 (*a*).

2. The prepositions **de, em** and **para** form no contraction in the written language with **o, a, os, as**, when these are weak object pronouns.

Tenho vontade de o [-d(i)-u] **fazer.** I feel like doing it.

Teimou em os [ɐj uʃ] **condenar.** He insisted on condemning them.

Pediu-me para o [p(ɐ)rɐ u] **fazer.** He asked me to do it.

3. When the infinitive is governed by some other verb then the pronoun may combine with the governing verb in accordance with rules (*a*) to (*c*) of § 91 above. This construction is too stylized for the beginner, however.

Desejam-nos ver. They wish to see us.
Começam-nos a detestar. They're beginning to detest us.

(c) The Past Participle

The weak object pronoun does not combine with a past participle but with its auxiliary (*e.g.*, **Tinha-o visto**, *I had seen him*). Students of Italian should also note that it may not be used in combination with an absolute past participle.

| Italian: **Lavatici uscimmo.** | Having got washed |
| Portuguese: **Tendo-nos lavado saímos.** | we went out. |

For the use of the reflexive see §§ 137–8.

93. ALTERNATIVE POSITION WITH NEGATIVES. In combinations of the type *short adverb* (or *subordinating conjunction* or *relative*) + *negative adverb* + *weak object pronoun* + *verb*, the order *negative adverb* + *weak object pronoun* is frequently reversed.

Ainda o não visitei. I haven't yet visited him.
Diz que o não fez. He says he hasn't done it (*or* didn't do it).
Vi o homem que o não quer fazer. I saw the man who doesn't want to do it.

94. CONTRACTION OF WEAK OBJECT PRONOUNS WITH VERB-FORMS. (*a*) **o, a, os, as** become **-lo, -la, -los, -las** when used after verb-forms ending in **r, s** or **z**.   The **r, s** or **z** fall.   A compensatory accent is required on the infinitive of the first and second conjugations, of verbs ending in **-pọr** (*i.e.*, the compounds of **pôr**), of verbs of the third conjugation ending in **-air** and **-uir,** and on **faz, traz, fẹz** and their corresponding forms in compound verbs.

falar+**o: falá-lo**	**unir**+**o: uni-lo**
falas+**o: fala-lo**	**contrair**+**o: contraí-lo**
falamos+**o: falamo-lo**	**atrair**+**o: atraí-lo**
falais+**o: falai-lo**	**distribuir**+**o: distribuí-lo**
aprendẹr+**o: aprendê-lo**	**faz**+**o: fá-lo**
pôr+**o: pô-lo**	**fẹz**+**o: fê-lo**
dispọr+**o: dispô-lo**	**traz**+**o: trá-lo**
compọr+**o: compô-lo**	**satisfaz**+**o: satisfá-lo**

NOTES.   1. **Traz** is part of the verb **trazẹr** (see § 142).

2. The form **quẹr** of the verb **querẹr** (see § 112) becomes **quẹre** before **o, a, os, as.**

3. **Tens**+**o** and **vens**+**o** become **tem-lo** and **vem-lo.**

(*b*) **o, a, os, as** become **-no, -na, -nos, -nas** when used after verb-forms ending in a nasal consonant or nasal vowel.

> **dão**+**o: dão-no**
> **falam**+**o: falam-no**
> **põe**+**o: põe-no**

NOTE: Clearly, **mandam-nos** can mean *they send them* or *they send us* (or *to us*).   Where ambiguity might arise it is usual to add **a ẹles** or **a nós** respectively for clarity.   For use of the personal **a** see § 227.

(*c*) When **nos** (*us*, [*to*] *us*) is used reflexively, *i.e.*, after a verb in the first person plural (and where in consequence it means *ourselves*, [*to*] *ourselves*) the final **s** of the verb falls: **lavamo-nos,** *we wash ourselves*.   For the use of the reflexive see §§ 137–8.

95. PRONUNCIATION: UNSTRESSED INITIAL (**h**)**o.**   Considerable difference of opinion exists with regard to the pronunciation of unstressed **o** in the initial position.   Much of this is caused by either regional or pedantic variants. However, the situation may be summarized quite simply as follows:

(*a*) generally, unstressed initial (**h**)**o**- is *closed*:

a **o**rigem, *origin*; o h**o**spital, *hospital*; a **o**pinião, *opinion*; **o**bt**e**r, *to obtain*;

(*b*) when followed by **pt, pç, ct, x** [ks] it is *open*:

o **o**ptimismo, *optimism*; a **o**pção, *option*; (o) **o**ctogenário, *octogenarian*; o **o**xigénio, *oxygen*;

(*c*) before the vowels **a, e** it is [u]:

o oásis [u¹aziʃ], *oasis*; o o**e**ste [u¹ɛʃtə], *west*;

(*d*) before the vowels **i, u** it is *closed*:

oitavo [oj¹tavu], *eighth*; o Out**o**no [o(w)¹tonu], *autumn*.

NOTES. 1. The addition of the negative prefix **in**- does not normally affect the basic principle of (*a*): **o**bservado, *observed*, hence in**o**bservado, *unobserved, unheeded*.

2. For regional variants see § 160.

VOCABULARY

agitar a mão	to wave (*intrans.*)	em cima	on top, upstairs
ambos, -as	both	em frente de	facing, opposite
ao + *infinitive*	on . . . ing	em linha	
o **a**utocarro	bus	r**e**cta	in a straight line
o bar	bar (*for drinks*)	encontrar	to find
cantar	to sing	ensinar	to teach
começar (a)	to begin (to)	esperar	to wait (for); to
compreen-	to understand,		hope
d**e**r	grasp	estar	to be in, be at
o condut**o**r	conductor (bus,		home
	tram)	estreito	narrow
disp**o**r (*like*	to arrange, dis-	o exame	exam, examina-
p**ô**r)	pose, set out		tion

gostar	to be very fond	passado	last
imenso de	of	um pouco de	a little, a bit of
infelizmente	unfortunately	respondẹr	to answer, reply
italiano	Italian	sạltar	jump
levar	to take (*from one place to another*)	sim	yes
		o sul	south
		tentar	to try to, try and
a maçada	bore, washout	tomar	
matar	to kill	assento	to take a seat
a moẹda	coin, piece (*of money*)	o tostão	ten centavos (*a coin*)
a paragem	bus stop, tram stop	visto que	seeing that, since

adẹus	good-bye	ir ⎫	go ⎫
adẹusinho	cheerio	vir ⎬ ao encontro	come ⎬
até à vista˙	so long, see you	etc. ⎭ de to	etc. ⎭
à espẹra de	waiting for		to/and meet
ir ⎫ tẹr com	to ⎰go ⎱ to/and	de tọdos	anyway, in any
vir⎭	⎱come⎰ meet	os mọdos	case

Study also the words listed in § 95.

EXERCISES

I. (*a*) *Pronounce the following:* hotéis, originário, optar, refrac-tário, vigilante, gigante, abstracto, distraído, exploração, satisfatório, hospitaleiro, inospitaleiro.

(*b*) *Study and translate:* Tem-no. Deram-lha. Ele dizia-mo. Gostávamos de fazê-lo. Tinha vontade de as ver. Não no-lo enviaram. Fala-lo. Manda-las. Fizemo-lo. Quem o viu? Ambos o disseram. Logo o vi. Também o fizeram assim. Recebendo-a. Em lhos dando. Ao vê-lo, parti. Não lhe escrevia ninguém. Não o estou a terminar. Depois de vo-lo dizer. Antes de dispô-las em linha recta. Vou-lhes explicar a décima lição. Fizeste-lo muito bem. Mandámos-lhes três cartas. Todos a viam. Até à vista.

(c) *Translate:* She wrote to us. We saw them. Who killed him? The man who received it. After sending it. I am not reading it now. We have arranged them in a straight line. Are you going to finish it? Immediately after doing it he began to sing. He has always tried not to do it (**não o fazer**). We always used to explain it to them. He has already looked for me. They were both waiting for me in the kitchen. We taught him a lot of songs. He drank only a little tea. *She* hasn't seen you (*masc. sing. fairly familiar*). We were going to visit you (*masc. pl. pol.*). We went to meet my mother. Good-bye. Cheerio.

II. (a) *Study and translate:* 1. O meu irmão esteve aqui ontem. Você viu-o? 2. Aprendeste muitas canções em Portugal? 3. V. Exª. esteve muito tempo no sul de Portugal, não é verdade? 4. Visto que vocês não compreendem esta poesia, vou explicar-lha. 5. Estava procurando as suas filhas para as levar ao novo restaurante grego. 6. Estive à tua espera duas horas, rapaz! 7. O que te responderam quando lhes falaste dessa ideia? 8. O que fez com o presente que lhe dei para a sua mãe? 9. Deu-o à sua irmã e ela mandou-o para Portimão. 10. Eu ia dar-lhos no dia seguinte antes de ir saudar os seus pais.

(b) *Translate:* 1. Why didn't you say good morning to them when you saw them in the park? 2. What did you give him last night when he went to your house? 3. Why didn't they send her to me? 4. We have already seen it three times. 5. Who told you that? 6. It was John who told me (so).[1] 7. When he saw us he understood why we were looking for him. 8. They all say they haven't seen him today. 9. They both used to send us to the hopsital every day. 10. Anyway, they've already given it to us.

III. (a) *Study and translate:* 1. Na quarta passada fui visitar Miguel, mas a irmã disse-me que não estava. 2. Nisto fui para a cidade esperando encontrá-lo no bar do seu amigo

[1] Forms in parentheses must be translated.

João. 3. Apanhei um autocarro na paragem que fica em frente da casa de Miguel. 4. Dei uma moeda de cinco tostões ao condutor e tomei assento em cima. 5. Logo o vi; andava por uma rua estreita com dois amigos. 6. Saltei do autocarro na paragem seguinte. 7. Quando me viram, os meus amigos agitaram a mão e vieram ao meu encontro. 8. Explicaram-me que iam ver um novo filme italiano ao Cinema Ritz. 9. Como gosto imenso de filmes italianos fui eu vê-lo também. 10. Mas infelizmente não gostámos; o filme foi uma maçada.

(b) *Translate:* 1. "Have you seen the new film at the Ritz?" "I've seen it, yes, but I didn't like [it].[1] 2. "Why not?" "It was a wash-out. Anyway, I don't like Italian films." 3. "When did you see it?" "Last Saturday." 4. "Did you call on Miguel this week?" "Unfortunately, no. We didn't have time, but we hope to go and see him soon." 5. "He told me he's finished his exams." 6. "Excellent! By finishing them he's going to have more time to (**para**) spend with his friends." 7. "Going into town?" "Yes, I am (**vou**). I'm going to catch the bus at the next stop." 8. "I don't understand why you have to go into town this morning." 9. "I've got to go and call on my uncle. He's not very well, unfortunately." 10. "O.K. See you. Cheerio!"

[1] Forms in square brackets must not be translated.

LESSON XV

96. RADICAL-CHANGING NOUNS AND ADJECTIVES. (*a*) *Nouns.* In Portuguese a number of masculine nouns ending in -o and with a closed -ọ- in the stressed radical syllable change the radical -ọ- to an open vowel, -ǫ-, in the formation of the plural.

o ǫvo, the egg	os ǫvos, the eggs
o pọrco, the pig	os pǫrcos, the pigs
o tijọlo, the brick	os tijǫlos, the bricks

There are some fifty of these nouns in all. With the above, the most common are: **ạlmọço** (*lunch*); **cọrpo** (*body*); **esfọrço** (*effort*); **espọso** (*husband*); **fọgo** (*fire*); **fọrno** (*oven*); **jọgo** (*game*); **ọlho** (*eye*); **ọsso** (*bone*); **pescọço** (*neck*); **pọço** (*well*); **pọrto** (*port*); **pọvo** (*people*); **sọgro** (*father-in-law*); **trọco** (*change*) [=money].

NOTES. 1. It should not be assumed that all nouns of the formation -ọ-o make their plural in this way, *e.g.*, **bọlo**, *cake*, *pl.* **bọlos**, *cakes*.

2. There is, however, a growing modern tendency for some words of this formation to acquire a radical change in the plural by analogy. Noteworthy in this context are **despọrtos** (*sports*) and **estọfos** (*upholstery*) which some speakers pronounce with an *open* radical ǫ.

(*b*) *Adjectives.* Similarly, a number of adjectives which in the masculine singular end in -o and have a closed -ọ- in the stressed radical syllable change the radical -ọ- to an open vowel, -ǫ-, in the formation of the masculine plural and the feminine singular and plural.

nọvo, young, new; *m. pl.* **nǫvos**; *f. sing.* **nǫva**; *f. pl.* **nǫvas**.

The other adjectives of this group are: **canhọto** (*left-handed*; *awkward*; *clumsy*); **chọco** (*broody*; *addled*; *stagnant*); **grọsso** (*thick*; *bulky*); **mọrno** (*warm*); **mọrto** (*killed*; *dead*); **pọrco** (*filthy*); **posto** (*put, placed, set*); **torto** (*crooked, twisted*); and all adjectives ending in **-oso**, *e.g.*, **formoso** (*beautiful*).

NOTE: It should not be assumed that all adjectives of the formation **-o-o** in the masculine singular make their other forms in this way, *e.g.*, **todo, todos, toda, todas,** *every, all.*

97. FURTHER CONTRACTIONS INVOLVING **de** AND **em**. So far we have seen that **de** and **em** form contractions with a following article or demonstrative. It will also be recalled that the contraction was optional in the *written* language (though NOT in pronunciation) in the case of **de** followed by the indefinite article, and in all the cases involving **em**. Similar contractions must now be observed in the case of a number of other words beginning with a vowel.

(*a*) **de**

(i) Where contraction *must* take place in the *written* language and in the *spoken* language:

$$\text{de} + \begin{cases} \textbf{aqui} & : \textbf{daqui,} \text{ from here, hence} \\ \textbf{aí} & : \textbf{daí,} \text{ from there, thence} \\ \textbf{ali} & : \textbf{dali,} \text{ from there, thence} \\ \textbf{acolá} & : \textbf{dacolá,} \text{ from there, thence} \end{cases}$$

(ii) Where contraction *may* take place in the *written* language and *must* take place in the *spoken* language:

algum, etc.	:	**dalgum**	or **de algum,** etc.
alguém (*someone*)	:	**dalguém**	or **de alguém**
algo (*something*)	:	**dalgo**	or **de algo**
algures (*somewhere*)	:	**dalgures**	or **de algures**
alhures (*elsewhere*)	:	**dalhures**	or **de alhures**
outro, etc.	:	**doutro**	or **de outro,** etc.
outrem (*other people*)	:	**doutrem**	or **de outrem**
outrora (*formerly*)	:	**doutrora**	or **de outrora**
além (*beyond*)	:	**dalém**	or **de além**
aquém (*on this side*)	:	**daquém**	or **de aquém**
entre (*between*)	:	**dentre**	or **de entre**

with **de +** applying to the bracketed group above.

(iii) Where contraction is optional in both spoken and written languages:

de + {
onde : **donde** or **de onde** [di-ˡŏndə], from where, whence

antes : **dantes** or **de antes** [di-ˡĕntəʃ], formerly (=**antes**); from before, of before
}

(b) **em**

Where contraction *may* take place in the *written* language and *must* take place in the *spoken* language:

em + {
algum, etc.: **nalgum**   or **em algum**, etc.

alguém   : **nalguém**   or **em alguém**

algo   : **nalgo**   or **em algo**

outro, etc. : **noutro**   or **em outro**, etc.

outrem   : **noutrem**   or **em outrem**
}

(c) *Demonstratives followed by* **outro**, *etc.*

The demonstratives usually contract with **outro**, etc., as exemplified below:

estoutro, *this other*; **essoutra** (*f.*), *that other*; **aqueloutras** (*f/pl.*), *those others*; *etc.*

These forms combine with the prepositions **de**, **em** and **a** in accordance with the rules already established for demonstratives.

(d) **de ora avante** (*henceforth*) may also be written **doravante** and *must* be pronounced thus.

98. USE OF WORDS IN § 97. (a) **aqui, aí, ali, acolá. Aqui** means *here* and is comparable to **este**, etc.; **aí** means *there* (near you) and is comparable to **esse**, etc.; **ali** and **acolá** mean *there* (remote) and are comparable to **aquele**, etc.

Other words for *here* and *there* are respectively **cá** and **lá**, which are used primarily with verbs of motion and in certain stock expressions.

Eu estou aqui, tu estás aí e ele está acolá.

I am here, you are there and he is over yonder.

Aqui e acolá havia grupos de operários a falar.
Here and there groups of workmen were talking.

Vem cá tọdos os dias.
He comes here every day.

Fui lá ontem, quarta-feira.
I went there yesterday, Wednesday.

Corrẹram pạra cá e pạra lá.
They ran hither and thither, to and fro, here and there.

Ẹu cá (*or* Cá por mim).
As for me (*or* For my part).

Lá está ẹle!	**Lá vai o ạutocarro.**
There he is!	There goes the bus.
Cá fọra.	**Lá dentro.**
Out here.	In there.
Cá em baixo.	**Lá em cima.**
(Here) downstairs.	(There) upstairs.

NOTE: As though they were object pronouns, **cá** and **lá** often precede infinitives introduced by a preposition.

    Gostamos imenso de lá ir.   We're very fond of going there.

    (*b*) **algo, ạlgures, alhures.** These words are rather literary and are replaced in day-to-day usage by **alguma cọisa, nạl-guma parte** and **noutra parte** respectively; **algo** is, however, also *commonly* used as an adverb meaning *somewhat*, *rather*. The expressions **um tanto** and **algum tanto** (both invariable) are also used in this sense.

Tem $\left\{ \begin{array}{l} \text{(algo)} \\ \text{ạlguma cọisa} \end{array} \right\}$ **mais** $\left\{ \begin{array}{l} \text{(barato)} \\ \text{barata} \end{array} \right\}$**?**

Have you anything cheaper?

Vou pạra outra parte.
I'm going somewhere else.

Dẹve estar $\left\{ \begin{array}{l} \text{nạlguma parte} \\ \text{ạlgures} \end{array} \right\}$**.**

He must be somewhere.

Ęstas casas estão algo caras.
These houses are a trifle expensive.

(c) **Outro, outrem, outrǫra.** **Outro** as well as meaning *other* also means *another*; it is only rarely found preceded by the indefinite article. **Outrem** (cf. French **autrui,** Italian **altrui**) means *other people,* and is most commonly found in proverbial expressions. It should be used only as the object of a verb or preposition. **Outrǫra,** unlike **antes** or **dantes** which refer to the recent past, is remote in meaning: *of yore, in olden times,* etc.

Outro sǫldado caiu mǫrto.   Another soldier fell dead.
Cobiçava sempre a propriędade doutrem.   He always coveted other people's property.
Os dias doutrǫra.   The days of yesteryear.

(d) **ąlém, ąquém.** The use of these two words is best illustrated by examples:

Ąlém dos confins da compreensão humana.
Beyond the confines of human understanding.

Muito ąquém das minhas esperanças.
Far short of my hopes.

Aqui e ąlém.   **Mais ąlém havia um casal.**
Here and there.   Further on there was a farmhouse.

99. PRONUNCIATION: **gu** AND **qu** BEFORE **e** AND **i.** Normally the **u** of **gu** and **qu,** although pronounced before **a** and **o,** is silent before **e** and **i.** There are, however, a number of words in which the **u** *is* uttered before **e** and **i.**

(a) **gu:**

o **agueiro,** *gutter*; **aguentar,** *to bear, put up with, stand*; a **ambiguidade,** *ambiguity*; **arguir,** *to censure; to infer, imply*; a **consanguinęidade,** *consanguinity*; **ensanguentado,** *blood-stained*; o **pinguim,** *penguin*; a **sangueira,** *pool of blood*; **sanguinário,** *sanguinary*; o **unguento,** *unguent, ointment*; any words related to, or derived from the above, and all words (mainly

of a scientific nature) beginning with **angui-**, **lingue-**, **lingui-**
and **ungui-**.

NOTES. 1. **o sangue**, *blood*, and **a sanguessuga**, *leech*, do not
belong to this group.

2. In the verbs **arguir, redarguir** (*to retort*) and all verbs
ending in **-guar**, the **u** before **e** or **i** carries an acute accent when
stressed, and is pronounced throughout their conjugation (see
§§ 211 and 216).

(*b*) **qu:**

antiquíssimo, *extremely ancient*; **cinquenta**, *fifty*; **delinquir,**
to be delinquent; **deliquescente**, *deliquescent*; **equestre**, *eques-*
trian; **frequente**, *frequent*; **a iniquidade**, *iniquity*; **a obliqui-**
dade, *obliqueness*; **sequestrar**, *to sequestrate*, *abduct, kidnap*;
Tarquínio, *Tarquin*; **tranquilo**, *calm, tranquil*; **ubiquitário,**
ubiquitous; any words related to, or derived from the above, and
all words (mainly of a scientific nature) beginning with **aqui-,**
equi-, querc-, quinque- (*both syllables*), and all words ending
in **-loquência, -loquente, -sequência, sequente**, *e.g.*, **gran-**
diloquente, *grandiloquent*; **a consequência**, *consequence*.

NOTES. 1. In the verb **delinquir** and in all verbs ending in
-quar, the **u** before **e** or **i**, carries an acute accent when stressed,
and is pronounced throughout their conjugation (see §§ 211 and 216).

2. A number of words beginning with **quo-**, namely, **a quota**,
quota; **o quociente**, *quotient*; **quotidiano**, *daily*, and related words,
have acceptable variants: **a cota, o cociente, cotidiano**, etc.

VOCABULARY

achar	to find; to think	**a caneca**	tankard, beer-
adormecer	to go to sleep,		mug, large
	fall asleep		glass
almoçar	to (have) lunch	**o cavalo**	horse
amiúde	often	**a cerveja**	beer
a pé	on foot	**cheio**	full
a bandeja	tray	**a compre-**	comprehension,
branco	white	**ensão**	under-
o caminho	way, path, road		standing

contar	to count, to tell	**a igreja**	church
correr	to run	**imediatamente**	immediately,
o criado	waiter		at once
o dedo	finger	**impossível**	impossible
delgado	thin, slim	**interessar**	to interest
o desporto	sport	**inútil**	useless
entrar em	to enter, go	**o lavrador**	peasant, farmer
	in(to),	**longe** (*adv.*)	far off, far away
	come in(to)	**melhorar**	to improve
as férias	holidays	**para**	(in order) to
francamente	frankly	**possível**	possible
a galinha	chicken; hen	**quase**	nearly, almost
a garrafa	bottle	**tinto**	red (*of wine*)
geralmente	generally	**voltar**	to (re)turn, go
o hábito	habit		back, come
a história	history; story		back
ibérico	Iberian		

estar encharcado até os/aos ossos	to be soaked to the skin
tomar o pequeno/primeiro almoço	to have breakfast
até domingo próximo	see you on/next Sunday
são horas de + *infinitive*	it is time to . . .
é (a) hora de (+ *definite article*) + *noun*	it is . . . time
à hora do almoço	at lunchtime
traga-me	bring me
traga-nos	bring us

Study also the words listed in §§ 96–99.

EXERCISES

I. (*a*) *Pronounce the following:* sangue, ensanguentado, arguí-mos, inaguentável, com frequência, tranquilidade, por con-sequência, a vida quotidiana, Rua do Ouro, a Idade de Oiro, quase ambíguo, ovos, treze animais, dezoito tijolos, essoutras mulheres, de entre eles.

(*b*) *Study and translate:* Onde estão os dias doutrora? Donde é você? Estes ovos são chocos. O Sr. tem troco? Os soldados corriam para cá e para lá mas nada encontravam. Estão a beber lá dentro no bar. Cá fora faz muito vento.

Cá por mim gosto muito de viajar no estrangeiro. Infelizmente isto está além da minha compreensão. Apanhámos
o primeiro autocarro que passava. Nós não gostávamos de
jogos e desportos. Ela estava um tanto cansada mas tentava
não o mostrar. As três raparigas entraram na igreja. Qual
é a sua melhor poesia? Traga-me uma garrafa de vinho
tinto. Até amanhã. Adeusinho! Vamos ter com Pedro
logo à noite.

(c) *Translate:* This house is made of brick[s]. I fell asleep
at once. That woman's beautiful fingers. It's lunchtime.
It's time to have breakfast. We made a great effort but it
was useless. The history of the Iberian peoples is very
interesting. We haven't seen her this morning. But it's
certain that she's somewhere nearby. We like her pretty
eyes. She wanted one of the other cakes. Bring us two
beers. She told me that my father was dead.

II. (a) *Study and translate:* 1. Todas iam para outra parte.
2. Não me interessavam os hábitos doutrem. 3. Da última
vez que te vi, almoçavas com Maria no novo restaurante
hindu. 4. Há uma velha casa de pasto aqui pertinho.
5. Todos os autocarros estavam cheios e tivemos de voltar a pé.
6. Os meus pais viveram dezoito anos em Paris. 7. O
criado levou-lhes duas canecas de cerveja. 8. Levou-lhas
numa bandeja. 9. Para ir àquela estação qual é o melhor
caminho? 10. Há alguém lá fora na rua; está tentando
entrar.

(b) *Translate:* 1. On entering the church I saw the priest.
2. Where are you going to spend [your] (the) holidays this
year? 3. The hospital is not very far from here. 4. He
is soaked to the skin. 5. We always used to have breakfast
at half past seven in the morning. 6. Who gave it to us?
7. I was coming through the park when I saw him. 8. He
said she thinks this shopkeeper has got something cheaper.
9. Our mother was laying the table when John came in.
10. Here and there there were pretty little houses.

III. (*a*) *Study and translate:* 1. A irmã deste soldado é muito formosa mas é algo delgada. 2. As ruas dessa cidade são muito porcas. 3. Todas estas raparigas são muito novas. 4. — Qual daqueles ovos é o pior? — É quase impossível dizer. 5. Está subentendido que vai chegar, apesar de todos os nossos esforços. 6. O lavrador era pobre, mas tinha três cavalos, oito vacas, um touro e vinte porcos. 7. Mas porque é que não tinha galinhas? É que não gostava de ovos! 8. A única coisa de que eu não gostava era que não me dava nunca os bons dias. 9. Amiúde nos contava uma história muito interessante. 10. Todos achámos que aquilo já não era possível.

(*b*) *Translate:* 1. Bring us two glasses and a bottle of white wine. 2. Frankly I think this is useless. 3. Peter's often playful but he is generally very hard-working. 4. She replied that my mother wasn't very well but that she was getting better. 5. He explained to us that he was going to call on John at half past ten on Sunday (in the) morning. 6. If the old shopkeeper is ill, it's because he works too much. 7. See you next Saturday at eight p.m. Cheerio! 8. His mother took him a glass of milk and two apples because he was hungry. 9. There goes the bus, come on. 10. It's useless to try and tell him something (**nada**)[1] when he's reading the (news)paper.

---

[1] As a general rule, negative adjectives function like **sem** and **antes de** [see § 76 (*e*)], *i.e.*, **é inútil = não é útil**.

LESSON XVI

100. RADICAL-CHANGING VERBS OF THE FIRST CONJUGATION.
(*a*) The radical or stem vowel of *any* verb of *any* conjugation is
stressed in nine instances:

  (i) the three persons singular and third person plural of the
      present indicative;
 (ii) the three persons singular and third person plural of the
      present subjunctive;
(iii) the singular (very familiar) of the imperative.

For the present subjunctive see § 179; for the imperative see
§ 194.

(*b*) The irregular verbs **dar, estar, crẹr** (*to believe*), **lẹr, sẹr,
tẹr, vẹr, pôr, ir, rir** (*to laugh*), **vir** and their compounds have
stressed radical vowel in the first and second persons plural of the
present indicative and in the *restricted* form (*i.e.*, of **vós**) of the
imperative *also*. Furthermore, the verbs **dar, ir** and their compounds have stressed radical *in addition* in the first and second
persons plural of the present subjunctive.

(*c*) The radical or stem vowel of many verbs of the first conjugation varies in quality in accordance with whether it is stressed
or unstressed. The vowels mainly in question here are **a, e, o**
and the diphthongs **ai** and **oi**. The vowels **i** [i] and **u** [u] are
affected to a lesser extent. The diphthongs **au** [aw], **ei** [ɐj], **ẹu**
[ew], **ou** [o(w)] and **ui** [uj] are NEVER affected by stress.

When unstressed, the vowels **a, e, o, ai** and **oi** are pronounced
in accordance with the rules given in the introduction for unstressed vowels; when stressed, they are *open*.

(*d*) In the scheme below the phonetic value of the *radical* is
shown in square brackets.

falar [ɐ], *to speak*: **falo** [a], **falas** [a], **fala** [a], **falamos** [ɐ],
falais [ɐ], **falam** [a];

levar [ə], *to carry*: **lęvo** [ɛ], **lęvas** [ɛ], **lęva** [ɛ], **levamos** [ə], **levais** [ə], **lęvam** [ɛ];

cortar [u], *to cut*: **cǫrto** [ɔ], **cǫrtas** [ɔ], **cǫrta** [ɔ], **cortamos** [u], **cortais** [u], **cǫrtam** [ɔ];

ensaiar [ɐj], *to try*: **ensaio** [aj], **ensaias** [aj], **ensaia** [aj], **ensaiamos** [ɐj], **ensaiais** [ɐj], **ensaiam** [aj];

bǫiar [oj], *to float*: **bóio** [ɔj], **bóias** [ɔj], **bóia** [ɔj], **bǫiamos** [oj], **bǫiais** [oj], **bóiam** [ɔj].

NOTE: For the acute accent on the radical-stressed flections of **bǫiar** see § 8 (*h*).

(*e*) All verbs ending in **-ear** and some verbs ending in **-iar** have radicals **e, i** both as [i] when unstressed and change them both to **ei** [ɐj] when stressed:

recear [i], *to fear*: **receio** [ɐj], **receias** [ɐj], **receia** [ɐj], **receamos** [i], **receais** [i], **receiam** [ɐj];

ǫdiar [i], *to hate*: **ǫdeio** [ɐj], **ǫdeias** [ɐj], **ǫdeia** [ɐj], **ǫdiamos** [i], **ǫdiais** [i], **ǫdeiam** [ɐj].

Like **ǫdiar** are **ansiar**, *to yearn*; **incendiar**, *to set fire to*; **mediar**, *to mediate*; **negociar**, *to negotiate*; **ǫbsequiar** [obze-kjar], *to favour*; *to present*; **premiar**, *to reward*; **remediar**, *to remedy*; in addition, **comerciar**, *to trade*, and verbs ending in **-enciar**, *e.g.*, **presenciar**, *to witness*, may optionally belong either to this group or to group (*l*) in § 101 below.

NOTE: **Ǫbsequiar** (and related words) is an exception to the rule that **s** is pronounced [s] after a consonant. The only other exception is the prefix **trans-** when followed by a vowel, *e.g.*, **o transeunte** [trɐ̃ziˈũntə], *passerby*.

101. SPECIAL CASES. (*This paragraph is largely for reference*)

(*a*) If the radical is followed by **m** + consonant or **n** + consonant (*not* **h**), it is always *closed*, in that it is a nasal vowel: **andar** [ɐ̃], *to walk, go*, **ando** [ɐ̃], etc.; **recomendar** [ẽ], *to recommend*, **recomendo** [ẽ], etc.; **comprar** [õ], *to buy*, **compro** [õ], etc. Similarly, **vingar** [ĩ], *to avenge*; **excomungar** [ũ], *to excommunicate*, etc.

(b) Before **m, n** or **nh,** radical **a** is always *closed*:

amar [ɐ], *to love,* **amo** [ɐ], etc.

But for many speakers the radical of **gạnhar,** *to gain, earn, win,* and related words, is *open* whether stressed or unstressed.

(c) Before **l** + consonant (*not* **h**), radical **a** is always *open*:

sạltar [a], *to jump,* **salto** [a], etc.

(d) Before **m** or **n,** radical **e** is [ə] when unstressed and *closed* when stressed:

condenar [ə], *to condemn,* **condẹno** [e], etc.

But the *stressed* radical of **remar,** *to row,* is open.

(e) Before **ch, lh, nh, j,** and **x** [ʃ], radical **e** is [ə] when unstressed and [ɐ] when stressed:

fechar [ə], *to close,* **fecho** [ɐ], etc.

But the verbs **engelhar,** *to wrinkle,* **grelhar,** *to grill,* and **invejar,** *to envy,* have stressed open radical **e.**

(f) Before **l** + consonant (*not* **h**), radical **e** is always *closed*:

esbẹltar [e], *to make slender,* **esbẹlto** [e], etc.

(g) Before **m, n,** or **nh,** radical **o** is [u] when unstressed and *closed* when stressed:

engomar [u], *to starch,* **engọmo** [o], etc.

But the stressed radical of **domar,** *to tame,* **somar,** *to add up,* and **tomar,** *to take,* is *open*: **dọmo** [ɔ], etc.

(h) Before **l** + consonant (*not* **h**), radical **o** is always *open*:

vọltar [o], *to return,* **vọlto** [ɔ], etc.

(i) Coming immediately before a flectional vowel, radical **o** is [u] when unstressed and *closed* when stressed:

soar [u], *to sound,* **sọo** [o], etc.

(j) *Miscellaneous Verbs.*

(1) **adạptar,** *to adapt*; **rạptar,** *to kidnap*; **empẹstar,** *infect*; **prẹgar,** *to preach*; **imprẹgnar,** *to impregnate*; **adọptar,** *to adopt*; **cọrar,** *to blush*; **descọrar,** *to bleach; to discolour*; **ọptar,** *to opt*; verbs ending in **-ạctar,** *e.g.,* **contạctar,** *to get in touch*; verbs ending

in -ectar, *e.g.*, **injectar**, *to inject*; and verbs with radical **ai**+consonant, *e.g.*, **pairar**, *to hover*; all have an *open* radical throughout their conjugation.

(2) **apoiar**, *to support*; and verbs with radical **oi**+consonant, *e.g.*, **pernoitar**, *to stay the night*; all have a *closed* radical throughout their conjugation.

(3) **obrar**, *to work, act, perform*; **obstar**, *to hinder, prevent*; **olhar**, *to look (at)*; **orar**, *to pray*; **orçar**, *to assess*; **ornar**, *to adorn*; all have *closed* unstressed radical and *open* stressed radical.

(4) **chegar**, *to arrive* (or *to suffice*), and its compounds, have unstressed radical [ə] and stressed radical [e].

(5) The verbs **herdar**, *to inherit*, and **errar**, *to err* (or *to wander*) have *open* stressed radical. The quality of the unstressed radical vacillates between a very closed [e] and a clipped [i].

NOTE: Nearly all these radical changes are in pronunciation only. The written language is affected only in the **boiar**, **recear** and **odiar** types.

102. COMPOUNDS OF IRREGULAR VERBS. Normally the compounds of irregular verbs exhibit the same irregularities as the simple verb.

The most common are:

dizer: condizer (*to match, tally*), **contradizer** (*to contradict*), **predizer** (*to predict, foretell*);

fazer: afazer (*to inure, accustom*), **desfazer** (*to undo, break up, destroy*), **satisfazer** (*to satisfy*);

ler: reler (*to re-read, read again*);

ter: abster-se de (*to abstain from*), **conter** (*to contain*), **deter** (*to detain, stop*), **entreter** (*to entertain*), **manter** (*to maintain*), **obter** (*to obtain*), **reter** (*to retain*), **suster** (*to sustain, hold up*);

ver: entrever (*to glimpse*), **prever** (*to foresee*), **rever** (*to see again*);

pôr: compor (*to compose*), **depor** (*to depose, put down*), **dispor** (*to dispose*), **expor** (*to expose*), **impor** (*to impose*), **propor** (*to propose*), **supor** (*to suppose*);

vir: convir (*to suit*; *to agree*), **intervir** (*to interfere, intervene*), **provir** (*to originate, stem*).

NOTES. 1. The verb **provêr** (*to provide, purvey*), though a compound of **vêr**, is regular in the preterite and the past participle.

2. For peculiarities in the use of the written accent in certain forms of the compounds of **têr, pôr** and **vir** see § 219.

VOCABULARY

Study the verbs listed in §§ 100–102 and revise the vocabulary of Lessons XI–XV.

EXERCISES

I. (*a*) *Pronounce the following:* boiais, ensaiamos, odeiam, incendeio, observávamos, obséquio, trânsito, pulso, persa, excomungado, ganhastes, saltou, remas, condena, agitou, fechavam, grelham, empestar, tomam, voltaram, soava, avistámos, pronunciaram, continuo, descorava, oramos, impregnaram, pairava, chegam, errais, entrevemos, negoceio.

(*b*) *Study and translate:* Relia. Mantinha. Supôs. Remedeiam. Sustê-la. Obtive-o ontem. Quem o desfez? Predisse o tempo. Condenam-nos a eles. Entreviram a luz. Mantivemo-la. Retemo-los. Tem-na. Compúnhamos. Não interveio. Em o revendo. Disse que o não satisfazia. Íamos compô-la. Quem lhe disse isso? Porque é que o entretinhas?

(*c*) *Translate:* Why did you close the door? When did they obtain it? They carry it. The aeroplane was hovering. They continued. We returned slowly. They envied him. They don't take them. She re-read it. When did he expose it to you? I am going to intervene tomorrow. Why do you hate her? She cut the bread. We were selling oranges. I don't like this hotel. We got in touch with the old guide.

They used to spend the night in London. They float. You support this idea, don't you? He said that we have kidnapped your elder sister. When did you arrive? Where do these books belong?

II. (a) *Study and translate:* 1. Aquele senhor vai levar o pacote ao correio, não é? 2. Foi Pedro que viu os aviões, não foi? 3. O primo do condutor teve de ir para o hospital. 4. Que alegre estava esse rapaz! 5. O seu tio estava a pescar no rio. 6. A senhora corou ao ver que não tinha razão. 7. A que horas é que parte o autocarro para Lisboa? 8. O lojista chegou à velha casa das três da tarde mas não estava ninguém. 9. A menina tem vontade de partir, não é verdade? 10. Ambos o viram ontem mas não lhes disse nada.

(b) *Translate:* 1. Which is the taller of the two brothers? 2. These two stories don't tally. 3. As soon as he saw me he waved. 4. The German soldiers kidnapped the two orphans. 5. Who is going to take (*use* **levar** *for conveying*, *never* **tomar**) these letters to the post-office? 6. I was re-reading the book when John came in. 7. This little boy is very playful. 8. It's very cloudy today, don't you agree? 9. There's somebody downstairs in the kitchen. 10. They all saw him when he closed the window.

III. (a) *Study and translate:* 1. A biblioteca fica perto da nossa casa? 2. Alguém está lá fora; vou ver quem é. 3. Ontem fazia muito vento e o céu estava carregado. 4. Tenho de voltar para casa porque vão sendo horas de almoçar. 5. O meu amigo não gosta de cerveja mas gosta imenso de vinhos. 6. Neste país está muito frio no Inverno. 7. O alemão vai chegar a 30 de Abril. 8. Este comboio vai a Lisboa às terças, quintas e sextas-feiras. 9. Outrora não havia muitos autocarros nesta cidade. 10. O livreiro mostra-me muitos livros importantes mas infelizmente não me interessam.

(b) *Translate:* 1. The walls of our house are made of brick. 2. When Alice arrived she was still soaked to the skin.

3. See you next Tuesday at a quarter to four. Cheerio!
4. Who's cut the pages of that book? 5. Michael's father always speaks very slowly. 6. Do you come here often? 7. Excellent! Bring us two large glasses of beer and a dish of mussels! 8. Your mother is grilling the tomatoes. 9. My father never used to earn much but we never went hungry. 10. I never contradict the opinions of other people.

*The Neuter Article, Ellipsis of a Noun, Special
Uses of the Definite Article, Omission of the
Definite Article, Unstressed Open* A

LESSON XVII

103. THE NEUTER ARTICLE **o.** (*a*) **O** joins with the masculine
singular form of an adjective to express the general quality of that
adjective without referring it to any specific noun: **o bom** (*what
is good, good things, goodness*), **o importante** (*that which is important, the important thing*), **o principal** (*the main thing*), etc.
Observe also the nouns **o bem e o mal** (*good and evil*) and the
expression **O mal é que** . . . (*The trouble is that* . . .).

Procurava sempre o impossível.   He always searched for the
impossible.

Isso é o mais importante.   That's the most important
thing.

O mal é que nunca chega a tempo.   The trouble is, he never
arrives on time.

O pior é que nunca me escreve.   What's worse/the worst
of it is, he never writes to me.

Diz-nos sempre $\left\{\begin{array}{l}\textbf{a mesma coisa}\\ \textbf{o mesmo}\end{array}\right\}$. He always tells us the

same (thing).

(*b*) In a similar sense **o** may be used also before an adverb.

pelo muito que trabalha, through the (great) amount of work
he does

apesar do devagar que avançávamos, in spite of the slowness
of our advance

NOTE: Students of Spanish should note that in indirect questions
como or **quão** are used before adjectives and **que** or **quão** before
adverbs to translate *how*. The neuter article is rarely used (cf.
Spanish **lo grave que** . . .). *How much* is translated by **quanto**.

Só percebęu $\begin{Bmatrix} \text{como era grave a} \\ \text{(quão grave era a)} \end{Bmatrix}$ doença quando recebęu a conta do médico.

He only realized how serious his illness was when he received the doctor's bill.

Vou perguntar quanto crescęu.

I'm going to ask how much he has grown.

104. ELLIPSIS OF A NOUN. A definite article used immediately before **que** or **de** usually corresponds to the English *the one(s)* or to a demonstrative pronoun. The neuter article **o** is used when there is no reference to a specific noun.

Os que trabalham mais, gąnham mais.

Those who work most earn most.

Que livro é ęste?   É o que me mandou o tęu irmão.

Which book is this?   It's the one your brother sent me.

Não lê o que escręve.

He doesn't read what (=that which) he writes.

os męus inimigos e os de vǫcê

my enemies and yours

os exercícios da primeira lição e os da quarta

the exercises of the first lesson and those of the fourth

NOTE: The demonstrative **aquęle**, *etc.*, and **aquilo** may frequently be used as alternatives to the definite article in the above types of clause or phrase.

105. SPECIAL USES OF THE DEFINITE ARTICLE. The definite article is required in Portuguese in the following cases where it is not used in English:

(1) With nouns used in a generalizing sense, *i.e.*, when *all* and not *some* is implied.

Os Portuguęses bębem vinho.   Portuguese drink wine (*i.e.*, *as a rule*).

O vinho não é caro em Portugal.   Wine is not dear in Portugal.

A liberdade não é a aspiração de tọdos os họmens.   Freedom is not the aspiration of all men.

NOTES.   1. The article is not normally used in this way after **gostar de,** *to like,* except when the noun is qualified by an adjective or adjectival clause or phrase.

Gostamos de flọres.   We like (all) flowers.
Gostamos das flọres.   We like the (*i.e.*, those) flowers.
Gostamos de vinho.   We like wine.

Gostamos dos vinhos $\begin{cases} \textbf{portuguẹses.} \\ \textbf{de Portugal.} \\ \textbf{que cultivam os Portuguẹses.} \end{cases}$

We like $\begin{cases} \text{Portuguese wines.} \\ \text{wines from Portugal.} \\ \text{wines grown by the Portuguese.} \end{cases}$

2. Students of other Romance languages should note that in Portuguese this generalizing use is frequently extended to expressions consisting of the framework *noun* + **de** + *noun*; the definite article is inserted between **de** and the second noun where other Romance languages omit it on the grounds that the second noun is partitive or that in combination with **de** (Italian **di**) its function is purely adjectival.   The student should carefully note such Portuguese examples as he meets them in the course of his reading.

o pedal da embraiagem, clutch-pedal
a Federação das Indústrias Britânicas, Federation of British Industries
a produção do carvão, coal-production; the production of coal
a escọva $\begin{Bmatrix} \textbf{de} \\ \textbf{dos} \end{Bmatrix}$ **dentes,** tooth-brush
o Cabo da Bọa Esperança, Cape of Good Hope
a estação $\begin{Bmatrix} \textbf{de} \\ \textbf{do} \end{Bmatrix}$ **caminho de fẹrro,** railway station

(2) With names of languages [but not, usually, after **de** or **em,** nor *need* it be used immediately after **aprẹnder** (*to learn*), **ensinar** (*to teach*), **entendẹr** (*to understand*), **estudar** (*to study*), **falar** (*to speak*), **sabẹr** (*to know*), **traduzir pạra** [*or* **em**] (*to*

translate into) and **vertęr em** (*to translate into*), nor when immediately following the subjects of these verbs].

O francês e o latim ajudam muito.　French and Latin help a lot.

Fala muito bem o inglês.　He speaks English very well.

but

Não falo alemão.　I don't speak German.

Quando aprendęu o Sr. hebręu?　When did you learn Hebrew?

Sei português.　I know Portuguese.

Uma lição de chinês.　A Chinese lesson.

(cf. **Uma lição de geografia.**　A geography lesson.)

Canta em italiano.　She sings in Italian.

NOTE: When **de** is used to indicate possession (*e.g.*, of qualities) the article must be used before the name of a language:

as dificuldades do russo, *the difficulties of Russian* (cf. **as dificuldades da geografia,** *the difficulties of geography*)

　(3) With the names of continents, countries and provinces: **a Ásia** (*Asia*), **a Itália** (*Italy*), **a Argentina** (*Argentina, the Argentine*), **a Alemanha** (*Germany*), **o Japão** (*Japan*), **a Andaluzia** (*Andalusia*), **a Estremadura** ([*Portuguese*] *Estremadura*).

But not with: **Portugal** (*Portugal*), **Cuba** (*Cuba*), **Flandres** (*Flanders*), **Marrǫcos** (*Morocco*), **Guatemala** (*Guatemala*), **Nicarágua** (*Nicaragua*), **São Sąlvadǫr** (*San Salvador*), **Aragão** (*Aragon*), **Castęla** (*Castile*), **Navarra** (*Navarre*) and **Trás-os-Montes;** nor with Portuguese overseas territories except **os Açǫres** (*the Azores*), **a Guiné** (*Guinea*) and **a Madeira** (*Madeira*).

It is sometimes also omitted after **de** and **em** before **África** (*Africa*), **Espanha** (*Spain*), **França** (*France*) and **Inglatęrra** (*England*).

It is, of course, omitted after a demonstrative adjective, *e.g.*, **ęsta Inglatęrra** (*this England*).

(4) Before many place-names which have a separate life as common nouns, *e.g.*, **o Rio de Janeiro** (*lit., the River of January*), **o Pǫrto** (*Oporto, lit., the Port*), **a Figueira da Fǫz** (*lit., the Figtree of the River-mouth*). Also used with the article are **o Cairo, a Covilhã, o Estoril, a Haia** (*the Hague*), **a Havana, o Havre** (*Le Havre*). This article is, however, usually omitted when the place-name is the subject of a sentence. In this respect **o Pǫrto** and **o Havre** are exceptions.

Vamos pạra a Covilhã. We're going to Covilhã.
(O) Rio é uma bẹla cidade. Rio is a beautiful city.
O Pǫrto fica no nǫrte de Portugal. Oporto is in the north of Portugal.

(5) Before a proper noun qualified by a descriptive adjective, adjectival clause or adjectival phrase.

o pǫbre (de) João, poor John
o Portugal que tanto amamos, the Portugal we love so much
a Lisbǫa modẹrna, modern Lisbon
a Londres de hǫje, contemporary London

Similarly before languages:

Não fala o português de Portugal. He doesn't speak European Portuguese (=the Portuguese of Portugal).

NOTES. 1. Where the qualifying element is a phrase or clause, English and Portuguese often coincide in using the article:

a Lisbǫa de hǫje, the Lisbon of today
a Sevilha que conhẹcem os estrangeiros, the Seville foreigners know
a Cartago de Dido e Eneias, the Carthage of Dido and Aeneas

2. The article is not used when the adjective is already considered to be part of the noun, e.g., **Nǫva Iǫrque,** *New York*, or when it is not a descriptive adjective, *e.g.*, **tǫdo Marrǫcos,** *all Morocco*, **ẹste Portugal,** *this Portugal*, **ẹsta Inglatẹrra,** *this England*, **que Alemanha?** *which Germany?*, **Londres inteira,** *the whole of London*. The article, however, must accompany a possessive adjective, *e.g.*, **o nǫsso Gil Vicente,** *our Gil Vicente* (the

great Portuguese playwright), and must accompany tǫdo in those cases where the proper noun is normally expressed with the article, e.g., tǫda a Inglatęrra, tǫdo o Brasil [see § 161 (c)].

(6) Before titles (but not in direct address, nor when the title is in apposition, nor when it is a foreign word, nor with **Dom, Dǫna, Santo, Santa, Frei, Sǫr** or **Sórǫr**).

> **a rainha Isabęl,** Queen Elizabeth, Queen Isabella
> **o general Eisenhower,** General Eisenhower
> **o presidente Kubitschek,** President Kubitschek
> **o senhǫr Cǫsta, a senhǫra Tǎvares,** Mr Costa, Mrs (or Miss) Tavares
> **o capitão Maia,** Captain Maia
> **o doutǫr Martins,** Doctor Martins

but **Bom dia, senhǫr professǫr.** Good morning, sir (= teacher).
> **o secretário, padre Avelino,** the Secretary, Father Avelino
> **lord Derby e sir Robert Peel,** Lord Derby and Sir Robert Peel
> **Herr Müller vai comprar a lǫja.** Herr Müller's going to buy the shop.
> **Santa Teręsa e São João da Cruz,** St Teresa and St John of the Cross
> **Frei Luís de Sousa e Sǫr Violante do Céu,** Brother Luís de Sousa and Sister Violante do Céu
> **Dom Pędro III e Dǫna Maria I,** King Peter III and Queen Mary I

NOTES. 1.Titles (except **Dom, Dǫna, Santo, Santa, Frei, Sǫr** or **Sòrǫr**) do not normally take a capital letter except in official documents and like matter.

2. **Santo** becomes **São** before a masculine singular Christian name beginning with a consonant.

> **Santo António, Santo Isidǫro, Santo Estêvão,** Saint Ant(h)ony, Saint Isidore, Saint Stephen

but **São Pędro, São Tomé, São Domingos,** Saint Peter, Saint
Thomas, Saint Dominic (*exception:* **Santo Tirso,** Saint
Thyrsus)

3. **Dom** is used before the Christian names of kings, members of
royal families, members of the higher nobility, and members of the
hierarchy of the Roman Catholic Church.   The feminine **Dǫna** is
of wider application and is used as a token of deference or respect
in all but the lowest levels of society, and is likewise used before
Christian names.   Where desired it may be preceded by the word
senhǫra, *e.g.,* (a Sra.) **D. Ana (Plácido).**

4. The following abbreviations are commonly used in writing:
**Sto. (Santo), Sta. (Santa), S. (São), Dr. (doutǫr), D. (Dom.),
D. (Dǫna), Fr. (Frei), Sr. (senhǫr), Sra. (senhǫra), Eng. (enge-
nheiro,** *engineer*).

5. *Doctor* (= *medical practitioner*) is translated by **médico,**
although **doutǫr** is used in address and before the surname.

(7) With parts of the body and with clothing the Portuguese
definite article usually translates the English possessive adjective,
the possessive only being retained where confusion might arise.
Students of Spanish in particular should note the constructions
with **tęr,** however.

Levantaram a cabęça.   They raised their heads.
but **Os sęus ǫlhos brilhavam.**   His eyes shone.

Onde deixaste o chapéu?   Where did you leave your hat?
but **Onde deixaste o męu chapéu?**   Where did you leave *my*
hat?

Tinha o nariz arrebitado.   Her nose was turned-up (*lit.,* She
had the nose turned-up).
Tinha o nariz grande.   She had a big nose (*lit.,* She had the
nose big).
Tinha (os) cabęlos prętos e (os) ǫlhos azuis.   She had black
hair and blue eyes.
Tinha uns cabęlos prętos e uns ǫlhos azuis maravilhǫsos
(*or* **uns ǫlhos azuis que encantavam**).   She had black
hair and two marvellous (*or* two enchanting) blue eyes.

NOTES. 1. *They raised their heads,* but each person has only one; therefore **a cabeça.** Similarly, **Abriram os olhos** (*They opened their eyes*), but **Todos abriram a boca** (*They all opened their mouths*).[1]

2. In some cases a weak indirect object is needed to make the ownership clearer.

Quebrei-lhe o braço direito.   I broke his (*or* her *or* your) right arm.

Tiraram-me o casaco.   They took my jacket off (*or* from me).

3. With **ter** the definite article must be used with a singular noun, whereas for the plural there are several constructions. **Uns (umas)** is used when some form of aesthetic judgment is being passed. If, however, the circumstances are accidental rather than inherent the definite article *must* be used: **Tenho os olhos cansados** (*My eyes are tired*).

(8) To indicate rate (the Portuguese definite article here translates the English indefinite article):

> **Vendem-no a três escudos o quilo.**   They sell it at three escudos a kilogramme.
>
> **Comprei-os a doze escudos a dúzia.**   I bought them at twelve escudos a dozen.

but with time-rate, the preposition **por** is used:

> **Ganha vinte escudos por dia.**   He earns twenty escudos a day.
>
> **cinquenta quilómetros por hora,** thirty miles an hour
> **seis vezes por semana,** six times a week

(9) The definite article *may* be used before Christian names and surnames to indicate familiarity and before surnames to indicate a sort of renown.

Onde é que está o João?   Where's John got to?
Está a falar com a Maria.   He's talking to our Mary.
Ouvi a Callas na Traviata.   I've heard Callas in *La Traviata.*
Onde é que está o Lopes?   Where's old Lopes got to?

---

[1] But note: **Apertaram as mãos** (*They shook hands*).

(10) The definite article is also used in Portuguese with meals and certain public institutions: o primeiro ạlmọço (*breakfast*), o ạlmọço (*lunch*), o chá (*tea*), o jantar (*dinner*), a ceia [ˈsɐjɐ] (*supper*); a escọla (*school*), o licẹu (*grammar school*), o colégio (*private school*), a universidade (*university*), o cárcere (*prison, jail*), also with a cidade (*town, city*) and a cama (*bed*) and in a number of idiomatic expressions too numerous to list here.

Às ọito sai pạra a escọla.   At eight he leaves for school.

Passei a manhã no licẹu.   I spent the morning in school.

Tomei o $\begin{Bmatrix} \text{pequẹno} \\ \text{primeiro} \end{Bmatrix}$ ạlmọço às sẹte.   I had breakfast at seven.

(11) For the use of the definite article in expressions of time and possession, see §§ 51, 69–72, 158.

106. OMISSION OF THE DEFINITE ARTICLE.   The definite article is used in English but omitted in Portuguese:

(1) Before a number in the title of a ruler.

João V (João quinto), John V (the Fifth)
Isabẹl II (Isabẹl segunda), Elizabeth II
Luís XIV (Luís catọrze), Louis XIV

(2) Usually before a noun in apposition, unless that noun is individualized.

Ao outro dia, vinte de Julho, parti pạra a Figueira.
   On the following day, the twentieth of July, I left for Figueira.

Depọis vem Beja, capital da província.
   Then comes Beja, the capital of the province.

but Estẹve também o sẹu pai, o professọr.
   His father, the teacher, was also there.

Cạmões, o grande escritọr português do século XVI
   Camoens, the great Portuguese writer of the sixteenth century

107. PRONUNCIATION: UNSTRESSED OPEN **a.** Unstressed **a** is
normally closed [ɐ]. In the following circumstances, however,
it is *open* [a].

(*a*) When followed by **-cci-, -cç-, -ct-, -pci- -pt-, -x-** [ks]:
fracçionário, *fractional*; a **acção,** *action*; **activo,** *active*;
capcioso, *captious*; **adaptar,** *to adapt*; **saxónico,** *Saxon*.
Exception: **os caractéres,** *characters*, and derivative words.

(*b*) In the verb **aguar,** *to water* and derivatives:

(*c*) In the endings **-ar, -al,** and **-ax:**
o **açúcar,** *sugar*; **César,** *Caesar*; **Setúbal;** o **clímax,** *climax*.

(*d*) When followed by 1+consonant (NOT **lh**):
alguém, *somebody*; **faltar,** *to be lacking*; **saltar,** *to jump*.

(*e*) In the diphthong **au:**
a **audição,** *audition*; **causar,** *to cause*.

(*f*) In the diphthong **ai** when this is followed by a consonant:
airado, *airy*; **pairar,** *to hover*:

(*g*) When carrying the grave accent:
à, àquele, etc.

(*h*) When an originally stressed **a** of a word acquiring certain
subsequent suffixes (see § 165).

(*i*) In a number of isolated words:
acerca de, *concerning*; **além,** *beyond*; o **alerta,** *alarm, alert*;
alertar, *to alert*; **amanhã,** *tomorrow*; **amém,** *amen* (or
ámen [ˈamen], in very learned usage); **um aparte,** *an aside*
(*remark*); **aquém de,** *on this side of*; **avante,** *onward*;
Camões, *Camoens*; **camoniano,** *pertaining to Camoens*; a
caveira, *skull*; **doravante** (also **de ora avante**), *from now on,
henceforth*; **jamais,** *never*; a **padaria,** *bakery*; o **padeiro,**
baker; **Sabor** (a proper name); **sadio,** *sound, healthful, whole-*

some; **Tavares** (a surname); **o vadio**, *idler, loafer, vagrant*; the
derivatives of **vadio**.

VOCABULARY

a África do Sul	South Africa	**os Estados Unidos**	U.S.A.
a aldeia	village	**o este**	east
a América	America (*continent*)	**a geografia**	geography
a América do Norte/Sul	North/South America	**o guardanapo**	napkin, serviette
americano	American (*especially* Latin-American)	**hábil**	able, skilful
		a Holanda	Netherlands, Holland
a amizade	friendship	**holandês**	Dutch
a aula	class, lecture; class-room, lecture-room	**já**	already, now, at once
		o leste	east
		a libra	pound
o Brasil	Brazil	**Moçambique**	Mozambique
o(s) cabelo(s)	hair	**o norte**	north
o Canadá	Canada	**norte-americano**	(North) American (*i.e.*, from U.S.A.)
canadiano	Canadian		
caro	dear, expensive		
cear	to have supper	**primeiro** (*adv.*)	first, firstly
a ceia	supper		
certo	(a) certain	**primeiro que tudo**	first of all
conhecer	to know, get to know, be acquainted with	**que vem**	next, coming
		o quilo (-grama)	kilo(gramme)
costumar	to be in the habit of, be accustomed to	**o quilómetro**	kilometre
		a revolução	revolution
		russo	Russian
crer (*conj. like* **ler**)	to believe	**sul-americano**	South American
curioso	curious, odd, strange; inquisitive	**a Suíça**	Switzerland
		útil	useful

Study also the words and phrases listed in §§ 103-107.

NOTE: Nouns of nationality are only written with capital initial letter when used generically, *e.g.*, **os Espanhóis,** Spaniards (*i.e.*, *all* Spaniards); **o sangue-frio do Inglês,** the Englishman's sangfroid.

EXERCISES

I. (*a*) *Pronounce the following:* atracção, tractor, adaptação, raptávamos, contactaram, invasor, relacionado, almíscar, causativo, pairou, pazada, radiotelefonia, padeiro, satisfação, caveira, obrava, olhei, Saxónia, alertaram, Alentejo, açúcar, norte-americano.

(*b*) *Study and translate:* Os Canadianos e os Norte-Americanos. O útil e o mais formoso. O bem e o mal. O bom e o mau. Esta revolução e a do século passado. Estas batatas e as que comemos ontem. O Inglês e o Russo. Não fala nem francês nem alemão. Vamos traduzir isto para o português. No Canadá e no norte dos Estados Unidos. O senhor Martins e a senhora Rodrigues. Uma chávena de chá e outra de café. É um professor muito hábil. Entrou em certa casa. Parte muito cedo para a cidade. Estive ontem com a senhora Dona Joana. A oeste e a leste.[1] Ao norte e ao sul.[1] Que línguas falam na Suíça? A mais de cem quilómetros por hora. Ele ganhava mil e cem escudos por semana. Tinha os olhos grandes. Ceiam sempre às onze da noite.

(*c*) *Translate:* South American. A terrible hunger. The nicest lecture-room. The possible. What is bad. All who work. He teaches me French and Dutch. How is Mrs Namora this morning? We know the markets of Brazil and of Spanish America. A thousand men and a hundred boys. Spain is in the south of Europe. This England. Eighteenth-century Holland. We walked round the building. They have had breakfast. Saint John. Saint Antony. Brother Michael. Seventeenth-century Oporto. He sold them to me at twenty escudos a kilogramme.

---

[1] Observe the difference in use of articles in these two examples.

II. (*a*) *Study and translate:* 1. Gosto muito dos vinhos franceses. 2. Não conhecemos nenhuma aula tão pequena como aquela. 3. O importante era terminá-lo antes da hora do chá. 4. Falou muito durante a ceia da sua viagem ao Japão. 5. Que triste ter de estar sempre a ensinar a mesma coisa! 6. Numa aldeia do sul de Portugal morava certo Sr. Magalhães. 7. Havana é a capital de Cuba. 8. Olhou para a janela mas não viu nada. 9. Estas lições são muito mais difíceis do que aquelas que estudávamos no ano passado. 10. Na semana que vem partimos todos para a África do Sul.

(*b*) *Translate:* 1. The important thing is to do it now before leaving for Spain. 2. His brother teaches French at the grammar school. 3. These books are much more difficult than last year's ones. 4. Spanish is more difficult than the geography we used to study at school. 5. What I don't understand is why he didn't write to us explaining what he was doing. 6. We are going to go first to France and Germany, and afterwards to Switzerland and Italy. 7. What's worse, he's going to leave at once. 8. The Cape of Good Hope is in South Africa. 9. The teacher has translated this book into Italian. 10. We are already acquainted with the difficulties of Portuguese.

III. (*a*) *Study and translate:* 1. A senhora dona Maria já pôs os guardanapos sobre a mesa? 2. As minhas irmãs não são tão altas como as do Filipe. 3. E o mais curioso é que esses senhores não crêem o que escreveram. 4. Durante sete anos o Magalhães ensinou alemão no liceu. 5. Camões esteve dois anos em Moçambique. 6. Os pais falam muito bem o espanhol e agora estão a ensiná-lo aos filhos. 7. Os Espanhóis costumam beber mais vinho do que os Ingleses porque o vinho é mais barato em Espanha que em Inglaterra. 8. Primeiro falou-nos da sua viagem para o Brasil e depois cantou-nos, em português, umas canções que lá aprendeu. 9. Disse num aparte que não gostava dos portugueses. 10. Faltavam oito minutos para as dez.

(b) *Translate:* 1. Her eyes were black and she had a flower in her hair. 2. Coffee is much dearer here than in present-day Portugal (= the Portugal of today). 3. At half past nine I have an Italian class. 4. For some people friendship is the most important of all the virtues. 5. But that has nothing to do with what he wrote to us last Tuesday. 6. I'm going to obtain a hundred pounds more in order to make the trip I was talking to you about last month. 7. Last year he was in South America and this year he is going to visit the United States. 8. The American told us that the supper was excellent. 9. The baker said Oporto is a very beautiful city. 10. It is the capital of the north of Portugal.

LESSON XVIII

108. RADICAL-CHANGING VERBS OF THE SECOND CONJUGATION. The rules for the radical changes of the second conjugation are the same as those for the first conjugation except that the radical **e** and **o** of the first person singular of the present indicative is always *closed*. When the radical vowel is followed by **m** + consonant or **n** + consonant, it is always *closed* by virtue of being nasalized. The phonetic value of the radical vowel is indicated in square brackets in the following scheme:

batẹr [ɐ], *to beat*: **bato** [a], **bates** [a], **bate** [a], **batẹmos** [ɐ], **bateis** [ɐ], **batem** [a];

devẹr [ə], *to owe*: **dẹvo** [e], **dẹves** [ɛ], **dẹve** [ɛ], **devẹmos** [ə], **deveis** [ə], **dẹvem** [ɛ];

movẹr [u], *to move*: **mọvo** [o], **mọves** [ɔ], **mọve** [ɔ], **movẹmos** [u], **moveis** [u], **mọvem** [ɔ];

lambẹr [ẽ], *to lick*: **lambo** [ẽ], etc.;

vendẹr [ẽ], *to sell*: **vendo** [ẽ], etc.;

rompẹr [õ], *to break, tear*: **rompo** [õ], etc.

109. SPECIAL CASES. (*a*) Before **l** + consonant, radical **o** is [ɔ] when unstressed:

dissọlvẹr [ɔ], *to dissolve*: **dissọlvo** [o], **dissọlves** [ɔ], etc.

(*b*) The three verbs **aquẹcẹr**, *to heat, warm*, **arrefẹcẹr**, *to cool* (*off*), and **esquẹcẹr**, *to forget*, have *open* **e** throughout.

(*c*) The two verbs **mexẹr**, *to stir*; *to fidget*, and **protegẹr**, *to protect*, have unstressed radical [ə], first person singular present indicative stressed radical [ɐ] or [e], and remaining stressed radicals of present indicative [ɛ]. For the orthographic change of **g** to **j** in **protejo** see § 209 (*b*).

mexẹr [ə], **mexo** [ɐ] or [e], **męxes** [ɛ], **męxe** [ɛ], **mexẹmos** [ə], mexeis [ə], **męxem** [ɛ];
protegẹr [ə]: **protejo** [ɐ] or [e], **protęges** [ɛ], **protęge** [ɛ], **protegẹmos** [ə], protegeis [ə], **protęgem** [ɛ].

The two verbs **elegẹr**, *to choose, elect*, and **regẹr**, *to rule, be in force*, behave like **protegẹr**.

(*d*) The verb **erguẹr**, *to erect, raise*, has first person singular present indicative **ẹrgo**, but open **e** for the remaining forms with stressed radical. The quality of the unstressed radical vacillates between a very closed [e] and a clipped [i]. Its compound **soẹrguẹr**, *to lift slightly, raise slightly*, is similar, but has [e] for the unstressed radical.

(*e*) The irregular verb **querẹr**, *to wish, want*, has first person singular present indicative **quẹro**. See § 112.

(*f*) For verbs in **-oẹr**, *e.g.*, **moẹr** [muˡer], *to grind*, see § 212.

NOTE: Apart from purely orthographic changes, none of the above radical changes involves any alteration in the written language. For the present subjunctive and very familiar imperative, see §§ 179, 194.

110. RADICAL-CHANGING VERBS OF THE THIRD CONJUGATION. The radical changes of the third conjugation involve more changes in the written language than those of the first and second conjugations. The rules for the third conjugation changes are similar to those of the second conjugation except that the radical **e** or **o** becomes **i** or **u** respectively in the first person singular of the present indicative.

When the radical vowel is followed by **m**+consonant or **n**+consonant, it is always *closed* by virtue of being nasalized. This does not impede, however, the change to **i** (there are no cases of radical **o** in verbs of this type). The phonetic value of the radical vowel is indicated in square brackets in the following scheme:

agir [ɐ], *to act*: **ajo** [a], **ages** [a], **age** [a], **agimos** [ɐ], **agis** [ɐ], **agem** [a];

servir [ə], *to serve*: **sirvo** [i], **serves** [ɛ], **serve** [ɛ], **servimos** [ə], **servis** [ə], **servem** [ɛ];

dormir [u], *to sleep*: **durmo** [u], **dormes** [ɔ], **dorme** [ɔ], **dormimos** [u], **dormis** [u], **dormem** [ɔ];

franzir [ẽ], *to wrinkle*: **franzo** [ẽ], **franzes** [ẽ], **franze** [ẽ], **franzimos** [ẽ], **franzis** [ẽ], **franzem** [ẽ];

sentir [ẽ], *to feel*: **sinto** [ĩ], **sentes** [ẽ], **sente** [ẽ], **sentimos** [ẽ], **sentis** [ẽ], **sentem** [ẽ].

NOTE: For the orthographic change of **g** to **j** in **ajo** see § 209 (*b*).

111. SPECIAL CASES.

(*a*) The verbs **polir**, *to polish*, and **sortir**, *to supply*, have **u** when the radical is stressed and **o** [u] when unstressed:

polir [u]; **pulo** [u], **pules** [u], **pule** [u], **polimos** [u], **polis** [u], **pulem** [u].

(*b*) Before **m** or **n**, radical **a** is always *closed*: **bramir** [ɐ], *to roar*, **bramo** [ɐ], etc.; **ganir** [ɐ], *to yelp*, **gano** [ɐ], etc.

(*c*) The present indicative of the verb **frigir** [i], *to fry*, is as follows:

frijo [i], **freges** [ɛ], **frege** [ɛ], **frigimos** [i], **frigis** [i], **fregem** [ɛ]. When in doubt use the verb **fritar**.

(*d*) Five verbs, **agredir**, *to attack*, **progredir**, *to (make) progress*, **transgredir**, *to transgress*, **denegrir**, *to denigrate*, and **prevenir**, *to anticipate*, *warn*, *forestall*, *prevent*, behave like **servir** except that the change of **e** to **i** takes place on *all* occasions when the radical is stressed:

agrido [i], **agrides** [i], **agride** [i], **agredimos** [ə], **agredis** [ə], **agridem** [i].

(e) Eight verbs, **acudir**, *to (run to) help*, **sacudir**, *to shake*, **bulir**, *to move, stir, budge*, **cuspir**, *to spit*, **fugir**, *to flee*, **subir**, *to go up, come up, bring up*, **sumir**, *to hide*, and **consumir**, *to consume*, have **ǫ** [ɔ] as the radical in the second and third persons singular and third person plural of the present indicative:

subo [u], **sǫbes** [ɔ], **sǫbe** [ɔ], **subimos** [u], **subis** [u], **sǫbem** [ɔ].

Notes. 1. **Entupir**, *to block up*, may optionally behave in this way.
2. The verbs **assumir**, *to assume*, **presumir**, *to presume*, and **resumir**, *to abridge, summarize*, do NOT behave like **sumir** and **consumir**.

(f) For a special radical change involving certain verbs in **-struir**, see § 215.

(g) For the verbs **delinquir**, **arguir** and **redarguir** see §216.

112. Two Irregular Verbs: **podęr** AND **queręr**. These two verbs present irregularities in the present indicative and the preterite. The irregular forms are in bold type.

(1) podęr, *to be able (can)* (cf. movęr)

pres. indic.: **pǫsso**, pǫdes, pǫde, podęmos, podeis, pǫdem
impf. indic.: podia, etc.
preterite: **pude, pudęste, pôde, pudęmos, pudęstes, pudę-ram**
gerund: podendo

(2) queręr, *to wish, want* (cf. devęr)

pres. indic.: **quęro**, quęres, **quęr** (*or* quęre), queręmos, quereis, quęrem *impf. indic.:* queria, etc.

preterite: **quis, quisęste, quis, quisęmos, quisęstes, quisę-
                ram**

gerund: querendo

NOTES. 1. For the use of **quęre**, see § 94 (*a*) note 2.

2. The verbs **podęr** and **queręr** do not take any preposition before a dependent infinitive.

Vǫcê quęr acompanhar-me ąmanhã? Do you wish to go with me tomorrow?

Ąmanhã não pǫsso (acompanhá-lo). I can't (go with you) tomorrow.

3. The English *can* is not normally translated with verbs of the senses.

Vês o męu irmão? Can you see my brother?

Ouviam-se as ondas sǫbre a praia. The waves could be heard on the shore. (For the *Reflexive Passive* see § 140.)

The use of **podęr** would emphasize the physical capability or incapability.

É muito vęlho e quase não pǫde vęr. He is very old and can hardly see.

4. *Can* implying knowledge or technique as opposed to pure physical ability is expressed by **sabęr**.

Sabes nadar (dançar, etc.)? Can you swim (dance, etc.)? (*i.e.*, Do you know how to?)

VOCABULARY

abrir	to open	**arrumar**	to put away,
achar	to find; to think		stow away,
acompanhar	to accompany,		stack away
	go with, come	**batęr (à**	to knock (at
	with	**pǫrta)**	the door)
ainda não	not yet	**o braço**	arm

178

brasileiro	Brazilian	**o leite**	milk
a cabeça	head	**levantar a**	to clear the
o carteiro	postman	**mesa**	table
chegar a	to arrive at, reach	**Martinho**	Martin
		mentir	to lie, tell lies
chegar tarde	to be (arrive) late	**minha senhora**	madam
chover	to rain	**muito obri-**	thanks very
a criada	maid	**gado (-a)**	much
custar	to cost	**não dever**	should not,
deixar	to leave (NOT *places*)		ought not to, must not
dever	to owe; ought, should, must	**a parte**	part
		a partida	departure
o embrulho	(large) parcel	**o pêssego**	peach
a empregada	maid; any female employee	**o preço**	price
		preferir	to prefer
		preparar	to prepare
o endereço	address	**quebrar**	to break
enquanto	while, whilst, (for) as long as	**o romance**	novel
		sempre que	whenever, every time (that)
o exército	army		
fazer compras	to do the shopping	**sentir (a) falta de**	to miss (*what is absent*)
ficar	to stay, remain, wait; to become	**tanto**	so much, *pl.* so many
		a toalha (de	
o governo	government	**mesa)**	tablecloth
ir às compras	to go shopping	**vir buscar**	to come and/to get, come for
ir buscar	to go and/to get, go for		

Study also the verbs listed in §§ 108–112.

EXERCISES

I. (*a*) *Pronounce the following:* comes, bebes, escrevo, sabemos, tivemos, acode, protegeis, mexo, conhecer, moveu, soergueu, elegeste, dormimos, despis, pulem, reaccionário, varapau, baptizamos, orlava, frigimos, agridem, pode, pôde, oásis.

(b) *Study and translate:* Não deves beber mais café. Você come pêssegos. Eu gosto de uvas. V. Exª. pode entrar. A Sra. chegou tarde. O menino está lendo um romance? Vais às compras depois? Qual é o seu endereço? Vamos levantar a mesa. Esqueceste o chapéu! Devemos partir já. Sinto a falta da minha mulher. Não tem vontade de trabalhar? Os preços vão sempre subindo.

(c) *Translate:* I want. They ought. We polish. Do you know them? They protected us. You go up. He lifted his arm slightly. He slept [for] three hours. She shook her head. We must not assume that. They are setting fire to the factory. I can't see. Can he sing? He went bankrupt. They warned me in time. We have fried the four eggs. What do we do now? We have put the cups away. I have broken his arm!

II. (a) *Study and translate:* 1. O Dr. Barros foi buscar o chapéu mas não o achou. 2. Ficámos na sala de estar enquanto o procurava. 3. Não deves comer tantos pêssegos. Vais ficar doente. 4. — Bom dia, minha senhora, como está? — Estou bem, muito obrigada, e você? 5. V. Exª. quer acompanhar-me à estação? 6. Os Brasileiros elegeram um novo presidente. 7. O ex-ministro serviu cinco anos no governo. 8. A empregada levantou a mesa e arrumou a toalha e os guardanapos. 9. O carteiro bateu à porta três vezes mas ninguém respondeu. 10. Abriu a porta e deixou o pacote numa cadeira.

(b) *Translate:* 1. Whenever (the) mother was preparing lunch, I would do the shopping. 2. The postman was late this morning but he gave me a parcel, two packets and five letters. 3. Coal production in this country went up last year. 4. The president has told the government that he fears a revolution. 5. Martin's mother is warming his supper in the oven. 6. The soldier missed his family while he was serving his country abroad. 7. We were all very

very fond of the novels of Aquilino Ribeiro. 8. They reached the railway station only five minutes before the departure of the train. 9. The maid has come to get the parcels I left on the table. 10. We could see only three aeroplanes in the sky.

III. (a) *Study and translate:* 1. O governo rege, o povo elege. 2. No sábado passado o carteiro chegou a casa por volta das seis da tarde mas a sua esposa não estava. 3. O cão ganiu quando viu o toiro. 4. Sou muito velho e quase não posso ver. 5. A criada ainda não está pronta a servir-nos. 6. Quem dividiu a Alemanha em duas partes ? 7. O presidente alertou o exército porque receava uma revolução. 8. O velho professor de línguas entrou devagar na aula e fechou a porta. 9. Vamos para a mesa, o jantar está pronto. 10. Ontem de manhã o tempo estava melhor e pudemos abrir as janelas.

(b) *Translate:* 1. I want to see what he has done. 2. Milk costs more than wine in many parts of Europe. 3. He lied when he said his mother was coming tomorrow morning. 4. She wants to warm the milk before going to bed. 5. They asked me what time it was and I told them it was half past nine. 6. It always rains when I want to go into town and visit my cousin. 7. They say that Italian people prefer coffee to tea but I don't understand why. 8. I prefer to buy them something for the house. 9. She undresses the children before preparing supper. 10. What time is it when he closes the shop and returns home ?

LESSON XIX

113. The student will probably, by now, have found difficulties in distinguishing between the Portuguese imperfect and preterite tenses, despite the general distinction suggested in § 84. Often shades of meaning difficult to express in English are indicated by the use of one tense rather than the other, and in translating from English to Portuguese it may be necessary to take into account a wider context than that of the mere sentence before one can decide which tense to use. It is a difficult problem at first but is one that, with practice and study of examples, should soon disappear. In the pages that follow we shall consider certain rather more difficult cases than those given in § 84, borderline cases where both tenses are possible in Portuguese but with differences of meaning. We shall consider cases first from the English side and then from the Portuguese.

(a) *English–Portuguese*

(i) *He was very happy when he saw his father.*

If we mean that he was already in a happy state of mind when he saw his father, then we shall use the imperfect (**Estava muito contente quando viu o pai**); if we imply that he became pleased because he saw his father, we are setting a beginning (*i.e.*, a time limit) to his happiness and we shall therefore use the preterite (**Ficou muito contente quando viu o pai**).

(ii) *The car was very cheap.*

If we mean that the price being asked for the car was a low one or that it was a cheap type of car, we are passing a neutral comment and shall therefore use the imperfect (**O carro era muito barato**); if, on the other hand, we are thinking of the moment at which the deal was proposed or accepted (*i.e.*, he offered it to me at a low price, or I bought it at a low price, or it cost me very little), the emphasis is on the price in its time limitations and we shall use the preterite (**O carro foi muito barato**).

(iii) *It was difficult to explain.*

If we are thinking only of the essential difficulty of explaining the problem irrespective of time limits within the past (*i.e.*, it was a difficult type of problem to explain), we shall use the imperfect tense (**Era difícil de explicar**); if, on the other hand, we are thinking of the difficulty someone experienced in explaining the problem at a given moment in the past, we shall use the preterite (**Foi difícil de explicar**).

(iv) *He was a very bad king.*

If we make this statement in a narrative sense, opening the way to details on his life, perhaps, or as a background to the happenings of his reign, we shall use the imperfect tense (**Era um rei muito mau**); but if we are thinking of his reign in its completeness, as a bygone moment in history, we shall use the preterite (**Foi um rei muito mau**).

(v) *She could not see her brother.*

If we mean that from where she was standing her brother was not in sight, we are indicating a state: **Ela não via o irmão**. (For the omission of **poder**, *to be able*, see § 112, Note 3.) If, on the other hand, we wish to stress that she made an effort to go and see her brother but that she met with a definite obstacle, then we must use the preterite (with **poder** now, to indicate the effort made): **Ela não pôde ver o irmão**.

(vi) *He had breakfast every morning at seven.*

Here there is repeated action, so that the imperfect tense would appear to be the obvious choice in Portuguese: **Tomava o pequeno almoço todas as manhãs às sete**. But suppose the action, though repeated, is ascribed to a limited period of time (his holidays, perhaps, or when he was in Portugal). There are then two possibilities, which bring us to the finest distinction of all between the preterite and the imperfect: if we wish to emphasize the completeness and pastness of the period of time in question, we shall use the preterite (**Tomou o pequeno almoço tǫdas as manhãs às sęte**); if we wish to present the same period narratively, as something living and progressing (cf. (iv) above), we shall use the imperfect.

(b) *Portuguese–English*

   (i) **João não encontrava o professǫr.**
      João não encontrou o professǫr.

In the first case John was having no luck in finding the teacher but he was still looking; in the second case, the search is over and the teacher remains unfound. The imperfect tense, then, indicates progression of the action; the preterite its completeness. In English these two examples might be rendered as *John could not find the teacher* and *John did not find the teacher* respectively, though the difference is less clear than in Portuguese for the first translation might also correspond to a Portuguese preterite (cf. (a) (v), above). Only by a free translation of the imperfect (*e.g.*, *John was not managing to find the teacher*) can we bring out the essential difference in English.

   (ii) **Não levava em conta o tempo que fazia.**
      Não levou em conta o tempo que fazia.

The imperfect **levava** indicates his state of mind, unconscious of weather conditions; the preterite **levou** emphasizes his lack of consideration for such conditions at a given moment: the moment in which he made his plans. Free English translations might be, respectively, *He was oblivious of the state of the weather* and *He did not take into account the state of the weather*.

   (iii) **Acompanhava-o o embǎixadǫr.**
      Acompanhou-o o embǎixadǫr.

In the first case the ambassador plays a less dynamic part in the proceedings, his presence being incidental to what was done during the tour (*The ambassador was with him*); in the second case the emphasis is on the action of the ambassador in going with him (*The ambassador went with him*). The imperfect presents the ambassador's presence in its vagueness, as little more than an accompanying state; the preterite presents it in its limits and its restriction to a given moment in the past.

(iv) **Falava alemão.**
     Falou-me em alemão.

In the imperfect we are interested in someone's ability to speak German (*He spoke* [=*was able to speak*] *German*); in the preterite the ability reveals itself in a definite action in the past (*He spoke to me in German*). In the first case, then, we have, as it were, a reservoir of potential action; in the second, a canalizing of that reservoir to a given end.

(v) **Sabia-o quando conheci o tẹu irmão.**
    Soube-o quando conheci o tẹu irmão.

(**sabẹr** = *to know* [for a fact]; **conhecẹr** = *to know* [be acquainted with].) In the first case (*I* [*already*] *knew about it when I made your brother's acquaintance*) the imperfect of **sabẹr** is used because I was already aware of it when and before I met the brother and there is *no* indication of when that state began; in the second case (*I got to know/found out about it* [*only*] *when I made your brother's acquaintance*) the preterite is used because my knowledge has now been given a time limit: the time at which I came to know the brother. Notice that the preterite **conheci** in both examples has been translated by *I made the acquaintance of*; **conhecia** would be translated by *I was (already) acquainted with*.

(vi) **Com quem estavas quando te chamei?**
     Com quem estivẹste ontem?

One might object here that the time covered by the imperfect **estavas** in the first sentence (*Whom were you with when I phoned you?*) is probably of shorter duration than that covered by the preterite **estivẹste** in the second. Once again it is a matter of the presence or absence of time limits and a sense of completeness. In the first case the action of being in someone's company is not confined to a point in time; it stretches without time limits on each side of the momentary action **chamei**. In the second example, on the other hand, the state of being is seen as a whole confined within the limits of the bygone **ontem**. **Com quem**

estavas ontem? is also possible, but the emphasis would not then be on the state of being in its completeness, but on its unprescribed duration, or as a setting for (*preterite*) actions more limited in time [cf. (*a*) (iv) above].

NOTE: In examples (*b*) (ii), (iii) and (iv) the imperfect may also, of course, indicate repetition of the individual definite action as well as suggest state as we have assumed. Thus, **Não levava em conta** may mean *He was not in the habit of taking into account*, and **Acompanhava-o o embaixador** may mean *The ambassador used to go* (or *come*) *with him*, and **Falava alemão** may mean *He used to speak German*. This use of the imperfect to indicate *repeated action* as opposed to *temporarily unlimited state* does not present difficulties and has been left out of account in the above examples. Also omitted above is the use of the Portuguese preterite as the means of translating the English perfect (*I have* + past participle), cf. § 83.

114. SPECIAL MEANINGS OF CERTAIN PRETERITES. The preterite of certain verbs often acquires a slightly specialized meaning:

Estive dois anos em Cambridge. I spent/stayed two years in Cambridge.

Tive uma grande surpresa. I got/received a great surprise.

Ele quis fazê-lo mas não pôde. He tried to do it but didn't manage to/succeed.

Foi então que eu soube que não vinha. It was then that I learned/found out that he wasn't coming.

Não quiseram considerá-lo. They refused to consider it.

Conheci-o pouco depois. I got to know him/made his acquaintance soon afterwards.

Houve um acidente. An accident occurred.

115. OMISSION OF THE INDEFINITE ARTICLE. The indefinite article is omitted in Portuguese in the following cases where it is used in English:

(1) Before an unqualified noun dependent on a negative (unless there is emphasis on the *one*ness of that noun).

> **Não tenho lápis nem papel.** I haven't a pencil or paper.
> **Não tinha recebido resposta.** He hadn't received a reply.

Saiu sem dizẹr palavra. She went out without saying a
word.

Entraram sem convite. They got in without an invitation.

but **Não tenho um irmão mạs dọis.** I haven't one brother
but two.

Não vimos nem um único monumento. We didn't see
a single monument.

Saiu sem dizẹr nem uma palavra. She went out without
saying a (single) word.

(2) Before an unqualified noun indicating nationality (or regional origin), rank or occupation, used after **sẹr** (*to be*) or **parecẹr** (*to seem, appear*).

É andaluz. He's an Andalusian.

O mẹu irmão ẹra professọr. My brother was a teacher.

Aquẹle senhọr parẹce ọficial. That gentleman looks like an
officer.

When the noun is qualified the article is normally used.

É um andaluz de fama universal. He is an Andalusian of
universal fame.

É um professọr que vale muito. He is a very good teacher.

Parẹce um ọficial muito bom. He seems a very good officer.

It is not used, however, in cases like the following:

Ẹra professọr de licẹu. He was a grammar-school teacher.

Parẹce ọficial de infantaria. He looks like an infantry officer.

The article is *not* used, then, when the person referred to is
attributed to a class; it *is* used when that person is picked out of
his class as an individual.

(3) Before a noun used in apposition, unless that noun is
strongly individualized.

**Acontecẹu ao fim do século XIX, época em que a
Espanha perdia as suas últimas colónias.** It happened
at the end of the nineteenth century, a period in which
Spain was losing her last colonies.

Depois falei com um tal Basto, professor de línguas no liceu. Then I talked to a certain Basto, a language teacher at the Grammar School.

but **Fui com o Sr. Sanches, um amigo da família.** I went with Mr Sanches, a friend of the family.

(4) With **cem,** (*a*) *hundred*, **mil,** (*a*) *thousand*, **meio,** *half* (*a*), **semelhante,** *such* (*a*), and **que!** *what* (*a*)!

cem couraçados, mil aviões e meio milhão de soldados, a hundred battleships, a thousand planes and half a million men

Que bela surpresa receber semelhante notícia! What a lovely surprise to receive such (a piece of) news!

NOTE: Observe the following distinction: **meia garrafa,** *half a bottle*; **uma meia garrafa,** *a half-bottle*.

(5) The adjectives **certo,** (*a*) *certain*, **outro,** (*an*)*other*, and **tal,** *such* (*a*), are only occasionally preceded by the indefinite article; usually it is omitted.

certa carta que lhe enviou outro amigo, a certain letter that another friend sent him

Surpreende-me tal sugestão. I'm surprised at such a suggestion.

NOTE: **Um tal** also exists with the meaning *a certain*: **um tal Sr. Lopes,** *a certain Mr Lopes*; **o tal** exists with the meaning *the afore-mentioned*: **a tal Sra. Costa,** *the afore-mentioned Mrs Costa*.

116. PRONUNCIATION: UNSTRESSED OPEN **e.** Unstressed **e** is normally *neutral* [ə]. In the following circumstances, however, it is open [ɛ].

(*a*) When followed by -**cç**-, -**ct**-, -**pci**-, -**pç**-, -**pt**-, -**x**- [ks], -**gn**-:
a ejecção, *ejection*; **o adjectivo,** *adjective*; **excepcional,** *exceptional*; **a excepção,** *exception*; **exceptuar,** *to except*; **sexual,** *sexual*; **impregnar,** *to impregnate*.

(b) In the endings -er, -el and -ex:

o carácter, *character*; terrível, *terrible*; o códex, *codex*.

(c) In words beginning (h)el-+consonant and (h)er-+b or v:

Elvira, *Elvira*; o herbívoro, *herbivore*; o ervanário, *herbalist*; helvético, *Helvetic*; but a ervilha [ir'viʎɐ], *pea.*

(d) When an originally stressed e of a word acquiring certain subsequent suffixes (see § 165).

(e) In aer- and retro- at the beginning of a word:

o aeroporto, *airport*; a retrospecção, *retrospection.*

(f) In a number of isolated words:

aquecer, *to heat*; arrefecer, *to cool (off)*; ave! *hail!*; o brejeiro, *loafer, rascal, urchin*; checoslovaco, *Czechoslovakian*; o credor, *creditor*; delgado, *thin*; empestar, *to contaminate, infect*; esquecer, *to forget*; exclusive, *exclusive* (adverb); o freguês, *customer*; Guilhermina, *Wilhelmina*; inclusive, *inclusive* (adverb); a mezinha, *potion, home-made remedy*; o pessimista, *pessimist*; a pletora, *plethora*; pregar, *to preach*; o relvado, *lawn*; relvoso, *grassy, turf-like*; Resende (*proper name*); a retórica, *rhetoric*; salve! *hail!*; o segeiro, *coach-maker*; selvagem, *wild, savage*; and all their derivatives; also the compound feminine demonstratives estoutra, essoutra, aqueloutra.

NOTE: The words gerar (*to generate*), geral (*general*) and a geração (*generation*) and derivatives are by some speakers pronounced with open e. This nowadays is generally regarded as pedantic.

VOCABULARY

o Alentejo	the Alentejo (*a province in Portugal*)	defender	to defend
		descobrir	to discover
		direito	right; straight (*adv.*)
a boca	mouth		
conhecido	known	esquerdo	left

excelente	excellent	**um pouco**	a little, a bit
extraordi-	unusual, extra-	**quanto**	how much, *pl.*
nário	ordinary		how many
a importân-		**o revólver**	revolver
cia	importance	**a Rússia**	Russia
o oficial	officer, official	**seguinte**	following, next
parecer	to seem, appear	**a sorte**	luck; fate
a perna	leg	**a surpresa**	surprise

não prestar (para nada) to be of no use (whatsoever)

Study also the words listed in §§ 115 (4) and (5) and 116.

EXERCISES

I. (*a*) *Pronounce the following:* objectivo, recepção, cível, sugestivo, carácter, caracteres, aeroporto, Checoslováquia, em-
pestou, retrógrado, Transportes Aéreos Portugueses, ecoou,
optimismo, pessimismo, revólver, cinquenta, adorável, revolver, questionário, linguístico, geralmente.

(*b*) *Study and translate:* Tivemos de o defender. Estávamos contentes. Ninguém o acompanhava. Soube-o da
parte da tarde. Não via bem. Íamos com os nossos pais.
Foram lá três ou quatro vezes. Sempre que púnhamos a
mesa. Enquanto subíamos. Uma África pouco conhecida.
Parece professor. Uma tal senhora Magalhães. De importância extraordinária. Uma meia garrafa.

(*c*) *Translate:* We used to quarrel. They visited her on
Tuesday afternoons (=on Tuesdays in the afternoon). We
wrote to them on Monday. I already knew him very well.
I got to know her in Spain. She was going home. They
sent it to us. I gave it to him. We were not buying any-
thing. On seeing him. Immediately after seeing him.
Before explaining it to her. I'm not going to do it either.
Half a potato. He's going to be a bus conductor. With
extraordinary luck. Of great importance for another friend.
He went straight to the bar. I gave him the revolver.

II. (a) *Study and translate:* 1. Quem eram os italianos que falavam com o teu primo? 2. Chegou de noite e na manhã seguinte partiu muito cedo para o sul. 3. Perguntei ao guia onde ficava a Sé Nova. 4. Esta senhora é alemã, mas conhece muitas canções andaluzas e catalãs. 5. Na quarta passada estive o dia todo sem fazer nada. 6. Íamos visitar a sé, mas não o fizemos. 7. É esta a casa de pasto onde servem esse vinho tão excelente? 8. Ela estava muito alegre porque os seus avós chegavam naquele dia. 9. A nossa ideia foi muito má porque não levámos em conta quão frio estava na capital. 10. Sempre que queria ler estas poesias, o meu pai dizia-me que não prestavam para nada.

(b) *Translate:* 1. This lady and gentleman spent several years in Holland studying the language. 2. "How old is the taller boy?" "He is eight or nine years old." 3. I am very keen to read the book that my uncle bought when he was in Oporto. 4. We all had to finish the ninth lesson before five o'clock. 5. The maid was showing Mrs Martins some peaches she bought at the market yesterday afternoon. 6. He was finishing the thirteenth chapter when we reached his house. 7. He refused to go and get the apples which his mother bought yesterday. 8. The first time that I stayed in Figueira da Foz I made the acquaintance of all his family. 9. He tried to go and help the old lady but he didn't succeed. 10. He is a very good soldier and they are going to make him an officer.

III. (a) *Study and translate:* 1. O velho lojista checoslovaco tinha muitos fregueses mas já não os tem. 2. Perguntei-lhe porque não me deu os bons dias ao ver-me esta manhã perto da praça. 3. Ao descobrir a verdade apanhei um comboio que ia para o Porto. 4. Quantas libras ficaram a V. Ex.ª depois de comprar tantos livros de poesias? 5. Estava triste porque via que ninguém lhe respondia. 6. Foi muito difícil explicar esta diferença ao meu avô. 7. — Donde são essas canções tão bonitas que você cantou ontem à noite? — São todas do norte do Alentejo. 8. Porque é que tens tanto medo? Eu nunca tenho medo. 9. — Estas flores são muito formosas, não são? — São, sim; sobretudo as amarelas. 10. Ficou muito contente ao saber que os seus pais o vinham visitar.

(*b*) *Translate:* 1. They left Oporto at about nine o'clock in the morning, had lunch at Figueira, and reached Lisbon a little before six in the evening. 2. It was very cold and windy when we arrived home and the windows were all open. 3. That is the wife of the Dutchman you were with yesterday morning. 4. Is this not the same girl I saw last year when I was visiting my uncle's new factory in Rio? 5. What's worse, in this country the king and queen have nothing to do with the laws. 6. I lived at his parents' whenever I visited São Paulo. 7. On seeing his elder brother, he went and asked him when he was leaving for Russia. 8. He has broken his right arm and his left leg. 9. After reading this book his eyes became very tired. 10. They got such a surprise that they all opened their mouths in astonishment (**com assombro**).

The Compound Tenses, the Irregular Verb
HAVER *and its Uses, Idiomatic Uses of* PARECER,
FICAR, SOBRAR, FALTAR *and* FAZER FALTA, *Un-*
stressed Open o

LESSON XX

117. THE PAST PARTICIPLE (English *bought, sold, lived,* etc.).
The Portuguese past participle forms are:

I. **-ar** verbs: stem plus **-ado (comprado, dado, estado).**
II. **-er** verbs: stem plus **-ido (vendido, sido, tido).**
III. **-ir** verbs: stem plus **-ido (partido, ido, unido).**

EXCEPTIONS: **gąnho** (gąnhar), **gasto** (gastar, *to spend*), **pago** (pagar
to pay), **feito** (fazęr), **escrito** (escrevęr), **visto** (vęr), **dito** (dizęr),
pǫsto (pôr), **vindo** (vir), **abęrto** (abrir), **cobęrto** (cobrir,
to cover), **descobęrto** (descobrir, *to discover*). Observe that **vindo**
is both the gerund and past participle of **vir.** See also § 225.

118. THE COMPOUND PERFECT TENSES. In Portuguese as in
English the compound perfect tenses are formed by some part
of the verb *to have* together with the past participle of the appropriate verb. The Portuguese auxiliary usually employed is **tęr,**
although in highly literary style this may occasionally be replaced
by the verb **havęr** (§ 126). Thus *I had bought* is rendered by
tinha comprado. It will, however, be recalled that *I have*
bought and *I bought* may both be translated by **comprei.** Although **tenho comprado** exists to render *I have bought*, its
function is highly specialized (see Lesson XXI) and it should *on*
no account be used at this stage.

119. THE PERFECT INFINITIVE (English *to have bought, to have*
sold, etc.). This is formed by the infinitive **tęr** (or **havęr,** see
above § 118) together with the appropriate past participle.

É um grande êxito tê-lo feito sǫzinho.
It is a great success to have done it alone.

Depǫis de tęr jantado fui passear.
After having dined I went for a walk.

120. The Past Gerund (English *having bought, having sold*, etc.). The gerund of **ter** (or **haver**, see above § 118) with the appropriate past participle.

Tendo perdido o comboio, apanhou a camioneta.
Having missed the train, he caught the motorcoach.

Observe that after a preposition the Perfect *Infinitive* is used, as in the second example in § 119.

121. The Pluperfect Indicative (English *I had bought, I had sold*, etc.). The imperfect of **ter** (or **haver**, see above § 118) with the appropriate past participle.

Ainda não tinha chegado. He still hadn't arrived.
Tinham-no visto três vezes. They had seen him three times.
O que tinha feito você? What had you done?[1]

122. The Synthetic Pluperfect Indicative. Apart from the foregoing there exists also a *synthetic* (or *simple*) pluperfect indicative which, although seldom used in speech, is common enough in literary style. It is formed by taking the third person plural of the preterite of any verb, removing **-ram** and substituting the endings **-ra, -ras, -ra, -ramos, -reis, -ram.** Accents are required on the preceding syllable in the first and second persons plural.

compra/ram:

   comprara, compraras, comprara, compráramos, compráreis, compraram;

vende/ram:

   vendera, venderas, vendera, vendêramos, vendêreis, venderam;

parti/ram:

   partira, partiras, partira, partíramos, partíreis, partiram;

[1] In all these perfect tenses and moods the past participle used after **ter** (**haver**) is invariable. An object pronoun which would follow the verb is placed between the auxiliary and the participle.

dę/ram:

   dęra, dęras, dęra, déramos, déreis, dęram;

fǫ/ram:

   fǫra, fǫras, fǫra, fôramos, fôreis, fǫram.

NOTE: The third person plural is rarely used owing to its identity with the third person plural of the preterite.

123. IDIOMATIC USES OF THE SYNTHETIC PLUPERFECT INDICATIVE. This tense possesses a number of idiomatic uses which are common to both conversation and the written language. In general, they are normally used only with reference to the first person.

Quisęra
Quiséramos $\Big\}$ + *infinitive* $\left.\begin{array}{c}\text{I}\\\text{We}\end{array}\right\}$ should like to . . .

Tomara ęu
Tomáramos nós $\Big\}$ + *infinitive*   If only $\left\{\begin{array}{c}\text{I}\\\text{we}\end{array}\right\}$ could . . .

Quem $\left\{\begin{array}{c}\textbf{me}\\\textbf{nos}\end{array}\right\}$ dęra + *infinitive*   If only $\left\{\begin{array}{c}\text{I}\\\text{we}\end{array}\right\}$ could . . .

Pudęra!   Rather!

— Quęres acompanhar-nos?   — Pudęra!
"Like to come with us?"   "Rather!"

From the obsolete verb **prazęr**, *to please*, has survived the expression

Prouvęra a Dęus que + *subjunctive* Would to God that . . .

124. THE PAST ANTERIOR. Students of other Romance languages should note that this tense has not been used in Portuguese since the fifteenth century.[1] It is the tense employed in French, Spanish and Italian to translate the English pluperfect indicative (*I had bought, I had sold*, etc.) in subordinate adverbial clauses of time when the main clause contains a preterite.[2] It is formed by

---

[1] In other words, such forms as **tęve feito**, **houve feito**, etc., are quite obsolete.

[2] When the main clause contains an *imperfect* indicative such forms as **tinha feito**, **havia feito** or **fizęra** are naturally all available for the subordinate clause.

the preterite of **avoir (être), haber, avere (essere)** with the appropriate past participle, although nowadays, especially in conversation, Spanish and Italian resort to the simple preterite. Conversational French has, of course, no use for the Past Anterior, nor for the Past Historic. In Portuguese, however, the past anterior is replaced by the synthetic pluperfect or by the preterite. If, however, in a sentence introduced by **mal** (*scarcely*, *hardly*), the second clause is introduced by **quando,** then the normal pluperfect may also be used in the **mal**-clause. **Mal** is under such circumstances to be regarded as an *adverb* introducing the *main* clause.

Quando o $\left\{{\text{fęz} \atop \text{fizęra}}\right\}$, fǫi-se embǫra.

When he had done it, he went away.

Mal o $\left\{{\text{terminou} \atop \text{terminara}}\right\}$, chegou o pai.

or

Mal o $\left\{{\text{terminou} \atop \text{tinha terminado} \atop \text{terminara}}\right\}$, quando chegou o pai.

Scarcely had he finished it, when his father arrived.

Contrast the following:

French: **Quand il l'eut fait, il s'en alla.**
Spanish: **Cuando lo hubo hecho, se fue.**
Italian: **Quando lo ebbe fatto, se ne andò.**

French: **À peine l'eut-il achevé que son père arriva.**
Spanish: **Apenas lo hubo terminado, (cuando) llegó su
       padre.**
Italian: **Appena lo ebbe finito, suo padre arrivò.**

125. GENERAL NOTE ON THE COMPOUND PERFECT TENSES. In combination with **tęr** (or **havęr**) the past participle is invariable (*i.e.*, does not agree with the subject, nor with any direct object).

(Elas) tinham partido.   They (*fem.*) had left.
Tinha-a visto.   He had seen her.

Contrast the French (**Elles étaient parties. Il l'avait vue**).
For a qualification of this rule, however, see § 130.

126. THE IRREGULAR VERB **havęr.**   (*a*) *Conjugation*:

pres. indic.:   **hei, hás, há, havęmos** (or, more rarely, **hęmos**),
              haveis (or, more rarely, **heis**), **hão.**
impf. indic.:   **havia,** etc.
preterite: **houve, houvęste, houve, houvęmos, houvęstes,
              houvęram.**

(*b*) *Uses:*

(i) It may be employed in literary Portuguese as the auxiliary for the formation of the compound tenses.   From the student's point of view, this is its *least* important function.

(ii) In **há** (*there is, there are*), **havia** (*there was, there were*), **houve** (*there was, there were*; *there has been, there have been*), **tinha havido** (*there had been*), **houvęra** (*there had been*), these forms correspond to the third person singular of the verb.   There is no plural form.   The infinitive can also be used in this sense.

Havia duas cǫisas de que não gostávamos.   There were two things we didn't like.

Houve muita confusão naquęle dia.   There was a lot of confusion that day.

Dęve havęr seis fregueses nęsta lǫja.   There must be six customers in this shop.

(iii) To indicate more visible states of the weather than those expressed by means of **fazęr** (see § 62).   The same third person singular forms are used as in (ii).

Há nevoeiro.   It is foggy.
Havia lua (*but* **Fazia luar**).   The moon was shining.
Há sǫl (*also* **Faz sǫl**).   The sun is shining (*also* It is sunny).

NOTE: The words **Sol** and **Lua** are written with a capital initial letter except (*a*) when they mean respectively *the heat of the sun*, *sunshine*, *sunlight*, and *moonlight*, (*b*) when they are plural.

(iv) **há** (*ago*) and **havia** (*before, ago, earlier*) followed by an expression of time.

Foi para o Pôrto há três dias. He went to Oporto three days ago.

Contou-nos que fôra para o Pôrto havia três dias. He informed us that he had gone to Oporto three days before.

NOTES. 1. There is a very widespread tendency for **há** to be used where **havia** would be more correct.

2. Less commonly **faz** and **fazia** may fulfil these functions of **há** and **havia**.

(v) In the expression **há** (**havia**, etc.) **que**+infinitive (*one must*).

Há que fazer mais. We (you, he, etc.) must do more.

NOTE: Students of Spanish accustomed to frequent use of Spanish **hay que**+*infinitive* should note that this, its Portuguese equivalent, is less commonly used. The expression **é preciso**+*infinitive* is to be preferred.

(vi) In **haver de**+infinitive, *to be* (*destined, obliged*) *to*.

O que havíamos de fazer? What *were* we to do?

For further observations on the use of this construction, see § 156 (*b*).

(vii) **Há ... para**+infinitive means (*something*) *to do* or *to be done*.

Há muito para estudar. There's a lot to study (*or* to be studied).

127. IDIOMATIC USES (**parecer, ficar, sobrar, faltar, fazer falta**). The use of these verbs often presupposes a change of sentence construction, the English subject becoming the indirect object of the Portuguese verb, and the English object becoming the Portuguese subject.

Thus **parecẹr** (*to seem, appear*), by such a change of construction, translates the English *to think* (*of*).

Parẹce que não o vamos vẹr. It looks as though we're not
going to see him.

Parecia-me inútil. I thought it was useless.

Que lhe parẹcem ẹstas fọtos? What do you think of these
photos?

Que lhe parẹce? What do you think?

Similarly:

	Basic Meaning	*Translates*
ficar	to remain, be left	to have (something) (left)
sobrar	to be more than enough	to have more than enough
fạltar	to be missing, lacking	to be short of, lack
fazẹr falta	to be necessary, needed	to need, miss

Ficam dọis problẹmas. There remain two problems.

Quantos cruzeiros te ficam? How many cruzeiros have you
got left?

Sọbram senhọres cọmo ẹle. There are too many gentlemen
like him.

Sọbram muitos pães. We have many loaves left.

Ainda fạltavam os dọis irmãos. The two brothers were still
missing.

Não lhes fạltou nunca nada. They have never gone short of
anything.

Faz-me falta muito dinheiro. I need a lot of money.

Ẹla faz-me muita falta. I miss her a great deal.

NOTE: With these verbs the order *verb–subject* is usual.

128. PRONUNCIATION: UNSTRESSED OPEN **o.** Unstressed **o** is
normally pronounced [u]. In the following circumstances, however, it is open [ɔ].

(a) When followed by -ct-, -pç-, -pt-, -x- [ks]:
ǫctogonal, *octagonal*; a ǫpção, *option*; ǫptar, *to opt*; o ǫxigénio, *oxygen*.

(b) In the endings -or and -ol:
júniǫr, *junior*; o álcoǫl, *alcohol* (pl. álcoǫis).

(c) When followed by l+consonant (NOT lh): vǫltar, *to return*; o sǫldado, *soldier*.

(d) In hyphenated words of the type anglǫ-sąxão, *Anglo-Saxon*; francǫ-prussiano, *Franco-Prussian*; lusǫ-brasileiro, *Luso-Brazilian*, etc.

(e) In the diphthong oi of words ending in -oidal:
esferǫidal, *spheroidal*.

(f) In the prefixes sota- and soto-:
o sǫtavento, *leeward*; sǫtopǫr, *to place underneath*.

(g) When an originally stressed ǫ of a word acquiring certain subsequent suffixes (see § 165).

(h) In a number of isolated words:
cǫrar, *to blush*, and its derivatives; nǫrmal, *normal*, and its derivatives; o cǫveiro, *grave-digger*; a cǫvinha, *dimple*; a dǫninha, *weasel*; o mǫrdǫmo, *majordomo*; vǫcê, *you*; also dǫrąvante (for de ǫra ąvante), *from now on, henceforth*; Cǫpacabana, *Copacabana*.

VOCABULARY

apęnas	only; hardly,[1] scarcely[1]; no sooner[1]	a Áustria	Austria
		o (bilhęte) postal	postcard
assim	thus; like this, like that	Brasília	Brasilia
assim que	as soon as	cobrir	to cover
		a condição	condition

[1] **Mal** is most commonly used to render these meanings; the prime meaning of **apęnas** is *only*.

contar	to tell; to relate; to count	**morrer**	to die
o cruzeiro	cruzeiro (*Brazilian monetary unit*)	**pegar em**	to seize, get hold of, pick up
		preciso	necessary; precise
desejar	to wish, want, desire	**o problema**	problem
		quinze dias	fortnight
diante de	in front of	**receber**	to receive
a dificuldade	difficulty	**Santos**	Santos
direçtamente	straight	**a tarefa**	task
logo que	as soon as	**a vida**	life
mal	hardly; no sooner; badly		

$$\text{não} \dots \begin{cases} \text{senão} \\ \text{mais que} \end{cases} \text{only [see § 67 (9)].}$$

Study also the words listed in §§ 117, 123, 126, 127 and 128.

EXERCISES

I. (*a*) *Pronounce the following:* adoptivo, sotopostas, álcoois, oito, dezoito, coloidal, normalizou, corou, coroou, extraordinário, poesia, ajaezar, saudávamos, satisfeito, russo-chinês.

(*b*) *Study and translate:* Não a tinha terminado. Tinham-no visto. Tendo-o feito. Tê-los coberto. Não me tinha satisfeito. Antes de o haver escrito. Escrevemos-lhe uma carta. Ainda não recebeu o bilhete postal. Houve uma dificuldade. Era preciso visitá-las. Havia lua. Há três anos. Havia dezoito meses. Já o descobrira. Quem me dera ter um carro assim! Não me ficam mais que duas libras. Sobram-lhe cem cruzeiros. Estivemos quinze dias em Brasília.

(*c*) *Translate:* We have almost finished. They had already arrived. What have they done? What had John said to Michael? When we had rested. She had visited them. Have you seen him? After having done it all. Having written to her. What had she discovered? After I had opened the door. We haven't visited anyone. He had protected his family. They had broken the table. As soon as I had read it. No sooner had I read it. They lacked nothing. He had two pencils too many. What did he think of our idea?

II. (a) *Study and translate:* 1. Tinha passado toda a manhã trabalhando no jardim. 2. Ninguém tinha chegado a tempo para lhes explicar todas as dificuldades. 3. Sobram-lhe libras, mas faltam-lhe cruzeiros. 4. Logo que partira de casa, foi à estação principal onde apanhou o comboio de Santos. 5. Apenas o vira quando lhe perguntei porque ficara tanto tempo (=so long) em casa. 6. É preciso levar em conta que em Janeiro e Fevereiro está muito frio em Madrid. 7. Ao chegar a Londres fui a casa duns senhores que tinha conhecido na Áustria. 8. Gostei imenso (=I enjoyed immensely, I have enjoyed very much) dos livros que o Sr. me comprou na França. 9. Com a morte de Filipe e Isabel já não lhe ficaram mais que dois filhos. 10. Ainda não chegou o telegrama que lhes mandei de Coimbra.

(b) *Translate:* 1. We had all already finished the third chapter when it struck four o'clock. 2. Both of us have seen her and explained the problem to her. 3. There were a lot of foreigners at the market today, weren't there? 4. After he had visited his aunt and uncle, he went to pay his respects to his grandmother. 5. His mother told us he had left for the Argentine a fortnight before. 6. I should like to visit South Africa in the spring but unfortunately I haven't the time. 7. For my parents Spain has always been the loveliest and most interesting country in (=of) Europe. 8. They had still not opened the doors when we got there. 9. It has been raining and foggy during the night. 10. I had scarcely read the first poem when my father seized the book and asked me where I had bought it.

III. (a) *Study and translate:* 1. Sempre que a minha mãe tinha coberto a mesa com a toalha, costumava entrar na cozinha a ir buscar os pratos e os copos. 2. Mal chegou a Paris, mandou-me um bilhete postal. 3. Logo que recebi o telegrama, fui directamente ao hospital. 4. Assim que o vi, soube que morrera o seu pai. 5. Que vida triste ter de morar em tais condições! 6. Ao vê-lo desejei contar-lhe que ia partir logo para a América, mas não pude. 7. Logo que entrara, o soldado pegou no revólver e tentou matar o capitão e o general. 8. Noutro dia, ao ver-nos diante da sua casa, acompanhou-nos à estação do caminho de ferro. 9. Contou-nos que fazia falta ao seu carro um novo pedal da embraiagem. 10. Nunca me fizeram tanta falta como agora as visitas daqueles amigos da minha juventude.

(b) *Translate:* 1. When we had all read the book we sent it to my brother. 2. I have opened the door but nobody has tried to come in. 3. We should all like to go and visit him in (a) Santos some day. 4. He was very tired through (**por**) having been working all day in the factory. 5. It is necessary to work harder (**mais**) in order to finish the task. 6. They spent almost the whole summer travelling round (=through) Switzerland and Italy. 7. I haven't read any of his novels, but I have read his poetry. 8. Martin told us that his father had only gone to sleep at half past three through having so much work to (**que, para** *or* **a**) do. 9. She asked me whom we were going to leave the dog with. 10. When his family went to live at Figueira, he was thirteen or fourteen years old.

LESSON XXI

129. THE PERFECT (CONTINUOUS). It has been seen that the English Perfect (*I have bought*) and the English Preterite (*I bought*) are both translated by the Portuguese Preterite (**comprei**). There does exist, however, in Portuguese a Perfect tense which is formed by means of the Present Indicative of **ter** and the relevant past participle, *e.g.,* **tenho comprado.**

This tense describes (i) a *continuous* or *constantly repeated action* which happened during a period which has not entirely elapsed; (ii) *a continuous state* which existed during a period which has not entirely elapsed.

Its nearest English equivalent is the Perfect Continuous, *e.g., I have been buying.*[1]

Tenho estado em Lisbọa.
   I've been (staying) in Lisbon.

Tem procurado em tọda a parte.
   He's looked (been looking) everywhere.

Têm viajado muito.
   They've done a great deal of travelling.

Têm viajado muito longe.
   They've travelled (been travelling) a long way.

Têm viajado muito ultimamente.
   They've been doing a good bit of travelling recently.

Não vou esquecẹr as lições que tenho recebido.
   I'm not going to forget the lessons I have received (been receiving).

---

[1] *I have been buying* may be translated even more precisely by

   tenho ${\begin{cases} \text{estado} \\ \text{andado} \end{cases}}{\begin{cases} \text{a comprar} \\ \text{comprando} \end{cases}}$.

Ęsta semana tenho visto a minha mãe tọdos os dias.
This week I've seen (been seeing) my mother every day.

Ęste mês tęmo-lo visto muitas vęzes.
We've been seeing a lot of him this month.

Tenho estado doente.
I've been ill (*recently* or *repeatedly*).

Não tem passado bem.
He hasn't been (keeping) well.

Tem estado um tempo muito mau.
It's been very bad weather.

But contrast the following:

Estive em Lisbọa três vęzes.
I have stayed in Lisbon three times.

Procurou no armário.
He has looked (taken a look) in the cupboard.

Sempre viajaram muito.
They have always travelled a lot.

Vi a minha mãe ęsta tarde.
I have seen my mother this afternoon.

Vimo-lo várias vęzes ęste mês.
We have seen him several times this month (*i.e.*, *sporadically*, *not at regular intervals*).

Assim o vi sempre.
I've always seen it this way.

Não o terminaste?
Haven't you finished it?

Já a visitou.
He's already visited her.

Ainda não chegaram.
They still haven't arrived.

Comprastę um chapéu ultimamente?
Have you bought a hat recently?

NOTES. 1. The expressions **sempre** and **várias vęzes** are regarded as tautologous with the Portuguese Perfect and are preferably used with the Preterite.

2. The Perfect Infinitive (§ 119), the Past Gerund (§ 120) and the Perfect Subjunctive (§ 180) are not of necessity limited to this *continuous* usage although naturally they may be used for this as well.

3. There exists also a rare tense formed with the Present Indicative of **havęr** and the appropriate past participle (*e.g.*, **hei comprado**). This is archaic, highly literary and must be avoided by the student. Its meaning is equivalent to the English Perfect (*I have bought*) and the Spanish Perfect (*he comprado*).

130. FURTHER USE OF **tęr** WITH PAST PARTICIPLE. A special use of **tęr** with the past participle, which bears absolutely no comparison to all the foregoing perfect tenses and moods, is that in which there is emphasis on the state arrived at rather than on the action. The past participle is then an adjective qualifying the direct object and agrees with it in number and gender.

Tens pensada a tua respọsta?

Have you thought out your reply? (*i.e.*, Have you got your reply ready thought out?)

Já lhe tínhamos preparada uma ceia de despedida.

We had already got a farewell dinner prepared for him.

Tinha escrita a carta *or* **Tinha a carta escrita.**

He had completed the writing of the letter (*i.e.*, He had got the letter written).

NOTE: In highly literary style the verb **deixar** may replace **tęr** in this construction.

131. OTHER WAYS OF TRANSLATING THE ENGLISH COMPOUND TENSES. (*a*) An English perfect tense indicating action begun in the past and *continuing in the present* is rendered by the Portuguese present.

Está aqui dęsde as cinco họras.

He has been here since five o'clock.

Dęsde quando estás aqui? *or* **Há quanto‾tempo estás aqui?**
How long have you been here?

$\left.\begin{array}{l}\textbf{Há}\\ \textbf{(Faz)}\end{array}\right\}$ **duas hǫras que estou aqui.**
I've been here for two hours.

Estou aqui há uma semana.
I've been here for a week.

Mǫro aqui $\left\{\begin{array}{l}\textbf{dęsde muito.}\\ \textbf{dęsde há muito.}\\ \textbf{de há muito.}\end{array}\right.$
I've been living here for a long time.

IMPORTANT NOTE: It is considered incorrect to use the Perfect Continuous in sentences of this type (*i.e.*, containing **dęsde, há** or **faz** in expressions of time).

(*b*) In corresponding cases in the more distant past a Portuguese imperfect translates an English pluperfect.

Estava ali dęsde as cinco hǫras.
He had been there since five o'clock.

Dęsde quando estavas ali? *or* **Havia quanto tempo estavas ali?**
How long had you been there?

$\left.\begin{array}{l}\textbf{Havia}\\ \textbf{(Fazia)}\end{array}\right\}$ **duas hǫras que estava ali.**
I'd been there for two hours.

Estava ali havia uma semana.
I'd been there for a week.

Morava ali $\left\{\begin{array}{l}\textbf{dęsde muito.}\\ \textbf{dęsde havia muito.}\\ \textbf{de havia muito.}\end{array}\right.$
I'd been living there for a long time.

but

Morei ali muito tempo.
  I lived there for a long time (*before realizing the truth, before selling up, leaving*, etc.).

Estive ali duas horas.
  I was there two hours (*and then left*).

132. Acabar de. The English *I* (*you*, etc.) *have just* with a past participle is translated by the present (occasionally preterite) tense of **acabar de** with an infinitive. Similarly, *I* (*you*, etc.) *had just -ed* is rendered by the imperfect of **acabar de** with the infinitive (occasionally by the synthetic pluperfect).

Acabo (Acabei) de o ver. I have just seen him.
Acabávamos (Acabáramos) de partir. We had just departed.

133. Mas, mas sim AND senão. *But*, introducing a positive statement set up in contradiction of a previous negative one, is translated by **mas**. Before a clause it is rendered by **mas sim.**

Não é alemã mas polaca. She is not German but Polish.
Não trabalha mas sim descansa. He is not working but resting.

Mas (or **mas sim** for emphasis) is also used in cases like the following:

Não vi a sua irmã esta manhã, mas vou vê-la da parte da tarde. I haven't seen your sister this morning, but I'm going to see her this afternoon.

Esta não é a sua irmã mas sim a sua prima. This isn't your sister but your cousin.

Senão is used as an *exceptive* particle after a negative:

Não fiz (outra coisa) senão dormir. ⎫ I did nothing (else)
Não fiz mais que dormir. ⎭ but sleep.

Não pensa senão em si próprio. He thinks of nothing but/only of himself.

Não me ficou senão um escudo.   I had only one escudo left.

Não me ficou outra cọisa senão partir.   There was nothing
for it but to leave.

Não tenho comido nenhuma outra cọisa senão pão e água.
I haven't been eating anything but bread and water.

Não é outra cọisa senão . . .   It's nothing but . . .

não $\left\{ \begin{array}{l} \text{só} \\ \text{sòmente} \end{array} \right\}$ . . . $\left\{ \begin{array}{l} \text{senão (também)} \\ \text{mạs também} \\ \text{mạs ainda} \\ \text{mạs até} \end{array} \right\}$ $\begin{array}{l} \text{not only . . . but} \\ \text{(also, as well)} \end{array}$

tanto . . . cọmo . . .   not only . . . but (also, as well)/both . . . and

**Tanto os estudantes cọmo os professọres estão a estudar
ẹste tẹxto.**   Not only the students but also the teachers are
studying this text.

Note also: **(vai) senão quando,** suddenly, all of a sudden, when
suddenly.

134. Two Irregular Verbs (irregular forms are shown in bold
type).

    sabẹr, *to know (for a fact)*

pres. ind.: **sei,** sabes, sabe, sabẹmos, sabeis, sabem

impf. ind.: sabia, etc.

preterite: **soube, soubẹste, soube, soubẹmos, soubẹstes,
        soubẹram**

past part.: sabido

    cabẹr, *to fit, be capable of being contained*

pres. ind.: **caibo,** cabes, cabe, cabẹmos, cabeis, cabem

impf. ind.: cabia, etc.

preterite: **coube, coubẹste, coube, coubẹmos, coubẹstes,
        coubẹram**

past part.: cabido

135. USES OF **saber** AND **caber.**

(a) **saber**

(1) **saber,** to know (for a fact) must be carefully distinguished from **conhecer,** to know (be acquainted with).

Sabe o caminho. He knows the way (in that he has been told where it lies or has seen it on a map).

Conhece o caminho. He knows the way (in that he has been along it and is acquainted with its every twist and turn).

(2) **saber** is used to translate can, to be able when this is equivalent to to know how to.

Não sei nadar. I can't swim (I don't know how to).

Não posso nadar. I can't swim (somebody or something prevents me).

(3) **saber** in the preterite usually translates learnt, found out (about).

Foi então que soube a notícia. It was then that I got to know, learnt, the news.

(4) **saber a** translates to taste of, taste like, smack of.

Este vinho sabe a tinta vermelha. This wine tastes like red ink.

Isto sabe a queimado. This tastes burnt.

NOTE: Similarly used is the verb **cheirar,** to smell.

    Cheira a enxofre. It smells of sulphur.

    Cheira a chamuscado (or **a chamusco**). It smells scorched.

(b) **caber**

(1) **caber (em),** to fit (in), go (in).

Este chapéu não cabe na caixa. This hat won't go in the box.

Caibo eu? Is there room for me?

(2) **caber por,** to be capable of passing through.

Esta mesa não cabe por aquela porta. This table won't go through that door.

(3) **cabẹr,** *to be fitting, proper.*

Não cabe aqui fazẹr comentários. This is not the time or place to pass comment.

(4) **cabẹr a,** *to befit, behove; to befall.*

Cabe a ⎫
É lá com ⎭ **você falar com ẹle.** It's up to you to speak to him.

Cabe-me dizẹr que ... It behoves me to say that ...

Coube-lhe a metade da herança. Half of the inheritance fell to him.

136. PRONUNCIATION: UNSTRESSED CLOSED e. Unstressed **e** is pronounced [e] in the following circumstances:

(*a*) In the diphthong **eu:**

a **Ẹurọpa,** *Europe;* BUT contrast **o chapèuzinho,** *little hat;* **o céu,** *sky.*

(*b*) In nouns ending in **-en:**

o **hífẹn,** *hyphen;* BUT plural **os hífenes** [ˈifənəʃ].

(*c*) Before **l**+consonant (NOT **lh**):

esbẹltar, *to make slender;* **fẹlpudo,** *shaggy;* BUT note: **o rẹlvado, rẹlvoso** (§ 116), **o hotẹlzinho** (§ 165).

(*d*) When nasalized in other than the final position:

vendẹmos, *we sell, we sold, we have sold;* **empregar,** *to use, employ;* BUT: **o họmem** [ˈɔmɐj], *man.*

(*e*) When in hiatus with another unstressed vowel:

ẹuropẹizar, *to europeanize.*

(*f*) When an originally stressed **ẹ** of a word acquiring certain subsequent suffixes (see § 165).

(*g*) In the endings **-eidade** and **-iedade:**

a **espontanẹidade,** *spontaneity;* a **solidariẹdade,** *solidarity.*

(*h*) In the compound words **ẹstoutro, ẹssoutro, aquẹloutro.**

211

VOCABULARY

acabar	to end, finish	a fruta	fruit
acabar de	to have just	o legume	vegetable
aceitar	to accept	a maneira	manner, way
acordar	to wake up	nessa altura	at that time
a álgebra	algebra	passar bem	to keep well
a amiga	friend (f.)	pelo menos	at least
bailar	to dance	o polícia	policeman
as batatas fritas	chips	a poltrona	easy chair, armchair
o bife	steak	o projecto	plan, project, scheme
o (carro) eléctrico	tram(car)	queimar	to burn (transitive)
cheirar (a)	to smell (of)	restar	to remain
concordar	to agree	seguir	to follow, to carry on
confessar	to confess		
a confiança	confidence, trust	a solução	solution
o convite	invitation	sonhar (com)	to dream (of)
cozinhar	to cook	suceder	to happen
dançar	to dance	o táxi	taxi
despertar	to wake up	tomar	to take (= receive, get)
disputar	to dispute, argue	ultima- mente	recently
então	then (= at that time)	a verdade	truth
esperar esperar por }	to wait for	a vila	township, small town

por toda a parte	everywhere
tenho dito!	so there! (also a form for ending a speech)
e lá se arranjam!	so there! that's that!

Study also the words listed in § 131–6 and revise the vocabulary of Lessons XVI–XX.

EXERCISES

I. (a) *Pronounce the following:* europeias, variedades, ajaeza-
ram, poesia, entrever, felpudo, líquen, hífenes, eufonia,
hotèizinhos, aqueloutros rapazes, relvosas, jacto, compacto,
sub-reptício, doravante, pletora, sadio, vadiice.

(b) *Study and translate:* Tenho coberto. Tendes feito. Têm-me dito. Tenho andado a procurar-te. Assim o acharam. Tem escritos os bilhetes postais. Estavam ali havia quinze dias. Desde quando é que você estuda a língua portuguesa? Quanto tempo moraste em Lisboa? Acabei de fazê-lo. Não me fica senão uma moeda de cinco tostões. Não sabia o caminho. Cabe-me dizer-lhe a verdade. Os ovos cheiravam mal.

(c) *Study and translate:* Steak and chips. I've seen him three times this week. He hasn't been keeping well. We saw her at the market recently. So there! We've been living here for three years. The teacher's got the lesson prepared. He never does anything but work. We had already been there three weeks. Good morning, Peter! Where've you been recently? I haven't seen you for a long time. Not only John but Michael as well.

II. (a) *Study and translate:* 1. A verdade é que não o temos visitado. 2. Não tínhamos mais confiança nesse senhor. 3. Temo-lo despertado às sete horas. 4. Morávamos nessa vila desde havia vinte e sete anos. 5. Qual tem sido a sua maneira de o fazer? 6. Este polícia segue-me de há muito. 7. Têm-me dito que isto não sucede muito. 8. Aquele homem tem-me explicado o seu projecto. 9. Faz três dias que leva os móveis para casa dos seus tios. 10. A sua avó mora desde há muito nesse hotel e tomou sempre no seu quarto as refeições todas.

(b) *Translate:* 1. We have all accepted his invitation. 2. They have been dreaming of doing this for many years. 3. The young Italian soldier told them that he had been studying algebra but could not understand it. 4. They have been following her for a quarter of an hour. 5. That conductor had been working on the buses for five years. 6. Peter's told me that you've been waiting in this bar for an hour. 7. I haven't seen him this week because he's been ill. 8. What's worse, she thinks of nothing but the holidays. 9. He told his mother that she couldn't cook because the potatoes smelled burnt. 10. The conductor told them that there wasn't room for them on the tram.

III. (a) *Study and translate:* 1. Esta semana tenho visitado não só os meus avós mas ainda todos os meus tios. 2. Foi só então que me coube confessar-lhes que não sabia o caminho. 3. O rapaz contou ao seu pai que todos estes ovos cheiram a choco. 4. Este lojista não vende legumes mas fruta. 5. Eu disse-lhe que moráramos ali trinta anos antes de ir morar para Vila Nova de Gaia. 6. O meu irmão acordava todas as manhãs às sete menos um quarto. 7. Estava a entrar no táxi vai senão quando avistei o teu amigo alemão. 8. Não me tem restado outra solução senão visitá-las todos os anos. 9. Não cabia ali disputar com V. Exª. mas sim dizer-lhe que não tinha tempo para coisas assim. 10. Foi apenas nessa altura que me confessou que tinham escrita a carta.

(b) *Translate:* 1. How long had they been living there when you went to visit them? 2. He doesn't know how to dance but at least he can sing. 3. Not only have I been ill recently but my wife hasn't been keeping well either. 4. We had just left when suddenly it began to rain. 5. She told me that the armchair wouldn't go through the door. 6. We've been waiting for them for three and a quarter hours. 7. It's up to him to confess that he's been looking everywhere. 8. It was only then that I told him something he's always wanted to know. 9. They both studied it [for] three years at Coimbra University. 10. What's worse, I can neither dance nor sing, but at least I have the courage to (de) confess it.

Weak Reflexive Object Pronouns and their Uses,
Translation of ELSE, *Four Irregular Verbs:*
TRAZER, MEDIR, PEDIR *and* OUVIR, *Plural of*
Nouns in -N *and* -ER, *Unstressed Closed* o

LESSON XXII

137. WEAK REFLEXIVE OBJECT PRONOUNS (English *myself, your-self*, etc.). The forms are the same for the direct and indirect object.

(1) (eu) **me** (to) myself **(nós)** **nos** (to) ourselves

(2) $\left\{\begin{array}{l}\textbf{(tu)} \quad \textbf{te}\\ \textbf{você,}\\ \text{etc.)} \quad \textbf{se}\end{array}\right\}$ (to) yourself $\left.\begin{array}{l}\textbf{(vós)} \quad \textbf{vos}\\ \textbf{(vocês,}\\ \text{etc.)} \\ \qquad\quad \textbf{se}\end{array}\right\}$ (to) yourselves

(3) $\left\{\begin{array}{l}\textbf{(ele)} \quad \textbf{se} \quad \text{(to) himself}\\ \\ \textbf{(ela)} \quad \textbf{se} \quad \text{(to) herself}\end{array}\right.$ $\left.\begin{array}{l}\textbf{(eles)} \quad \textbf{se}\\ \\ \textbf{(elas)} \quad \textbf{se}\end{array}\right\}$ (to) themselves

These are positioned in relation to the verb in the same way as other weak object pronouns, and are likewise atonic. Whether used as direct or indirect objects they precede other weak pronouns. The combination of **se** with the weak direct object pronouns **o, a, os, as** is never found.

> **Viu-se no espelho.** He saw himself in the mirror.
>
> **Estes senhores já se me apresentaram.** These gentlemen have already introduced themselves to me.

but **Enviaram-no a si próprios.** They posted it to themselves (see § 146).

138. VERBS USED REFLEXIVELY (English *I cut myself, He sees himself*, etc.). (*a*) A reflexive verb is one in which the direct or indirect object refers back to the subject of the verb.

Pedro cortou-se. Peter (has) cut himself.

O autor reserva-se o direito de fazê-lo. The author reserves (to himself) the right of doing it.

Lavámo-nos. We (have) washed ourselves.

NOTE: Students of Spanish accustomed to the Spanish types of construction like: **Nos lavamos las manos; Se puso el sombrero,** etc., should note that it is rare for the indirect "possessive" *reflexive* object pronoun to be used in Portuguese in such circumstances.

Lavámos as mãos.	We (have) washed our hands.
Pôs o chapéu.	He (has) put on his hat.

Lavámo-nos as mãos would mean that the action was reciprocal (*We (have) washed one another's hands*).

Quebrei o braço direito.	I broke (have broken) my right arm.
Quebrei-lhe o braço direito.	I broke (have broken) his right arm.

(*b*) Certain transitive verbs in Portuguese have a corresponding reflexive form where two different verbs are used in English.

deitar	to throw; to pour; to dump
deitar-se	to lie down; to go to bed (*lit.*, to dump oneself down)
levantar	to raise
levantar-se	to get up; to rise (*lit.*, to raise oneself)
pôr	to put
pôr-se	to set (*of the sun*)

Similarly:

chamar	to call
chamar-se	to be called (*lit.*, to call oneself)

Ele deita-se antes de mim, e eu levanto-me depois dele.
He goes to bed before I do, and I get up after he does.
O Sol pôs-se às oito horas.   The sun set at eight o'clock.
Chamo-me Ilídio Ferreira.   My name is Ilídio Ferreira.

NOTE: A reflexive infinitive may take other pronouns than the **se** with which it is listed in vocabularies. Thus, *before sitting down* will be translated as **antes de me sentar, antes de se sentar,** etc., according to the person it refers to.

139. REFLEXIVE PRONOUNS USED WITH RECIPROCAL SENSE (English *we see each other*). (*a*) The Portuguese reflexive pronoun refers back to the subject of the verb. It may, however, indicate interaction between different parts of a plural subject. This is the reciprocal sense of the reflexive pronoun.

> **Vimo-nos ontem.**   We saw each other yesterday.
> **Odeiam-se.**   They hate one another.

(*b*) In the above examples the Portuguese is unlikely to give rise to confusion with the purely reflexive use of the pronouns (*We saw ourselves yesterday, They hate themselves*). Admittedly there is a special use of **ver-se** which renders *to find oneself*, e.g., **Vimo-nos em apuros** (*We found ourselves in difficulties*), but that is another matter. However, a case like **Felicitam-se** might equally well be interpreted as *They congratulate themselves* or *They congratulate one another*. The addition of **um ao outro** (fem. **uma à outra**) or, in the case of several persons, **uns aos outros** (**umas às outras**) will make it clear that the latter sense is desired. The adverb **mutuamente** (*lit.*, *mutually*) may also fulfil the function of these expressions.

Todos se felicitaram uns aos outros.   They all congratulated
  each other.
Feriram-se um ao outro.   They wounded each other.
Elogiaram-se mutuamente.   They praised one another.

NOTES. 1. Whatever the term of reciprocity added after the verb, the weak reflexive pronoun is still required.

2. There is also a means of emphasizing that it is the purely reflexive (and *not* the reciprocal) sense that is required, but this will be explained later.

140. THE "REFLEXIVE PASSIVE". The reflexive in Portuguese frequently gives passive sense to an active verb, thus translating the English passive or the English *one* (*people, you, we*, etc., cf. French *on*, German *man*) with the corresponding active verb. For further comments on this theme see §§ 223-4.

O meu filho chama-se Pedro.   My son is called Peter.

Estes fatos vendem-se muito baratos.   These suits are being sold very cheap.

Aqui fala-se inglês.   English (is) spoken here.

Não se ouvia nada.   There was nothing to be heard.

Necessita-se rapaz.   Boy needed (*shop-sign*).

Diz-se que não vai vir.   It is said he is not coming.

Pode-se fazer isso depois?   Can one do that afterwards?

Não se pode entrar.   One (*or* you) can't go in.

Deve-se tentar chegar cedo.   One (*or* you) must try to arrive early.

141. TRANSLATION OF *else* (see also § 133).

(*a*) **noutra parte** ⎫
       alhures (*rare*) ⎬   somewhere else, else-where

em qualquer outra parte ⎫
noutra parte qualquer ⎬   anywhere else

em nenhuma outra parte   nowhere else

por ⎫ **todas as (de)mais partes**   everywhere else
em ⎭

For *motion towards*, **para** or **a** replace **em, n-**;
For *motion from*, **de, d-** replace **em, n-**.

dalhures ⎫ (*rare*)   from somewhere else
de alhures ⎭

(*b*) **outra coisa** ⎫
       mais alguma coisa ⎬   something else

qualquer outra coisa ⎫
outra coisa qualquer ⎬   anything else

mais nada ⎫
nada mais ⎭   nothing else

tudo o mais ⎫
todo o resto ⎭   everything else

(c) outra pessǫa
   mais ạlguém   somebody else
   ạlguém mais

   quạlquęr outra pessǫa
   outra pessǫa quạlquęr   anybody else

   mais ninguém
   ninguém mais   nobody else

  (*but* **nenhum outro,** not one other, no other, no one else)
    tǫdos os (de)mais   everybody else

(d) **que mais?**   what else?

   aliás
   doutro mǫdo ...   or else ..., otherwise ...

   Que outra cǫisa é senão ...?   What else is it but ...?

NOTE: It will be observed from (b) and (c) above that **mais** may precede or follow the word it modifies. Further examples will clarify this:

João tem três anos (de *or* **a) mais do que Pędro.**
João tem mais três anos do que Pędro.   } John is three
João é (de) três anos mais vęlho do que Pędro.   years older
João é mais vęlho três anos do que Pędro.   than Peter.

142. FOUR IRREGULAR VERBS: **trazęr, medir, -pedir** and **ouvir**; the irregular forms are in bold type.

    trazęr, *to bring*; *to wear*

pres. indic.:   **trago,** trazes, **traz,** trazęmos, trazeis, trazem
impf. ind.:   trazia, etc.
preterite: **trouxe, trouxęste, trouxe, trouxęmos, trouxęstes,**
           trouxęram (x = [s])
gerund: trazendo
past part.:   trazido

    medir, *to measure* (cf. servir)

pres. ind.:   **męço,** mędes, męde, medimos, medis, mędem
impf. ind.:   media, etc.

preterite: medi, etc.
gerund: medindo
past part.: medido

Like medir are conjugated pedir (*to ask for*), expedir (*to send, despatch*), despedir (*to dismiss*) and impedir (*to prevent*).

ouvir, *to hear*

pres. ind.: ouço *or* oiço, ouves, ouve, ouvimos, ouvis, ouvem
impf. ind.: ouvia, etc.
preterite: ouvi, etc.
gerund: ouvindo
past part.: ouvido

143. PLURAL OF NOUNS (cont.). (*a*) Nouns ending in **n** (usually words of a scientific or technical nature and somewhat rare); the plural is made by adding **-es**:

o íman [ˈimɐn], *magnet*   os ímanes [ˈimɐnəʃ], *magnets* [1]
o hífẹn [ˈifen], *hyphen*   os hífenes [ˈifǝnǝʃ], *hyphens*
o cânọn [ˈkɐnon], *canon* (*rule*)   os cânones [ˈkɐnunǝʃ], *canons*

Note the changes in vowel quality of the endings **-ẹn** and **-ọn** when made plural. This is typical of all words with these endings.

(*b*) Nouns ending in unstressed **-ẹr**: add **-es** to form the plural:

o cadávẹr, *corpse*   os cadáveres [-ǝrǝʃ], *corpses*
o revólvẹr, *revolver*   os revólveres [-ǝrǝʃ], *revolvers*

Note the change in vowel quality of the ending **-ẹr** when made plural. This is typical of all words ending in unstressed **-ẹr**. (Contrast **a mulhẹr, as mulhẹres.**)

One word of this group has an irregular plural:

o carácter [kɐˈra(k)tɛr], *character*; os caractẹres [kɐrɐˈterǝʃ], *characters*. Note the **a** of the derived words: **característico** (*characteristic*), **a característica** (*characteristic*), **caracterizar** (*to characterize*), and **a caracterização** (*characterization*).

---

[1] In popular speech, this word is pronounced [iˈmẽ]; it is also often written **imã** (with plural **imãs**). These forms are incorrect.

144. PRONUNCIATION: UNSTRESSED CLOSED **o**. Unstressed **o** is pronounced [o] in the following circumstances:

(a) In the diphthongs **ou** and **oi**:

o Qutǫno, *autumn*; Qutubro, *October*; bǫiar, *to float*; apǫiar, *to support*; *but* note **-ǫidal**, *e.g.*, **esferǫidal**, *spheroidal.*

(b) When nasalized:

ponderǫso, *ponderous*; **o pombal,** *dovecote.*

(c) When initial (see § 95).

(d) When an originally stressed **ǫ** of a word acquiring certain subsequent suffixes (see § 165).

(e) In the prefix **sobre-** (this is resisted by some speakers):

sǫbretudo, *especially*; **sǫbrecarregar,** *to overload.*

(f) In the concessive adverb **tǫdavia,** *still, yet, nevertheless, even so.*

(g) In nouns ending in **-on**:

o cânǫn, *canon, rule*; BUT plural **os cânones** [ˈkɐnunəʃ].

VOCABULARY

antes que		**a derrǫta**	defeat
(*conj.*)	before	**desiludido**	disappointed
apanhar	to pick up	**despedir-se**	to take one's
aproximar-		**(de)**	leave (of), say
se de	to approach		goodbye (to)
a árvore	tree	**divertir**	to amuse
a bagagem	luggage	**divertir-se**	to amuse one-
a banheira	bath, bath-tub		self, enjoy
cair	to fall		oneself
o capital	capital (*money*)	**o dǫno**	owner
a chegada	arrival	**enganar**	to deceive
o cientista	scientist	**a falta**	lack
depǫis que		**ficar**	to stay, remain;
(*conj.*)	after		to become

frẹsco	cool, cold; fresh	percebẹr	to understand; to perceive
o guarda-chuva	umbrella	perdẹr	to lose
ir(-se)		a polícia	police
embọra	to go away	reconhecẹr	to recognize, acknowledge
lavar	to wash		
a luva	glove	a respọsta	answer, reply
ọlhar ọlhar pạra }	to look at	a reunião	meeting
		o salão	sitting-room
o pé	foot	seguro	sure, certain
a pensão	boarding house	sentar-se	to sit down
pensar	to think; to intend to	sentir-se	to feel (of oneself)
pensar de	to think of (opinion)	o silêncio	silence
		tarde (adv.)	late
pensar em	to think of (meditation)	vestir	to dress
		vestir-se	to get dressed

pintar de }
vestir de } branco, vẹrde, etc.
to paint }
to dress in } white, green, etc.

Study also the words listed in §§ 137, 138 (b), 141–4.

EXERCISES

I. (a) *Pronounce the following:* abdómen, cânones, caracteres, caracterizou, os esfíncteres, ímanes, apoiei, coloidais, trouxeste, voltáreis, ponderosas, pombalino, sobrecarregado, boiar, bóio, todavia, observação, obsequeia, trânsito, cadáver, peço, guarda-chuva.

(b) *Study and translate:* Outra coisa qualquer. Tudo o mais. Doutro modo. Em todas as demais partes. Vestiram-se. Não quis deitar-se. Levantámo-nos. Olharam-se. Sentou-se. Tem-se perdido. Assim se faz. Não se deve responder assim. Expedimo-lo. Temo-la expedida. Não o oiço bem. Lavei as mãos. Lavou-lhes os pés. Não se via nada. O que é que se diz do novo projecto? Iam aproximando-se da vila. Ensina-se grego. Trouxe-me um relógio.

(c) *Translate:* Somewhere else. Everybody else. They have measured. We've got the luggage despatched. I get dressed. We warm ourselves. I have broken his arm. She broke her leg. They have taken their leave. He is going to bring me a pear. She was approaching the building. The sun set at nine o'clock. They all congratulated each other. German spoken here. One couldn't recognize him. You used to get a good meal here (= One used to eat well here). One doesn't understand anything else of what they say. Still, what else could he do before arriving?

II. (a) *Study and translate:* 1. Parece que durante aquela viagem se descobriram coisas muito interessantes para os cientistas. 2. Ao acordar pela manhã, sentiu-se muito mais contente e fez projectos para os dias que pensava ficar ali. 3. Entrámos na sala de jantar e sentámo-nos sem dizer nada. 4. Nunca se sabe o que pensa a gente quando não se lhes pergunta. 5. Acordou às sete mas apenas se levantou um quarto de hora mais tarde. 6. Caiu ao voltar da universidade e partiu-se-lhe o relógio que lhe haviam comprado os seus avós. 7. Dizem que na China a gente se veste de branco quando morre alguém. 8. Foi-se embora sem dizer nada à polícia nem ao dono da pensão. 9. A gente procurava-o por toda a parte mas não o achava. 10. A tua mãe disse que devias lavar-te antes de mim.

(b) *Translate:* 1. He slept [for] an hour and, on waking, asked for a glass of cold water. 2. At these hours of the evening, when the tourists have all gone away, the gardens are left (= remain) in silence. 3. Everybody else thinks that he got up at six in the morning and went to bed at eleven o'clock at night. 4. They all got dressed and went to lunch at a friend's. 5. Never have there been so many aeroplanes nor so many soldiers as since the visit of President Juscelino Kubitschek. 6. "One can think one thing and say something else." "One can, yes, but one mustn't." 7. Catalans who think this about their boorish neighbours are deceiving themselves. 8. We have both been more than a year without seeing each other. 9. Yet we write to one another every week. 10. We have got the bathroom measured and we think the new bath isn't going to fit!

III. (a) *Study and translate:* 1. Ao chegar, viu que todas o esperavam lá em baixo no salão. 2. Partiu uma perna ao cair duma árvore. 3. Ao outro dia, ao partir da reunião, fui cear com uma amiga norte-americana. 4. Não disseram nada quando se encontraram depois do primeiro almoço. 5. Tem-se dito amiúde que nós Ingleses somos os grandes turistas do mundo, mas agora me parece que o são os Norte-americanos. 6. Foi nessa altura que se soube o que fizera o ex-ministro ao ver segura a sua derrota. 7. Aproximava-me da capital senão quando me senti sem forças para (strength to) seguir com o projecto. 8. O Miguel é mais novo cinco anos do que o seu irmão, não é? 9. A verdade é que nem se sabe como se vai fazer. 10. Depois da minha chegada não se ouviu mais nada.

(b) *Translate:* 1. He got dressed somewhat slowly, thinking of the reply he had to give to the prime (=first) minister. 2. Why have you not brought me the wine I asked you for yesterday? 3. He usually gets up at six thirty, but he also goes to bed very early at night. 4. We amused ourselves making paper aeroplanes and I think the children enjoyed themselves as well. 5. He put on his hat and coat, picked up his gloves and umbrella and went away. 6. We both looked at one another in silence [for] a few moments but didn't recognize one another. 7. It was not known how they had managed to (=been able to) finish it so early. 8. It is not known who did it first but it is thought that it was some minister disappointed by the lack of capital. 9. When anybody else arrived he would always get up and go away. 10. One mustn't think things like that, because they aren't true.

LESSON XXIII

145. PREPOSITIONS.

(a) Simple Prepositions

a	to; at (*of time*)	**para**	for, by (*of time*),
ante	before		in order to,
após	after		towards
até	until, as far as,	**por**	by, through
	(up) to	**segundo**	according to
com	with	**sem**	without
contra	against	**sob**	below, under,
de	of, from, about		beneath
desde	since, from	**sobre**	on, upon, about
em	in, on, at		
entre	between,		
	among(st)		

(b) Compound Prepositions

à frente de	at the front of	**dentro de**	inside, within
além de	besides; beyond	**depois de**	after
antes de	before	**detrás de**	(from) behind
ao ⎫ redor	around, about	**diante de**	in front of,
em ⎭ de			before
atrás de	behind		
através de	through, across	**em cima de**	on top of
à ⎫		**em frente**	facing, opposite;
em ⎬ volta around, about		**de**	in front of
por ⎭ de		**fora de**	outside, out of
		longe de	far from
debaixo de	under, beneath	**perto de**	near, close to
defronte de	facing, opposite	**por cima de**	over, above

NOTES. 1. For the relationship between the adverb and the preposition in these latter cases, note the following examples:

225

Quem está diante? Who is in front?

Estou diante desta senhora. I'm in front of this lady.

Morava muito longe. He lived a very long way away.

Morava muito longe daqui. He lived a very long way from here.

2. Many of the same adverbs (and others) may be *preceded* by **de** and then serve as adjectives.

   a parte de fora, the outside part
   a Espanha de hoje, present-day Spain
   os (lá) de dentro, those inside (there)

3. Certain prepositions join with **que** to form a compound conjunction: **desde que,** *since*; **até que,** *until*; **para que,** *in order that*; **sem que,** *without*; observe also: **antes que,** *before*; **depois que,** *after*.

Não o vi desde que chegou. I haven't seen him since he arrived.

The word **segundo** is also used as a conjunction in the sense of *as, according to what*:

segundo diz o nosso professor, according to what our teacher says

Mas, segundo creio, é impossível. But it's impossible, in my opinion.

(c) Possible Confusions

(1) *Before:* time (**antes de**), place (**diante de, ante**).

Diante de indicates more physical position than **ante** which introduces an element of the English *in the presence of, when confronted by.* **Perante** is a very common alternative to this latter.

Terminou-o antes de chegar. He finished it before getting there.

Um pajem ia diante do rei. A page boy walked before the king.

Compareceu ante o juiz. He appeared before the judge.

(2) *At:* time (**a**), place (**a** for movement, **em** for position), metaphorical sense (**ante,** cf. (1) above).

Fizeram-no todos ao mesmo tempo. They all did it at the same time.

A que hǫras chegou à reunião?   What time did he arrive at
the meeting ?

Vamos comęr ao nǫvo restaurante gręgo.   Let's go and eat
at the new Greek restaurant.

Estive na exposição.   I was at the exhibition.

Ficou muito triste ante ęsta idęia.   He was very sad at this
idea.

(3) *About:* time (**por, á vǫlta de** and **por vǫlta de;** in Brazil
lá para), place (**ao redǫr de, em redǫr de** and **à rǫda de**),
concerning (**de, sǫbre,** also **acęrca de,** also **em** may be found
after **falar**).   In the last sense **sǫbre** and **acęrca de** indicate a
fuller, more authoritative treatment than **de**.

Chegou pelas (à vǫlta das) duas hǫras.   He arrived about two
o'clock.

Havia uma taipa ao redǫr do jardim.   There was a wall about
the garden.

Falou da (na) sua viagem.   He talked about his trip.

Falou sǫbre a (acęrca da) sua viagem.   He talked about
(gave a talk on) his trip.

O que disse da sua irmã?   What did he say about his sister ?

Li um livro sǫbre a Alemanha.   I read a book about Germany.

NOTE: *About* (and *around*) meaning *approximately* is usually translated either by the plural indefinite article: **umas cem libras** (*about
a hundred pounds*), or by **cęrca de.**

(4) *After:* time (**depǫis de, após**), succession (**após**).

Depǫis de o visitar, fui pạra casa.   After visiting him I went
home.

Após a guęrra, elegęram outro govęrno.   After the war they
elected another government.

um após outro, [1] one after another

dia após dia, day after day

------

[1] Also **um atrás do outro.**

(5) *From:* **desde** is rather more emphatic than **de**; it is usually balanced by **até** (*to*). **Até** is sometimes followed by **a**, particularly before the *feminine* definite article.

das cinco às oito horas, from five o'clock to eight

desde as cinco até às oito horas, from five o'clock until eight

Tinha trabalhado desde a uma.   He had worked from one o'clock.

De Sintra a Lisboa fui de comboio.   From Sintra to Lisbon I went by train.

Fui a pé desde Sintra até Lisboa.   I walked (all the way) from Sintra to Lisbon.

(6) *On:* physical position (**em, sobre**), figurative sense (**sobre**). In the former case the difference is small, **sobre** being rather more emphatic than **em**. **Sobre** and **em cima de** often serve to avoid the ambiguity that may occur with **em** (meaning *in* as well as *on*).

Os pratos estão na (*or* sobre a) mesa.   The plates are on the table.

Está sobre o (em cima do) armário.   It is on (on top of) the cupboard.

Escreveu alguma coisa sobre a Revolução.   He wrote something on the Revolution.

NOTE: For *on* with days of the week and dates see §§ 70–71.

(7) *Under:* physical position (**debaixo de, sob**), figurative sense (**sob**). In the former case **debaixo de** (cf. English *underneath*) is slightly more concrete than **sob**.

Encontrei-o debaixo da mesa.   I found him under(neath) the table.

Estavam a brincar sob as árvores.   They were playing under the trees.

Estavam sob o mando de Napoleão.   They were under Napoleon's command.

(8) *Through:* = *on account of* (**por**); otherwise (**por, através de**). In the latter sense **por** is usual; **através de** indicates greater length or penetration.

pelo que lhe tinha dito o seu pai, through what his father had told him

Viemos pelo parque. We came through the park.

Escapou pela janela. He escaped through the window.

Através da névoa enxergou um casal. Through the mist he could make out a farmstead.

Através de todo o livro nota-se a mesma coisa. Through-(out) the whole book one notices the same thing.

(d) The preposition **por** (*through*) may add a notion of means, movement or direction when it is used before a compound preposition indicating place (or before the corresponding adverb). In these circumstances **em cima** and **debaixo** lose their first element, and **detrás** may do so.

Saltou por cima da taipa. He jumped over the wall.

Cinco soldados sustinham o escudo por baixo. Five soldiers held the shield firm (from) underneath.

Depois atacaram por (de)trás da companhia C. Then they attacked from behind C Company.

Examinei a casa com muito cuidado por dentro e por fora. I examined the house very carefully inside and out.

Os corvos pairavam por cima das árvores. The crows were hovering above the trees.

146. STRONG PERSONAL PRONOUNS. Besides the weak object pronouns or *con*junctive pronouns (that join *with* the verb, §§ 88–89 and 137), there are in Portuguese two series of strong or *dis*junctive personal pronouns (*i.e.*, pronouns that stand *apart from* the verb): the reflexive series and the non-reflexive series. In the first persons and the second persons the two series coincide.

		Reflexive	*Non-Reflexive*
(1)	(ęu)	mim	mim
(2)	(tu)	ti	ti
	(vǫcê, *etc.*)	si	vǫcê, *etc.*, *or* si[1]
(3)	(ęle)	si	ęle
	(ęla)	si	ęla
(1)	(nós)	nós	nós
(2)	(vós)	vós	vós
	(vǫcês, *etc.*)	si	vǫcês, *etc.*, *or* si[1]
(3)	(ęles)	si	ęles
	(ęlas)	si	ęlas

147. USE OF THE STRONG PERSONAL PRONOUNS. (*a*) The disjunctive pronouns are used after prepositions. The reflexive series is used if the prepositional object refers back to the subject of the verb; the non-reflexive forms if the prepositional object refers to some person other than the subject. The adjectives **męsmo** or **próprio** (inflected where appropriate) may, for emphasis, be added to a reflexive pronoun and, more rarely, to a non-reflexive pronoun.

Faço-o pạra mim (męsmo/próprio). I do it for myself.

O męu irmão fá-lo pạra mim. My brother does it for me.

Tens confiança em ti (męsmo/próprio)? Have you got confidence in yourself?

Tọdos estamos a pensar em ti. We are all thinking of you.

Vǫcê esquęce-se de si (męsma/própria). You (*fem. sing.*) are forgetting (about) yourself.

Não podęmos esquęcęr-nos de vǫcê (*or* si). We can't forget you.

Tem bastante pạra si (męsma/própria). She has enough for herself.

Não tenho bastante pạra ęla. I haven't enough for her.

Não nos fiamos de nós (męsmos/próprios). We don't trust ourselves.

Estavam a falar de nós. They were talking about us.

[1] After a preposition **si** is used more frequently than **vǫcê(s)** (except in Brazilian).

Vocês estão sempre pensando em si mesmos/próprios.
You're always thinking of yourselves.

Construíram-no para os Srs. (*or* **si**).   They (have) built it for
you.

Discutiram-no entre si.   They (have) discussed it amongst
themselves.

Construiu-o para eles.   He (has) built it for them.

(*b*) The preposition **com** joins with the disjunctive pronouns
mim, ti, si, nós and **vós** to give respectively **comigo, contigo,
consigo, connosco** and **convosco**.[1]

Desejava estudá-lo comigo.   He wanted to study it with me.
Discutiram-no contigo?   Did they discuss it with you?
Desejo falar consigo.   I wish to speak with you.
Brincaram connosco.   They (have) played with us.
Posso contar convosco?   May I count on you?

(*c*) The prepositions **de** and **em** contract with the disjunctive
pronouns **ele, ela, eles** and **elas** as shown below.   The contractions made by **em** are not always observed in writing but *must*
be observed in speech.

> **de: dele, dela, deles, delas**
> **em: nele, nela, neles, nelas**

Estávamos falando deles.   We were talking about them.

Não temos mais confiança $\begin{cases} \textbf{em ela} \\ \textbf{nela} \end{cases}$.   We have no further
confidence in her.

(*d*) When a weak *direct* object pronoun is in the first or second
person (*i.e.*, **me, te, nos, vos**), a weak *indirect* object pronoun is
replaced by **a** with a strong pronoun.

> **Manda-me a você.**   He sends me to you.
> **Ele recomendava-nos a eles.**   He recommended us to
> them.

but **Deparavam-se-lhe duas carreiras.**   Two careers offered
themselves to him.

---

[1] *But* **com nós mesmos,** *with ourselves,* etc.

(e) The use of the disjunctive personal pronoun is not of course limited to persons.

O edifício aluiu-se por si mẹsmo. The building collapsed of its own accord.

Víamos o rio e pouco a pouco nos aproximávamos dẹle. We could see the river and gradually we were drawing near to it.

as águas do Tejo e ẹste castẹlo que se reflẹcte [rrə ˈflɛtə] **nẹlas,** the waters of the Tagus and this castle (that is) reflected in them

The neuter pronoun **isso** exists for cases where the prepositional object does not refer to a specific noun.

Não estou cẹrto disso. I'm not sure of it.

Está muito contente com tudo isso. He's very pleased with it all. (N.B. For **tudo** see § 161.)

148. PRONUNCIATION: **ọi** AND **ou.** In many Portuguese words **ọi** and **ou** are interchangeable in both spelling and pronunciation, yet in many other words this optional alternation is not possible and in a few others obsolescent or obsolete. Brazil and the North of Portugal tend to favour **ou;** elsewhere **ọi** is generally preferred.

(a) Alternation of **ou** for **ọi** is possible in all words ending in **-ọiça, -ọice, -ọiço, -ọira, -ọiro, -ọita, -ọito**[1] and all derivatives.

(b) Likewise alternation of **ọi** for **ou** is possible in all words ending in **-ouça, -ouce, -ouço, -oura, -ouro, -outa, -outo** and all derivatives.

(c) Alternation of **ou** for **ọi** (and vice versa) is also found occasionally in the following words: **dọido,** *mad*; **frouxo,** *slack, floppy*; and their derivatives.

(d) The former alternatives for **dọis,** *two*, **a cọisa,** *thing*, **a nọite** (and its derivatives), *night*, are now considered obsolescent or obsolete.[2]

(e) Alternation is not possible in any other words.

---

[1] Except **ọito** and **dezọito.**

[2] Exceptional is the expression **cousíssima** (*or* **cọisíssima**) **nenhuma** (*nothing whatsoever, absolutely nothing*).

VOCABULARY

a ajuda	help	julgar	to judge; to think
ajudar	to help		
algumas		junto	together
vezes	sometimes	ao lado de	beside, at the side of
o andar	floor, storey		
o cacau	cocoa	o letreiro	notice
o centro	centre	o lugar	place, spot
a chave	key	a manteiga	butter
o chocolate	chocolate	a ópera	opera
construir	to build	o {pequeno	
de per si	by himself, etc.	primeiro}	
dinamarquês	Danish; Dane	almoço	breakfast
o erro	error, mistake	reagir	to react
escolher	to choose, pick	repetir	to repeat
examinar	to examine, look at	a saída	exit, way out
		segundo	according to (what)
forte	strong, loud		
importar	to matter; to import	surpreender	to surprise
		unicamente	only, solely, just
o intérprete	interpreter		

além disso   besides, in addition

o Sr. não se importa $\begin{Bmatrix} de + inf. \\ que + subj. \end{Bmatrix}$ would you mind $\begin{Bmatrix} \text{-ing} \dots \\ \text{if} \dots \end{Bmatrix}$?

antes de mais nada⎫
primeiro que tudo⎭   before all else, first of all

Study also the words listed in §§ 145, 146 and 148.

EXERCISES

I. (a) *Pronounce the following:* infracção, hífenes, características, afoitado, baloiçar, espelho, tenha, vejamos, ideia, onomatopeico, entreaberto, norte-americano, trouxéreis, mouro, moita, lã cardada, efectuaríamos, frouxidão, endoidecido.

233

(b) *Study and translate:* Ganhava menos que tu. Ganhei mais de duas mil libras por ano. Estavam atrás da sua tia. Além do Largo da Carioca. Diante de vocês. Escreviam-no para si mesmos. Comprei-a para ela. Não devemos pensar tanto em nós mesmos. Segundo (o que) dizem os seus pais. Fizemo-lo sem ajuda de ninguém. Com os doentes nunca se sabe. Vamos consigo. Parecia-lhes a eles um grande erro. Estamos a pintá-lo de verde. O Sr. não se importa de se levantar?

(c) *Translate:* Around twelve o'clock. With us. For you. He did it (by) himself. Are they all sure of it? We've come without her. Facing the station. Not very far from the old post-office. Near here. In front of the cathedral. Without thinking of his mother. She made it for herself. Can we go with you? After the meeting. We have no more confidence in them. Behind them. He used to drink more than I did. They arrived after him. Besides sending him a postcard. The next door neighbours and those opposite. They were all repeating it amongst themselves. What does it matter to you? Would you mind coming here?

II. (a) *Study and translate:* 1. Li um livro muito interessante sobre as viagens duns alemães através da Espanha. 2. Estes rapazes não sabem nadar mas sim sabem dançar e além disso fazem-no muito bem. 3. É-lhe impossível escolher entre aqueles chapéus. 4. Não sabia como reagir perante tais opiniões. 5. Víamos a Sé Nova de fora da cidade, não muito longe donde moras tu. 6. Depois de dizer isto foi ter com uns amigos que tínhamos conhecido na reunião. 7. Como bons turistas tivemos de examinar todos os antigos monumentos do lugar por dentro e por fora. 8. Além disso falou contra o projecto unicamente porque mora perto do centro da cidade. 9. O gato saltou sobre a mesa com o cão atrás. 10. Os seus amigos iam chegando uns após outros, alguns tristes, outros mais alegres.

(b) *Translate:* 1. I went with him to see if I could help him.

2. He was looking for the exit when someone seized him from (**por**) behind. 3. I usually arrive before my brother but he generally goes away long (=much) after I do. 4. They both wanted to leave Seville on Wednesday at 4 p.m. 5. Until that day we had never arrived after him. 6. Next year (**No ano que vem**) they are all going to come with us. 7. He had taken his wife and children to have lunch in a small Greek restaurant that he knew near the main station. 8. They were sitting (=seated) in front of the door preparing the vegetables for dinner. 9. Over the door I could see a small notice but I couldn't read it. 10. If he arrived on time we all used to go to the pictures together.

III. (*a*) *Study and translate:* 1. É inútil dizer-lhe isso, visto que nunca pensa senão em si. 2. Quem é que estava contigo quando chegaram os meus pais? 3. Ele não quis responder porque já não lhe era possível. 4. Ficou muito surpreendida perante tal opinião e não pôde convencê-lo do seu erro. 5. Todos estamos contra tal projecto, porque julgamos que se vai ter de trabalhar mais. 6. Parece que o Doutor Martins, ao não receber resposta, teve de pedir a chave aos vizinhos. 7. Quisemos vê-lo antes da partida do comboio. 8. Ela chegou ao hotel às nove e pediu um quarto no terceiro andar. 9. Perguntou-lhes porque nem sempre faziam a mesma coisa. 10. Quem foi que construiu as casas em frente?

(*b*) *Translate:* 1. "What's the date?" "It's the first of July." 2. We discovered him beside the armchair asleep (=sleeping). 3. Besides German, which is the language of his country, this interpreter speaks English, Dutch and Danish. 4. I told him that the postman had spoken to me about this a fortnight before. 5. They have bought a house outside the town, but it is very old and many of the windows are broken. 6. For (**Ao**) breakfast we had coffee and (**com**) milk and ate bread and (**com**) butter. 7. Sometimes they have supper after the theatre or the opera. 8. In the city we usually have dinner at seven o'clock at night. 9. In Portugal and Brazil there are a lot of people who take chocolate or cocoa instead of coffee. 10. But in our family John and Philip prefer to have tea if it is not too strong.

*The Future and Conditional Tenses, More on
the Possessives,* PEDIR *and* PERGUNTAR, *Variants
in Pronunciation*

LESSON XXIV

149. THE FUTURE TENSE (English *I shall buy, you will buy*, etc.).
The future is formed by adding to the *infinitive* the endings **-ei,
-ás, -á, -ęmos, -eis, -ão.** This applies to verbs of all three
conjugations.

I. **comprar**	II. **vendęr**	III. **partir**
comprarei	venderei	partirei
comprarás	venderás	partirás
comprará	venderá	partirá
compraręmos	venderęmos	partiręmos
comprareis	vendereis	partireis
comprarão	venderão	partirão

Compraręmos uma lǫja.   We shall buy a shop.
Venderei jornais.   I shall sell newspapers.
Partirão ąmanhã.   They will depart tomorrow.

150. THE CONDITIONAL (English *I should buy, you would buy*, etc.).
The conditional is formed by adding to the *infinitive* the endings
-ia, -ias, -ia, -íamos, -íeis, -iam.   The same endings are used
for the three conjugations.

I. **comprar**	II. **vendęr**	III. **partir**
compraria	venderia	partiria
comprarias	venderias	partirias
compraria	venderia	partiria
compraríamos	venderíamos	partiríamos
compraríeis	venderíeis	partiríeis
comprariam	venderiam	partiriam

Ęle disse que o compraria.   He said he would buy it.
Venderíamos muitos mais, mąs não tęmos.   We should sell
a lot more, but we haven't [any].
Pąra onde iria o Sr.?   Where would you go to?

237

NOTE: In cases where confusion could not arise, the conditional is often replaced by the imperfect indicative.

151. THE FUTURE PERFECT (English *I shall have bought, you will have bought*, etc.). The future perfect is formed by the future tense of **ter** together with the past participle of the verb.

Amanhã terá lido tudo.   Tomorrow he'll have read everything.
Terá podido fazê-lo?   Will he have been able to do it?

152. THE CONDITIONAL PERFECT (English *I should have bought, you would have bought*, etc.). The conditional perfect is formed by the conditional of **ter** together with the past participle of the verb.

Disse que o teria comprado.   He said he would have bought it.
Teria partido, mas o seu irmão chegou às oito.   He would have left, but his brother arrived at eight o'clock.

153. IRREGULAR FUTURES AND CONDITIONALS. Three verbs add the respective endings to a stem other than that of the infinitive.

	Future	*Conditional*
fazer	farei, farás, fará, etc.	faria, farias, faria, etc.
trazer	trarei, trarás, trará, etc.	traria, trarias, traria, etc.
dizer	direi, dirás, dirá, etc.	diria, dirias, diria, etc.

The verb **pôr** loses its accent in the formation of these tenses:

pôr	porei [pu'rɐj], porás, porá, etc.	poria, porias, poria, etc.

154. A SPECIAL USE. The Portuguese future may indicate supposition or probability with present time, the conditional with imperfect past time, the future perfect with perfect past time and the conditional perfect with pluperfect past time.   English usage frequently coincides.

Ęle estará a trabalhar cọmo sempre e ęla (estará) a divertir-se por aí com as suas amigas.   I suppose he's working the same as ever, and she's probably out gallivanting with her friends.

Que họras seriam quando se fọram embọra?   Seriam duas họras.   What time would it be when they left? It would be/was about two o'clock.

Terás visto o nọvo filme, não (terás)?   I suppose you've seen the new film, haven't you?

Não teria terminado a lição quando ęu o vi.   He probably hadn't finished the lesson when I saw him.

155. WEAK OBJECT PRONOUNS WITH FUTURE AND CONDITIONAL. Where the weak object pronoun would normally follow the verb, in the case of the future and conditional it is inserted between the infinitive part and the ending.

Comprá-lo-ei ạmanhã.   I shall buy it tomorrow.
Fá-lo-iam mais tarde.   They would do it later.
Trá-lo-ás na semana que vem?   I expect you'll be bringing it next week?
Dir-lho-ei outra vęz.   I shall say it to you again.
Pô-los-á na mẹsa.   He'll put them on the table.

156. OTHER WAYS OF TRANSLATING THE ENGLISH *shall, will, should, would.*   (*a*) An interrogative *shall* introducing or asking for a suggestion must be translated by the Portuguese present tense; a corresponding affirmative *shall* may be so translated in conversational style.

Deixamo-lo pạra ạmanhã?   Shall we leave it until tomorrow?
O que faço agọra?   What shall I do now?
Vou (*or* Irei) ẹsta tarde se possívẹl.   I'll go this afternoon if possible.

(*b*) The English *shall, will, should* and *would* emphasizing action as intended or destined to take place is usually translated by the present or imperfect of **havẹr de.** The monosyllabic parts of **havẹr** are inseparable from **de** and are linked to it by a hyphen.

Promẹto-lhe que hei-de recusá-lo.   I promise you I shall refuse it.

O que hei-de ẹu fazẹr?   What am *I* supposed to do?

Ẹu estava cẹrto (de) que ẹle havia de vọltar.   I was sure he would return.

Note: The English emphatic forms indicating obligation or determination (strictly *I will, you shall, he shall,* etc.) are also rendered by **havẹr de.**

(*c*) *Should* implying duty or obligation is translated by some part of **devẹr,** *to have to, must* with the pure infinitive.

Isto $\begin{cases} \text{dẹve} \\ \text{devia} \\ \text{deveria} \\ \text{(devẹra)}^1 \end{cases}$ levar-se em conta.   This should be taken into account.

Devias tẹr-lhe dito a verdade.   You should have told him the truth.

Note: In the first example the present indicative implies that something *is to be* taken into account, the other three tenses that it *ought to be* (but may not be).

(*d*) English *will* and *would*, especially in questions and negations, may indicate disposition (*to be willing*) rather than future action.   In such a case the verb **querẹr** is used in Portuguese (also **estar dispọsto a,** *to be disposed to,* and, in negative sentences, **negar-se a,** *to refuse to*).

O Sr. quẹr dizẹr-me onde é que ẹle está?   Will you tell me where he is?

Não quẹr ir; não está dispọsto a ir; nẹga-se a ir.   He won't (is unwilling to, refuses to) go.

---

[1] This form is highly literary and should not be imitated.

Não queria fazê-lo; não estava disposto a fazê-lo. He
wouldn't (was unwilling to) do it.

Não quis fazê-lo; negou-se a fazê-lo. He wouldn't (was unwilling to, refused to) do it.

NOTE. In the last two examples **não queria** and **não estava
disposto a** indicate a state of unwillingness; **não quis** and **negou-
se a** suggest downright refusal.

157. AVOIDANCE OF THE SPLIT FUTURE AND CONDITIONAL. The
split future and conditional (see § 155) are not favoured in in-
formal conversation, being rather literary in tone. They may
usually be avoided either:

(a) by including a *subject pronoun* (this word-order, however,
is regarded by some purists as a Brazilianism):

$$\text{Eu o} \begin{Bmatrix} \text{escreverei} \\ \text{escreveria} \end{Bmatrix}. \quad \text{I} \begin{Bmatrix} \text{shall} \\ \text{should} \end{Bmatrix} \text{write it.}$$

or

(b) by using **haver de** + *infinitive*:

$$\begin{Bmatrix} \text{Hei-de} \\ \text{Havia de} \end{Bmatrix} \text{escrevê-lo.} \quad \text{I} \begin{Bmatrix} \text{shall} \\ \text{should} \end{Bmatrix} \text{write it.}$$

or

(c) by using **ir** + *infinitive* in the case of the future only:

Vou escrevê-lo. I am going to write it.

or

(d) by using the present tense to replace the future, particularly in conjunction with some adverb or adverbial phrase of
futurity:

Vejo-o amanhã.   I'll see you tomorrow.
Levo-os imediatamente.   I'll bring them at once.

Cf. § 156 (a), particularly the last example.

or

241

(e) by using the imperfect tense to replace the conditional, provided that the context admits of no ambiguity:

Se fosse possível eu matava-os! Were it possible I'd kill them!

158. MORE ON THE POSSESSIVES. (a) *Omission of the definite article.* (i) The definite article is optionally omitted before singular nouns referring to family relatives:

O meu pai⎫
Meu pai⎬ é soldado. My father is a soldier.

But not in the plural:

Os meus pais estão mortos. My parents are dead.

(ii) It is omitted after **ser** and similar verbs (*e.g.*, **parecer,** *to seem*) except when distinction of ownership is made:

Este livro é meu. This book is mine.
but **Este é o meu livro.** This is my book.

Este livro é o meu, mas esse é o teu. This book is *mine*, but that's *yours*.

Este é o meu livro, mas esse é o teu (livro). This is *my* book, but that's *yours* (*your* book).

(iii) It is omitted in a number of stock expressions:

a meu ver, a teu ver, etc.	in my opinion, in your opinion, etc.
em meu lugar, em teu lugar, etc.	instead of me, instead of you, etc.
por minha causa, por tua causa, etc.	for my sake, for your sake, etc.
a meu cargo, a teu cargo, etc.	in my charge, in your charge, etc.

(iv) It is omitted in vocative expressions:

Bom dia, minha senhǫra, pǫsso ajudá-la? Good morning, madam, may I help you?

Bǫa tarde, (męu) senhǫr, passou bem? Good afternoon, sir, how are you?

(v) It is occasionally omitted in refined literary style.

(*b*) *The possessive used after the noun.* It has been seen that the possessive may be used after the noun with the indefinite article, *e.g.*, **um amigo męu,** *a friend of mine.* This feature is occasionally found in certain expressions with the definite article in order to give special emphasis. This tendency is most common in poetry, prayers and songs:

o Padre-nǫsso, the Lord's Prayer

O pão nǫsso de cạda dia dai-nos hǫje. Give us this day our daily bread.

(*c*) *The use of* **o dęle,** *etc.* **O sęu, a sua,** etc. are often ambiguous, *e.g.*, **o sęu livro** may mean

$$\left.\begin{array}{l}\text{his}\\\text{her}\\\text{your}\\\text{their}\end{array}\right\} \text{book}$$

For this reason, it is often necessary to replace **o sęu,** etc., with some other expression:

$$\text{o livro}\left\{\begin{array}{l}\text{dęle}\\\text{dęla}\\\text{de vǫcê, etc.}\\\text{dęles}\\\text{dęlas}\end{array}\right\}$$

(*d*) In some cases the simple omission of the possessive in Portuguese (*He has gone out with his father:* **Saiu com o pai**) is preferable, provided that the meaning is clear.

159. Pedir AND **perguntar.** As these two verbs are often confused, some clarification of their distinctions is necessary. Both verbs mean *to ask*. The distinction is that **pedir** means *to request*, **perguntar** *to inquire*.

Pediu-me cinco libras esterlinas. He asked me for a fiver.

Perguntou-me se tinha cinco libras esterlinas. He asked me if I had a fiver.

Pediu-me para lhe dar cinco libras esterlinas. He asked me to give him a fiver.

Perguntou-me pelas cinco libras esterlinas. He asked me about the fiver.

Both verbs take an indirect object for the person asked.

Perguntar por is used to render *to ask about, ask after, ask for* (a person):

Perguntei por sua mãe. I asked after (or for) your mother.

To ask for a person is also rendered by **pedir para ver** or **pedir para falar com**:

Está uma senhora lá em baixo que pede para falar com V. Exa. There's a lady downstairs asking for you, sir.

160. VARIANTS IN PRONUNCIATION. Below are listed the principal variants in the speech of educated Portuguese citizens. These are mainly of regional origin, though they should not be regarded as dialectal.

(*a*) Stressed **e** before palatals is [ɐ] in Central Portugal, [e] elsewhere:

o espelho [əʃˈpɐʎu], [əʃˈpeʎu], *mirror*.[1] It is in fact pronounced [e] by the majority of speakers.

(*b*) The sound [rr] is replaced by [ɹɹ] in Setúbal and by many inhabitants of Lisbon:

morrer [muˈrrer], [muˈɹɹeɹ], *to die*.

---

[1] In the mouths of some speakers [ɐ] becomes [ɐj]: [əʃˈpɐjʎu].

(c) The graph **ou,** pronounced [o] in Central and Southern Portugal, is pronounced [ow] in some parts of the North:

o Out**ọ**no [oˈtonu], [owˈtonu], *autumn.*

(d) Although initial unstressed (**h**)**o** is pronounced [o] in most of Central and Southern Portugal, the variants [ɔ] and [u] are to be found in many areas, especially in the North:

ocupar [okuˈpar], [ɔkuˈpar], [ukuˈpar], *to occupy.*

(e) Unstressed initial **ex** followed by a vowel, normally pronounced [iz], is by some speakers rendered as [ɐjz].   This is sometimes regarded as an affectation:

exacto [iˈzatu], [ɐjˈzatu], *exact.*

VOCABULARY

acontec**ẹ**r	to happen, occur	faz**ẹ**r uma	
agradecido	grateful, thankful	mala	to pack a case
		a mala	(suit)case, bag
o ano	school year, academic year	a necessidade	necessity, need
escolar	demic year		
o ano l**ẹ**ctivo	academic year	pensar	to consider, ponder over
casar com	to get married to		der over
concordar		poupar	to save (*money*)
em	to agree to	principiar	to commence
a criança	child	res**ọ**lv**ẹ**r	to solve; to resolve
enganar	to deceive, mislead		solve
		ridículo	ridiculous
enganar-se,		tencionar (+	
estar	to be mistaken, wrong	*infinitive*)	to intend (to)
enganado		a viúva	widow

é uma verg**ọ**nha	it's a disgrace
não vale a p**ẹ**na	it's not worth the trouble
cumprir (com) o s**ẹ**u dev**ẹ**r	to do one's duty
aos cat**ọ**rze anos	at the age of fourteen

algo
um tanto } rather, somewhat, a
algum tanto trifle . . .

Study also the words and expressions listed in §§ 156 and 158–60.

EXERCISES

I. (a) *Indicate the variations in pronunciation of the following words:* Tejo, venho, ocorrera, Outubro, outeiro, oculista, Olhão, examinou, fartura, armário, fecham, tenho.

(b) *Study and translate:* Terão que pensá-lo. Fá-lo-ei amanhã. Não poderás ir ter com ele. Você expor-se-á a ter de lhe responder. Concordaremos em ir juntas. O que terá acontecido? Deveriam dizer-nos alguma coisa. Deixo-o para a quarta? Dir-se-ia que é ridículo. Seria uma vergonha. Estaríamos todos a pensar em ti. Gostaria imenso de o fazer. Iremos todos consigo. Trar-lho-ei na sexta. A nosso ver. Hás-de fazê-lo desde já.

(c) *Translate:* We shall see. They will do. He will see. He *shall* see. The child will appear. Everything else. He'll want to know. I'll bring it tomorrow. We said she would go and see him. They will all sit down here. What would you say? What time will it be? For her sake. He must be ten or eleven years old. At fifteen years of age. I'll see you on Friday morning (**de manhã**). I ought to do it today. But I don't feel like it. Will it fit? Shall I come back tomorrow? They will clear the table. He ought to have done it.

II. (a) *Study and translate:* 1. Abro a porta ou deixo-a fechada? 2. Quando dará de comer às crianças? 3. Tomaremos muito cedo o primeiro almoço e às sete menos um quarto estaremos na Estação de Santa Apolónia. 4. Ó Isabel, ajudas-me a fazer estas malas? 5. Trago-lhe uma faca e um prato ou prefere tomar café primeiro? 6. O que havíamos nós de fazer enquanto se vestia? 7. Teremos de preparar toda a lição para a segunda de manhã. 8. Eu gostaria imenso de ir em teu lugar, mas é-me impossível. 9. Está um rapaz lá fora que está a pedir para falar consigo, minha senhora. 10. Fá-lo-iam apenas por tua causa e não por causa dela.

(*b*) *Translate:* 1. I cannot acknowledge the necessity of such a scheme. 2. He said that they were all friends of his. 3. I'll wind the clock up tomorrow morning. 4. Why wouldn't the American soldiers occupy the capital? 5. She said she would bring it to me on Wednesday. 6. I should like to know why she can't bring it at once. 7. You ought to have found another way of solving all these difficulties. 8. It's ridiculous to save all that money just for his sake. 9. If you think I'm doing it just for him, you're mistaken. 10. I shall ask him about his aunt because I know she hasn't been keeping too (**muito**) well.

III. (*a*) *Study and translate:* 1. Aos trinta anos casou com uma viúva muito rica. 2. Como estarão um tanto cansados, dormirão muito bem. 3. Achar-me-ás sempre ao lado dos que cumprem o dever. 4. Amanhã passarão o dia fora de casa. 5. Em que dia principiará o ano escolar? 6. Parece-me que principiará a um de Setembro. 7. Enganouse; pensava que terias vinte e cinco anos. 8. Falarei consigo amanhã de tarde? 9. Amanhã eu levantar-me-ei cedo, porque vamos dar um passeio no campo. 10. Parecia-lhe que nos pediria os cem escudos que lhe devíamos desde havia tanto tempo.

(*b*) *Translate:* 1. Would you like to spend the months of June and July in Madeira? 2. I intend to visit his uncle next week. 3. He would get up early in the morning but he thinks it is not worth while. 4. At forty years of age he would never get up early in the morning but would stay in (**na**) bed until a quarter to nine. 5. We shall always be (*use* **estar**) grateful to you for your help. 6. He said that he would write to all of us (= to us all): to you from Argentina, to Manuel from Brazil, and to me from Nicaragua.

247

7. Shall we write him a letter explaining what we intend to do? 8. "What time would it be when you reached the station?" "It was just half an hour after midnight." 9. What *could* he do on receiving such a telegram? 10. Immediately after sending me the postcard he left for Vila Real (*no article*).

LESSON XXV

161. THE USES OF **tǫdo** (*every, all*) AND **tudo** (*everything*).

(*a*) When **tǫdo** is followed by a noun, the definite article (or a demonstrative) is always interposed between the form **tǫdo** and the noun:

tǫdo o prédio	all the building; every building
tǫdas as mulhęres	all (the) women
tǫdos ęstes hǫmens	all these men

(*b*) When **tǫdo** means *the whole* it is frequently found after the noun:

tǫdo o dia⎫
o dia tǫdo⎭ all day, the whole day

(*c*) When **tǫdo** is accompanied by a pronoun or followed by a demonstrative, numeral or other word not normally accompanied by the definite article, the definite article is not used:

nós tǫdos⎫
tǫdos nós⎭ all of us, we all

tǫdos ęstes	all these
tǫdos três	all three (of them)
tǫdo Portugal	all Portugal

but **tǫdo o Brasil,** all Brazil; **tǫdos os três dias** (= **de três em
três dias**), every three days

(*d*) *Some useful expressions*

em⎫
por⎭ **tǫda a parte**   everywhere

249

em⎱ tǫdas as (de)mais partes	everywhere else
por⎰	
tǫda a gente⎱	everybody
tǫdos　　　 ⎰	
tǫda a (de)mais gente⎱	everybody else
tǫdos os (de)mais　　 ⎰	
tǫdo o hǫmem que ...	every man who ...

(*e*) The singular forms **tǫdo** and **tǫda** may be used adverbially:

Ęste chapéu está tǫdo sujo.	This hat's all dirty.
A sua camisa está tǫda molhada.	His shirt's (all) wet through.

This construction is not possible in the plural.

(*f*) When **tǫdo** is used pronominally as the direct object of a verb, the corresponding weak object pronoun must also be expressed; this construction does NOT apply to **tudo**.

Vi-os tǫdos.　　I saw them all *or* all of them.

(*g*) The pronoun **tudo** is neuter and limited in use. It may be used in combination with other neuter pronouns but not with neuter adjectives.

Vi tudo.	I saw it all *or* all of it *or* everything.
tudo isto	all this
tudo isso	all that (*dem.*)
tudo aquilo	all that (*dem.*)
tudo o mais	everything else, all else (*but* **tǫdo o ręsto**)
tudo o que ⎱	all that (*rel.*), everything that
(tudo) quanto ⎰	
primeiro que tudo	first of all, before all else

NOTE: **Tǫdo** fulfils the function of the neuter before neuter adjectives (see § 103): **tǫdo o lindo**, *everything beautiful, all that is beautiful*; **fazęr tǫdo o possívęl**, *to do all possible, do one's best*. It is also neuter in the following idioms:

ao tǫdo, *in all, altogether*; **de tǫdo**, *totally, at all*; **de tǫdo em tǫdo**, *out and out, completely*.

162. THE USE OF **ambos** (*both*). Like **tǫdo, ambos** is followed by the definite article when describing a noun, but not when accompanying a pronoun or a demonstrative.

ambos os sǫldados	both (the) soldiers
ambas ęstas mulhęres	both these women
ambos nós⎫ **nós ambos**⎭	both of us, we both
de ambos os lados da rua	on both sides of the street

NOTE: *Both* is also often rendered by **os dǫis (as duas)**.

163. THE VERB **cręr**, *to believe*. This irregular verb is identical in its conjugation to **lęr**, *to read*. Owing to its phonetic similarities to the verb **queręr**, *to wish, want*, it is rarely used in other than the present tense. Its other tenses are normally replaced by those of **acreditar**. This latter verb is usually followed by **em** when its object is a noun, noun-clause or disjunctive pronoun.

Crê o que dizes. He believes what you say.
Mal o pǫsso acreditar. I can scarcely believe it.
Não acreditei nas suas palavras. I didn't believe his words.
Cǫmo pǫdes acreditar nisso? How can you believe that?
Acreditaste no que ęu disse? Did you believe what I said?

164. ADVERBS. (*a*) Many adverbs are formed by the addition of **-mente** to the feminine singular of the corresponding adjective (cf. English *-ly*).

sevęro	severe	**sevęramente**	severely
intenso	intense	**intensamente**	intensely
geral	general	**gerąlmente**	generally

NOTES. 1. The pronunciation of the adjective-part of the adverb is NOT affected by the shift of stress to the first **e** of **-mente.**

2. The *masculine* singular of national and regional adjectives in **-ês** is used in the formation of the corresponding adverbs:

portuguesmente, in a Portuguese fashion

(*b*) If two or more such adverbs come together, **-mente** is normally placed only after the last of the series, the others being represented by the relevant form of the adjective.

Trabalhava intensa e constantemente. He used to work intensely and constantly.

(*c*) An adverb in **-mente** is frequently avoided by the use of **com** with the corresponding noun, or by the phrases **duma maneira** or **dum modo** with an adjective, or by some other prepositional phrase.

com frequência, frequentemente	frequently
por fim, finalmente	finally
por completo, completamente	completely
dum modo eficaz, eficazmente	effectively

(*d*) An adjective is often used in Portuguese where English has an adverb.

Estes livros vendem-se muito baratos. These books sell very cheaply.

165. SUFFIXES. (*a*) The stressed vowel of a word retains the same quality on addition of the suffix **-mente** or any suffix beginning with **z,** *e.g.,* **-zinho, -zinha; -zito, -zita; -zarrão, -zona; -zada; -zeiro; -zista; -zudo.** Any word originally carrying an accent loses it. The stress is in all cases transferred to the relevant syllable of the suffix.

cego	blind	cegamente	blindly
cortês	polite	cortêsmente	politely
enérgico	energetic	energicamente	energetically
pobre	poor	pobrezinho	poor little
a pêra	pear	a perazinha	little pear
o pé	foot	o pezito	little foot
o homem	man	o homenzarrão	great lout
má	bad (f.)	a mazona	slut
o pé	foot	pezudo	big-footed

(b) Before **z**, final **-m** becomes **n**, and nouns ending in **-ão** or **-l** form their plural in the original body of the word as well as in the suffix. The internal final **-s** drops before the **z**.

o homem	os homens	o homenzarrão	os homenzarrões
man	men	great lout	great louts
o pão	os pães	o pãozinho	os pãezinhos
bread	loaves	roll	rolls
o hotel	os hotéis	o hotelzinho	os hoteizinhos
hotel	hotels	guest-house	guest-houses

(c) There are a vast number of suffixes in Portuguese.[1] At this stage, however, the student should merely learn the most common ones, *i.e.*, the adverbial **-mente**, the diminutives **-inho, inha** (**-zinho, -zinha**), the augmentatives **-ão, -ona,** and the collective **-ada** (**-zada**). This last suffix very often corresponds to the English *-ful*. The augmentative and diminutive suffixes should be used with the greatest caution by a foreigner.

(1) *Diminutives.* The suffix **-inha** (**-zinha**) is used to modify feminine words; **-inho** (**-zinho**) modifies all others. Words ending in unstressed **-o** or unstressed **-a** lose this ending and substitute **-inho** or **-inha** respectively. Words with other endings *normally* add **-zinho** or **-zinha**.

[1] For a complete study, see J. H. D. Allen, Jr., *Portuguese Word Formation with Suffixes*, the Linguistic Society of America, Philadelphia, 1941.

a casa, house	a casinha, cottage
o rato, rat	o ratinho, mouse
a pedra, stone	a pedrinha, pebble
perto, nearby	pertinho, quite close by
baixo, low	baixinho, very soft(ly)
o rapaz, boy	o rapazinho, little boy
o irmão, brother	o irmãozinho, little brother
o avô, grandfather	o avozinho, grandpa
o animal, animal	o animalzinho, little animal
a mãe, mother	a mãezinha, dear old mum
devagar, slowly	devagarinho, very slowly

(2) *Augmentatives.* The normal augmentative suffix is **-ão**, which confers masculine gender and absorbs vowel endings. The suffix **-ona** (feminine) is only used for people (*i.e.*, women) and is even then not the only choice in some cases.

o papel, paper	o papelão, pasteboard
a caixa, box	o caixão, coffin; chest
a carta, letter	o cartão, cardboard; card
	o sensaborão, boorish man, lout
sensabor, insipid, lacking in taste, boorish	a sensaborona, boorish woman
a mulher, woman	a mulherona⎱ hefty woman; o mulherão⎰ virago

(3) *The suffix* **-ada.** Examples will suffice to indicate the use of this suffix.

a bacia, basin	a baciada, basinful
a colher, spoon	a colherada, spoonful
o boi, ox	a boiada, herd of oxen
o forno, oven	a fornada, batch
a pá, shovel	a pazada, shovelful
o rapaz, boy	a rapaziada, gang of lads; prank

166. The Use of the Grave Accent. The grave accent is used in the following circumstances:

(a) In the contraction of the preposition **a** with the feminine forms of the definite article and with all forms of the remote demonstrative:

     à, às; àquęle, àquęla, àquęles, àquęlas, àquilo.

(b) until April 1971 in replacing an original acute accent of a word acquiring the suffix **-mente** or any suffix beginning with **z** [see § 165 (a)].

(c) in the representation of a small number of poetic or dialectal forms which lie beyond the scope of this work, *e.g.*, **ò** for **ao**, **prò** for **pąra o**, **prèguntar** for **perguntar**, etc.

VOCABULARY

apesar de	in spite of	**a época**	period, time
apresentar	to introduce, present	**examinar**	to examine
		excessivo	excessive
o cafęzal	coffee-plantation	**o fato**	suit
		o herói	hero
o carvão	coal	**imediata-**	immediately, at
o casaco	jacket, coat	**mente**	once
conciso	concise	**imediato**	immediate
considerar	to consider	**dęste lado**	on this side
o coração	heart	**a libra**	pound
derradeiro	last, very last	**o prédio**	building
o diręctor	headmaster; director, manager	**preocupar**	to worry (*transitive*)
a dúvida	doubt	**o remédio**	remedy
a elegância	elegance	**restar**	to remain, be left over
engraçado	funny, amusing; quaint, cute	**a situação**	position, situation

sumo	extreme	**total**	total, utter
tal como	such as	**o trabalho**	work
a tempera-		**verdadeiro**	true, very
tura	temperature	**a visita**	visit, visitor
a tempo	in time, on time		

> **ao que (me) parece** ⎫
> **do que me consta** ⎰ apparently, as it seems (to me)
> **no dia imediato** (on) the following day
> **se bem me lembro** if I remember rightly

Study also the words and expressions listed in §§ 161–5.

EXERCISES

I. (a) *Pronounce the following:* geralmente, severamente, erroneamente, energicamente, pezudo, pazada, homenzarrões, hoteizinhos, velhinho, pertinho, ratinho, somente, sozinha, animaizinhos, rapariguinha.

(b) *Give the plural of the following:* mão, mãe, país, cais, vírus, capitão, órfão, pãozinho, avozinho, avô, útil, o mal, o real, perazinha, carácter, esfíncter, cânon, íman, hífen.

(c) *Translate:* Both of us. All of us. All else. Everything beautiful. Nothing else. Thirteen in all. Solely. Frequently. Cheerfully. In a completely natural way. Finally. In the Portuguese manner. Every four days. This suit's all dirty. Very slowly.

II. (a) *Study and translate:* 1. Toda a demais gente julgava que a ideia era ridícula. 2. Todo o homem sabe fazer tais coisas sem dificuldade. 3. O seu casaco estava todo sujo, mas foi visitar o director do liceu. 4. Depois de visitar a fábrica o primeiro ministro escreveu no livro de visitas: Vi tudo. 5. Farei todo o possível para terminar o trabalho a tempo. 6. Havia prédios de ambos os lados da rua.

7. Estavam a falar com nós ambos, quando chegou a velhota. 8. Primeiro que tudo, desejava apresentar-lhe um velho amigo meu que conheço desde há vinte anos. 9. Falou clara e concisamente e, além disso, com suma elegância. 10. Já não nos restava mais remédio senão aceitar o projecto tal como o haviam preparado eles.

(b) *Translate:* 1. He told us that they were all going to leave immediately. 2. Without doubt, this is not the best time to (para) get to know the (o) Algarve. 3. Immediately after finishing dinner he left for a walk round the oldest part of the city. 4. This little boy is only thirteen years old, but he walks much faster than his brothers who are all older than he [is]. 5. Waiter![1] Bring us some rolls and butter. 6. How many spoonfuls of sugar do you take with your tea? 7. It is the best time of the year to study the trees and flowers of this part of Germany. 8. You should look at this funny little car I've bought. It only cost me fifty pounds. 9. Naturally everything he says is utterly ridiculous. 10. Apparently there used to be lots of rats and mice in this building.

III. (a) *Study and translate:* 1. Tudo o mais que o preocupara até então não tinha agora importância nenhuma. 2. O meu amigo não se importa de fazer isso? 9. Ao despir-se António considerou todas as dificuldades da sua situação. 4. No dia seguinte, ao sair da fábrica, dei com um velho amigo meu 5. Também ele queria ir para a linda casinha do Manuel. 6. Também tenho pensado nisso; mas, quando fico em casa, ganho menos, já se sabe. 7. Capital da Beira Alta, verdadeiro coração da Beira, Viseu é uma das mais características cidades portuguesas. 8. Os piores momentos para Félix eram as terças e quintas-feiras quando o José vinha passar os serões em família. 9. Pensava-se outrora

---

[1] In Portuguese this is rendered by **Faz favor** or **Fazia favor** (= *Excuse me, please*). Any other formula is considered impolite.

que a temperatura desta região era excessivamente baixa.
10. A mãe disse-me baixinho que o avozinho estava a
dormir.

(b) *Translate:* 1. If I remember rightly, it was only then that
I got to know your little brother. 2. If only I could read
all of them! I would then (**então**) know what to do.
3. The fact is that I hadn't time to do all that and carry
out my duties as well. 4. Every time I saw him he would
tell me the idea was of no avail whatsoever. 5. Michael,
bring us a shovelful of coal for the fire. 6. Everybody knew
that the plan was a washout, in spite of what he said. 7. He
explained to us very slowly that his elder brother was working
on a coffee-plantation in Angola. 8. All four of them said
they could scarcely believe it. 9. I have looked at all of them
and this is the one I prefer. 10. All those who have read
the last chapter will know where the hero died.

LESSON XXVI

167. PERSONAL PRONOUNS (FORMS). There are three classes of
personal pronoun in Portuguese: subject pronouns, weak object
(*or* conjunctive) pronouns, and strong object (*or* disjunctive) pronouns. The object pronouns may be further classified into
reflexive and non-reflexive, and into direct object and indirect
object. The forms corresponding to these different classes may
thus be tabulated as follows:

Subject	Weak Object Pronoun			Strong Object Pronoun	
	reflexive	*non-reflexive*		*reflexive*	*non-reflexive*
	i.o/d.o.	*i.o.*	*d.o.*		
1. ęu	me	me	me	mim	mim
2. { tu	te	te	te	ti	ti
vǫcê, *etc.*	se	lhe	o, a	si	vǫcê, *etc.* (*or* si)
3. { ęle	se	he	o	si	ęle
ęla	se	lhe	a	si	ęla
1. nós	nos	nos	nos	nós	nós
2. { vós	vos	vos	vos	vós	vós
vǫcês, *etc.*	se	lhes	os, as	si	vǫcês, *etc.* (*or* si)
3. { ęles	se	lhes	os	si	ęles
ęlas	se	lhes	as	si	ęlas

NOTES. 1. Reflexive pronouns are those which refer back to the
subject of the verb.

2. The forms in rectangles are the variables in the weak object
pronoun series; the remaining weak object pronouns are invariable
whether reflexive, non-reflexive, direct, indirect, masculine or
feminine.

3. The forms surrounded by dotted lines are those strong object
pronouns which are not identical to the corresponding subject
pronoun.

4. Note the alternative **si** (= *you*) to **vǫcê, vǫcês, o Sr., a Sra.**,
etc., in the strong object pronoun series. It is hardly ever used in
Brazilian Portuguese.

168. THE SUBJECT PRONOUN. The subject pronoun in Portuguese is generally omitted, except in the second person polite (*e.g.*, **o senhọr**) and fairly familiar (*i.e.*, **vọcê**) forms where it is often present. In the other persons it is used for emphasis and to avoid possible ambiguity.

Ẹla queria comprar ạlguma cọisa, mạs ẹle não tinha dinheiro. She wanted to buy something but he hadn't any money.

169. THE WEAK OBJECT PRONOUN. (*a*) If there are two weak object pronouns with the same verb, they range themselves in the following order of precedence: **se**, *indirect object*, *direct object*.

Apresentavam-se-me duas possibilidades. Two possibilities were open to me.

Devọlvẹu-mo ontem. He gave it back to me yesterday.

(*b*) In certain cases where it replaces a noun the weak pronoun object may translate the English *some, any* or *one(s)*.

Há-os muito bons; há-as muito bọas. There are some very good ones.

Manteiga? Duvido que o Sr. a encontre por aqui. Butter? I doubt whether you'll find any round here.

(*c*) A noun or adjective complement is indicated by the neuter and invariable **o** (English *so*, no word, or repetition of noun or adjective).

Estão muito alẹgres e também o estavam ontem. They are very cheerful and they were (so *or* very cheerful) yesterday too.

Ọra bem, diz-me cá: é tua amiga ou não o é? Right now, let's have it: is she a friend of yours or isn't she?

(*d*) The English neuter *it* when referring to an idea, statement, event, etc., is likewise translated by the invariable neuter **o**.

Acho-o difícil de crẹr. I find it difficult to believe.

Mal ẹle o disse, ẹu soube-o lọgo. I knew it the moment he said it.

But observe: this *it* is not to be translated in sentences of the type *I found it difficult to believe* + noun, pronoun or noun-clause; *I consider it impossible to achieve* + noun, pronoun or noun-clause, etc.

Achei difícil crẹr tais coisas. I found it difficult to believe such things.

Julgo impossívẹl completar o trabalho no tempo combinado. I consider it impossible to complete the job in the time agreed on.

Julgou ridículo acreditar nisso. He considered it ridiculous to believe that.

Acha fácil crẹr que isto é verdade. He finds it easy to believe that this is true.

Julga ilógico crẹr em Dẹus. He considers it illogical to believe in God.

Acha insuportávẹl que saiam juntos. He finds it intolerable that they should go out together.

170. STRONG OBJECT PRONOUNS. (*a*) These forms are used in Portuguese after a preposition.

Colocou-se diante de mim. He placed himself in front of me.

Ẹu estava atrás do mẹu pai. I was behind my father.

Guardou-o pạra si. He kept it for himself.

Mẹsmo or **próprio** may be added to the pronoun for emphasis:

Comprei-o pạra mim próprio. I bought it for myself.

Fê-lo por si mẹsma. She did it by herself.

(*b*) The English preposition *to*, however, followed by a personal pronoun usually corresponds to the Portuguese weak indirect object pronoun.

Deu-o a sẹu pai; dẹu-lho. He gave it to his father; he gave it to him.

But notice the following uses of **a** + strong pronoun:

(1) For clarity or emphasis, to *repeat* an object already expressed with the verb in weak-pronoun form.

Disse-lho a ęle não a ti. I told *him* not *you*.
Vi-o a ęle não a ęla. I saw *him* not *her*.

Note that this construction applies both to direct and indirect objects. For amplification of the rules for the use of personal **a** before a direct object see § 227.

(2) To *replace* a weak indirect object pronoun when the direct object is **me, te, nos** or **vos** [see § 90, NOTE 2 and § 147 (*d*)].

Mandaram-me a ti. They sent me to you.
Apresentaram-nos a ęla. They introduced us to her.

(3) After a verb of motion to emphasize movement.

Veio a mim. He came to me.

(*c*) *Two Notes in Conclusion*

(1) Distinguish carefully between the use of the strong-pronoun series in the following examples:

Subject	*Reflexive*	*Non-Reflexive*
Fi-lo ęu męsmo.	**Fi-lo pąra mim.**	**Fê-lo pąra mim.**
I made it myself.	I made it for myself.	She made it for me.
Fê-lo ęla męsma.	**Fê-lo pąra si męsma.**	**Fi-lo pąra ęla.**
She made it herself.	She made it for herself.	I made it for her.

(2) *By oneself, by myself, by himself*, etc., can usually be translated by **por**+strong reflexive pronoun (+**męsmo** or **próprio**), and by the adjective **só**. When the pronoun is **si** it is usually followed by **só(s)**. But when the meaning is *alone, in solitude*, **sozinho** must be used. Note also **de pęr si** (*of his (one's) own accord*).

Fi-lo $\begin{Bmatrix} \textbf{por mim męsma} \\ \textbf{(ęu) só} \end{Bmatrix}$. I (*fem.*) did it by myself.

Fizęram-no $\begin{Bmatrix} \textbf{por si sós} \\ \textbf{(ęlas) sós} \\ \textbf{de pęr si} \end{Bmatrix}$. They (*fem.*) did it by themselves.

but only **Morava sozinha.** She lived by herself.

171. Further Avoidance of Restricted Form of Address. It has been observed that **vós, vos, vosso,** etc., and the corresponding second person plural verb forms are nowadays restricted to sermons, public address and prayers to the Deity in the Roman Catholic Church, and that a group of persons who would individually be addressed as **tu** are collectively addressed as **vocês.** Similarly, nowadays, if **tu** is combined as a subject with any other third person (noun or pronoun), the third person plural of the verb is used, although this is contrary to normal grammatical canons.

Tu e ela sabem a minha opinião. You and she know my opinion.

Pedro e tu têm de cumprir com o seu dever. Peter and you have got to do your duty.

172. Use of Four Verbs: levar, trazer, ir and vir. The student should carefully note that **levar** and **ir** are sometimes used to translate the English *to bring* and *to come* respectively. **Trazer** and **vir** are normally used only when motion towards the speaker or narrator is involved; otherwise they should be avoided.

— Faz favor!   — Vou já, já, senhor!

— Traga-me duas cerve-   — Levo-as imediatamente,
    jas.   senhor.

"Waiter!"   "Coming, sir!"

"Bring me two beers."   "I'll bring them at once, sir."

173. Two Irregular Verbs: perder (*to lose*) **and valer** (*to be worth*). These two verbs are irregular only in the first person singular of the present indicative: **perco** and **valho** respectively.

VOCABULARY

atravessar	to cross	**calar(-se)**	to keep (*or* be) quiet
o balcão	(shop) counter		
barbear-se	to (have a) shave	**capaz**	capable, able
		colocar	to put, place, set

convençer	to convince	**prático**	practical
guardar	to guard; to keep; to put away	**preferir**	to prefer, would rather
a guerra	war	**tentar**	to attempt (to); to tempt
insistir (em)	to insist (on)	**ter prazer**	to have pleasure
a licença	permission	**em**	in
meter	to put, place, set	**último**	last, latest, most
oportuno	opportune		recent
pouco a pouco	little by little, gradually	**o valor**	value

custar (trabalho) a alguém ⎫
a fazer   ⎭ to be an effort for someone to do

Study also the verbs listed in § 173 and revise the vocabulary of Lessons XXI–XXV.

EXERCISES

I. (a) *Study and translate:* Não o temos visto. Comeram-nas todas. Tinha-nos mandado a você. Ela estava atrás dele. Ajudaram-nos muito a nós. Não no-lo mandou nem a ele nem a mim. Quisera dá-lo ao senhor. Eu fui-me embora sem ela. Falaste primeiro connosco. Estava-mas mostrando. Nunca pensa senão em si próprio. Eu comprei-o para si. Insistimos nisso. Não são capazes de o terminar? Comprámo-lo para ele. Tu e ela partiram antes de mim. A nós mandaram-nos a ti. Julgo impossível fazê-lo agora.

(b) *Translate:* I told him so. I have given it to her. They'll have gone without her. They saw you. You looked for *him*. She was looking at them. I taught it to them. We went with her. Are you going to wait for him or not? There used to be some very nice ones. He did it after me. They introduced me to him. She would have made it for us. She took them all to him. I have kept it for myself. He's done it all on his own. They took him with them but left me here alone. Are you his friends? We are. First of all they crossed the street.

II. (a) *Study and translate:* 1. Ao chegar a Manaus, não lhe restavam mais que três mil e quinhentos cruzeiros. 2. Fizemos todo o possível para convencê-lo, mas não queria deixar sozinha a sua mãe. 3. Visto que você não gosta de falar de política, vamos falar de religião. 4. Tem pouca confiança nos nossos projectos, mas eu julgo que os seus não têm nenhum valor extraordinário. 5. Pediu licença para visitá-los na manhã seguinte. 6. Não lhes parece que seria ainda mais prático principiar com o que estudávamos na semana passada? 7. Ela pensa muito em si e muito pouco noutrem. 8. Mas não deve ir-se embora sem se despedir dos meus pais. 9. Não acho oportuno fazer tal agora. 10. Apesar do trabalho que tem, é-lhe impossível continuar assim.

(b) *Translate:* 1. It was a great (**muito**) effort for me to get up this morning. 2. Little by little he managed to understand what the foreigners were saying to him. 3. They waited for him until the following Friday and then left for Germany. 4. The difficult thing is to solve the problem without asking anybody for help. 5. "Shall we walk?" "If you don't mind (*use* **importar**) I'd rather go by (= **de**) car." 6. Without doubt, the minister will not accept the policy that the rest wish to follow. 7. We have been waiting for her for over two hours. 8. The coffee cost me about fifty escudos a kilogramme. 9. He told us he would rather go with you. 10. I shall have great pleasure in sending you my latest book of poems.

III. (a) *Study and translate:* 1. É que eu também já me sentia mal e queria ir para a cama. 2. É preciso ver isso tudo antes de fazer mais nada. 3. A sua mulher era brasileira e ele vivia em Portugal. 4. Não estou disposto a repetir agora o que já tenho dito mil vezes. 5. O ex-soldado contou-me tristemente que tinha perdido tudo durante a guerra. 6. Não valia a pena fazer mais sem a ajuda do pai dela. 7. Era ridículo pensar assim! Não podia explicar o que sentia naquele momento. 8. Como ela, em vez de lhe responder

da mesma maneira, nada dissera, ficara muito contente.
9. A Maria quase perdeu a coragem ao vê-lo no táxi. 10.
Ao vê-lo o rapazinho deixou a mãe e correu alegre ao seu
encontro.

(b) *Translate:* 1. I consider it ridiculous to attempt to do
such things without the help of others. 2. He couldn't tell
her what he felt in his heart. 3. It was of no use whatsoever
putting the table near the window. 4. Whenever we entered
the shop he was [standing] behind the counter. 5. My
father always shaves in front of a mirror. 6. I made it for
her, but I'm going to give it to her sister. 7. Aren't you
capable of keeping quiet, boy? 8. I'll bring the books to
your room at once, sir. 9. He introduced me to her and she
presented me to her mother. 10. Every Saturday morning
Martin's father used to go into town in his car (in order) to
do the shopping for the whole family.

LESSON XXVII

174. VERBS WITH AN INFINITIVE. Used with a dependent infinitive some verbs take no preposition (**mandou-me fazê-lo,** *he ordered me to do it*), whilst others are followed by **a, de, em, por, com** or **para (ajudou-me a fazê-lo,** *he helped me to do it*; **insistiram em fazê-lo,** *they insisted on doing it*; **esforçou-se por fazê-lo,** *he strove to do it*; **conta com fazê-lo,** *he's counting on doing it*; **preparou-se para fazê-lo,** *he got ready to do it*).

(1) *Verb + Pure Infinitive* (*i.e.,* without a preposition)

(i) A few verbs when used *impersonally,* with the infinitive as the real subject of the sentence.

Alegra-me vê-la. I'm pleased to see her (*lit.,* To see her cheers me).

Agrada-me
Apetece-me } **vê-la.** I like to see her (*lit.,* To see her appeals
Apraz-me to me).

Faz falta
Precisa } **estudar mais.** It's necessary to study more (*lit.,*
É preciso To study more is needed).

Esqueceu-me levar-to. I forgot to bring it to you (*lit.,* To bring it to you escaped me).

Lembrou-me fazer isso. I remembered to do that (*lit.,* To do that occurred to me).

Parece-me tê-la visto. I seem to think I've seen her (*lit.,* To have seen her seems to me).

Convém-nos fazê-lo. It is best that we do it. It is a good (*or* wise) thing for us to do it (*lit.,* To do it is fitting for us).

Cabe-nos
Compete-nos } **fazê-lo.** It behoves us to do it (*lit.,* To do it
Cumpre-nos is incumbent upon us).
Incumbe-nos

(ii) The verbs of the senses **ver** (*to see*), **ouvir** (*to hear*) and **sentir** (*to feel; to sense; to hear*). These verbs take a *direct* object,

267

but when the dependent infinitive has a *noun* object, they may—
and frequently do—take an *indirect* object.

Vi-o chegar.	I saw him arrive.
Vi o homem chegar.	I saw the man arrive.
Vi chegar o homem.[1]	I saw the man arrive.
Vi-o ⎫ **matar seu filho.** **Vi-lhe** ⎭	I saw him kill his son.
Vi ⎰ **o** ⎱ **homem matar seu filho.** ⎱ **ao** ⎰	I saw the man kill his son.
Vi-o matá-lo.	I saw him kill him.
Vi o homem matá-lo.	I saw the man kill him.

The infinitive may have passive sense after these verbs in which
case it must come *immediately* after the verb on which it is dependent.   Only a weak pronoun object may intervene.

Vi matar seu filho.	I saw his son killed.
Vi-o matar.	I saw him killed.
Ouvi cantar esta canção.	I've heard this song sung.
Ouvi dizer que . . .	I've heard (it said) that . . .
Ouvi falar de . . .	I've heard (tell) of . . .
Senti abrir a porta.	I heard the door (being) opened.
but **Senti abrir-se a porta.**	I heard the door open.

These three verbs may also be used with **a** + *infinitive* (as all
other verbs of perception *must* be).   Under such circumstances
the implication is that the observed action is *in progress* without
any notion of completion.   For this construction a direct object
is always used.   The passive may *not* be rendered this way.

Vi-o a atravessar a rua.   I saw (*or* watched) him cross*ing* the
street.

Ouvi o homem a cantar esta canção.   I heard (*or* listened to)
the man sing*ing* this song.

Encontrei o carpinteiro a trabalhar.   I found the carpenter
working.

---

[1] This word order is not possible of course when the dependent infinitive has an object.

NOTE: **Vi-o atravessando a rua** (*I saw him crossing the street*) is also found, particularly in Brazilian Portuguese. In European Portuguese it tends to be avoided, although it is by no means excluded. Purists claim, however, that it can only mean *I saw him (as I was) crossing the street.*

(iii) The verbs **deixar** (*to let, allow to, permit to*), **fazer** (*to make*) and **mandar** (*to order to, command to, send to*). These verbs take a *direct* object, but when the dependent infinitive has a *noun* object, they may—and frequently do—take an *indirect* object.

Não deixaram o homem terminar.   They didn't let the man finish.

Fi-lo partir.   I made him leave.

Mandaram-nos fazê-lo.   They ordered/sent us to do it.

Deixei-o ⎫
Deixei-lhe ⎬ **terminar o trabalho.**   I let him finish the work.

Observe that when **fazer** has a *noun* object, this follows the infinitive: **Fiz partir o homem,** *I made the man depart.* Should the infinitive in turn have an object, the construction is abandoned [See § 181 (*a*)]. The infinitive may have passive sense after these verbs, in which case it must come *immediately* after the verb on which it is dependent. Only a weak pronoun object may intervene.

Mandei-o fazer ⎫
Mandei fazê-lo ⎬.   I ordered it to be done, I had it done.

Mandou buscar o médico.   He sent for the doctor.

Fez abrir a janela.   He had the window opened.

(iv) The verbs **aconselhar** (*to advise to*) and **permitir** (*to permit to*). These verbs operate in the same way as those in (iii) above, but with the difference that they should always take an *indirect* object.[1]

Aconselhei-lhe partir.   I advised him to leave.

Permiti ao homem ficar.   I permitted the man to stay.

---

[1] Its use with a *direct* personal object, *plus* **a** *plus infinitive* is not recommended

(v) Certain other verbs when the subject is the same as that of the infinitive. The most common are:

acreditar	to believe (that)	**ousar**	to dare to
ameaçar	to threaten to	**parecer**	to seem, appear to
anelar	to long to		
buscar	to seek to	**pensar**	to intend to; to think (that)
confessar	to confess to -ing		
conseguir	to manage to	**poder**	to be able to, can
costumar	to be wont to	**preferir**	to prefer to, would rather
crer	to believe (that)		
decidir	to decide to	**pretender**	to intend to; to claim to
desejar	to desire, wish to		
determinar	to determine to	**procurar**	to try to, try and
dever	to have to, must	**prometer**	to promise to
dizer	to say (that)	**propor-se**	to propose to
esperar	to hope to	**querer**	to want to
evitar	to avoid -ing	**resolver**	to resolve to
intentar	to intend to	**saber**	to know how to
julgar	to think (that)	**sentir**	to regret to, be sorry to
lograr	to succeed in -ing		
		soer (*rare*)	to be wont to
merecer	to deserve to	**temer**	to fear to
negar	to deny -ing	**tencionar**	to intend to
oferecer	to offer to	**tentar**	to try to, try and

Decidiu não casar com ela. He decided not to marry her.

Parecem duvidar do que digo. They seem to doubt what I say.

Você prometeu não dizê-lo a ninguém. You promised not to tell anyone.

Ela não sabe dançar. She can't dance.

Sinto muito ter de dizer-lhe isto. I regret very much having to tell you this.

NOTES. 1. This construction should be used in Portuguese even where the English has two finite verbs, except that in less literary language a **que** clause is usual after verbs of saying and thinking.

Sinto não podęr acompanhá-lo.　I'm sorry I can't go with you.

Julgo $\begin{Bmatrix} \text{tê-lo visto} \\ \text{que o vi} \end{Bmatrix}$ **nąlguma parte.**　I think I've seen him somewhere.

2. **Ameaçar** is sometimes followed by **com**; **anelar** is sometimes followed by **por**.

3. Students of Spanish should note that nowadays **devęr** rather than **devęr de** translates the *must* of supposition: **Dęvem sęr três hǫras** (*It must be three o'clock*).

4. **Pensar em** renders *to consider -ing*.

(vi) The verbs **ir** (*to go, go and, be going to*) and **vir** (*to come to, come and*).

Vou trabalhar naquęla fábrica.　I'm going to work in that factory.

Vim vęr a senhǫra.　I've come to see you.

Both these verbs are used with a following gerund to indicate the gradualness of an action: **cǫmo ęu ia dizendo** (*as I was saying*), **veio correndo** (*he came running*). **Ir a**+infinitive is occasionally to be found as a stylized literary variant of the more normal **ir**+infinitive; it is also so used dialectally.[1] However, the expression **Vamos a vęr** is a quite normal alternative for **Vamos vęr** (*Let's see*).

Vir a+infinitive is used in a non-literal sense to imply *finally*, and is particularly found in the locutions **vir a sęr** (interchangeable with **chegar a sęr**) and **vir a significar**.

Quando veio a aparecęr?　When did he finally appear?

Veio (*or* **Chegou**) **a sęr rei.**　He came to be (*or* He became) king.

O que vem a significar isso?　What does that come to mean? (*i.e., What is the ultimate significance of that?*)

---

[1] The same applies to **vir a**+infinitive.

NOTE: Ir and vir may very occasionally be followed by para to indicate purpose, particularly when the dependent infinitive does not immediately follow ir and vir:

Fui a casa dos meus avós para lhes dar um presente.
I went to my grandparents' (in order) to give them a present.

(2) *Verb + a + Infinitive*

(i) All other verbs implying motion to a given end, and verbs of stopping for a given end:

Saiu a falar com meu pai. He went out to talk to my father.

Enviaram-me a entregar-lho. They sent me to hand it over to him.

Sentámo-nos a comer. We sat down to eat.

Subiu a ver o que se passava. He went up to see what was happening.

Volta a ver-nos amanhã. He's coming back to see us to-morrow.

Deteve-se a olhar para trás. He stopped to look back.

NOTES: 1. All verbs of this type may also be followed by para (*in order to*) + infinitive, particularly, but not exclusively, to express strong intention. **Correr** (*to run*) may also be used with a pure infinitive without any intervening preposition.

2. For **mandar**, *to send*, see § 174 (1) (iii); **mandar para** + infinitive may also be used, however, to render *to send to*.

3. The verb **voltar a**, besides meaning *to return and*, also means *again*; this function is also fulfilled by **tornar a**:

Voltou ⎱ **a gritar da mesma maneira.** He shouted again in
Tornou ⎰ the same way.

(ii) Verbs of helping, authorizing, learning, teaching, enabling and accustoming, all of which take a *direct* object:

ajudar a	to help to	**habilitar a**	
autorizar a	to authorize to	(*or* **para**)	to enable to
aprender a	to learn (how) to	**acostumar a**	to accustom to
ensinar a	to teach (how) to	**afazer a**	to accustom to
		habituar a	to accustom to

Ajudámos o homem a descer. We helped the man to get down.

Ensinei-o a falar inglês. I taught him to speak English.

(iii) Certain verbs of forcing, inviting and exhorting, all of which take a *direct* object:

animar a	to encourage to, urge to	**incitar a**	to incite to
		induzir a	to induce to
compelir a	to compel to	**levar a**	to cause to
convidar a		**obrigar a**	to oblige to
(*or* **para**)	to invite to	**persuadir a**	to persuade to
forçar a	to force to		

Animaram-no a continuar. They urged him to continue.

Compeliram o homem a partir. They compelled the man to leave.

(iv) Verbs of beginning:

começar a	to begin to	**meter-se a**	to set about -ing
desatar a	to burst out -ing	**pôr-se a**	to start to, -ing
entrar a	to set about -ing	**principiar a**	to begin to
largar a	to set about -ing	**romper a**	to start to, -ing

Começa a chover. It's beginning to rain.

Desatou a chorar. She burst out crying.

NOTE: Other less common verbs of beginning are **dar a, deitar a** and **empeçar a**.

(v) *Reflexive* verbs of deciding:

decidir-se a to decide to   **resolver-se a** to resolve to

NOTE: When used non-reflexively these verbs are used without an intervening proposition. Thus:

Decidiu
Decidiu-se a} **ir embora.** He decided to go away.

(vi) Certain other verbs (most of which are reflexive), the most common being:

acostumar-se a	to get used to -ing	habituar-se a	to get used to -ing
aspirar a	to aspire to	negar-se a	to refuse to
atrever-se a	to dare to	ocupar-se a	to busy oneself -ing
compro-meter-se a	to undertake to	opor-se a	to object to -ing
divertir-se a	to amuse oneself -ing	resignar-se a	to resign oneself to -ing
entreter-se a	to amuse oneself -ing	tardar a	to take a long time -ing
expor-se a	to expose oneself to -ing		

Como te atreves a falar-lhe dessa maneira? How do you dare to speak to him in that way?

Negou-se a acompanhar-nos. He refused to come with us.

Não tardou muito a chegar. It wasn't long before he arrived.

NOTE: **tardar** may also be followed by **em** before a dependent infinitive.

(vii) Three constructions may have either the *gerund* or **a** +*infinitive* to express the dependent verb of English, the latter construction being more common:

continuar $\begin{Bmatrix} \text{a fazer} \\ \text{fazendo} \end{Bmatrix}$ to continue $\begin{Bmatrix} \text{to do} \\ \text{doing} \end{Bmatrix}$

levar tempo $\begin{Bmatrix} \text{a fazer} \\ \text{fazendo} \end{Bmatrix}$ to take time $\begin{Bmatrix} \text{to do} \\ \text{doing} \end{Bmatrix}$

passar (o) tempo $\begin{Bmatrix} \text{a fazer} \\ \text{fazendo} \end{Bmatrix}$ to spend (the) time doing

(viii) The impersonal verb **custar** (*to be difficult*) may optionally be followed by **a**:

Custou-me muito (a) fazer isso. I found it very difficult to do that.

(3) *Verb* + **de** + *Infinitive*

(i) Verbs that indicate separation from an action (*i.e.*, leaving off, finishing, etc.):

acabar de	to finish -ing	**fartar-se de**	to grow tired of -ing
cansar-se de	to grow tired of -ing	**guardar-se de**	to take care not to
cessar de	to cease -ing		
deixar de	to leave off -ing stop -ing	**parar de**	to cease -ing
		terminar de	to finish -ing
não deixar de	not to fail to, be sure to		

Acabou (*or* **Terminou**) **de o lêr.** He finished reading it.

Cansou-se de não fazer nada. She grew tired of doing nothing.

NOTE: **Acabar de** also means *to have just* (§ 132).

(ii) Verbs that indicate forgiveness for,[1] or exemption, prevention or dissuasion from an action. They are followed by a *direct* object:

desculpar de	to forgive for -ing	**impedir de**	to prevent from -ing
dissuadir de	to dissuade from -ing	**isentar de**	to exempt from -ing
empecer de	to prevent from -ing	**proibir de**	to forbid to, prohibit from -ing
escusar de	to excuse from -ing		

Dissuadi-a de ir sozinha. I dissuaded her from going alone.

Escusei o homem de terminá-lo. I excused the man from finishing it.

(iii) The verbs **acusar** and **encarregar**. They are followed by a *direct* object:

---

[1] But **perdoar** (*to pardon, forgive*) takes *indirect object* + **o** + *perfect infinitive*: **Perdoei-lhe o ter-me insultado** (*I forgave him for insulting me*).

acusar de   to accuse of -ing   **encarregar de**   to entrust
with -ing

Acusei-o de tẹr-me roubado cem escudos.
I accused him of having stolen 100 escudos from me.
Encarregaram os sọldados de protegẹr as casas.
They entrusted the soldiers with protecting the houses.

(iv) Certain other verbs of which the most common are:

alegrar-se de	to be glad to	**maravilhar-se de**	to wonder at -ing, marvel at -ing
arrependẹr-se de	to repent of -ing	**necessitar de**	to need to
contentar-se de	to content oneself with -ing	**ọlvidar-se de**	to forget to
desesperar de	to despair of -ing	**não podẹr deixar de**	not to be able to help -ing
encarregar-se de	to undertake to	**precisar de**	to need to
envergo-nhar-se de	to be ashamed of -ing	**recordar-se de**	to remember to
esquẹcẹr-se de	to forget to	**tẹr de**	to have to
fọlgar de	to rejoice in -ing	**tẹr (o) tempo de**	to have (the) time to
gostar de	to like to, -ing	**tratar de**	to deal with -ing, see about -ing
havẹr de	to be to, have to		
jạctar-se de	to boast of -ing	**tratar-se de**	to be a question of -ing
lembrar-se de	to remember to		

Não se lembrou de tê-lo visto.   He didn't remember having
seen him.
Alẹgro-me muito de conhecê-lo.   I am very pleased to know
you.
Encarregou-se de falar com ẹle.   He undertook to have a
talk with him.
Não pọsso deixar de aprovar a sua ạcção.   I cannot (help)
but approve of his action.

NOTES. 1. **Necessitar** and **precisar** are sometimes used without **de**.

2. **Ter de** is interchangeable with **ter que** (though this latter is more common in Brazilian Portuguese).

3. **Ter (o) tempo de** is interchangeable with **ter (o) tempo para**.

4. **Contentar-se de** is interchangeable with **contentar-se com**.

(4) *Verb* + **em** + *Infinitive*

Important verbs that take **em** are:

comprazer-se em	to take pleasure in -ing	**fazer mal em**	to do badly (*or* wrong) to
concordar em	to agree to	**hesitar em**	to hesitate to
consentir em	to consent to	**insistir em**	to insist on -ing
consistir em	to consist in -ing	**pensar em**	to think of -ing
convir em	to agree to	**perseverar em**	to persevere in -ing
empenhar-se em	to insist on -ing	**persistir em**	to persist in -ing
fazer bem em	to do well (*or* right) to	**porfiar em**	to persevere in -ing
		teimar em	to insist on -ing
		vacilar em	to hesitate to

Ele empenha-se em fazer a mesma coisa. He insists on doing the same.

Fazes mal em o não ajudar. You do wrong not to help him.

Não hesitou em aceitar tal condição. He did not hesitate to accept such a condition.

(5) *Verb* + **por** + *Infinitive*

Important verbs that take **por** are:

acabar por	to finish, end up (by) -ing	**estar por**	*see* § 74 (*b*)
anelar por	to long to	**lutar por**	to fight, struggle to
começar por	to begin by -ing	**pelejar por**	to fight to
esforçar-se por	to strive to	**principiar por**	to begin by -ing
		suspirar por	to sigh, yearn to

| terminar | to finish, end up | **trabalhar** | |
| **por** | by -ing | **por** | to work to |

Esforça-se por fazê-lo bem. He strives to do it well.
Acabou por se matar. He ended up by killing himself.

(6) *Verb* + **com** + *Infinitive*

Common verbs that take **com** are:

| conformar-
se com | to resign one-
self to -ing | **sonhar com**
contar | to dream of -ing |
| | | **(com)** | to count on -ing |

Sonhava com morar no campo. He dreamed of living in the country.
Conforma-se com anotar os exemplos. He resigns himself to jotting down the examples.
Contava (com) partir cędo. I was counting on leaving early.

(7) *Verb* + **pąra** + *Infinitive*

| preparar-se | | **servir pąra** | to serve to |
| **pąra** | to prepare to | **estar pąra** | see § 74 (*b*) |

Ęste instrumento sęrve pąra medir a fǫrça do vento. This instrument serves to measure the force of the wind.

NOTES. 1. See also § 174 (2) (i), (ii), (iii) and 3 (iv).
2. The verb **pedir** is also used with **pąra** + infinitive; it has two meanings: *to ask to*, and *to ask permission to*. Similarly used is the rarer verb **rogar** (*to ask*).

Pedi ao hǫmem pąra sair. {
I asked the man to go out.
I asked the man('s) permission to go out.[1]
}

[1] To avoid possible confusion the word **licença** may be inserted:
   Pedi-lhe licença pąra sair.

3. In very colloquial usage, the verbs of command **dizẹr** and **dar ọrdem** may take **pạra** + infinitive or even **de** + infinitive in the case of **dizẹr**. Like **pedir** and **rogar** they take an indirect object.

Disse
Dei ọrdem } ao sọldado pạra entrar.   I { told } the soldier
                                           { ordered } to come in.

VOCABULARY

Study all the verbs and constructions listed in § 174.

EXERCISES

I. (*a*) *Study and translate:* Encarregou-se de no-la enviar. Consenti em não dizer nada a ninguém. Conseguiu chegar a tempo. Animei-o a seguir. Impeço-o de ir. Aconselhei-lhe a voltar cedo. Vimo-lo matar. Esforçou-se por terminá-lo. Fi-lo sair. Resignámo-nos a não o ver. Envergonhei-me de o ter pensado. Arrependeu-se de tê-lo feito. Eles propõem-se fazê-lo já. Alegra-me ver-te. Alegro-me de ver-te. Peço licença para sair.

(*b*) *Translate:* I let her go alone. We were sorry to have to leave. He feared to come. She has just come in. Are you trying to do the same thing? I succeeded in visiting her. She advised the soldier to go away. He wouldn't let me in. We avoided looking at her. They saw him kill the captain. She repented of having told him so. The captain told the soldier to come in. He forbade him to do it again. The little old lady hesitated to get off the bus.

II. (*a*) *Study and translate:* 1. Nunca deixo de dizer-lhes quanto faço com os meus filhos. 2. Foi só nessa altura que principiou a sentir-se doentinha e a insistir em voltar para casa. 3. Alguns dias acorda-me às sete e meia e outros deixa-me continuar a dormir até por volta das oito. 4. Não pôde encontrá-los e agora sentiu muito ter-lhes contado o que dizia o telegrama que lhe havia enviado seu pai. 5. Porque é que teima em crer que eu quero enganá-lo? 6. O simples facto é que me custa muito trabalho a acostumar-me à ideia de morar sozinha numa vila tão pequena como esta. 7. Tem-se dito que ela fez muito mal em não responder à carta que lhe expedíramos. 8. Precisa procurar ter tudo já feito para a semana que vem. 9. Quando soube isto disse-me que ia resignar-se a voltar para a cidade. 10. Todos gostámos da ideia de ir passar o Verão para casa dos tios.

(b) *Translate:* 1. In my opinion he's going to take a long time to arrive. 2. I had just finished reading the last chapter when she came to say good-bye. 3. His wife insisted on inviting Mr and Mrs Costa to lunch with us. 4. If I remember aright, I seem to think I've seen her somewhere. 5. I forgot to tell him that my uncle wanted to come and see me. 6. We have promised not to say anything to anybody. 7. It was at that time that Mary was beginning to teach him to speak French. 8. We have heard that your aunt has been a trifle ill. 9. As David's mother wasn't feeling well (*use* **sentir-se**) we decided to send for the doctor immediately. 10. A year ago I thought you weren't working [hard] enough and now it surprises me to see you working so hard (*use* **tanto**).

III. (a) *Study and translate:* 1. Eram quase onze horas da noite quando ela se decidiu a voltar para casa. 2. Também ele voltara a ter vontade de correr para casa. 3. Miguel! continuava a não encontrar as palavras que desejava. 4. Estive a pensar nas cartas e como agora, com a guerra, tardam muito a chegar. 5. Por tua causa não se atrevera a dizer nada a ninguém. 6. Quando a via atravessar da porta à cozinha, erguia-se da poltrona e corria ao seu encontro. 7. Resolvi-me a voltar para a Praça dos Restauradores e pus-me a andar pela Avenida da Liberdade. 8. Agrada-me sempre descansar após um dia de muito trabalho. 9. A ideia consiste em ir comprando casas para logo as vender mais caras. 10. Estávamos cansadas da visita e de andar todo o tempo falando de coisas tão pouco importantes.

(b) *Translate:* 1. I asked him how long it would take the train to arrive. 2. She speaks Spanish and now she is beginning to learn Catalan. 3. We attempted to persuade him to believe that all this is true. 4. I am pleased to know you don't regret having helped me to do so. 5. Both boys agreed to wait until next week. 6. What will you do, seeing that your father refuses to help you? 7. All three of them long to visit Morocco, but they won't be able to go. 8. How will they prevent him from telling it to his mother? 9. He ordered them to go and see him at once. 10. As I promise to say nothing to your father, will you undertake to come back tomorrow?

LESSON XXVIII

175. ADJECTIVES AND NOUNS WITH AN INFINITIVE. (*a*) An adjective or noun is followed by the pure infinitive only when that infinitive can be considered as the real subject of the sentence. This is frequently the case after verbs such as **ser, tornar-se,** and **parecer.**

É fácil fazer isto. It is easy to do this (To do this is easy).
É impossível vê-lo hoje. It is impossible to see him today.
Não parecia difícil fazê-lo. It did not seem difficult to do it.
Parece prudente deixá-lo sòzinho. It seems wise to leave him alone.
Não vale a pena fazê-lo. It is not worth while doing it.
É meu dever dizer-lhe a verdade. It is my duty to tell him the truth.

(*b*) If the infinitive cannot be considered as the subject of the finite verb a preposition must be used. This preposition is usually **de.**

Isto é fácil de fazer. This is easy to do.
Tornou-se-nos impossível de fazer. It proved impossible for us to do.
É meu o dever de lhe dizer a verdade. The duty of telling him the truth is mine.
Tinha medo de nos ver. He was afraid of seeing us.
São horas de ir-nos embora. It is time for us to go.
Tenho o costume de a visitar. I'm in the habit (*lit.,* have the habit) of visiting her.

(*c*) Prepositions other than **de** are used in certain limited cases, of which the following are the most important.

282

(1) **A** is normally used after the noun **tendência** (*tendency*), and with certain adjectives most of which indicate tendency (imposed or from within) towards a given action, or which are numerical adjectives.

acostumado a	accustomed to
afeiçoado a	fond of -ing
atento a	attentive to -ing
convidado a (*or* **pạra**)	invited to
decidido a	determined to
dispọsto a	prepared to, willing to
entretido a	busy -ing
inclinado a	inclined to
ọbrigado a	obliged to
ọcupado a	busy -ing

o primeiro (único, último) a   the first (only one, last one) to

NOTE: The corresponding nouns usually take **de**: **o costume de trabalhar** (*the habit of working*), **a ọbrigação de gạnhar a vida** (*the obligation to earn one's living*).

(2) **Em** is used in the following expressions:

tẹr empenho em	to insist on -ing
tẹr gọsto em	to be pleased to
tẹr prazẹr em	to be pleased to
tẹr prẹssa em	to be in a hurry to
havẹr inconveniente em	to be a snag in
vẹr inconveniente em	to see a snag in

Tem empenho em fazẹr a mẹsma cọisa.   He insists on doing the same.

Não há inconveniente em pensá-lo.   There is nothing against thinking it.

(3) **Pạra** is used:

(i) in expressions of motive and aim.

Não tem motivo pạra chorar.
He has no cause for tears (*lit.*, weeping).

Não é mais que um pretẹxto pạra não ir.
It is only a pretext for not going.

É o passo mais sério que se dẹu pạra chegar a uma solução.
It is the most serious step that has been taken to reach a solution.

(ii) in expressions of suitability and adequacy.

Não tẹve fọrças pạra o fazẹr.
He hadn't the strength to do it.

Tenho o necessário pạra vivẹr.
I have what is necessary to live on.

É um momento ọportuno pạra lhe falar.
It is a suitable moment to talk to him.

Ẹra uma cọisa íntima demais pạra discutir diante de teste-munhas.
It was too intimate a matter to talk of in front of witnesses.

Tem o ouvido pouco apto pạra apreciar ẹstes matizes.
His ear is ill-suited to the appreciation of these nuances.

(4) **Por** is used with nouns expressing haste and striving, and usually after **contente**.

Não fẹz nenhum esfọrço por aclarar a sua própria atitude.
He made no effort to clarify his own attitude.

Ẹu estou contente por/de/em estar aqui.
I'm glad to be here.

176. VERBS, ADJECTIVES AND NOUNS WITH A CLAUSE. A verb, adjective or noun which takes a preposition before an infinitive *may* take the same preposition before the **que** that introduces a corresponding noun clause. It is quite optional and may be omitted, particularly in conversation.

Lembrou-se (de) que não estavas.   He remembered you were not in.

É uma prọva (de) que ẹla me ama.   It is (a) proof that she loves me.

Estou cẹrto (de) que o conhẹces.   I am sure you know him.

NOTE: If the noun clause can be considered as the subject of the main verb no preposition is used.

É cęrto que vǫltou já. It is certain that he has already come back (That he has already come back is certain).

177. THE USES OF eis. The interjection **eis** (*this is, see here*) is followed by nouns, noun clauses, weak pronoun objects or adverbs. Before the weak pronoun objects **o, a, os, as** it behaves in the same way as verb-forms ending in **r, s** or **z**. Its use is somewhat literary.

Eis os resultados da sua tolice. Behold the results of their folly.

Eis o que queria dizęr. This is what I meant.

Ei-lo aqui. Here he is.

Eis cǫmo se faz a ǫperação. This is how the operation is carried out.

178. THE IRREGULAR VERBS jazęr AND prazęr. (*a*) **jazęr,** *to lie* (positionally). This verb is irregular only in the third person singular of the present indicative: **jaz.** Formerly there were other irregularities also, but these have now been replaced by regular forms. The verb is somewhat rare.

Aqui jaz fulano. Here lies so-and-so.

(*b*) **prazęr,** *to be pleasing.* This verb is obsolete and survives only in the noun **o prazęr** (*pleasure*) and in the expressions

$$\left.\begin{array}{l}\textbf{Praza}\\\textbf{Prouvęra}\end{array}\right\} \textbf{a Dęus que} + subjunctive \quad \text{Would to God that...}$$

It is irregular in the third person singular of the present indicative: **praz;** and in the preterite: **prouve.** Its compounds, **aprazęr** (*to be pleasing*), **comprazęr** (*to be pleasing*), **desprazęr** (*to be displeasing*) and **comprazęr-se em** (*to take pleasure in*) are not entirely obsolete, though somewhat literary, and are conjugated similarly. Their preterites are usually avoided.

Apraz-me muito sabęr isso. I'm pleased to know that.

Comprazia-se sempre em acompanhar-me. He always took pleasure in going with me.

VOCABULARY

Study the words and constructions listed in §§ 175–8.

EXERCISES

I. (a) *Study and translate:* Parecia-me difícil acabá-lo. Tem empenho em contar-mo. Sou afeiçoado a fazer tal. Temos todos o costume de tomar em conta o tempo que faz. Pareceu-lhe mais prudente partir. O primeiro soldado a ver o general. Aqui jaz Vasco da Gama. É muito fácil cozinhar uma galinha. Eis porque se decidira a voltar para casa. Aprouve-lhe muito saber da chegada dela.

(b) *Translate:* It proved impossible to begin the work. I found myself obliged to call on him. He is the only one not to know it. The habit of studying hard. He had no cause to do it. We made every effort to speak to her. It's not an opportune moment for taking such a step. They are very pleased to hear he's gone. He was always looking for a pretext for arguing with us. It's useless to try and discuss it with him. I'm sure he won't come.

II. (a) *Study and translate:* 1. Eis porque não lhe agrada a ideia de falar contigo. 2. Sou muito afeiçoado a discutir semelhantes projectos, mas não estou acostumado a aguentar tanta confusão. 3. Se bem me lembro, ias contando-me que não valia a pena seguir com o trabalho. 4. Na terça passada explicou-me que era seu o dever de dizer-me o que acontecera. 5. Principiou por negar tudo quanto já se dissera acerca do problema. 6. Ao terminar a tarefa viu-se obrigado a confessar que eu tivera razão. 7. Apesar de todas as dificuldades que o preocupavam conseguiu ficar atento aos problemas de outrem. 8. A seu ver é inútil continuar assim sem falar com ninguém. 9. Disse-me que a questão era séria demais para se discutir diante dos filhos. 10. Bem sei que não vês inconveniente algum nas relações que tens connosco, mas deves confessar que as coisas podem tornar-se difíceis para todos.

(b) *Translate:* 1. It's of no use whatsoever talking like that, especially if he doesn't know her. 2. Such a nuance is too difficult to grasp. 3. In spite of his tendency to be optimistic, he thinks he can see a snag in deceiving his mother in this way. 4. He refused to agree with what I had said. 5. Mary was the last to arrive at the party and the first to leave. 6. The soldier's corpse lay in the field for a long time without being discovered. 7. Herr Müller didn't appreciate the importance of entrusting the Danes with carrying on with the project. 8. Martin doesn't seem to understand the value of going to bed early. 9. It's not easy to prevent the child from crying when he insists on doing so. 10. It was only then that she remembered that she had to go to the post-office.

III. (a) *Study and translate:* 1. Foi o primeiro a saber que alguém tentava liquidar a sua mulher. 2. Os jornais norte-americanos continuavam a falar de fome e de frio na Europa. 3. Um inglês nosso conhecido explicou-nos que o seu país não podia continuar assim. 4. Nessa noite não fora para a cidade, mas António lembrava-se de que ele havia ido lá na noite anterior. 5. O velhote contou-me que o vira entrar, de manhãzinha, na fábrica. 6. Mas, pelas palavras que ouvia, pareceu a José que eles não diziam tudo quanto pensavam. 7. Ela confessou-nos que ainda não tinha o necessário para comprar um carro novo. 8. Estou decidida a fazer todo o possível para resolver este problema. 9. Estávamos com muita pressa em partir, porque nao queríamos perder[1] o comboio. 10. Ele diz que me ama, mas parece-me que me está enganando.

(b) *Translate:* 1. When the waiter brought him a bottle of champagne he began to repent of what he had said. 2. It was useless to long to be a teacher because he knew he wasn't very clever. 3. He took the horse to the water but unfortunately he couldn't make it drink. 4. When Michael

---

[1]**perder,** to lose; to miss (*trains, buses, planes, etc.*).

entered the classroom he came to understand the folly of his actions. 5. He decided that it would be much wiser to let his daughter go to bed later. 6. The teacher felt it was useless but he told the boy he didn't like his attitude. 7. At times it proved easy to find a pretext for not working as hard as he should. 8. What displeased him more than anything (=all) was that he hadn't even got the strength to lift the dining-room chairs. 9. He told us that that was how (**que ęra assim cǫmo**) the operation would finally be carried out. 10. Surely he can find another way of earning his living!

LESSON XXIX

179. THE FORMATION OF THE PRESENT SUBJUNCTIVE. (*a*) The Present Subjunctive is formed, *with seven exceptions*, by taking the stem of the first person singular of the present indicative (be it regular, irregular or radical-changing) and adding the following endings:

I. **-ar** verbs: **-e, -es, -e, -ęmos, -eis, -em.**
II. **-ęr** verbs: **-a, -as, -a, -amos, -ais, -am.**
III. **-ir** verbs: **-a, -as, -a, -amos, -ais, -am.**

(*b*) Radical-changing verbs conserve in the present subjunctive the quality of the radical vowel of the *first person singular* of the present indicative, whenever the radical is stressed. Whenever the radical is unstressed, the quality of the radical vowel is the same as it would be in similar circumstances in the present indicative. This will be made clear by the following scheme which illustrates regular, radical-changing, and irregular verbs.

comprar: compro: compre, compres, compre, comprę-mos, compreis, comprem.

vendęr: vendo: venda, vendas, venda, vendamos, ven-damos, vendais, vendam.

franzir: franzo: franza, franzas, franza, franzamos, franzais, franzam.

levar: lęvo: lęve, lęves, lęve, levęmos, leveis, lęvem.

bǫiar: bóio: bóie, bóies, bóie, bǫięmos, bǫieis, bóiem.

devęr: dęvo: dęva, dęvas, dęva, devamos, devais, dęvam.

movęr: mǫvo: mǫva, mǫvas, mǫva, movamos, mo-vais, mǫvam.

tẹr:	tenho:	tenha, tenhas, tenha, tenhamos, tenhais, tenham.
pôr:	pọnho:	pọnha, pọnhas, pọnha, ponhamos, po- nhais, pọnham.
pedir:	pẹço:	pẹça, pẹças, pẹça, peçamos, peçais, pẹçam.

(c) The **recear** and **ọdiar** types behave as follows:

| recear: | receio: | receie, receies, receie, receẹmos, receeis, receiem. |
| ọdiar: | ọdeio: | ọdeie, ọdeies, ọdeie, ọdiẹmos, ọdieis, ọdeiem. |

The irregular verbs **crẹr** and **lẹr** do not behave similarly:

| crẹr: | creio: | creia, creias, creia, creiamos, creiais, creiam. |
| lẹr: | leio: | leia, leias, leia, leiamos, leiais, leiam. |

(d) Radical-changing verbs of the third conjugation which have a radical change of **e** to **i** or **o** to **u** in the first person singular of the present indicative exhibit this change in all six forms of the present subjunctive.

servir:	sirvo:	sirva, sirvas, sirva, sirvamos, sirvais, sirvam.
sentir:	sinto:	sinta, sintas, sinta, sintamos, sintais, sintam.
despir:	dispo:	dispa, dispas, dispa, dispamos, dispais, dispam.
agredir:	agrido:	agrida, agridas, agrida, agridamos, agridais, agridam.
dormir:	durmo:	durma, durmas, durma, durmamos, durmais, durmam.
polir:	pulo:	pula, pulas, pula, pulamos, pulais, pulam.

(e) The *seven* exceptions referred to in (a) are the following:

dar:	dou:	dê, dês, dê, dêmos, deis, dêem.
estar:	estou:	esteja, estejas, esteja, estejamos, estejais, estejam.
ser:	sou:	seja, sejas, seja, sejamos, sejais, sejam.
ir:	vou:	vá, vás, vá, vamos, vades, vão.
haver:	hei:	haja, hajas, haja, hajamos, hajais, hajam.
saber:	sei:	saiba, saibas, saiba, saibamos, saibais, saibam.
querer:	quero:	queira, queiras, queira, queiramos, queirais, queiram.

180. THE PERFECT SUBJUNCTIVE.   This is formed by the present subjunctive of **ter** with the appropriate past participle.   It need *not* have any of the continuous functions of its indicative counterpart.

> **que tenha comprado**   that I (may, should) have bought
> **que tenhas vendido**   that you (may, should) have sold

NOTES: 1. There exists also a perfect subjunctive formed with **haver** as the auxiliary, *e.g.*, **haja comprado**; this is archaic, highly literary and should be avoided by the student.   It is the subjunctive equivalent of **hei comprado** (§ 129, note 2).

2. The English perfect subjunctive [*that I (may, should) have bought*] is also sometimes rendered by the Portuguese Imperfect Subjunctive [see Lesson XXX and especially the first example of § 185 (b)].

181. THE USE OF THE SUBJUNCTIVE.   The subjunctive is most frequently used in subordinate clauses in which the action of the verb is not presented as a fact or reality, but rather as a hypothesis or possibility.   It is thus used:

(a) After verbs, adjectives and nouns that imply influence on other people or things (*i.e.*, expressions of wanting, requesting, permitting, forbidding, causing, necessity, etc.). The desired or forbidden or necessary action is not at the moment a fact; it must be made one, or prevented from becoming one.

Deseja que me vá embǫra. He wants me to go away.

Prefiro que o faças tu. I prefer *you* to do it.

Está a pedir que se faça isto. He's asking for this to be done.

Não devęmos permitir-lhe que vá. We must not let him go.

Proíbe a sęu filho que vǫlte. He forbids your son to come back.

Faręmos (com) que se alua a ponte. We shall make the bridge collapse.

Diz-lhe que se vá embǫra. Tell him to go away.

Vou mandar-lhe que o faça hǫje. I'm going to order him to do it today.

Deseja persuadir-me que os acompanhe. He wants to persuade me to go with them.

É preciso que ęles vão (*subj.*) **também.** *They* must go too.

É preciso que falęmos com o ąutǫr. It is necessary for us to speak to the author.

NOTES: 1. In sentences of the type *I prefer to go, He asks to go, He let himself fall*, where the wanting, requesting, etc., is aimed at one's own actions, Portuguese uses an infinitive construction:

   Prefiro ir, Pęde pąra ir, Deixou-se cair.

2. The infinitive construction may be used also with certain verbs of advising, making, ordering, requesting, telling and permitting even where the influence is on another person's actions.

Aconselho-lhe fazê-lo. **Aconselho-lhe que o faça.**	I advise him to do it.
Faço-o fazê-lo. **Faço (com) que o faça.**	I make him do it.
Mando-o fazê-lo. **Mando-lhe que o faça.**	I order him to do it.
Pęco-lhe pąra fazê-lo. **Pęco-lhe pąra o fazęr.** **Pęco-lhe que o faça.**	I request him to do it.

Digo-lhe pąra fazê-lo.
Digo-lhe pąra o fazęr.   }   I tell him to do it.
Digo-lhe que o faça.

Permito-lhe fazê-lo.   }   I permit him to do it.
Permito-lhe que o faça.

Observe carefully the constructions with **fazęr,** the use of prepositions where there are any, and whether the verb in question takes a direct or indirect object.

3. Verbs of preventing and forbidding have two possible constructions: either with *direct object* + *de* + *infinitive*, or with *indirect object* + **que** + *subjunctive*.

Impeço o hǫmem de vir.   }   I prevent the man from
Impeço ao hǫmem que venha.   coming.

Proíbo o hǫmem de vir.   }   I forbid the man to come.
Proíbo ao hǫmem que venha.

4. Verbs implying stimulus to action [see § 174 (2) (iii)] may take **a** + *infinitive* or (**a**) **que** + *subjunctive*. The verb **levar** may take only **a** + *infinitive*, however.

Anima			urges	
Compęle			compels	
Convida			invites	
Fǫrça	o hǫmem	a vir *or* (a) que venha.	forces	He ... the man to come.
Incita			incites	
Induz			induces	
Ǫbriga			obliges	
Persuade			persuades	

but only **Lęva o hǫmem a vir.** He causes the man to come.

Remember that **convidar** *can* be used with **pąra** instead of **a.**

5. The verbs **implorar** (*to implore*), **suplicar** (*to entreat*) and **ǫrdenar** (*to order*) are used only with *indirect object* + **que** + *subjunctive*.

Imploramos			implore	
Suplicamos	ao hǫmem que o faça.	We	entreat	the man to do it.
Ǫrdenamos			order	

6. Verbs of wanting, preferring and needing *someone else* to do something may take only **que** + *subjunctive*.

Desejo			I want		
Prefiro	}	que o faça.	I prefer	}	him to do it.
Preciso			I need		

Observe that **Preciso que o faça** implies: *I have need that he should do it.* **Preciso dęle pąra fazê-lo/o fazęr** has a different nuance: *I need him in order (to help me) to do it.*

(*b*) When the statement in the subordinate clause is presented as probably or certainly contrary to fact.

Duvido que venha. I doubt whether he will come (*i.e.*, the statement *he will come* is probably false).

Nęga que seja assim. He denies it is so (*i.e.*, the statement *it is so* is presented as false).

É incrívęl que ęle tenha dito cǫisas assim. It is incredible that he should have said things like that.

Não é cęrto que ęle esteja a trabalhar. It isn't true that he's working.

Não creio que se resǫlva dęsse mǫdo. I don't think it will be solved in that way.

Não paręce que esteja com razão. It does not seem that he is right.

Contrast:

Não duvido que virá. I don't doubt that he will come (*i.e.*, the statement *he will come* is considered to be true).

Creio que não irá. I think he will not go (*i.e.*, the statement *he will not go* is probably true).

Estou convencido (de) que o veręmos. I'm convinced we shall see him.

É evidente que não podęmos ir. It is obvious that we cannot go.

Paręce que está com razão. It seems that he is right.

NOTES. 1. After an open question the indicative is usual:
    (Não) crês que é verdade? Do(n't) you think it's true?

though a subjunctive may occasionally be used to indicate particular doubt.

2: After the negative imperative (see § 195) of a verb of *thinking* or *saying*, the indicative is used:

Não creias que sou maluco.   Don't think I'm mad.

(*c*) After impersonal expressions other than those which emphasize that something is *true* or *evident*.

É possível, provável, estranho, lógico, natural, etc.,
$\left\{\begin{array}{l}\textbf{que o faça}\\\textbf{que o tenha feito}\end{array}\right\}$.

It's possible, probable, strange, logical, natural, etc.,
$\left\{\begin{array}{l}\text{that he should do it}\\\text{that he has (}or\text{ should have) done it}\end{array}\right\}$.

but **É verdade, evidente, certo, óbvio, manifesto,** etc.,
$\left\{\begin{array}{l}\textbf{que o faz}\\\textbf{que o fez}\end{array}\right\}$.

It's true, evident, certain, obvious, clear, etc.,
$\left\{\begin{array}{l}\text{that he does it}\\\text{that he has done (}or\text{ did) it}\end{array}\right\}$.

(*d*) After subordinating conjunctions when they introduce future or otherwise hypothetical action.

Avisar-te-ei $\left\{\begin{array}{l}\textbf{assim}\\\textbf{logo}\end{array}\right\}$ **que se vá embora.**
I shall let you know as soon as he goes.

but **Despeço-me** $\left\{\begin{array}{l}\textbf{assim}\\\textbf{logo}\end{array}\right\}$ **que se apresenta seu pai.**
I take my leave as soon as his father appears.

Não iremos enquanto não responda à nossa carta.
We shall not go as long as he does not answer our letter.

but **Não o vemos enquanto seu primo está em Madrid.**
We don't see him while his cousin is in Madrid.

Ficarás aqui até que venha.
You will stay here until he comes.

but **Ficam de pé até que sai o presidente.**
    They remain standing until the president leaves.

Fazem-no em segrędo de maneira que ęle não saiba.
    They do it in secret so that he will not know.

but **Fazem-no em segrędo, de maneira que ęle não sabe.**
    They are doing it in secret with the result that he does not
    find out.

Quando
Sempre que } **o veja dar-lhe-ei os bons dias.**

When
Whenever } I see him I'll wish him good morning.

but **Quando**
Sempre que } **o vejo dou-lhe os bons dias.**

When
Whenever } I see him I wish him good morning.

NOTE: **Lǫgo que, assim que, enquanto, sempre que** and especially **quando** are also, and much more commonly, followed by the
future subjunctive [see § 190 (*a*)], when used with reference to future
action.

(*e*) After the expressions **onde quęr que** (*wherever*), **cǫmo
quęr que** (*however*) and **quem quęr que** (*whoever*), when they
introduce future or otherwise hypothetical action.   In practice
the subjunctive tends also to be used even when this is not the
case.   For all general purposes, therefore, the student should
avoid the use of the indicative in this construction.

Onde quęr que vivam os hǫmens haverá estupidęz.
    Wherever men live there will be stupidity.

Ęla não o conhęce, quem quęr que seja.
    She doesn't know him, whoever he is.

**Pąra onde quęr que vá o Inglês, compǫrta-se sempre cǫmo
na sua própria casa.**
    Wherever the Englishman goes, he always behaves as if in his
    own home.

Cọmo quẹr que ⎱ se estude o projẹcto, chẹga-se
De quạlquẹr maneira que⎰ sempre à mẹsma conclusão.

However ⎱ one studies the plan, one always arrives at
In whatever way⎰ the same conclusion.

NOTE: **Quạlquẹr** in the last example is the adjective or pronoun
which translates (*any*) *what(so)ever, whichever*. Its plural is
quạisquẹr. Note also the expressions **quạlquẹr que seja** (*whatever is* or *may be*) and **o que quẹr que seja** (*whatever it is* or *may be*).

Insisto em fazê-lo, quạisquẹr que sejam as suas ọbjẹcções.
I insist on doing it, whatever his objections (are [*or* may be]).

Não gọsto dẹstas invenções modẹrnas, rádio, televisão ou o que quẹr que seja.
I don't like these modern inventions, radio, television or whatever it may be.

(*f*) After expressions of the formula **por** (+**mais** *or* **muito**)
+*adjective or adverb*+**que** (*however*), **por**+**mais** *or* **muito -a
-os -as**+*noun*+**que** (*however much, however many*), when they
indicate future or otherwise hypothetical action. In practice, the
subjunctive tends also to be used even when this is not the case.
For all general purposes, therefore, the student should avoid the
use of the indicative in this construction.

Não o creio por muito que mo digas.
I don't believe it however much you tell me so.

Por muito longe que seja já não pọdem tardar muito.
No matter how far it may be, they can't take much longer now.

Por mais que digas, estás muito nervọso.
No matter how much you say, you're very nervous.

Nunca o esquẹcerá por muitos anos que viva.
However many years he lives he'll never forget it.

Por muito atrevido que seja o projẹcto, há-de tẹr êxito.
No matter how daring the plan is, it's bound to succeed.

(*g*) After certain conjunctions and related phrases which *always* take the subjunctive.

(1) **antes (de) que** (*before*), **primeiro que** (*before*), **a fim (de) que** (*in order that*), **para que** (*in order that*), because with these conjunctions the action of the subordinate clause is never a reality at the time of the action of the main clause.

Chęga sempre $\begin{Bmatrix} \text{antes} \\ \text{primeiro} \end{Bmatrix}$ que ęu me vá embǫra.

He always arrives before I go away.

Escręve-nos amiúde $\begin{Bmatrix} \text{pąra} \\ \text{a fim} \end{Bmatrix}$ que sąibamos onde está.

He writes to us frequently so that we may know where he is.

(2) **sem que** (*without*), **não (é) que** ([*it is*] *not that*), **não é porque** (*it is not because*), for the action of the subordinate clause is rejected as contrary to fact, or, in the latter instances, if not contrary to fact, then at least irrelevant.

Fá-lo sem que o ajude ninguém.
He does it without help from anybody.

Não (é) que o ache antipático.
(It is) not that I find him unlikeable.

Ǫdeiam-se um ao outro e não é porque sejam rivais.
They hate one another and it is not because they are rivals.

NOTE: Similarly, the subjunctive is used after **ou porque ... ou porque ...**, *either because ... or because ...*, for the explanation in the subordinate clause is open to doubt.

Não vai ęste ano, ou porque não pǫssa ou porque não queira.
He's not going this year, either because he can't or because he won't.

(3) **com a condição que** (*on condition that*), **sǫb condição que** (*on condition that*), **contanto que** (*provided that, so long as*), **a não sęr que** (*unless*), **a męnos (de) que**[1] (*unless*), **(no) caso** (*in case*), **no caso que** (*in case*), **pąra o caso que** (*in case*),

---

[1] Regarded by some as a Gallicism.

because the subordinate clause presents a mere hypothesis or condition.

Dar-lho-ei sǫb condição que o guarde pạra sua mãe.
I shall give it him on condition that he keeps it for his mother.

Lá irei contanto que não me acompanhe ninguém.
I shall go there provided that nobody goes with me.

É cẹrto que virá, a não sẹr que mǫrra antes.
It's certain that he'll come, unless he dies beforehand.

Vamos andando, no caso que nos veja.
Let's be going in case he sees us.

(4) **embǫra, ainda que, pǫsto que, se bem que, conquanto,** all of which render *although, even though* or *even if,* regardless of whether the verb expresses a fact or a hypothesis; the conjunctions **ainda se, ainda quando** and **mẹsmo que,** which all translate *even if,* likewise always take the subjunctive.

Fá-lo-ei ainda que ẹle esteja aqui agǫra mẹsmo.
I shall do it even though he *is* here.

Fá-lo-ei, mẹsmo que ẹle esteja aqui.
I shall do it, even if he's here.

(5) **tạlvẹz** (*perhaps*), provided that the verb follows; here the subjunctive is used in a main clause.

Tạlvẹz não seja verdade.   Perhaps it's not true.

but **Não é verdade, tạlvẹz.**

Tạlvẹz fǫsse (*impf. subj.*) **melhǫr adiar a reunião pạra outro dia.**
Perhaps it would be better to postpone the meeting till another day.

(*h*) After relative words when the antecedent is hypothetical (*i.e.,* not a specific person or thing).

Estou a procurar ạlguém que me engraixe os sapatos.
I'm looking for someone to clean my shoes.

Não há ninguém que pense como eu.
There's nobody who thinks as I do.

Não há obstáculo que se não possa vencer.
There is no obstacle that cannot be overcome.

Conheces algum inglês que me ensine a língua inglesa?
Do you know any Englishman who will teach me his language?

Todo o estrangeiro que fale assim é despedido do escritório.
Any foreigner who talks like that is shooed out of the office.

NOTE: If the antecedent is accepted as a reality no subjunctive is used, for the relative clause then becomes a statement of fact. Thus, with the above compare **Conheço alguém que lhe engraixa os sapatos, Este é um obstáculo que se não pode vencer.**

(*i*) Finally, the subjunctive is used in clauses dependent on expressions of emotion. Here the action of the subordinate clause is often a reality, but it is a reality subordinated to the emotion expressed; hence the subjunctive.

Sinto que você se vá embora.
I'm sorry you're going.

Alegro-me (de) que esteja aqui.
I'm glad he's here.

Estranha-me
Estranho } **que se comporte assim.**
I'm surprised he behaves like that.

Está com medo (de) que o tornem a encontrar.
He's afraid lest they find him again.

NOTES. 1. Compare also impersonal expressions like:
É estranho que o tenha feito. It's strange that he has (should have) done it.
See § 181 (c).

2. The verb **estranhar** has two meanings: to *surprise* and *to be surprised at.*

182. VERBS ENDING IN -uzir. Verbs ending in **-uzir** are irregular only in that the third person singular of the present indicative does not end in **-e.**

luzir, *to shine*: pres. ind. **luzo, luzes, luz, luzimos, luzis, luzem.**

produzir, *to produce*: pres. ind. **produzo, produzes, produz, produzimos, produzis, produzem.**

VOCABULARY

Study all new words and constructions used in §§ 179–82.

EXERCISES

I. (*a*) *Supply the first and third persons plural of the present subjunctive of the following verbs:* andar, prevenir, abster, fixar, caber, provar, prover, provir, vestir, boiar, apoiar, cear, ler, negociar, dar, luzir, viajar, subir, dormir, servir, mentir.

(*b*) *Study and translate:* Digo-lhe que vá embora. Não achamos que estejas enganada. Ele deseja que produzamos mais. É natural que venha. Será melhor que se saiba como. Precisa que consintam em fazê-lo. Primeiro que entremos. Sob condição que a condenem. Sem que ninguém pense assim. Até que to peçamos. Prefere que aprendas a nadar. É possível que isto seja verdade. É necessário que não se arrependam do que fizeram. Talvez seja pior assim. Conquanto ele não possa falar consigo agora.

(*c*) *Translate:* Either because he's rich or because he's hardworking. Until she leaves. Before he comes back. Provided he finishes it. So long as he understands the difficulties of the situation. It is true that he doesn't feel like going with us. I implore you to take me to him at once. Unless he makes the manager understand. In order that he may say so. Even if he gives it to me tomorrow morning.

However much you want to do it. Anybody who thinks this must be very clever. We're glad he's been receiving Spanish lessons.

II. (*a*) *Study and translate:* 1. Aconselhamos-lhe que o considere bem primeiro que seja tarde demais. 2. O que importa que as pessoas não tenham as mesmas ideias acerca da religião e da política contanto que vivam felizes uns com os outros? 3. Por muito que procuremos fazê-lo, ainda nos será impossível. 4. Não há nada que mais me apraza do que saber que ele chegou a casa hoje. 5. Não convém que saibamos o que fez com o livro que lhe demos. 6. Também te parece mal que sintamos que esteja a morrer um amigo nosso? 7. Não é verdade que te foste embora logo depois? 8. Gosto imenso de Portugal mas não porque seja português. 9. Estamos a procurar um guia que nos mostre os monumentos mais importantes da cidade. 10. Vamos deixar aqui a nossa bagagem, para o caso que tenhamos de voltar.

(*b*) *Translate:* 1. He says he won't give me the book he promised me unless I go and visit him. 2. We prefer to remain here in case they come. 3. It's quite probable that she'll get here tomorrow morning. 4. Since your wife's like that it's not worth the trouble your spending the winter here. 5. You must promise me that you won't do that again without my knowing it. 6. I doubt whether it will rain, although the sky *is* somewhat overcast. 7. I am very pleased that they've been having such (**tanta**) luck. 8. I think this plan is ridiculous even if he decides to continue. 9. However often you write to him, you'll get no reply. 10. But I don't think she's unlikeable even if she does argue with everybody.

III. (*a*) *Study and translate:* 1. Aconselho-te que deixes de ir à fábrica e que trabalhes comigo em casa. 2. Vou pedir a esse criado que nos traga uma garrafa de vinho do Porto e dois cálices. 3. Não te estranhará que te fale do que tenciona fazer o teu irmão? 4. Tem-se exposto a que todos pensem mal dele. 5. Parece que não agrada à sua tia que se vá embora. 6. Não vejo inconveniente em que o saibas contanto que não o repitas a ninguém. 7. Não encontra ninguém que esteja disposto a ajudá-lo nisso. 8. Sua mãe está acostumada a que todos os filhos façam o que querem. 9. Será mais prático que partamos já, já. 10. Sinto muito que costumes levar tanto tempo a chegar à estação.

(b) *Translate*: 1. But is it possible that you still don't understand? 2. I want you to stay and help me with the meeting. 3. I'm afraid he won't be able to come. 4. There is no man, however bad he may be, who is not inclined at times to help little children. 5. I'm not saying your scheme is impossible. 6. I promise you it won't happen again. 7. I think it unlikely that he'll succeed in persuading his mother to let him go before Thursday. 8. But we shall go now even if it rains all night. 9. His father forbids him to study in the lounge. 10. The general is encouraging the soldiers to set fire to all the houses in (=of) the village. I'm surprised the army permits such a thing (**tal**).

LESSON XXX

183. THE FORMATION OF THE IMPERFECT SUBJUNCTIVE. The imperfect subjunctive is formed by taking the third person plural of the preterite of any verb, removing **-ram** and substituting the endings **-sse, -sses, -sse, -ssemos, -sseis, -ssem.** Accents are required on the preceding syllable in the first and second persons plural.

compra/ram:

 comprasse, comprasses, comprasse, comprássemos,
 comprásseis, comprassem;

vendẹ/ram:

 vendẹsse, vendẹsses, vendẹsse, vendêssemos, vendês-
 seis, vendẹssem;

parti/ram:

 partisse, partisses, partisse, partíssemos, partísseis, par-
 tissem;

dẹ/ram:

 dẹsse, dẹsses, dẹsse, déssemos, désseis, dẹssem;

fọ/ram:

 fọsse, fọsses, fọsse, fôssemos, fôsseis, fọssem.

184. THE PLUPERFECT SUBJUNCTIVE. The pluperfect subjunctive is formed by the imperfect subjunctive of **tẹr** (very occasionally in highly literary style by that of **havẹr**) with the past participle of the appropriate verb.

que tivẹsse comprado, that I might (should) have bought, that
 I had bought

185. THE USE OF THE IMPERFECT AND PLUPERFECT SUBJUNCTIVE.
(*a*) The imperfect and pluperfect subjunctives are used in the
same conditions as the present and perfect subjunctives (see § 181)
but generally after different tenses of the main verb. Thus, the
present, future, perfect continuous and future perfect are followed
by the present or perfect subjunctive, and the imperfect, preterite,
conditional, pluperfect and conditional perfect by the imperfect
or pluperfect subjunctive.

Present and Perfect Subjunctives

Desejo que o vejas. I want you to see it.

Estranha-me que não o tenhas visitado. I'm surprised you
haven't been visiting him.

Pedir-te-á que o faças. He'll ask you to do so.

Tenho-lhes dito que o não façam. I've been telling them
not to do it.

Ter-lhe-á dito que não vá. He'll have told him not to go.

A ver se o terminamos antes que nos vejam. Let's see if we
(can) finish it before they see us.

Imperfect and Pluperfect Subjunctives

Pedia-nos que o fizéssemos. He used to ask us to do so.

Não acreditava que o tivesse feito assim. I didn't think he
would have done it like that.

Mandou-me que o terminasse. He (has) ordered me to
finish it.

Foi-se embora sem que eu tivesse chegado. He went (*or*
has gone) off without my having arrived.

Seria preciso que você lho dissesse. It would be necessary
for you to tell him so.

Insistira (em) que não viessem. He had insisted that they
shouldn't come.

Tê-lo-ia feito assim para que se não inteirasse ninguém.
He would have done it like that so that nobody should find out.

(*b*) The above division is not absolute. Thus, where the
action of the subordinate clause is definitely past, an imperfect

subjunctive is used where the tense of the main verb would suggest a present subjunctive.

Espero que o leitor $\begin{Bmatrix} \textbf{tenha entendido} \\ \textbf{entendesse} \end{Bmatrix}$ **agora.** I trust the reader has now understood.

É possível que não fosse tão ruim como se dizia. He might not have been as bad as people said.

Tê-lo-á estranhado que não estivesses. He must have been surprised you weren't there.

Sinto que estivesse doente. I'm sorry he was ill.

(*Contrast:* **Sinto que tenha estado doente.** I'm sorry he's been ill.)

Conversely, where the action of the subordinate clause is clearly present or future, a present subjunctive may be used where the main verb would suggest an imperfect subjunctive.

O que fizeste para que pense assim? What did you do (*or* have you done) that he should be thinking thus?

Pediu-me que te fale. He (has) asked me to talk to you (*implies:* and I'm going to do so now).

Não lhe disse nada que não seja verdade. I didn't tell (*or* haven't told) him anything that isn't true.

Não quis acreditar que eu não tenha passado bem. He refused to believe that I haven't been keeping well.

186. FURTHER OBSERVATIONS ON THE SUBJUNCTIVE IN SUBORDINATE CLAUSES. (*a*) The subjunctive *may* be used in subordinate clauses dependent on *affirmative* verbs of *thinking*, especially when it is intended to imply that the statement contained in the subordinate clause has been proved incorrect or is open to doubt:

Julguei que não tivesses vindo. I thought you hadn't come (*but you had*).

Cuidei que viesses ontem. I thought you came (*or* would come) yesterday (*but you didn't*).

(b) The subjunctive *may* be used in subordinate clauses dependent on verbs expressing *ignorance*, when it is intended to give extra emphasis to the degree of ignorance.

Nem sabia que tivęssem chegado.
I didn't even know they'd arrived.

Ainda ignorava cǫmo se chamasse.
I didn't even know what his name was.

Sem sabęr qual fǫsse . . .
Without knowing which one it was . . .

(c) The subjunctive is commonly used after the verbs **esperar,** *to hope*, and **supǫr,** *to suppose*, but they may be followed by an indicative in the subordinate clause if there is a strong probability of realization of the hope or supposition.[1] The verbs **fingir,** *to pretend*, and **imaginar,** *to imagine*, are always followed by an *indicative*.

Espęro que virão.   I hopę they'll come.
Supǫnho que morrerá.   I suppose he'll die.

$$\text{Ęu} \begin{Bmatrix} \textbf{fingia} \\ \textbf{imaginava} \end{Bmatrix} \textbf{ que ęle estava mǫrto.} \quad \text{I used to} \begin{Bmatrix} \text{pretend} \\ \text{imagine} \end{Bmatrix}$$
he was dead.

(d) In past narrative (but much less commonly in a present context) the conjunction **cǫmo** usually takes a subjunctive when used causally.

Vǫltaram pạra casa cǫmo estivęssem derreados.
They returned home as (because) they were worn out.

(e) In a subordinate clause introduced by **que** which precedes the main clause, the verb of the subordinate clause *may often be* in the subjunctive even when this is not required by the type of verb used in the main clause.

Que ęstas três cǫisas estivęssem na arca do testamento di-lo São Paulo na epístola aos Hebręus.
That these three things were in the ark of the covenant is stated by Saint Paul in the epistle to the Hebrews.

[1] But the elliptical **esperar que,** *to wait until*, which is sometimes found in the place of **esperar até que,** must always take the subjunctive.

Que possa isto suceder, e que já tenha sucedido, o Profeta Jeremias o afirma.

That this can happen, and that it has already happened (*or* been happening), is affirmed by the Prophet Jeremiah.

187. THE IRREGULAR VERB **rir**, *to laugh.* (*a*) The irregular forms are shown in bold type.

pres. ind.: **rio, ris, ri,** rimos, **rides, riem.**
pres. subj.: ria, etc.
impf. ind.: ria, etc.
preterite: ri, etc.
fut. ind.: rirei, etc.
gerund: rindo
past part.: rido

(*b*) **rir(-se) de,** *to laugh at*; **sorrir,** *to smile,* is a compound of **rir**; note also **sorrir(-se) com,** *to smile at*.

VOCABULARY

acender	to light; to switch on	**escapar**	to escape
		o estudante	student
adorável	adorable	**exigir**	to demand
afinal	after all; finally	**existir**	to exist
ainda	still, yet; even	**mesmo** (*adv.*)	even; just
até	until, till; even	**o mestre**	
a camisa	shirt	(**-escola**)[1]	(school)master
cioso	jealous	**namorar-se**	to fall in love
cuidar	to think	**de**	with
cumprir	to fulfil, accomplish	**o noivo**	fiancé; bridegroom
de modo que + *indic.*	so that, with the result that	**o objecto**	object
		a ocasião	
devolver	to give back	**a oportunidade**	opportunity
o dinheiro	money		
dirigir-se	to make one's way	**o operário**	workman, worker
emprestar	to lend	**a pergunta**	question

[1] This word nowadays has a pejorative ring. For normal purposes use **o professor.**

fazẹr uma pergunta	to ask a question	**restituir**	to give back
regressar	to return, go back, come back	**o ruído**	noise
		a sinceri- dade	sincerity
o represen- tante	representative	**suspirar (por)**	to sigh (for), long (for)
		tornar	to give back

de vẹz em quando	from time to time
quanto antes	as soon as possible
contudo⎫ **porém** ⎬ **tọdavia** ⎭	however, nevertheless
pedir ⎫ **tomar** ⎭ **emprestado**	to borrow

Study also the verbs listed in §§ 186 (c) and 187.

EXERCISES

I. (a) *Give the first and third persons plural of the imperfect subjunctive of the following verbs:* fazer, haver, caber, saber, dar, aprender, estar, ler, pôr, poder, trazer, rir, produzir, ver, prover, vir, provir.

(b) *Study and translate:* Antes que to desse. Para que ninguém o soubesse. Mandei-lhe que o fizesse do mesmo modo. A fim que não reagisse assim. Duvido que o visse! Não desejavam que nos fôssemos embora. Seria melhor que não dissésseis nada a ninguém. Cuido que não chegasse antes de mim. Espero que vissem tudo. Pedi-lhe que entrasse. Imploro-lhe que não ria tanto. De modo que ele regressou.

(c) *Translate:* Not because he asked me for it. We insisted on his speaking to his father. We advised him to see it. He was used to its being done like this. Wherever he went. Provided he arrived on time. In order that they might understand. It was natural he should go back. He asked the waiter to bring him steak and chips, as he was very hungry. If only I could finish it before he comes! The king smiled at this strange reply. I have borrowed it. Even if she were not so jealous.

II. (a) *Study and translate:* 1. Ela evitava falar-lhe do noivo, para que não discutisse os projectos dele. 2. Para ver melhor, pedira à Teresa que acendesse a luz do salão. 3. Margarida suspirava de vez em quando e os ouvidos dela pareciam atentos à noite, à chuva e aos ruídos lá de fora. 4. Francisco estranhava que, parecendo João tão inteligente, acreditasse naquilo. 5. Ao entrar em casa, como encontrasse sozinha a senhora Oliveira, fizera-lhe uma pergunta terrível. 6. Já não iria ter com ela, mesmo que os seus pais se fartassem de esperar. 7. Todas as manhãs, ao dirigir-se para a fábrica, esperava que Mariano lhe levasse o embrulho. 8. A Maria ia andando e pensando que talvez àquela hora o primo ainda não tivesse comido nada. 9. Espero que os senhores chegassem a tempo. 10. Por muito que se esforçasse, por mais que lutasse com os dois homens, não conseguiu escapar.

(b) *Translate:* 1. Nevertheless, it was natural that he should think only of his own family. 2. We didn't know how to prevent his managing to speak to the minister. 3. You already heard him demand last night that you should stay until Friday. 4. I want to beg him to reconsider the answer he gave to our representative. 5. Until that time, he had neither left his village nor did he know there existed, outside books, countries where [any] other language but (**que**) Portuguese was spoken. 6. It is evident that he has thought about you a lot. 7. We ordered him to repeat what he had said to the officer. 8. Although they can no longer defend their former policy, they continue to convince people of their sincerity. 9. We tried hard (=strove) to keep the secret but we couldn't prevent the truth being known after all. 10. She would be adorable even if she were not so cheerful.

III. (*a*) *Study and translate:* 1. Que isto fosse verdade, já o julgávamos saber. 2. Como estivesse namorado dela, não tinha tempo para mais nada. 3. O mestre-escola insistira em que as crianças voltassem quanto antes. 4. Talvez fosse com esse dinheiro que contava comprar outra loja. 5. Parecia-lhe, agora, não ser necessário mentir porque tudo havia corrido bem e Joaninha estava mesmo como ele desejava. 6. Não vi nenhuma camisa de que gostasse. 7. Receávamos que ele não chegasse cedo. 8. Não seria possível que a fizesse a Maria. 9. Sinto muito que o senhor tenha estado doente. 10. Não duvido que o pai dela era feliz.

(*b*) *Translate:* 1. It was important for me to have the suit the following morning. 2. I did not think that I would see you today. 3. He went into the church without knowing exactly what he was intending to do. 4. He asked me if it was possible for him to have the vegetables before next week. 5. The workmen couldn't help smiling at such an answer. 6. He studied very hard so that he learned his lesson well. 7. She said that she would give a book to the student who learned to speak Portuguese. 8. We will never learn to speak this language unless we get an opportunity to hear it spoken. 9. She said they could all go to the pictures so long as they came back before eleven p.m. 10. I was going to ask him to give me back the object I had lent him.[1]

---

[1] If **restituir** is used, remember § 8 (*c*).

*The Future and Future Perfect Subjunctives
and their Uses, Conditional Sentences, Three
Irregular Verbs:* PROVER, REQUERER *and* RE-
FLECTIR

LESSON XXXI

188. THE FORMATION OF THE FUTURE SUBJUNCTIVE. The future
subjunctive is formed by taking the third person plural of the
preterite of any verb, removing **-ram** and substituting the endings **-r, -res, -r, -rmos, -rdes, -rem.**

compra/ram:

   comprar, comprares, comprar, comprarmos, comprardes, comprarem.

vendę/ram:

   vendęr, vendęres, vendęr, vendęrmos, vendęrdes, ven-
dęrem.

parti/ram:

   partir, partires, partir, partirmos, partirdes, partirem.

dę/ram:

   dęr, dęres, dęr, dęrmos, dęrdes, dęrem.

vię/ram (from **vir**):

   vięr, vięres, vięr, vięrmos, vięrdes, vięrem.

vi/ram (from **vęr**):

   vir, vires, vir, virmos, virdes, virem.

fǫ/ram:

   fǫr, fǫres, fǫr, fǫrmos, fǫrdes, fǫrem.

189. THE FUTURE PERFECT SUBJUNCTIVE. The future perfect
subjunctive is formed by the future subjunctive of **tęr** (very
occasionally in highly literary style by that of **havęr**) with the
past participle of the appropriate verb.

Se não tivęres recebido as flǫres ąmanhã ...

   If you've not received the flowers by tomorrow ...

190. The Use of the Future Subjunctive. It should be understood that, whereas in Spanish the future subjunctive is a dying tense confined to stock expressions and legal jargon, its Portuguese counterpart is a very healthy tense and that in modern times its use is increasing. It is used in subordinate clauses (adverbial, relative or conditional) which refer to an indefinite or hypothetical future.

(a) *Adverbial Clauses.* The use of the future subjunctive in adverbial clauses depends on the subordinating conjunction which introduces the clause. In subordinate adverbial clauses which refer to an indefinite or hypothetical future there are three classes of subordinating conjunction: (i) those that require future subjunctive; (ii) those that usually require future subjunctive, but which may be used with present subjunctive instead; (iii) those that require present subjunctive.

   (i) **quando,**[1] *when*; **segundo,** *according as, depending on whether*; **conforme,** *according as, depending on whether*; **(assim) como,** *(just) as*;

   (ii) **enquanto,** *while, (for) as long as*; **assim que,** *as soon as*; **logo que,** *as soon as*; **depois que,** *after*; **sempre que,**[2] *whenever*;

   (iii) all others (*e.g.*, **até que,** *until*; **antes que,** *before*; etc.).

Dir-lho-ei quando o vir.
   I'll tell him when I see him.

Segundo a operação se tornar mais ou menos necessária, teremos que adaptar os nossos planos.
   We shall have to adapt our plans in accordance with the extent to which the operation becomes necessary.

Assim que $\left\{\begin{array}{l}\textbf{chegar}\\\textbf{chegue}\end{array}\right\}$, diga-lhe que venha ver-me.
   As soon as he arrives, tell him to come and see me.

---

[1] **Quando** is to be found on odd occasions in literary style with the present subjunctive, especially with conditional sense.

[2] **Sempre que** + *subjunctive* is also occasionally used to render *provided that*; under such circumstances it may never be used with the future subjunctive.

V. Exa. pọde arranjá-lo cọmo quisẹr.
You may arrange it as you like, sir.

Fico aqui até que ẹla venha.
I'm staying here until she comes.

(b) *Relative Clauses.* The future subjunctive is used regularly in relative clauses which refer to an indefinite or hypothetical future.

Dar-me-ás metade do dinheiro que gạnhares, quando começares a trabalhar na nọva fábrica.
When you start work at the new factory you will give me half the money you earn.

Será punido tọdo o rapaz que não fizẹr os sẹus devẹres.
Any boy who doesn't do his homework will be punished.

Seja o que fọr. Whatever it is (*or* may be).	**Seja qual fọr.** Whichever it is (*or* may be).
Seja cọmo fọr. However it is (*or* may be).	**(Esteja) onde estivẹr.**[1] Wherever he is (*or* may be).
Seja quem fọr. Whoever it is (*or* may be).	**Seja quando fọr.** Whenever it is (*or* may be).
Seja quanto fọr. However much it is (*or* may be).	**Sucẹda o que sucedẹr.** Happen what may.
Venha o que viẹr. Come what may.	**Venha quando viẹr.** Whenever he may come; come when he may.
Custe o que custar. Cost what it may; at all costs.	**Diga o que dissẹr.** Say what he will; whatever he says.

NOTES. 1. The future subjunctive ought never to be used in relative clauses introduced by expressions like **quem quẹr que,**

---

[1] In practice the first word of this expression is omitted.

por muito que, etc. [see § 181 (*e*) and (*f*)].   Observe the following
constructions:

Defendê-lo-ei contra {**quem quẹr que venha.**
{**quem viẹr.**

I shall defend him against {all comers.
{whoever comes.

Por muitos họmens que emprẹgues   }
Sejam quantos fọrem os họmens que empregares }'
   nunca poderás cumprir a tarẹfa.
   You'll never be able to complete the task no matter how many
   men you employ.

2. In secondary sequence [see § 185] the equivalents of such expressions as **seja o que fọr, venha quando viẹr,** etc. take both
verbs in the imperfect subjunctive:

Fọsse o que fọsse.
   Whatever it was (*or* might be).

Viẹsse quando viẹsse.
   Whenever he came (*or* might come); come when he might.

**Explicou que, vọltasse o sọldado quando vọltasse, nunca
   tornaria a falar com ẹle.**
   She explained that, whensoever the soldier might come back, she
   would never speak to him again.

(*c*) *Conditional Clauses.* The future subjunctive is used in
subordinate conditional clauses of indefinite or hypothetical future
time, when the subordinating conjunction used is **se,** *if.* The
verb in the main clause is usually in the future indicative or the
imperative (or similar command form, se §§ 194–6).   There is,
however, an increasing tendency to use the future subjunctive in
the subordinate clause, even when the main clause contains a
present indicative. This is particularly the case: (i) when an
adverb phrase of futurity is used, (ii) when one makes a rule or
generalization which will, for the most part, affect future conduct.

Se ęsse malandro tornar a vir cá, matá-lo-ei (*or* mato-o)!
If that scoundrel comes here again, I'll kill him!

Se Dęus quisęr, chegarei a tempo.
With luck, I'll get there on time.

Se ąlguém vięr, diga-lhe que não estou.
If anyone comes, tell them I'm out.

— Vais pąra a cidade ąmanhã? — Se tivęr tempo.
" Going into town tomorrow?" "If I've got time."

Se examinarmos (*for* examinamos) a carta da Ęurǫpa, vęmos que o continente se compõe de vários países.
If we examine the map of Europe, we (shall) see that the continent is composed of several countries.

191. USE OF THE FUTURE PERFECT SUBJUNCTIVE. The use of this tense is not very frequent; it is similar in usage to the future subjunctive, but serves to indicate an interval of time between the action of the subordinate and that of the main clause.

Se não tivęr recebido ąmanhã a carta de Miguęl, telegrafarei pąra Paris.
If I've not received Michael's letter by tomorrow, I'll cable Paris.

192. CONDITIONAL SENTENCES. Portuguese conditional sentences fall into three categories, *future conditions* (as already described above), *open conditions*, and *remote conditions*.

(1) If the condition is open, the indicative is used.

Se trabalho, cǫmo mais. If I work, I eat more.
Se trabalhava, comia mais. If I worked, I ate more.
Se comęu a empada, fǫi porque tinha fǫme. If he ate/has eaten the pie, it was because he was hungry.

(2) If the condition is felt to be remote, perhaps even contrary to fact, the imperfect or pluperfect subjunctive is used.

Se comęsse ęsta empada, ficaria doente. If he ate/were to eat this pie, he would fall ill.

Se estivęsse a comęr ęsta empada agǫra męsmo, estaria a comê-la com muito gǫsto. If he were eating this pie right now, he would be enjoying it.

Se tivęsse comido a empada, agora estaria doente. If he had eaten the pie, he would now be ill.

Se tivęsse comido a empada, teria ficado doente. If he had eaten the pie, he would have been ill.

NOTES. 1. It will be noted that the imperfect or pluperfect subjunctive is used in the subordinate clause of all remote conditions. The choice, as exemplified, is usually determined by the degree of remoteness.

2. The subordinating conjunctions **ainda que** (*even if*), **ainda quando** (*even if*), and **męsmo que** (*even if*) may also be used in remote conditions.

3. In highly literary style, the verbs of both clauses (*or* either clause) of a remote condition may be represented by the synthetic form of the pluperfect indicative.

Se o fizęra ǫutra vęz, fǫra castigado.
If he did it again, he would be punished.

4. The future indicative and conditional tenses are found in **se** clauses only when the **se** can be translated by the English *whether*.

    Não sei se trabalhará ąmanhã. I don't know if (*or* whether) he will work tomorrow.
    Não sabia se trabalharia. I didn't know if (*or* whether) he would work.

but **Se trabalhar ąmanhã, comerá mais.** If he works tomorrow, he will eat more.
    Se quisęsse (*or* **Se estivęsse dispǫsto a**) **trabalhar, gąnharia mais.** If he would work he would earn more.

5. The subordinating conjunction **cǫmo se** (*as if, as though*) is always followed by either imperfect subjunctive or pluperfect sub-

junctive, in accordance with the degree of remoteness of the comparison.

Fá-lo cọmo se não soubẹsse cọmo.
He does it as if he didn't know how to.

Comportava-se cọmo se não tivẹsse recebido a carta.
He was behaving as though he hadn't received the letter.

6. *As if, as though* is rendered by **cọmo (que)** when there is no dependent finite verb.

Estacou cọmo (que) estupefacto.
He halted as if stupefied.

Fẹz um gẹsto cọmo (que) pạra dissuadi-la.
He gestured as though to dissuade her.

7. Students of Spanish should note that in reported versions of an original future condition the verb of the *if*-clause appears in Portuguese in the Imperfect *Subjunctive.* Contrast:

Se viẹres, irei (*Spanish: Si vienes, iré*).   If you come, I'll go.
Ẹla disse que se viẹsse, iria (*Spanish: Ella dijo que si venía, iría*).
She said that if he came, she'd go.

8. The conjunction **se** is *never* followed by the present subjunctive.[1]

9. Remember that the Conditional Tense may often be replaced by the imperfect indicative (see § 150, note 2).

193. THREE IRREGULAR VERBS. (*a*) **provẹr,** *to provide*, and **requerẹr,** *to request, require.* Though compounds respectively of **vẹr** and **querẹr**, these two verbs are conjugated rather differently:

provẹr is irregular only in the present indicative in which it resembles **vẹr:**
provejo, provês, provê, provẹmos, provẹdes, provêem; (*pres. subj.* **proveja,** etc.);

requerẹr also is irregular only in the present indicative, but differs from **querẹr** in the first person singular:
requeiro, requẹres, requẹr *or* **requẹre, requerẹmos, requereis, requẹrem;** (*pres. subj.* **requeira,** etc.).

[1] Except occasionally after **não sabẹr.**

318

(b) **reflęctir,** *to reflect* (all meanings). This radical-changing verb has silent **c** throughout; a preceding **e** is always open. The present indicative is as follows:

reflicto [rrəf'litu], **reflęctes, reflęcte, reflęctimos, reflęctis, reflęctem.**

VOCABULARY

abraçar	to embrace, hug	**o exercício**	exercise
acrescentar	to add	**fitar**	to stare (at)
admirar	to admire	**fumar**	to smoke
anteontem	the day before yesterday	**gastar**	to spend (*money*)
argentino	Argentinian	**o mar**	sea
arranjar	to arrange, put right	**meridional**	southern
		o México	Mexico
austríaco	Austrian	**a mǫrte**	death
castigar	to punish	**a notícia**	(piece of) news
o cavalheiro	gentleman	**pagar**	to pay (for)
o chęfe	chief, head, boss	**a paisagem**	scenery,
o clima	climate	[pɐi-]	landscape
a conta	bill, account	**o perigo**	danger, peril
a cǫr	colour	**pouco**	shortly
corrigir	to correct; to mark	**depǫis**	after(wards)
		poucos	not many; few
dar-se conta (de)	to realize	**a província**	province
declarar	to declare	**de** {**repente** / **súbito**}	suddenly
desprezar	to scorn, despise	**sęr mentira**	to be untrue; to be a lie
o empregado	clerk, employee		
entregar	to hand in, hand over, pass, deliver	**suficiente**	sufficient
		suíço	Swiss
		a taça	(champagne) glass
escondęr	to hide		
a espǫsa	wife	**tęr êxito**	to be successful
a estad(i)a	stay, sojourn	**tornar-se**	to become
exclamar	to exclaim	**vǫltar-se (pɐra)**	to turn, turn round (to, towards)
o exemplar	copy (*of book, etc.*)		

demais
demais a mais
aliás } besides, moreover, in addi-
além disso   tion
além do que

esperar (dizer, julgar) que {sim / não} to hope (say, think) {so / not

dęste (doutro, de tal) mǫdo } in this (in another, in such a)
dęsta (doutra, de tal) maneira } way

Study also the words listed in §§ 190 (*a*), (*c*) and 193, and revise the vocabulary of Lessons XXVI–XXX.

EXERCISES

I. (*a*) *Give the first and second persons plural of the future subjunctive of the following verbs:* provar, prover, provir, estar, caber, rir, pôr, querer, poder, pedir, ir, trazer, fazer, dizer.

(*b*) *Study and translate:* Quando o vires. Logo que os abraçarmos. Segundo me admirares ou não. Assim como quiserdes. Depois que se voltarem para nós. Enquanto eu viver. Venha o que vier. Custe o que custar. Conforme o arranjarem. Se o vir, dir-lho-ei. Disse-me que julgava que sim.

(*c*) *Translate:* As soon as he arranges the colours. After we arrive home I shall send for the doctor. If he comes I shall go. If he were to come in now he would punish you severely. If the job became difficult it wasn't because I was feeling ill. She didn't know whether or not he would provide it. At all costs. I shall pay it to him however much it is. I hope not.

II. (*a*) *Study and translate:* 1. Ainda que pagasse a conta era tarde demais. 2. Logo que se der conta disso hás-de esconder a chave. 3. Quando o suíço vier a esta mesa traga-nos uma garrafa de champanhe e duas taças. 4. Depois que tiverem corrigido os exercícios vão fumar lá fora. 5. Logo

que tiver escrita a carta irá ter com o seu amigo austríaco.
6. Por mais dinheiro que gastes, se não o fizeres doutro modo
todos te desprezarão. 7. De repente, Pedro voltou-se para
o argentino e disse-lhe que, no sábado seguinte, partiria dali.
8. Se tu soubesses o que eu estou sentindo! 9. De vez em
quando o chefe da polícia levantava os olhos da mesa e fitava-
os, como se soubesse o que eles pensavam. 10. Tinha-lhes
declarado que, se Deus quisesse, chegariam a tempo aqueles
cavalheiros.

(b) *Translate*: 1. If I'm successful I'll send you a telegram.
2. The next time I meet him I'll hand him the other copy.
3. "Besides," exclaimed the clerk, "if he had done it the
day before yesterday we would all have realized the danger."
4. I'm not sure that my father's going to be pleased when he
knows this. 5. I shall not go with them until I'm sure they
want me to (=they desire it). 6. Besides, if you'd been at
home you would have had no need to ask anyone. 7. If
you run into him (*use* **dar com**) while you're in Mexico
perhaps you'll tell him that it's a long time since I received
news of him (**notícias suas**). 8. However, if this were
untrue I should not be here now. 9. Not many days
after her death I realized that it would be impossible to
carry on. 10. If he is right we shall have to accept the
new scheme.

III. (a) *Study and translate*: No ano que vem, minha esposa e
eu esperamos passar alguns dias em Portugal durante o mês
de Julho. Custe o que custar, ficaremos lá uns quinze dias
pelo menos. Tencionamos visitar o Algarve, que é a província meridional do país, visto que gostamos imenso do
clima e da paisagem. Há três anos estivemos uma semana
na Praia da Rocha a tomar banhos de sol e de mar e tanto
gostámos da nossa estada que estamos com saudades de
regressar. Mas é preciso acrescentar ao mesmo tempo que,
se fizer demasiado calor, voltaremos quanto antes para
Lisboa ou ainda para o norte, para o Porto, onde moram
muitos amigos nossos, tanto portugueses como ingleses.

(*b*) *Translate:* The day before yesterday I ran into a friend of mine as I was getting on (*use* **entrar**) the bus on my way home.   I asked him where he was going to spend [his] (the) holidays this year, as I knew that he was very fond of visiting the Iberian countries.   He told me that if he managed to save up sufficient money he intended to spend a month in Spain and hoped to visit Seville and Granada and perhaps do some sun- and sea-bathing at Málaga if he had time. "Before I go," he declared, "if I can find a good teacher, I'm going to learn a little Spanish, because, even though I've been there three times, I don't speak a word!"

LESSON XXXII

194. THE FORMATION OF THE IMPERATIVE. (*a*) Portuguese imperative forms exist only for the **tu** and **vós** persons, *i.e.*, for the grammatical second person. The singular imperative may be readily obtained for nearly all verbs, including irregular and radical-changing verbs, in that it is identical to the third person singular of the present indicative. The plural imperative is also readily obtained by removing the final -**s** from the second person plural of the present indicative.

	Singular	*Plural*
comprar:	compra	comprai
vendẹr:	vende	vendei
partir:	parte	parti
dar:	dá	dai
vẹr:	vê	vẹde
ir:	vai	ide
levar:	lẹva	levai
movẹr:	mọve	movei
servir:	sẹrve	servi
subir:	sọbe	subi

(*b*) There are, however, alternative singular forms for all verbs with infinitive ending in -**azẹr**, -**dizẹr** or -**uzir**, *e.g.*, **fazẹr: faz** or **faze.**

fazẹr:

Faz-me } o favọr de fechar a pọrta.   Do me the favour of
Faze-me }   closing the door.

Faze-o }
Fá-lo }   com muito cuidado.   Do it very carefully.

323

(c) The imperatives of the verb **ser** are respectively **sê** and **sęde.**

(d) The imperative singular of **ouvir** is regular: **ouve.** However, it is often replaced by **ouça** (or **ọiça**) when special (vocal) emphasis is required. A popular plural form, **ouvide,** is also found.

(e) The imperative singular of **queręr** is historically **quęr.** Its use is limited to the construction **quęr ... quęr ...,** *either ... or ...,* and *whether ... or (whether) ...*

Visitá-lo-ęmos quęr à ida quęr à vinda.
We'll visit him either on the way there or on the way back.

Quęr tenha feito isso quęr não, não tenho mais confiança nęle.
Whether he's done that or not, I've no further confidence in him.

Não vou sair, quęr chọva quęr não.
I'm not going to go out, whether it rains or not.

Não poderá fazê-lo, quęr queira quęr não.
She won't be able to do it, whether she wants to or whether she doesn't.

NOTE: Observe the use of the subjunctive whenever a finite verb follows.

(f) Weak object pronouns follow the imperative. See above (b).

195. COMMANDS AND EXHORTATIONS (English *Do this, Let's go, Let him try (if he dare),*[1] *May you regret it*). The imperative and the present subjunctive supply between them the Portuguese command and exhortative forms. The imperative is used only in affirmative commands and only then with the **tu** and **vós** persons. Elsewhere the subjunctive is used, *i.e.,* in negative commands with the **tu** and **vós** persons, in both affirmative and negative commands with such persons as **o Sr., vọcê, V. Exa.,**

[1] Note that *let* in such cases does indicate exhortation and not permission, for which **deixar** or **permitir** would be used.

os Srs., vọcês, etc., and in all exhortations. The conjunction **que** generally introduces exhortative forms in the third person. Weak object pronouns follow the verb in all cases except when it is introduced by **que** or when the clause is in the negative, in which case they precede the verb.

Compra ẹstes lápis.	Buy these pencils.
Compra-os.	Buy them.
Não compres ẹstes lápis.	Don't buy these pencils.
Não os compres.	Don't buy them.
Compre (o Sr.) ẹste lápis.	Buy this pencil.
Não compre (o Sr.) ẹste lápis.	Don't buy this pencil.
Escrevamos nós.	Let *us* write.
Que vivam muitos anos.	May they live many years.
Que vendam ẹles os lápis.	Let *them* sell the pencils.
Que os vendam ẹles.	Let *them* sell them.
Que abram ẹles a pọrta.	Let *them* open the door.
Que abra a pọrta João.	Let *John* open the door.

NOTES. 1. If the subject is expressed it follows the verb and, if heavily stressed, it may follow a short direct object (cf. last example).

2. **Que** + subjunctive may be used with exhortative sense for the **tu** and **vós** persons.

Que tenhas bọa viagem.   May you have (*or* Have) a good journey.
Que pelejeis pela vọssa pátria, Portuguẹses!   Portuguese, fight for your country!

This is less abrupt than the simple imperative without **que**.

3. The first person plural command form tends to be replaced, especially in conversation, by **vamos** + infinitive.

> **Vamos atravessar a rua.**   Let's cross the road.
> **Vamos sentar-nos aqui.**   Let us sit down here.

196. REQUESTS, *please, will* AND *would*. (*a*) These are normally translated into Portuguese by using **querẹr** interrogatively or by using **fazẹr (o) favọr de** or **tẹr a bondade de** imperatively.

Quẹres trazẹr-me um cọpo de água?
   Please will you bring me a glass of water?

Faça (o) favǫr de examinar isto.
Would you please have a look at this?

Tenha a bondade de passar-me o vinho.
Would you mind passing the wine, please?

NOTE: **Faz favǫr de** can be used generally for all purposes, singular or plural, familiar or polite.

(b) For very polite requests **queira** (pl. **queiram**) is used (cf. French **veuillez**).

Queira passar por aqui, minha senhǫra.
Kindly step this way, madam.

(c) The expression **(se) faz favǫr** is very commonly used to soften a command. It is invariable. **Por favǫr** is also used.

    Abra a pǫrta, se faz favǫr. Please open the door.
    Dǫis cafés, se faz favǫr! Two coffees, please!

197. THE OPTATIVE ǫxalá (que). Close to the exhortative is the use of the subjunctive after **ǫxalá (que)** (*oh that! may! would that!*). If the wish is expressed as an open possibility the present or perfect subjunctive is used; if it is felt to be remote or contrary to fact or likely to prove so, the imperfect or pluperfect subjunctive is employed. The synthetic pluperfect indicative may replace the imperfect subjunctive in this construction.

Ǫxalá não venha ǎmanhã! Heaven prevent his coming tomorrow!

Ǫxalá (que) não tenham falado com ęle! Let's hope they haven't talked (been talking) to him!

Ǫxalá (que) o $\begin{Bmatrix} \text{pudęsse} \\ \text{pudęra} \end{Bmatrix}$ terminar! If only I could finish it!

Ǫxalá não o tivęsses feito! Would that you had not done it!

Note also the constructions listed in § 123. The locution **queira Dęus que** is a widely used equivalent of **ǫxalá (que)** also.

198. THE COMPARATIVE (English *faster, dirtier, more intelligent, more slowly*). (*a*) The comparative of a Portuguese adjective or adverb is formed by placing **mais** (*more*) before the simple form.

uma pessǫa mais simpática, a nicer person
um rapaz muito mais inteligente, a much cleverer boy
Ęste é mais alto do que aquęle. The latter is taller than the former.
Irei mais tarde. I shall go later.
Faze-o mais devagar. Do it more slowly.

(*b*) Notice, however, the following irregular comparatives:

Adjectives		*Adverbs*	
bom	**melhǫr**	**bem**	**melhǫr**
good	better	well	better
mau	**piǫr**	**mal**	**piǫr**
bad	worse	badly	worse
muito	**mais**	**muito**	**mais**
a lot of	more	a lot	more
pouco	**męnos**	**pouco**	**męnos**
little, few	less, fewer	little	less

NOTES. 1. The adjective **grande** (*big, great*) has only one correct comparative form, **maiǫr**, but **pequęno** (*little, small*) has **menǫr** and **mais pequęno.**[1] Students of Spanish should note that **maiǫr** and **menǫr** are only very rarely used to translate *older* (*elder*) and *younger*.

2. Used as adjectives, **mais, męnos** and the derivative **somęnos** (*of little worth, scant*) are invariable. Before a singular abstract noun **mais** and **męnos** may sometimes alternate with **maiǫr** and **menǫr** with little real difference in meaning:

uma ǫbra de $\begin{Bmatrix} \text{maiǫr} \\ \text{mais} \end{Bmatrix}$ **importância,** a work of $\begin{Bmatrix} \text{greater} \\ \text{more} \end{Bmatrix}$ importance

uma ǫbra de $\begin{Bmatrix} \text{menǫr} \\ \text{męnos} \end{Bmatrix}$ **importância,** a work of $\begin{Bmatrix} \text{lesser} \\ \text{less} \end{Bmatrix}$ importance

uma ǫbra de somęnos importância, a work of scant importance

---

[1] In general, **mais pequęno** is used in expressions involving *physical* size, whereas **menǫr** is to be preferred for figurative or abstract expressions.

3. **Antes** exists with the meaning *rather*.

Tem tipo inglês antes que francês. He seems English rather than French.

4. In conjunction with past participles the English adverbs *better* and *worse* are rendered by **mais bem** and **mais mal** respectively.

Ęsta igreja fọi mais bem construída do que a outra. This church was better built than the other one.

199. TRANSLATING THE ENGLISH *than*. (*a*) *Than* is usually rendered by **que** or **do que,** but chiefly the latter. **Do que** is obligatory if the second element of comparison contains its own verb.

Ęste lápis escrẹve melhọr do que julgava. This pencil writes better than I thought.

Bẹbe mais do que cọme. He drinks more than he eats.

Compra mais livros do que vende. He buys more books than he sells.

(Students of Spanish should contrast this last example with the Spanish **Compra más libros de los que vende.**)

(*b*) *More than* and *less than* before an indication of quantity or number are translated by **mais de** and **mẹnos de.**

Estẹve aqui mais duma họra. He was here for more than an hour.

Tem mẹnos de quinze anos. He is less than fifteen years old.

NOTE: **Não ... mais que** means *only*: **Não tem mais que dọze anos** (*He is only twelve years old*), but **Não tem mais de dọze anos** (*He is not more than twelve years old*).

200. OTHER TERMS OF COMPARISON.

tão ... cọmo	as ... as
tanto(s) ... cọmo	as much ... as; *pl.* as many ... as
quanto mais/mẹnos ...	the more/less ...
tanto mais/mẹnos	the more/less

É tão alta cọmo sẹu irmão. She is as tall as her brother.

Vọcê não trabalha tanto cọmo ẹla. You don't work as hard as she does.

Ẹle tem tantas irmãs cọmo ẹu. He has as many sisters as I have.

Bebẹmos tanta água cọmo vinho. We drink as much water as wine.

Quantas mais vantagens tinha, (tantas) mais exigia. The more advantages he had, the more he demanded.

Quanto mais difíceis são os exemplos, (tanto) mais devagar os traduzo. The more difficult are the examples, the more slowly I translate them.

Quantos mais livros vende, (tantos) mẹnos lhe sọbram. The more books he sells, the fewer he has left.

Quanto maiọr fọr a dificuldade, (tanta) mais satisfạção terẹmos ao vencê-la. The greater the difficulty, the more satisfaction we shall have in overcoming it.

NOTES. 1. In the construction **quanto ... tanto**: (i) **quanto** and **tanto** decline when used as adjectives (*i.e.*, immediately before **mais** or **mẹnos** + noun) and are invariable when used as adverbs (before **mais** or **mẹnos** + adjective or adverb); (ii) **tanto (-a, -os, -as)** is more often omitted than used; (iii) the **mais** may be contained in an irregular comparative (cf. last example: **maiọr = mais grande**).

2. The following construction is also noteworthy, involving **tão ... quanto** which replaces **tão ... cọmo** when a second finite verb is introduced:

João é tão aplicado quanto Maria é preguiçọsa. John is as industrious as Mary is lazy.

Não é tão fácil quanto parẹce. It's not as easy as it looks.

201. THE SUPERLATIVE (English *fastest, dirtiest, most intelligent, mọst slowly*). (*a*) The superlative in Portuguese is the same as the comparative, except that, as in English, the article is used with it more often than with the comparative. Unlike French, Portuguese never duplicates the article when the adjective follows the noun.

Êste é o mais inteligente.
This is the most (*or* more) intelligent one.

(*but* **Êste é mais inteligente.**
This one is more intelligent.)

Qual é o rapaz mais inteligente?
Which is the most (*or* more) intelligent boy?

É a melhor das suas poesias.
It is the best of his poems.

É o pior que tenho visto.
It is the worst I've seen.

Foram os dias mais felizes da sua vida.
They were the happiest days of his life.

Qual é a sua filha mais bonita?
Which is his prettiest daughter?

Qual é a filha mais bonita das duas?
Which is the prettier daughter?

Ésta é a mais bonita (das duas).
This is the prettier one.

Contrast: **Ésta é mais bonita.**
This one is prettier.

É o homem mais rico do país.
He's the richest man in the country.

NOTES. 1. The English *in* after a superlative is best translated by **de.**

2. When *most* means *the majority of* or *the greater part of* it is translated by **a maioria de** or **a maior parte de.** If it is the subject of the sentence and refers to several individuals it takes a plural verb.

A maioria dos meus amigos dirão a mesma coisa.
Most of my friends will say the same.

A maior parte das mulheres sabem cozinhar bem.
Most women know how to cook well.

but **Quem tem mais amigos?**
    Who's got most friends?

and **Quem tem o maiọr número de amigos no Gabinẹte?**
    Who's got most friends in the Cabinet?

(*b*) With the superlative of an adverb the article is used only when there follow some qualifying elements.

Fọi ẹle quem o fẹz mais devagar.
    It was he who did it most slowly.

but **Fê-lo o mais devagar que pôde.**
    He did it as slowly as he could.

A vẹr quem termina mais deprẹssa.
    Let's see who finishes soonest.

but **Terminará o mais deprẹssa que pudẹr.**
    He will finish as soon as he can.

Ẹssas cọisas acontẹcem quando mẹnos se pensa.
    Those things happen when one least expects.

but **O que impọrta é que acontẹçam o mẹnos possívẹl.**
    The important thing is that they should happen as little as possible.

(*c*) The absolute superlative (which intensifies rather than compares) is formed by adding **-íssimo** to the last consonant of the simple adjective (with loss of stem accent and with change of spelling where necessary to preserve the consonant sound). Many absolute superlatives are irregular in their formation (cf. their Latin counterparts). Some adjectives possess two absolute superlatives, one of popular derivation, and one of learned derivation based on Latin.

rápido	**rapidíssimo**	**rapidissimamente**
quick	most quick	most quickly
rico	**riquíssimo**	
rich	extremely rich	
feio	**feiíssimo**	
ugly	exceedingly ugly	

pio	piíssimo
pious	most pious
feliz	**felicíssimo**
happy	extremely happy
antigo	**antiquíssimo** [-kw-]
ancient	exceedingly old
mau	**malíssimo** *or* **péssimo**
bad	exceedingly bad
fácil	**facilíssimo** *or* **facílimo**
easy	very easy indeed
pobre	**pobríssimo** *or* **paupérrimo**
poor	extremely poor

Esta lição é dificílima.   This lesson is most difficult.

São um par felicíssimo.   They are a most happy pair.

É um senhor riquíssimo.   He is a most wealthy gentleman.

NOTE: **Muitíssimo** translates *very much*.

202. TRANSLATION OF COMPARATIVE PLUS INDEFINITE WORD. The English *comparative + than + indefinite word* is normally translated into Portuguese by *comparative* + **(do) que** + *negative*.

Conhece Lisboa melhor que ninguém.

He knows Lisbon better than anyone.

Estudávamos isso mais que nenhuma outra coisa.

We studied that more than anything else.

VOCABULARY

adquirir	to acquire	**o assunto**	matter, subject
advertir	to warn; to notice	**o bacalhau**	cod, codfish
		belo	lovely, beautiful
antes	before; rather	**um bocado**	a little, a bit
anunciar	to announce; to advertise	**(de)**	(of)
		a bondade	goodness, kindness
o arroz	rice		
assar	to roast, grill	**cada** (*adj.*)[1]	each

[1] *Each* (*pron.*) and *each one* are to be translated by **cada um(a)** or **cada qual**, though **cada** alone is admissible in expressions of rate (*e.g.*, **Comprou-os a cinco cruzeiros cada,** *She bought them for five cruzeiros each*).

a carne	flesh; meat	o ombro	shoulder
com certeza	certainly	oxalá (que)	would (that), if only
conduzir	to lead; to drive		
consolar	to console	pois	well; then; so
depressa	quickly, fast	por aí	that way
a dose	dose, portion	por ali	that way
a ementa	menu	por aqui	this way
encomendar	to order (*food, books, groceries, etc.*)	que [1]	for, because
		o queijo	cheese
		rápido	quick; quickly; fast
estúpido	stupid		
a faca	knife	a salada	salad
o favor	favour	seco	dry
o feijão	(runner, haricot, French) bean	a(s) sobremesa(s)	dessert
o garfo	fork	a sopa	soup
indicar	to indicate, point out	telefonar	to telephone
		o tipo	type, sort, kind
a lista	list; menu	usar	to use; to wear
a maioria	majority	a uva	grape
mal-passado	rare, underdone	o vinho do Porto	Port wine
a montanha	mountain		
nascer	to be born	a vista	view, sight

depois em seguida então logo pois	then, after that, next
faz(ia) favor com licença dá-me licença	excuse me, (*asking permission, etc.*)
sinto muito perdão desculpe	sorry, excuse me
como?	pardon? (= what did you say?)

[1] Often without English equivalent: **Vamos embora que são horas de partir** (*Come on; it's time we were off*).

333

EXERCISES

I. (*a*) *Study and translate:* Dize-me onde está ele. Compre-mos outro. Que façam a mesma coisa. Ide-vos embora. Tenha a bondade de mo mostrar. Quer trazer-me um bocado de pão? Queira falar mais devagar. Faça favor de indicar qual é. Ficaremos aqui quer venham quer não. Que o anunciem eles. Não o conduzas por aqui. Vamos consolá-lo. Oxalá o pudera advertir! É a vista mais bela que conhecemos. Fê-lo melhor do que esperáveis, não é verdade? Não tenho mais que um irmão. Não temos mais duma irmã. Quantos mais livros se lêem, mais se sabe. É a montanha mais alta do país.

(*b*) *Give the four possible renderings of the following:* Come in (*e.g.*, entra, entre você, entrai, entrem vocês). Eat it. Don't drink it. Ask for another. Be good. Don't do that. Go to bed. Be careful. You do the same (thing). May you be lucky. Bring me a knife, fork and spoon. Don't waken him.

(*c*) *Translate:* The more books he read the more he knew. The more he knew the less he spoke. He was not so good as to explain (**que** + *subjunctive*) what he had acquired. They are not so stupid as to believe that. This is the worst thing he has done. If only I had been born three years later! Kindly give me your address, madam. Please don't discuss matters of this sort. This is as practical as that is ridiculous. Excuse me. Sorry!

II. (*a*) *Study and translate:* 1 Enquanto tivermos cabeça sobre os ombros, usemo-la como devemos. 2. — O que me aconselhas que faça? — Faz o que quiseres. 3. Quando a vires, diz-lhe que o pense bem, que um marido como ele não se encontra todos os dias. 4. São dificílimos os pri-meiros capítulos deste livro, mas já os vamos entendendo. 5. Não deixe o senhor de a visitar quando estiver em Braga. Seguro que estará. 6. É preciso falar com ele. Que te veja, que te diga o que tenciona fazer ao chegar à capital.

7. Ó Miguel, telefone ao médico que estou doente.   8. Tome uma colherada depois de cada refeição.   9. Tenha a bondade de me dizer qual é o melhor caminho para ir à estação do caminho de ferro do Cais do Sodré.   10. Que a traga ela já, que não temos muito tempo.

(b) *Translate:* 1. If he comes back tell him I'm not in to (**para**) anybody.   2. He's not as stupid as he looks. — He couldn't be!   3. I don't understand Portuguese well; please don't speak so quickly.   4. Read three lessons and then write four exercises.   5. Let me see it and I'll tell you if it's yours or not.   6. Don't tell me I'm the only one to realize what he's trying to do.   7. Don't think that this building is better built (**construído**) than that one.   8. In my opinion he dances better than anybody.   9. Tell me: is the important thing that they should do it as little as possible?   10. It seems to me to be better to carry on like this rather than to waste (=lose) time asking so many questions.

III. (a) *Study and translate:*

— Os senhores já pediram?

— Ainda não. Pois bem, deixe ver a ementa. Vamos escolher. Primeiro, para mim sopa, e salada de tomates para o meu amigo, apenas meia dose. Depois, como peixe, traga-nos bacalhau com feijões.

— E como carne, senhor?

— Vejamos. Pois ... eu vou comer galinha assada com arroz, mas o meu amigo preferia bife com batatas fritas, malpassado.

— Está dito, senhor, com certeza. Querem alguma coisa de beber?

— Queremos, sim. Faça favor de trazer-nos uma garrafa de vinho tinto seco. E também, como sobremesa, queríamos queijo do Alentejo e uvas.

— Muito bem, senhores; muito obrigado.

(b) *Translate:* Last night my wife and I went out for dinner to a restaurant in the Rua Primeiro de Dezembro, (which is) called the Leão d'Ouro.[1] First of all I ordered a glass of white Port for my wife and a tankard of beer for myself. Then we asked the waiter to bring us the menu. My wife ordered tomato salad and I chose soup. As we had already eaten well at lunchtime we decided not to have (**comer**) fish. For the meat course (**Como carne**) we both chose steak with roast potatoes and vegetables. During the meal we drank a half-bottle of dry white wine, and finished up by having cheese and drinking white coffee (**café com leite**). When we had paid the bill we both agreed that one can eat very cheaply (**barato**) in Lisbon.

[1] = Golden Lion.

LESSON XXXIII

203. THE FORMATION OF THE INFLECTED INFINITIVE. The inflected infinitive is formed by adding to the infinitive the following endings: *(none)*, **-es**, *(none)*, **-mos**, **-des**, **-em**. The verb **pôr** loses its circumflex on the addition of the extra syllable.

comprar, comprares, comprar, comprarmos, comprardes, comprarem;

pôr, pọres, pôr, pọrmos, pọrdes, pọrem.

NOTES. 1. The first and third persons singular have no added flection. This is clarified in § 204 (*b*) (2) Note 2.

2. The inflected infinitive and future subjunctive are identical in form only in those verbs which have a regular preterite (see § 188).

3. The inflected infinitive is sometimes called the "personal" infinitive; neither description is entirely satisfactory.

204. THE USES OF THE INFLECTED INFINITIVE. (*a*) As a preamble to the uses of the inflected infinitive it is first necessary to state the uses of the non-inflected infinitive. These are threefold; it is used:

(1) whenever the infinitive indicates general action, as if it were an abstract noun, or when there is no thought of any agent, *e.g.*:

Estudar ⎱ **aproveita.** To study is profitable. Study(ing) is
O estudar ⎰ profitable. It is profitable to study.
Querẹr é podẹr. Where there's a will, there's a way (*lit.*, To wish is to be able).

NOTE: When the infinitive is the subject of a sentence it may be preceded by the definite article.

(2) whenever the infinitive is dependent on some other verb (see § 174), flection only being permissible when the infinitive is

337

so far removed from its auxiliary and its own subject as otherwise to obscure the sense.

Vi-os atravessar a rua onde morava o sęu tio Bernardo, họmem de grande influência política naquęla época, e depọis tomar/tomarem pela Avenida da Liberdade.

I saw them cross the road in which there lived their Uncle Bernard, a man of great political influence at that time, and then turn into the Avenida da Liberdade.

(3) whenever the infinitive is introduced by an independent preposition,

(i) provided the subject of the infinitive is the same as that of the main verb;

Depọis de chegar, viram as ruínas.
After arriving (*or* After they arrived), they saw the ruins.

but: **Depọis de chegarem, fugimos.**
After they arrived, we fled.

but (ii) the inflected infinitive, however, is necessary if its subject is expressed [see also (*b*) (1) below];

Depọis de ęles chegarem, viram as ruínas.
After arriving, they saw the ruins.

and (iii) the inflected infinitive is also available even if its subject is not expressed [see also (*b*) (2) note 1 below].

Depọis de chegarem, viram as ruínas.
After arriving, they saw the ruins.

(*b*) The uses of the inflected infinitive are threefold also; it is used:

(1) whenever the infinitive is accompanied by its own subject

(noun or pronoun), whether this be the same as the subject of an adjacent verb, or whether it be different.

Ao chegarem $\left\{\begin{array}{l}\textbf{os soldados}\\\textbf{eles}\end{array}\right\}$, $\left\{\begin{array}{l}\textbf{o povo fugiu}\\\textbf{viram as ruínas}\end{array}\right\}$.

When $\left\{\begin{array}{l}\text{the soldiers}\\\text{they}\end{array}\right\}$ arrived, $\left\{\begin{array}{l}\text{the people fled}\\\text{they saw the ruins}\end{array}\right\}$.

NOTE: It would be incorrect to say **Ao chegar** $\left\{\begin{array}{l}\textbf{os soldados}\\\textbf{eles}\end{array}\right\}$, . . .

(2) whenever it is necessary to individualize the agent, and to refer the action to a specific person, either to avoid confusion, or to clarify the thought. The infinitive *must* agree with the person we have in mind, if the subject of the adjacent verb is different.

Ao chegarem, $\left\{\begin{array}{l}\textbf{o povo fugiu}\\\textbf{viram as ruínas}\end{array}\right\}$.

When they arrived $\left\{\begin{array}{l}\text{the people fled}\\\text{they saw the ruins}\end{array}\right\}$.

NOTES. 1. It would be incorrect to say **Ao chegar, o povo fugiu,** unless **o povo** were also the subject of **chegar,** which in this example would be nonsensical. It *is* permissible, however, to say **Ao chegar, viram as ruínas,** it being understood that the subject of **chegar** is also that of **viram.**

2. When reference is made to the first or third person singular and the subject of the adjacent verb is *another* person, it is necessary to *include* the appropriate pronoun:

Ao chegar $\left\{\begin{array}{l}\textbf{eu}\\\textbf{você}\\\textbf{ele}\end{array}\right\}$, **o povo fugiu.** When $\left\{\begin{array}{l}\text{I}\\\text{you}\\\text{he}\end{array}\right\}$ arrived, the people fled.

Similarly:

Ao chegar o soldado, $\left\{\begin{array}{l}\textbf{o povo fugiu}\\\textbf{viu as ruínas}\end{array}\right\}$.

When the soldier arrived, $\left\{\begin{array}{l}\text{the people fled}\\\text{he saw the ruins}\end{array}\right\}$.

(3) whenever the author *intentionally wishes* to throw into relief the person to whom the infinitive refers; see (*a*) (2) above.

Vi-os atravessar a rua onde morava o sẹu tio Bernardo, họmem de grande influência política naquẹla época, e depọis tomarem pela Avenida da Liberdade.

I saw them cross the road in which there lived their Uncle Bernard, a man of great political influence at that time, and then turn into the Avenida da Liberdade.

(*c*) Further examples should amply illustrate the uses of this construction, which is unique to Portuguese. The subject, when expressed by means of a noun or pronoun, nearly always follows the infinitive, except after a preposition. When the inflected infinitive (or " personal " infinitive in the case of the first and third persons singular) is the subject and precedes the finite verb, or when it is the direct object of the sentence, it *must* be preceded by the definite article. Notice how these locutions may often be a means of replacing complicated subordinate clauses.

O patinar ẹu é perigọso. It is dangerous for me to skate.
O patinares (tu) é perigọso. It is dangerous for you to skate.
É uma vergọnha (o) não sabẹrmos lẹr. It's shameful that we can't read.
Fui-me embọra sem me vẹrem. I went off unseen by them.
Ao vẹrem-me, saíste. When they saw me, you went out.
Dei-te os livros pạra os lẹres. I gave you the books so you'd read them.
Não é pạra ẹu dizẹr. It's not for me to say.
Ajudámo-los por estarem derreados. We helped them because they were dog-tired.
Não convém (o) dizẹrmos isso aqui. It is not becoming for us to say that here.
Agradeci-lhes o tẹrem defendido mẹu filho. I thanked them for having defended my son.
Perdoou-lhes o havẹrem-nos ọfendido. He forgave them for having offended us.

(d) The verb **parecẹr** (*to seem*) may be used personally with infinitive, or impersonally with inflected infinitive.

Parẹces não querẹr ir. }
(Tu) parẹce não querẹres ir. } You don't seem to want to go.
(Parẹce que não quẹres ir is also possible of course.)

(e) The inflected infinitive is also found after verbs of saying, thinking and knowing. This construction is rare and should not be used by the student, although he should be able to recognize it. The definite article is not used in this construction.

Dissẹmos sẹrem maliciọsos. We said they were malicious.
Julgamos estares cansada. We think you're tired.
Sabem tẹrmos partido. They know we've left.

(f) As a formal imperative, particularly in business correspondence, **é favọr** + *inflected infinitive* is to be found:

É favọr enviarem cem toneladas de farinha.
Please send one hundred tons of flour.
É favọr os senhọres passageiros não cuspirem.
Passengers are requested not to spit.

205. IDIOMS WITH **andar**. (a) **andar** is frequently employed instead of **estar** to form the *continuous* or *progressive* tense:

Há quatro anos que ando { **a vendẹr** / **vendendo** } **ạutomóveis.**

I've been selling cars for four years.

(b) **andar** is frequently employed instead of **estar** to indicate a continual or successive state of being:

andar aborrecido, melancólico, preocupado, triste, etc.
to be bored, melancholy, worried, sad, etc.

(c) **andar em** is used to render habitual attendance at a place of learning:

andar na escọla, no colégio, na universidade, etc.
to go to (to attend) school, college, university, etc.

(*d*) The following should also be noted:

andar bom	to be well (*of health*)
andar mau	to be ill (*of health*)
andar bem	to go well, prosper
andar mal	to go badly
andar mal de dinheiro	to be hard up, be short of money
andar **ir** } **de mal a piọr**	to go from bad to worse
andar **ir** } **nos trinta**	to be getting on for thirty (*years of age*)
andar **estar** } **na casa dos trinta**[1]	to be thirtyish, thirty-odd
Vamos andando!	Let's be going!

Note also:

Vamos lá!	Let's be going!
Vamos embọra!	Let's be off!

206. THE REITERATIVE REPLY. In Portuguese it is customary not to answer a question by a curt **sim** (*yes*) or **não** (*no*), but rather by reiterating the main verb of the question in the appropriate person (accompanied optionally by **sim** or **não**).

— **Falou com o catedrático?**   — **Falei, sim, senhọr.**
  "Did you speak to the professor?"   "Yes, I did."

— **Já fọste a Santos?**   — **Fui.**
  "Ever been to Santos?"   "Yes."

— **Tens mẹdo?**   — **Não tenho, não.**
  "Afraid?"   "No, no."

VOCABULARY

ạlguma vẹz	ever; sometimes	**apagar**	to switch off; to put out, extinguish
ạlgumas vẹzes	sometimes		
o alojamento	lodging, accommodation	**aproveitar**	to be profitable; to profit by

[1] Note also **tẹr sẹus trinta anos** (*to be a good thirty*); the expression **casa** here means *section, group.*

o assento	seat	famoso	famous
bastar	to be enough, suffice	o fim	end; aim, object
		a gorjeta	tip, gratuity
breve (adj.)	brief, short	hospedar-se	to lodge, put up
a camio-neta	motor-coach; lorry	inteiro	entire, whole
		o interesse	interest
o carro de {aluguel aluguer}	taxi	já	already; now; ever; at once
		livre	free, unoccupied, empty
a casa de hóspedes	guest-house, boarding house	o motorista	driver, motorist
		parar	to stop
cavaquear	to chat	a península	peninsula
célebre	famous	a pensão	boarding-house
cessar	to cease, stop	perigoso	dangerous
chegar	to be enough, suffice	o poeta	poet
		a possibili-dade	possibility
a costa	coast	a praia	beach
cruzar	to cross	realizar	to bring about, carry out
curto	short, brief		
a custo	with difficulty	a roupa	clothes
a discussão	discussion	o salário	wage(s)
diversos	various	a serra	saw; mountain range
em lugar de	in place of		
em vez de	instead of	simpático	nice, likeable
encantador	charming	o táxi [ˈtaksi]	taxi
enfim	at last; in short	zangado	angry
esquerdo	left		

é pena   it is a pity, a shame

longe de mim seja + *infinitive*   far be it from me to ...

no
pelo } caminho   en route, on the way

de novo
novamente } again, once more
outra vez

Study also the expressions and idioms listed in § 205.

EXERCISES

I. (a) *Study and translate:* Sem me verem. Para o fazeres. É perigoso fazermos isso. Depois de terem acabado. Ao chegardes. Já não aproveitava partirmos cedo. Antes de ele entrar. É preciso irmos embora. Por serem muito ricos. São horas de eu partir. É pena tu não saberes ler. Este dinheiro é para nós gastarmos. Anda zangada comigo. Já está na casa dos quarenta. Todos parece terem muita pressa.

(b) *Translate, using the personal/inflected infinitive where possible:* I shall speak to him before we leave. It is possible that they do not know it. This book is for me to read. It is not for you to say. I went in without their hearing me. I shall leave after they have arrived. I have some exercises for you to mark. It is a pity that he has no money. They both passed without coming to see me. Before rising from the table. "Ever been to Cacilhas?" "Yes, three times."

II. (a) *Study and translate:* 1. Nós fizemos o trabalho em vez de eles o fazerem. 2. Apaga sempre a luz antes de eu adormecer. 3. Ando a considerar a possibilidade de tu realizares os meus projectos. 4. Antes de se levantarem da mesa, uma das raparigas pediu um copo de água para eu beber. 5. Julgava que fosses fazer isso antes de voltares para a aldeia. 6. Há muitos dias que ando a pensar nisto. 7. Temos andado a fazer compras. 8. Ao chegarem à porta, vinha de dentro segundo grupo, a Maria e os seus avós, o tio Frederico, mais homens e mais mulheres. 9. Em vez de trazeres os pãezinhos que eu te tinha pedido, traz um bocado de queijo para o Joãozinho comer. 10. Quando, finalmente, a criada atravessou a praça, havia lá, como todas as tardes, grupos de operários a cavaquearem.

(b) *Translate, using the personal/inflected infinitive where possible:* 1. But nobody answered him, because words were useless. 2. It would be better for us to wait until he arrives. 3. His wage did not suffice for the two [of them] to eat nor for her to buy the clothes they so much needed. 4. I stopped going to school five years ago. 5. Gentlemen lift the seat. 6. Far be it from us to arrive at such a conclusion. 7. We made our way along the narrow street, without knowing quite (**exąctamente**) why, nor where we were going. 8. Sometimes we have breakfast in (**na**) bed before getting up. 9. It is dangerous for us to behave like this in this country. 10. He was worried because we hadn't written to him.

III. (*a*) *Study and translate:* Ao chegarmos ao Porto e por não termos alojamento apanhámos um táxi, perguntando ao motorista se nos podia recomendar um bom hotel ou pensão. Explicámos-lhe que só desejávamos hospedar-nos num hotel barato, visto que não pensávamos passar mais de dois ou três dias no Porto. Respondeu-nos que, por serem duas horas da noite, a custo acharíamos um quarto livre, que quase todos os hotéis e pensões estariam cheios, sobretudo por ser Junho. Parámos em cinco hotéis e casas de hóspedes até que enfim descobrimos uma pequena casa de hóspedes onde o dono nos ofereceu um quarto com duas camas. O quarto estava limpo e era baratíssimo, sendo o preço sòmente quarenta escudos por dia, primeiro almoço e jantar inclusive. Sem hesitar, aceitámos, pagámos ao motorista, dando-lhe uma boa gorjeta, e fomos deitar-nos imediatamente.

(*b*) *Translate, using the personal /inflected infinitive where possible:* Three days after our arrival in Lisbon we got up early in the morning, having decided to visit the left bank of the Tagus. We had intended to go to the Costa da Caparica, where there is an excellent beach, in order to do some sun- and sea bathing. However, on arriving at Cacilhas, we were about to cross the main square with the aim of catching one of the motor-coaches which so frequently cross the peninsula, when a taxi-driver approached us and offered to take us round the whole peninsula for only three hundred escudos each. After a brief discussion we accepted and got

in (*use* **entrar**) the taxi.   Our driver was very likeable and
pointed out various things of interest en route.   Several
times we stopped to admire the view, or the scenery of
the Serra da Arrábida.   We had lunch at the Portinho da
Arrábida at a charming little restaurant with a view towards
the sea.   In the afternoon we continued our journey along
the coast and visited Setúbal where we saw the monument dedicated to Bocage, the famous eighteenth-century
poet so much admired by William Beckford.   We finally
arrived at Cacilhas at about half past four.

LESSON XXXIV

207. ORTHOGRAPHY-CHANGING AND RELATED VERBS. It is a regular tendency of Portuguese verbs to preserve throughout their conjugation the consonantal sound at the end of the *stem* (as it stands when we cut off the infinitive ending **-ar, -ęr, -ir**). Hence before certain vowels of the flectional suffix a change in the spelling of the end of the stem is required. This applies not only to regular verbs but to irregular verbs also.

208. **-ar** VERBS. Before flectional **e** these changes occur:

(*a*) Verbs in **-car** change **c** to **qu** to keep the [k] sound:

> **ficar,** *to remain*

> *preterite:* fiquei, ficaste, ficou, *etc.*
> *pres. subj.:* fique, fiques, fique, fiquęmos, fiqueis, fiquem

(*b*) Verbs in **-gar** change **g** to **gu** to keep the [g] or [g] sound:

> **chegar,** *to arrive*

> *preterite:* cheguei, chegaste, chegou, *etc.*
> *pres. subj.:* chęgue, chęgues, chęgue, cheguęmos, chegueis, chęguem

(*c*) Verbs in **-çar** omit the cedilla from the **c,** as being superfluous:

> **caçar,** *to hunt*

> *preterite:* cacei, caçaste, caçou, *etc.*
> *pres. subj.:* cace, caces, cace, cacęmos, caceis, cacem

NOTE: There is no orthographic change in **-jar** verbs because both **g** and **j** may represent the [ʒ] sound before **e.**

> **viajar,** *to travel*
> *preterite:* viajei, viajaste, viajou, *etc.*
> *pres. subj.:* viaje, viajes, viaje, viajęmos, viajeis, viajem

209. **-ęr** AND **-ir** VERBS. Before flectional **o** or **a** the following changes occur:

347

(*a*) Verbs in **-cer** change **c** to **ç** to keep the [s] sound:

> **conhecer,** *to know*

pres. indic.: conheço, conheces, conhece, *etc.*
pres. subj.: conheça, conheças, conheça, conheçamos, conheçais, conheçam

(*b*) Verbs in **-ger** and **-gir** (regular or not) change **g** to **j** to keep the [ʒ] sound:

> **eleger,** *to choose*

pres. indic.: elejo, eleges, elege, *etc.*
pres. subj.: eleja, elejas, eleja, elejamos, elejais, elejam

> **dirigir,** *to direct*

pres. indic.: dirijo, diriges, dirige, *etc.*
pres. subj.: dirija, dirijas, dirija, dirijamos, dirijais, dirijam

> **fugir,** *to flee*

pres. indic.: fujo, foges, foge, *etc.*
pres. subj.: fuja, fujas, fuja, fujamos, fujais, fujam

(*c*) Two rare verbs, **extorquir,** *to extort*, and **retorquir,** *to retort*, change **qu** to **c**:

pres. indic.: exturco, extorques, extorque, *etc.*
pres. subj.: exturca, exturcas, exturca, exturcamos, exturcais, exturcam

(*d*) Verbs in **-guer** and **-guir** (regular or not) omit their unpronounced **u**:

> **erguer,** *to erect*

pres. indic.: ergo, ergues, ergue, *etc.*
pres. subj.: erga, ergas, erga, ergamos, ergais, ergam

> **seguir,** *to follow, carry on*

pres. indic.: sigo, segues, segue, *etc.*
pres. subj.: siga, sigas, siga, sigamos, sigais, sigam

210. Changes Involving the Written Accent.   Apart from the orthographical changes given above, certain verbs require changes involving the inclusion of a written accent.   Verbs ending in **-oer, -air,** and **-uir** require *both* an orthographical change *and* an accent change.

211. Verbs in **-guar** and the few very rare verbs in **-quar** require an acute accent on stressed **u** before flectional **e.**[1]   It should also be noted that unstressed **u** [w] is pronounced before flectional **e** (see § 99) just as before flectional **o** and **a.**

    averiguar, *to ascertain, find out*

preterite: averiguei [-ˈgwɐj], averiguaste, averiguou, *etc.*

pres. subj.: averigúe [-ˈgui], averigúes, averigúe, averiguemos
             [-ˈgwemuʃ], averigueis [-ˈgwɐjʃ], averigúem

    antiquar, *to antiquate, make out-of-date*

preterite: antiquei [-ˈkwɐj], antiquaste, antiquou, *etc.*

pres. subj.: antiqúe [-ˈkui], antiqúes, antiqúe, antiquemos
             [-ˈkwemuʃ], antiqueis [-ˈkwɐjʃ], antiqúem

212. Verbs ending in **-oer** change to **i** [j] the **e** of the endings of the second and third persons singular of the present indicative; the result is an open diphthong written **ói.**   In addition, in the conjugation of such verbs, an acute accent is required on stressed flectional **i.**

    moer, *to grind*

pres. indic.: moo, móis (*for* moes), mói (*for* moe), moemos, moeis,
             moem

impf. indic.: moía, moías, moía, moíamos, moíeis, moíam

preterite: moí, moeu, *etc.*

past part.: moído

213. Verbs ending in **-air** have first person singular of the present indicative in **-aio,** and change to **i** [j] the **e** of the endings of the second and third persons singular of the present indicative, the result being an open diphthong written **ai.**   In addition, in the

---

[1] In Brazilian Portuguese, the stress-pattern is different in verbs of this type: **averíguo, averíguas,** etc.

conjugation of such verbs, an acute accent is required on stressed flectional **i** *except* in the:

(i) infinitive
(ii) gerund
(iii) third person singular of the preterite
(iv) first and third persons singular and first and second persons plural of the future subjunctive and inflected infinitive.

cair, *to fall*

pres. indic.:	caio, cais (*for* caes), cai (*for* cae), caímos, caís, caem
pres. subj.:	caia, *etc.*
impf. indic.:	caía, caías, caía, caíamos, caíeis, caíam
preterite:	caí, caíste, caiu, caímos, caístes, caíram
impf. subj.:	caísse, *etc.*
syn. plupf.:	caíra, *etc.*
fut. subj.: *infl. inf.:* }	cair, caíres, cair, cairmos, cairdes, caírem
gerund:	caindo
past part.:	caído

214. Verbs ending in **-uir** change to **i** [j] the **e** of the endings of the second and third persons singular of the present indicative; the result is a closed diphthong written **ui**. In addition, in the conjugation of such verbs, an acute accent is required on stressed flectional **i** *except* in the:

(i) infinitive
(ii) gerund
(iii) third person singular of the preterite
(iv) first and third persons singular and first and second persons plural of the future subjunctive and inflected infinitive.

possuir, *to possess*

pres. indic.:	possuo, possuis (*for* possues), possui (*for* possue), possuímos, possuís, possuem
impf. indic.:	possuía, possuías, possuía, possuíamos, possuíeis, possuíam
preterite:	possuí, possuíste, possuiu, possuímos, possuístes, possuíram

impf. subj.:   possuísse, *etc.*
syn. plupf.:   possuíra, *etc.*
fut. subj.:⎫   possuir, possuíres, possuir, possuirmos, possuirdes,
infl. inf.:⎭   possuírem
gerund: possuindo
past part.:   possuído

215. Of the verbs ending in **-struir,** three, **construir** (*to build, construct*), **destruir** (*to destroy*) and the obsolescent **estruir** (*to destroy*), may be conjugated like **possuir** or may have alternative second and third persons singular, present indicative, in **-óis** and **-ói,** and third person plural, present indicative, in **-oem.** The other verbs in **-struir,** *i.e.,* **instruir** (*to instruct*) and **obstruir** (*to obstruct*) are conjugated like **possuir.**

   destruir, *to destroy*

prés. indic.: destruo, destruis *or* destróis, destrui *or* destrói, destruímos, destruís, destruem *or* destroem

216. The verbs **delinquir** (*to be delinquent, transgress*), **arguir** (*to censure; to infer, imply*) and **redarguir** (*to retort*), in all of which the **u** is pronounced (see § 99), require an acute accent on *stressed* **u** before flectional **e** or **i**; they are otherwise conjugated like **possuir.**

   arguir, *to censure; to infer, imply*

pres. indic.: arguo, argúis [-ˈguiʃ], argúi [-ˈgui], arguímos, arguís, argúem

217. (*a*) A number of verbs have radical **i** or **u** preceded by a vowel with which it does *not* form a diphthong. Such verbs take an acute accent on the **i** or **u** in the forms stressing the radical. A comprehensive list of such verbs includes:

   enraizar [ɐi], *to take root;*
   europeizar [ei], *to europeanize;*
   judaizar [ɐi], *to make Jewish;*

abaular [ɐu], *to camber*;
apaular [ɐu], *to make marshy*;
saudar [ɐu], *to greet*; *to salute*;
coibir [ui], *to curb*;
proibir [ui], *to prohibit, forbid.*

pres. indic.: saúdo, saúdas, saúda, saudamos, saudais, saúdam
pres. subj.: saúde, saúdes, saúde, saudemos, saudeis, saúdem

NOTE. Contrast such verbs as ajaular and enjaular, *to cage up*; ensaiar, *to try*; boiar, *to float*; causar, *to cause*; louvar, *to praise*; deitar, *to throw*, etc., etc., where the radical *is* a diphthong.

(*b*) Similarly behave a number of verbs with radical iu, ui and eu. A comprehensive list of such verbs includes:

amiudar [iu], *to redouble*;
esmiuçar [iu], *to shatter*; *to (express in) detail*;
arruinar [ui], *to ruin*;
cuidar [ui], *to believe, think*;[1]
reunir [iu], *to gather together.*

pres. indic.: reúno, reúnes, reúne, reunimos, reunis, reúnem
pres. subj.: reúna, reúnas, reúna, reunamos, reunais, reúnam

218. The otherwise regular verbs, coar, *to filter*, parar, *to stop*, and pelar, *to peel*, have slight modifications in the present indicative [see § 8 (*c*) and (*d*)]:

côas, côa; pára; pélo, pélas, péla.

219. Compounds of the irregular verbs ter, vir and pôr exhibit the following features:

(*a*) The second and third persons singular of the present indicative of compounds of ter and vir carry an acute accent on the stressed radical.

ter: tens, tem, but conter (*to contain*): conténs, contém;
vir: vens, vem, but convir (*to fit, suit*): convéns, convém.

---

[1] Some vacillation occurs in the pronunciation of this verb in the forms where the radical is stressed. The accent is generally omitted nowadays. Thus both cuído ['kwiðu] and cuido ['kujðu], etc., are found.

(b) The infinitive of the compounds of **pôr** does not carry the circumflex accent, *e.g.*, **compor**, *to compose*; but note **compô-lo,** *to compose it.*

VOCABULARY

abotoar	to button (up)	**o emprego**	job
o acordo	agreement	**o ensaio**	essay
de acordo	in agreement	**estabelecer**	to establish, set up
algarvio	(of the) Algarve (*adj.*)	**o gerente**	manager
andar de farda	to wear uniform	**o jeito**	skill, knack; way
antigamente	formerly	**justificar**	to justify
aparecer	to appear	**lustroso**	shiny
apertado	tight, close-fitting	**não obstante**	notwithstanding
aplacar	to appease, pacify	**a obra**	work (*e.g., literary*)
apresentar-se	to appear	**a ortografia**	spelling, orthography
atrair	to attract	**perseguir**	to pursue; to persecute
as calças	trousers		
o casaco	coat, jacket	**publicar**	to publish
conceder	to concede, grant	**a quinta**	farm, country estate
concluir	to conclude	**rasgar**	to tear (up)
a conduta	conduct, behaviour	**a regra**	rule
		sentir	to regret
confundir	to confuse	**o sobretudo**	overcoat
contrariar	to go against	**sossegar**	to calm, relieve
dar graças (a)	to thank	**substituir**	to substitute
		tropeçar	to stumble
desagradar	to displease	**uns quantos**	a number of
o desgosto	displeasure	**utilizar**	to use, utilize
desta {**feita** / **vez**}	on this occasion	**verificar-se**	to take place
		a vontade	will
distinguir	to distinguish	**zangar-se (com)**	to get angry (with)
efectuar	to bring about		
em baixo	at the bottom, below		

353

NOTE: The verb **parecer** means *to appear* in the sense of *to seem*; the verbs **aparecer** and **apresentar-se** mean *to appear* in the sense of *to come into view, emerge*.

EXERCISES

I. (*a*) *Give the first person singular of the present subjunctive of:* aparecer, viajar, redarguir, tropeçar, distinguir, perseguir, estabelecer, atrair, publicar, substituir, averiguar, sossegar, moer, reunir, saudar, contrariar, efectuar, verificar-se.

(*b*) *Study and translate:* Cheguei ontem. Até que mo ofereça. Contanto que o não publiquem. Oxalá que justifiquem a sua conduta. Primeiro que consiga aplacá-la. Zanguei-me e rasguei a carta. Ao saírem do café.[1] Caiu morto. Possuíam uma pequena quinta. A fim que averigúe o que se verificou. Não porque o conheças. Proíbe-me que saia. Siga lendo. Foi assim que concluímos o ensaio. Contêm pêssegos.

(*c*) *Translate:* I threatened him. Don't deny it. So long as he doesn't destroy it first. I handed him the book. She wants me to ascertain what happened. Without their contributing anything. It was this that attracted me. It is possible he will begin tomorrow morning. We thanked him for everything. Devote yourself to more important things. Even if he manages to bring it about. Unless we oblige them to pay. I doubt whether he will desire it. Even if he appears now.

II. (*a*) *Study and translate:* 1. Ficámos todos de acordo em que a mudança se efectuasse deste jeito. 2. Convém que saibam todos como o gerente pôde contrariar a vontade dos empregados. 3. Quanto melhor conheço o Algarve, mais gosto dele e mais ganas sinto de ir estabelecer-me ali. 4.

---

[1] Note that the verb **sair** may mean *to go out, to come out,* or *to depart*; similarly **sair** (**de**), (*to leave*).

Aproximei-me da janela onde estava ela, e rapidamente, sem que me visse ninguém, entreguei-lhe a carta. 5. Contudo eu o que fiz para que V. Exª. me dedique uma das suas melhores poesias? 6. Quando assim me ouvi chamar pela primeira vez, julguei terem-me confundido com outra. 7. A ideia consiste em irmos construindo bons hotéis por todo o país para assim atrairmos os turistas estrangeiros. 8. Nesta obra têm-se seguido as regras de ortografia estabelecidas pelo Acordo Luso-Brasileiro do ano de 1945. 9. Concederam-nos licença para cá trabalharmos, mas apenas sob condição que não utilizemos senão os livros que autorizarem eles. 10. — São muito formosas estas flores. — Pois eleja a Sra. as que quiser, contanto que me deixe umas quantas para minha esposa.

(b) *Translate:* 1. No sooner had I seen the soldiers than I began to run towards them. 2. If he had not appeared then she would have become very angry. 3. I published my first book three years ago. 4. Notwithstanding the skill he showed on this occasion, let someone justify his previous bad behaviour! 5. If it's true he possessed so much money, why couldn't he buy a new overcoat? 6. Frankly he doesn't attract me at all with his torn trousers and filthy jacket, whatever other virtues he may possess. 7. You can carry on working in this shop on condition that you don't ruin everything with your bad behaviour. 8. Down below she saw three men appear from behind the house. 9. If you think *I* persecute you, just wait till the manager finds out about this! 10. Formerly he worked on a small farm near Évora where he found out a lot about the antiquated customs of the region.

III. (a) *Study and translate:* Quando desci da camioneta em Lagos, voltei a olhar o meu fato. Durante o serviço militar, como andava de farda, poupara-o; apesar disso, já estava lustroso e ficava-me, agora, apertado. As calças sobretudo desagradavam-me. Mostravam-se mais estreitas em baixo do que as usadas nas grandes cidades. Era pena que eu não pudesse ir bem vestido, pois quem sabia se o tio Carlos não me arranjaria um emprego na fábrica? Abotoei o casaco e pus o chapéu. Não obstante o desgosto que me produzia o fato, sentia-me muito mais feliz do que das duas outras vezes que viera a Lagos. A cidadezinha algarvia não me impunha agora aquele medo que eu tinha, perante ela, antes de conhecer Lisboa e Coimbra. Lagos parecia-me, desta feita, muito mais pequena do que antigamente.

(b) *Translate:* The train was on the point of leaving the platform when I began to regret that I had promised my sister to take the parcel. Two little old women, who had been shopping, got in and looked with surprise at the strange object. If only it had fitted in my suitcase! There was only one thing left for me to do. I would wait in the train until everybody else got out. As soon as we had arrived in Santos, I took down my overcoat and put it on slowly, so as to give the others time to depart. As I left the station I had a good mind to go straight into the nearest café, order a cup of coffee and then go away leaving the parcel under the table. But, what was worse, who would believe that I had lost such (**tão**) a large object by accident (**sem me dar conta**)? It was then that the policeman spoke to me.

SER, ESTAR *and* FICAR *with the Past Participle,*
Avoidance of the Passive, Irregular Past
Participles

LESSON XXXV

220. Sẹr AND estar WITH THE PAST PARTICIPLE. **Sẹr** and **estar** may both be used with a past participle, **sẹr** to introduce *action* (*i.e.*, the passive voice) and **estar** to indicate *state* resulting from such action. In both cases the past participle agrees in number and gender with the subject of the sentence. The agent of a passive voice is introduced by **por.**

Ẹste livro fọi escrito por um português. This book was written by a Portuguese.

Está escrito em português. It is written in Portuguese.

A lição fọi muito bem explicada. The lesson was explained very well (*e.g.*, *by the teacher*).

A lição está bem explicada. The lesson is well explained.

Tinha sido convencida. She had been convinced.

Fọi convencida. She was convinced (*action*) (*e.g.*, *by his arguments*).

Estava convencida. She was convinced (*state*).

As árvores são cortadas na Primavẹra. The trees are cut in (the) spring.

As árvores estão cortadas. The trees are (=have been) cut.

Fọi acompanhado pelo embạixadọr. He was accompanied by the ambassador.

(Implies action on the part of the ambassador; the ambassador *went* with him, showed him round perhaps.)

Estava acompanhado pelo embạixadọr. He was accompanied by the ambassador.

(The ambassador takes a less active part in the proceedings: the ambassador *was* with him, formed part of the attendance.)

NOTE: In certain cases an English present participle may indicate state. In Portuguese the past participle must be used. Common examples of this are:

ajoelhado	kneeling	**deitado**	lying down
apoiado	leaning	**pendurado**	hanging
sentado	sitting	**reclinado**	reclining

Estavam sentados à mesa.   They were sitting at the table.
Vi-a apoiada numa bengala.   I saw her leaning on a stick.

221. A SPECIAL USE OF **ser.**   If the result of a previous action can be considered as lasting or permanent in nature, then it is frequent for **estar** to be replaced by **ser,** the participle then functioning like an adjective. This construction is usually optional.

O telhado $\begin{Bmatrix} \text{está} \\ \text{é} \end{Bmatrix}$ coberto com telhas.

> The roof is covered with tiles (*It's a tile-covered roof*).

but **O telhado está coberto de neve.**

> The roof is covered with snow (*only temporarily*).

A cabeça $\begin{Bmatrix} \text{está} \\ \text{é} \end{Bmatrix}$ coberta com cabelo.

> The head is covered by hair (*by natural law*).

but **A sua cabeça está coberta de chagas.**

> His head is covered with sores (*presumably curable*).

$\begin{Bmatrix} \text{São} \\ \text{Estão} \end{Bmatrix}$ casados.[1] $\begin{Bmatrix} \text{São} \\ \text{Estão} \end{Bmatrix}$ mortos.

> They're married.   They're dead.

NOTES.   1. In impersonal expressions involving the use of the past participle it is normal only to use **ser:**

Isso é proibido.   Era sabido (*or* conhecido) que ...
That is forbidden.   It was well known that ...

For the use of **estar** in impersonal expressions see § 79 (2).

2. Often very akin to these uses of **ser** is **ficar,** whenever used

---

[1] **Ser casado** stresses marital status ; **estar casado** tends to be used with expressions of duration.

in the sense of *to continue to be*: **Fica entendido que** ... (*It's understood that* ...).

   3. **Sẹr feito de,** *to have become of*

   O que é feito dẹle?   What has become of him?

222. A SPECIAL USE OF **ficar.**   The verb **ficar** is normally the correct choice when translating the English *to be + past participle* (or *adjective*), whenever one describes the inception of an emotion in cases where the past participle is not followed by the preposition *by* or its Portuguese equivalent (usually **por**).

Fiquei assombrado ao ouvir as notícias.   I was astonished to hear the news.

Vai ficar satisfeito com o relatório.   He's going to be pleased with the report.

Ficou contente com a chegada dos sẹus pais.   She was pleased at the arrival of her parents.

Tinha ficado desiludido quando se fọram embọra os artistas.   He had been disappointed when the artists left.

but **Fui desiludido pelas notícias.**   I was disappointed by the news.

NOTE: By analogy, the preterite of **estar** is usually replaced by that of **ficar** when in combination with a past participle or adjective.

Ẹra Pẹdro quem $\begin{Bmatrix}\text{estava} \\ \text{(ficava)}\end{Bmatrix} \begin{Bmatrix}\text{desiludido} \\ \text{triste}\end{Bmatrix}$.

It was Peter who was $\begin{Bmatrix}\text{disappointed} \\ \text{sad}\end{Bmatrix}$ (*imperfect*).

Fọi Pẹdro quem ficou $\begin{Bmatrix}\text{desiludido} \\ \text{triste}\end{Bmatrix}$.

It was Peter who was $\begin{Bmatrix}\text{disappointed} \\ \text{sad}\end{Bmatrix}$ (*preterite*).

223. AVOIDANCE OF THE PASSIVE VOICE.   The passive voice—**sẹr** (*to be*) + *past participle*—is used rather less in Portuguese than in English, and the English passive may often be better rendered into Portuguese by other means.

(a) Where the agent is expressed (*i.e.*, the doer of the action: 'written by *a Portuguese*,' 'accompanied by *the ambassador*') the true passive is more frequent than in other cases. Nevertheless, it is often avoided by transposing the verbs into the active voice and making the agent the subject. In such cases inversion of the order *subject–verb* is very occasionally used to indicate exceptional, passive-type emphasis. In cases where inversion is used, it is necessary (1) that the grammatical object be a weak object pronoun, or (2) that, if the grammatical object is a noun, it be preceded by "personal" **a** (see §227) and be placed *before* the verb.

O embaixador acompanhou-a **Acompanhou-a o embaixador**	She was accompanied by the ambassador.

O embaixador acompanhou a rainha **À rainha acompanhou o embaixador**	The queen was accompanied by the ambassador.

Inversions of type (2), which involve placing the direct noun-object *before* the verb (as in the second example above), should in general be avoided by the student, except when both subject and object are abstract nouns.

(b) Where there is no particular agent expressed or implied, the passive is generally avoided by one of the following means:

(i) by the use of a Portuguese reflexive (the most common solution); the person or thing undergoing the action is expressed as the *subject*; inanimate subjects *follow* the verb.

As crianças chamam-se João e Maria. The children are called John and Mary.

Vendem-se livros naquela loja. Books are sold in that shop.

Cortam-se as árvores na Primavera. The trees are cut in (the) spring.

NOTES. 1. This construction always functions correctly for inanimate objects; when the action is done to persons or living beings, the reflexive must be used guardedly. If there is the slightest possibility of confusion with either the true reflexive or the reciprocal reflexive, then some *other* construction *must* be adopted to indicate that the sense required in a given context is passive.

2. In colloquial usage it is common to find constructions such as **Vende-se livros** used instead of **Vendem-se livros**; this is considered incorrect by purists. However, if a modal auxiliary (such as **devęr** or **podęr**) is used with an accompanying infinitive, the auxiliary may stand quite correctly in either the singular or the plural in circumstances such as the above.

Dęvem-se⎫
Dęve-se ⎬ examinar ęstes tęxtos.   These texts must be examined.

Pǫdem-se⎫
Pǫde-se ⎬ justificar as suas ącções.   His actions can be justified.

(ii) by using the verb actively in the third person plural, thereby giving the sentence an indeterminate subject (*they, people*).

Explicaram muito bem a lição.   The lesson was explained very well.

Convencęram-na.   She was convinced.

Cǫrtam as árvores na Primavęra.   The trees are cut in (the) spring.

(iii) by introducing **a gente** (*one, people*) as an indeterminate subject (less common than solutions (i) and (ii); used principally when the verb is already reflexive and the use of a further reflexive pronoun as in solution (i) therefore impossible).

A gente não se dá conta da sua importância.   Its importance is not realized.

(**Não se dá conta** means *he does not realize*, and **não se se dá conta** is not possible).

(iv) by the use of **é preciso** + *infinitive* (to indicate admonition or obligation).

É preciso cortar as árvores na Primavęra.   The trees are to be cut in (the) spring.

224. TRANSLATION OF THE ENGLISH DATIVE PASSIVE (*I was given a book, Mary was sent a letter*, etc.). This common English construction, which builds the passive upon what is really an indirect object, is impossible in Portuguese. It must be rendered into Portuguese either (1) by recasting in such a form as *A book was given to me, A letter was sent to Mary*, etc., and by placing the new subject *after* the verb (its best position in these circumstances) or (2) by resorting to the use of **a gente** or an indeterminate third person plural in an active sentence. Also available, but to an extent limited by conditions of euphony, is a reflexive passive construction in which the object *given, sent*, etc. becomes the subject of a reflexive verb.

Fọi-me dado		
A gente dẹu-me	um livro.	I was given a book.
Dẹram-me		
Fọi enviada		
A gente enviou	uma carta a	Mary was sent a letter.
Enviaram	Maria.	
Enviou-se		
Fọi-lhe dita		
A gente disse-lhe	a verdade.	He was told the truth.
Dissẹram-lhe		

225. IRREGULAR PAST PARTICIPLES (cont.). Besides their regular past participle, some verbs have another which is irregular, derived either from the Portuguese verb or from the corresponding Latin verb. Thus:

> **enxugar,** *to wipe, dry*, has **enxugado** and **enxuto**
> **frigir,** *to fry*, has **frigido** and **frito**
> **juntar,** *to bring together*, has **juntado** and **junto**

As a rule, it is the regular participle of such verbs that is employed with the auxiliary to form the perfect tenses of the individual verb. The irregular forms are adjectival in their nature and are used only in the passive construction or merely as a participial adjective modifying a noun.   The three usages function thus:

Active: **Ęla tinha juntado uma grande fortuna.**
        She had amassed a great fortune.

Passive: **Aquęla fortuna fǫi junta só a custo.**
        That fortune was amassed only with difficulty.

Adjectival: **Tǫda ęssa grande fortuna junta pertence a uma única pessǫa.**
        All that great amassed fortune belongs to one single person.

Common verbs with double past participles are listed here; only the irregular forms are given.

aceitar	(*to accept*)	aceite *or* aceito
acendęr	(*to set alight, light, switch on*)	acęso
afligir	(*to grieve, afflict*)	aflito
aspergir	(*to sprinkle*)	aspęrso
assentar	(*to settle*)	assente
elegęr	(*to elect, choose*)	eleito
entregar	(*to hand over, pass, deliver*)	entręgue
envǫlvęr	(*to wrap, wrap up*)	envǫlto
enxugar	(*to wipe, dry*)	enxuto
fixar	(*to fix*)	fixo
frigir	(*to fry*)	frito
imprimir	(*to print*)	impręsso
isentar	(*to exempt*)	isento
juntar	(*to amass, bring together, join*)	junto
matar	(*to kill*)	mǫrto
morręr	(*to die*)	mǫrto
prendęr	(*to fasten, catch, seize, capture*)	pręso
rompęr	(*to tear, burst, break asunder*)	rǫto
sąlvar	(*to save*)	salvo

soltar	(*to set loose*)	solto
sujeitar	(*to subject, hold fast*)	sujeito
suspender	(*to suspend, hang up*)	suspenso
torcer	(*to twist, bend*)	torto

NOTES. 1. The participle **morto** translates both *dead* and *killed* (active and passive); the participle **morrido** translates *died*; **matado** is rare, is usually applicable only to animals and translates *slaughtered*. Remember that **morto** (as also **torto**) is radical-changing.

Meu pai $\begin{Bmatrix} é \\ está \end{Bmatrix}$ **morto.**   My father is dead.

Meu pai tinha morto o soldado.   My father had killed the soldier.

Meu pai foi morto pelo soldado.   My father was killed by the soldier.

Meu pai tinha morrido.   My father had died.

2. The verbs listed as exceptions in § 117 have only the one (irregular) past participle. The compounds of such verbs form their past participles similarly.

feito (fazer)   hence **satisfeito** (satisfazer), *satisfied*
escrito (escrever) hence **descrito** (descrever), *described*
visto (ver)   hence **previsto** (prever), *foreseen*
dito (dizer)   hence **contradito** (contradizer), *contradicted*
posto (pôr)   hence **composto** (compor), *composed*
vindo (vir)   hence **contravindo** (contravir), *contravened*
coberto (cobrir)   hence **encoberto** (encobrir), *hidden*

But **prover** (§ 193), *to provide*, has **provido**; note also **desprovido** (*destitute*) and **desabrido** (*insolent, disagreeable*). Note that **composto**, etc., like **posto**, is radical-changing.

VOCABULARY

o afecto	affection	a ameaça	menace, threat
a alegria	joy, cheerfulness	antigo	old, former, ancient
alugar	to hire, rent; to let	o apartamento	apartment, flat

364

o aspecto	appearance, aspect	o jornalista	newspaperman, journalist
bater (com)	to bang	o lábio	lip
a bengala	(walking-)stick	a lágrima	tear
a cara	face	o leitor	reader
o chão	floor, ground	longo	long, lengthy
comprido	long, lengthy	maçar	to irk; to bore
decerto	certainly, for certain	o milionário	millionaire
dedicar	to dedicate	morder	to bite
desaparecer	to disappear	não bem	no sooner
despender	to spend (money); to waste [1]	o nordeste	north-east
a direcção	direction; address	a organiza-ção	organization
distribuir	to distribute	outorgar	to grant
a electrici-dade	electricity	o parente	relative, relation
o engano	deception	passar	to pass, to spend (time)
enorme	enormous	passar-se	to happen, take place
a extremi-dade	extreme, end	perfeito	perfect
extremo	extreme	político	political
gastar	to spend (money); to waste [1]	o princípio	beginning
		o quadro	picture
as infor-mações	information	queixar-se	to complain
o inimigo	enemy	revelar	to reveal
		o sentimento	feeling
		situar	to situate
		o sudoeste	south-west
		a temporada	while, spell

de costume — as a rule, usually
em primeiro lugar — in the first place

Study also the verbs and past participles listed in §§ 220 and 225.

EXERCISES

I. (a) *Study and translate:* Esta poesia foi escrita por Fernando Pessoa. Enviaram-me um sobretudo. Não se sabia quem era. É proibido falar. Não se via nada. A gente atreve-se

[1] *To waste* (*money*) is **desperdiçar** (**dinheiro**) *or* **malgastar** (**dinheiro**).

a tudo. Está pendurada atrás da porta. Foram vistos na semana passada. Acusam-me sem razão. Encarregam-lhes a maior parte do trabalho. Surpreendeu-me o aspecto da escola. O coração encheu-se-me de alegria. Vendem-se apartamentos. Ambas são casadas. Fiquei desiludida ao vê-los desaparecer. A conta foi paga por Henrique. A porta é pintada de verde. O fogo está já aceso. O general foi preso pelos inimigos. A pobre mãe ficou desprovida. Recife fica no nordeste do Brasil.

(b) *Translate:* It was translated by him. What has been done? Has it been published yet (**já**)? The plan hasn't been accepted. He was seen last night. He has been granted permission to leave. Nothing has been decided. The bill's already paid. She was kneeling on the ground. Pictures hung on the walls. As soon as it was realized what had happened. He had killed her three minutes before. If only we had been told earlier! A new president has been elected. What insolent behaviour! She is the only one to be exempt.

II. (a) *Study and translate:* 1. Já sabiam que nem com ameaças nem com lágrimas podia conseguir-se nada. 2. A obra foi dedicada por ele com todo o afecto ao seu antigo professor de grego. 3. Como queres que convençamos a outrem se não estivermos convencidos nós mesmos? 4. A Península Ibérica fica situada no extremo sudoeste da Europa. 5. Estão muito surpreendidos de que não os deixem entrar a ver o que se passa. 6. Ficaram muito contentes ao saberem que se ia publicar o meu livro. 7. Na outra extremidade da mesa estava sentada uma tal senhora Rodrigues, muito conhecida, conforme me disseram, por um livro que escrevera acerca da situação política no Brasil ao princípio do século XIX. 8. Fiquei surpreendida ao saber que a mãe fora morta pelo filho mais novo. 9. Foi-lhe enviado um telegrama, disseram-me, em que leu que seu pai já não está satisfeito com a sua conduta. 10. A gente não costuma tomar em conta quão importante é a boa organização do trabalho.

(*b*) *Translate:* 1. We regret that the letters can't be distributed any longer. 2. Flats to let. 3. Certainly I think that he has been deceived, but don't you think the deception was justified by his own conduct? 4. The doctor was called straight away but it was too late for him to do anything (coisa alguma). 5. Without doubt these problems are difficult but they are not so difficult that they cannot be solved by a good student. 6. The door was opened by a very old gentleman leaning on a stick. 7. He was sent a letter this morning but it is not known where he is now. 8. It has been announced that the government will do everything possible to reach an agreement. 9. But after the bill had been paid we all returned home. 10. Suddenly the husband was heard approaching, and evidently he was not alone.

III. (*a*) *Study and translate:* Não bem o Ilídio acabara de escrever a segunda carta quando a esposa entrou na sala de jantar a pedir-lhe a chave do carro. Ela disse-lhe que ia para a cidade para comprar uns poucos presentes para os amigos e os parentes deles. Ao entregar-lhe a chave, o Ilídio olhou-a duma maneira severa. Os olhos da Teresa negavam-se a encontrar os do marido e a cara nada revelava dos seus sentimentos. Talvez estivesse um pouco mais pálida que de costume, mas aproximara-se dele da direcção da janela e a luz achava-se atrás dela. Oxalá lhe explicasse a ele o que a maçava! Seguro que havia alguma coisa grave desta vez. Noutra época ela ter-lhe-ia contado tudo, mas já não valia a pena pensar naqueles tempos. Jã sucedera muita coisa desde os primeiros anos. Mas agora nao see podia queixar, claro. A Teresa esteve a hesitar uma temporada como se quisesse dizer-lhe algumas palavras; pois, a morder o lábio, voltou-se e saiu batendo com a porta.

(*b*) *Translate:* One night two young newspapermen were told to visit a famous millionaire so that they could ask the latter to give them some information for their newspaper. The millionaire received them at once in his luxury flat, and as soon as they were seated, one of the journalists explained to him the object of their visit, saying politely: "In the first place will you please tell us how you have succeeded in amassing such (**tão**) an enormous fortune? I'm sure it'll be of great interest to our readers for them to understand that."

The rich man smiled at this question and replied, "Unfortunately the story is a very long one and so, instead of wasting electricity, I'll tell you about it with the lights out." Both the journalists got up quickly, and before leaving the flat one said, "You need not say any more; now we understand perfectly."

LESSON XXXVI

226. Por AND para. (*a*) Despite the clear distinction between **por** and **para** suggested by the English renderings in § 145 these two words are often confused by the non-native speaker of Portuguese, especially since both may translate the English preposition *for*. It is important to understand from the beginning their essential difference: **por** most frequently indicates the source or means of an action (English *by, through, out of, for, because of,* etc.); **para,** on the other hand, denotes principally its direction, destination, purpose or suitability (English *for, to, towards, in order to,* etc.).

Porque tomaste o meu canivete? Why (=through what cause) did you take my pen-knife?

Tomei-o por meu irmão. I took it because of my brother (*e.g., lest he hurt himself with it*).

... por necessidade. ... out of necessity.

... por não ter aqui o meu. ... because I didn't have mine here (*lit.,* through not having mine here).

... porque não estavas. ... because you weren't here.

Deixá-lo-ei por tua causa. I'll leave it for you (=on your account, *e.g., so that I can be with you*).

Saí de Lisboa por Almada. I left Lisbon via Almada.

Para que tomaste o meu canivete? Why (=for what purpose) did you take my pen-knife?

Tomei-o para meu irmão. I took it for my brother (*i.e., for his use*).

... para uma aula de desenho. ... for an art class.

... para afiar o meu lápis. ... to sharpen my pencil.

Deixá-lo-ei para ti. I'll leave it for you (*i.e., so that you can have it*).

Saí de Lisboa para Mafra. I left Lisbon for Mafra.

POR:

Foi atropelada por um carro.
She's been knocked down by a car.

Quatro por cinco são vinte.
Five fours are twenty.

Escolhẹram-no pela sua experiência.
They chose him for his experience.

Faço-o pelo amọr que lhe tenho.
I do it out of the love I bear you.

Felicitou-me pelo nascimento de mẹu filho.
He congratulated me on the birth of my son.

Gạnhámos por estarmos bem treinados.
We won because we were well trained.

Soubẹmo-lo por carta.
We learnt about it by letter.

Prendẹram-me pelos braços.
They held me fast by my arms.

Ataquei-o por trás.
I attacked him from behind.

PARA:

Vou pạra Lisbọa (pạra casa).
I'm off to Lisbon (off home).

Avançou pạra a janẹla.
He advanced towards the window.

Estava a vestir-se pạra o baile.
She was dressing for the dance.

Estão-se a preparar pạra sair.
They're getting ready to go out.

Está a estudar pạra um exame.
He's studying for an examination.

Mạs ẹstes não são pạra ti.
But these are not for you.

Aproveitei a ọcasião pạra o conhecẹr pessoạlmente.
I took advantage of the occasion to get to know him personally.

Pạra que precisam de tanto dinheiro?
What do they need so much money for?

Não tinha bastante pạra comprar outro pạra si próprio.
He couldn't afford (hadn't enough) to buy himself another.

É muito apropriado pạra ẹsse fim.
It is well-suited to that end.

(b) *Translating the English "for"*

The English *for* is translated by **pạra,** except in the following cases where **por** is used:

(i) When *for* indicates a causal relationship (*i.e., because of, on account of*).

Admirámo-lo pela sua confiança.
We admired him for his confidence.

Desprẹza-me pelas minhas crenças.
He scorns me for my beliefs.

Tem-nos simpatia pela ajuda que lhe dẹmos.
He is fond of us for the help we have given him.

Faço tudo por ẹla.
I do it all for her.

contrast **Faço-o pạra ẹla.**
I make it for her (*i.e.,* destined for her, for her use).

Trago-o pạra vọcê.
I bring it for you.

(ii) When *for* indicates exchange or substitution.

Paguei cem escudos por ẹsta camisa.
I paid a hundred escudos for this shirt.

Faço-o por mẹu irmão.
I am doing it for (=in place of) my brother.

contrast **Comprei-a pạra mẹu avô.**
> I bought it for my grandfather.

Fạço-o pạra mẹu irmão.
> I am making it for (=destined for) my brother.

(iii) when *for* indicates *on what occasion*.

Presenteou-mo pelo mẹu aniversário.
> He gave it me for my birthday.

É frequente comẹr-se isto pelo Natal.
> This is eaten a lot for (*or* at) Christmas.

contrast **Nós fá-lo-ẹmos pạra ạmanhã.**
> We shall do it for tomorrow.

> **Pạra quando o necessitas?**
> When do you want it for?

(iv) When *for* indicates for how long something is (or was) intended.

Irei pạra a Espanha por quinze dias.
> I shall go to Spain for a fortnight.

contrast **Está a poupar dinheiro pạra quando se reformar.**
> He is saving up for when he retires.

NOTE: In general the English *for* indicating space of time is best translated by **por** when the action of the verb marks the mere entering into the space of time; otherwise (*i.e.*, when the action of the verb covers the whole space of time) **durante** is used, or no preposition.

> **Convidou-me pạra a sua casa por um mês.** He invited me to his house for a month.
> **Vou pạra Lisbọa por ọito dias.** I am going to Lisbon for a week.

but **Trabalharei durante quinze dias.** I shall work for a fortnight.

> **Estive dọis mẹses em Lisbọa.**⎫ I was in Lisbon
> **Estive em Lisbọa durante dọis mẹses.**⎭ for two months.

The only important exceptions to this are **por um momento** (*for a moment*) and **por um instante** (*for an instant*):

> **Por um momento (um instante) julguei que não vinha.** For a moment (an instant) I thought he wasn't coming.

372

(v) when *for* introduces an object for which one has gone or been sent.

Enviou o sęu filho à farmácia por um frasco de remédio.
She sent her son to the chemist's for a bottle of medicine.

NOTE: If the object of one's movement is a person the above construction is best avoided.

Mandaram $\begin{Bmatrix} \text{buscar} \\ \text{chamar} \end{Bmatrix}$ o médico.   They sent for the doctor.

(vi) when *for* introduces the object of an emotion.

Mǫstram um grande afęcto pelo męu pai.
They show great affection for my father.

But see below § 227 (vii) also.

(vii) when *for* indicates support *for* (*i.e.*, on behalf of, in favour of, cf. § 174 (5)), or striving *for*.

Falou pela monarquia.   He spoke for the monarchy.
Votaram pelos comunistas.   They voted for the Communists.
Pelejavam pelo dinheiro.   They were fighting for the money.
Morręram pela pátria.   They died for their country.
Qptou por partir imediatamente.   He elected to leave at once.
Esfǫrça-se por acabá-lo.   He strives to finish it.

227. THE USES OF PERSONAL **a.**   Unlike its Spanish equivalent, the Portuguese personal **a** is nowadays exceedingly limited in its uses.   These are as follows:

(i) In cases of a double direct *noun* object.

Pędro coroou rainha à sua amante mǫrta.
Pedro crowned his dead mistress queen.

Elegęram presidente a Kubitschek.
They elected Kubitschek president.

NOTE: In the case of the verb **chamar,** when this means *to call* (*names*), the person involved is the indirect object and the name the direct object.

Chamaram idiọta ao rapaz.
>They called the boy an idiot.

Chamaram-lhe idiọta.
>They called him an idiot.

contrast **Elegẹram-no presidente.**
>>They elected him president.

(ii) In the reciprocal **um ao outro,** etc. [§ 139 (*b*)].

As raparigas amam-se umas às outras.
>The girls love one another.

(iii) Before the relative pronoun **quem** when this is the direct object [see § 232 (*c*) (2)].

(iv) Frequently though optionally before Christian names and surnames in the direct object.

Ontem vi a $\begin{Bmatrix} \textbf{Silva} \\ \textbf{João} \end{Bmatrix}$.   I saw $\begin{Bmatrix} \text{Silva} \\ \text{John} \end{Bmatrix}$ yesterday.

(v) To avoid possible confusion between subject and object.

Ama-os cạda um.   Each one loves them.
Ama-os a cạda um.   He loves them, every one.
Tratei-o cọmo họmem de bem.   I treated him as a gentleman should.
Tratei-o cọmo a (um) họmem de bem.   I treated him like a gentleman.

Students of Spanish should observe the following:

A paz sẹgue a guẹrra.   Peace follows war.
À paz sẹgue-se a guẹrra.   After peace (there) comes war.
Ninguém vê.   Nobody can see.
Não vê ninguém.   He can't see anyone.

(vi) Before a disjunctive pronoun reinforcing or clarifying a conjunctive direct object pronoun of the same clause.

Vimos (a) João e Miguẹl mạs não nos viram a nós.
>We saw John and Michael but they didn't see *us*.

Viram-nos a nós mạs evitaram-nos a ẹles.
>They saw *us* but avoided *them*.

(vii) Somewhat analogously after a limited number of nouns and adjectives expressing emotional or similar relationships.

o amǫr a Dęus.   **a ǫbediência à lei**
love for God   obedience of the law

o respeito $\begin{Bmatrix} \textbf{aos} \\ \textbf{pelos} \end{Bmatrix}$ **vęlhos**   **temente a Dęus**
                                   God-fearing
respect for the aged

but **anęlo por** (*longing for*), **entusiasmo por** (*enthusiasm for*), **ódio de** (*hatred of*), **mędo de** and **temǫr de** (*fear of*), etc.

228. SPECIAL USES OF PREPOSITION + INFINITIVE.

(i) **a** + infinitive: to express condition (English *if*).

A sabęr isso, não lhe diria nada.
If I knew that I wouldn't tell him anything.

A continuares assim, que farás?
What will you do if you carry on like that?

(ii) **com** + infinitive: to express concession (English *although*)[1] and means (English *by -ing*).

João, com sęr o mais vęlho, nem por isso deixa de me parecęr o męnos inteligente. John, although he is the eldest, nevertheless appears to me to be the least intelligent.

Não se pęrde nada com fazęrmos-lhe uma visita. We lose nothing by paying him a visit.

(iii) **por** + infinitive: to express cause (English *because*).

Fi-lo assim por não sabęr onde estava. I did it like that because I didn't know where he was.

NOTE: When **por** is introduced by **estar** or **ficar** the infinitive expresses incompletion. The infinitive has passive sense.

O gira-discos está por consertar. The record-player has yet to be mended.

Ęsta lição ainda fica por terminar. This lesson still remains
$\begin{cases} \text{to be finished.} \\ \text{unfinished.} \end{cases}$

[1] This construction is nowadays considered old-fashioned.

375

VOCABULARY

admirável	admirable	o limiar	threshold
o aeroporto	airport	a literatura	literature
afastar-se	to go away	o maciço	clump
agradável	pleasant	melancólico	melancholy
a alma	soul	a memória	memory;
aumentar	to increase		memoire
cheio (de)	full (of); fed up	monótono	monotonous
	(with)	moreno	dark (*of skin*)
cinzento	grey	mouro	Moor; moorish
a colina	hill	o número	number
o defeito	defect	a nuvem	cloud
derrotar	to defeat	oblíquo	oblique
a descrição	description	a obra-prima	masterpiece
devoto	devout	ocorrer	to occur
distinto	distinct	parecido	similar
encaminhar-	to make one's	o passado	past
se	way	o pastor	shepherd
o escritor	writer	a pátria	homeland, (na-
o escultor	sculptor		tive) country
estéril	sterile	a paz	peace
estimar	to esteem	profundo	deep, profound,
falso	false		sound
a fama	fame	o respeito	respect
a folha	leaf	retirar-se	to retire, with-
formular	to formulate		draw
a frase	sentence;	rezar	to pray
	phrase	rodear	to surround
idêntico	identical	o secretário	secretary
improvável	improbable,	a torre	tower
	unlikely	transpor	to cross
insignifi-		tratar	to treat
cante	insignificant	a tristeza	sadness
o instante	instant	vago	vague
insubsti-		o vento	wind
tuível	irreplaceable	a voz	voice

ao } pelo } contrário	on the contrary
a sós	all alone

à pressa	in haste
cada vez mais	more and more
cada vez menos	less and less
na {verdade / realidade}	in fact; as a matter of fact
para sempre	for ever
para todo (o) sempre	for ever and ever
por {conseguinte / consequência}	consequently
por exemplo	for example
por um lado	on the one hand
por outro lado	on the other hand

Revise the vocabulary of Lessons XXXI–XXXV.

EXERCISES

I. *Study and translate:* Trabalha por ser pobre. Trabalha para ser rico. Deixemo-lo para então. Estuda para escultor. Fazia frio para Abril. Para que se retirara? Porque não o trouxeste? O comboio está para partir. Estou em dizer-lhe que não. Por muito que lho dissessem. Guardei-o para o dia seguinte. Não há nada que eu possa fazer por você. Admiravam-se um ao outro. Afastaram-se um do outro. Elegeram secretário a Andrade. À guerra segue-se a paz. Estima-as a cada uma. Os dois irmãos, com serem muito parecidos, não eram exactamente idênticos. Rodeado de colinas.

(b) *Translate:* They have been defeated by the Moors. A hundred and fifty kilometres an hour. Who is this book for? For an instant she thought she was all alone. I am tired through having studied so much. She was fed up with formulating so many insignificant projects. The idea occurred to him that the fame of the two writers would increase more and more. They both hated each other. On the contrary, she treated him with extreme respect. However admirable his conduct may have been. They appointed Salazar prime minister. They prayed devoutly for the shepherd's soul. What, for example, is the number of his flat?

II. (a) *Study and translate:* 1. Tudo quanto se pode fazer por esta pobre senhora está feito já. 2. Por um lado, lembro-me bem dos seus defeitos; mas por outro lado, não consigo chamar à memória as suas características mais agradáveis. 3. Procurarei estudar a lição amanhã de manhã, conquanto diga Filipe que conta com tê-la terminada para esta noite. 4. Na verdade estou convencida de que esta é uma obra-prima da literatura portuguesa, mas tem sido mal compreendida pela gente. 5. — Mas é muito velho este livro. Porque é que o meu amigo não o substitui por outro? — Mas é um livro insubstituível para mim. 6. Saímos do Porto para Santo Tirso mas passámos primeiro por Leça. 7. Por não termos tempo para perder, tomei à pressa o meu café. 8. Por conseguinte acho falsas e estéreis as ideias deste grupo de escritores. 9. Apesar das profundas lições que me ensina o passado, decidi-me a ficar para sempre na pátria. 10. Por fim cheguei a admirá-la pela muita confiança que tinha em si mesma.

(b) *Translate:* 1. Will you please do it for my brother? 2. She is loved by all who know her. 3. I punished him for having sold all his books for a few cruzeiros. 4. But I've not been asking them to do it for her; now it is for me. 5. You have not been told the whole truth; consequently your conclusions are utterly false. 6. It appears that he has been punished for not having told them what he had seen. 7. They slept soundly all night and were wakened on the following morning by their aunt's voice. 8. This is too difficult for me to do; certainly I'm not going to be able to get it finished for next Monday. 9. Although they both saw us we didn't see them. 10. Not one of them seems to grasp what he's come to this country for.

III. (a) *Study and translate:* Logo que a Gabriela chegou à porta da pequena igreja de Santo Eleutério, acompanhada do tio e da avó, no relógio da torre deram devagarinho cinco horas da tarde. A igreja ficava situada numa colina e rodeada dum maciço de árvores. Era nos primeiros dias de Dezembro.

O céu, carregado de nuvens, que corriam para o nordeste batidas dum vento frio, estava duma tristeza monótona. Às vezes, uma nuvem mais escura, cinzenta e pesada cobria o céu e a chuva caía então obliquamente. Quando passava a chuva um vento forte levantava as folhas amarelas de Outono. As antigas paredes escuras da igreja aumentavam o seu aspecto melancólico. Antes de entrarem esteve a Gabriela com a cabeça caída sobre o ombro da avó a chorar. Abraçaram-se e logo transpuseram o limiar.

(b) *Translate:* The difficult thing was that I had never seen this man before, and I did not even know what language he would speak when we met. I had the vague idea that he was from a European country, but I could not remember whether Michael had said he was Italian, French or Swiss. It would not matter, of course, if the man spoke English, but I was afraid that he would know only his own strange tongue, whatever that was, for Michael had said quite distinctly that he had never been abroad before, and had added something which I did not hear, though I thought it was something like "small, fat and very dark". As I made my way to the airport I repeated to myself all the sentences I could remember in French. They did not seem very apt, and he was unlikely to want to know that I had left the pen of my aunt in the garden. I also realized that he might not even be French, or speak it. And how was I going to recognize him? In spite of the description that Michael had given me, the task seemed almost impossible.

LESSON XXXVII

229. VERBS THAT TAKE A DIRECT OBJECT IN ENGLISH OR PORTUGUESE. (*a*) In general, verbs that take a direct object in English also take a direct object in Portuguese and vice versa.

Conhęces Lisbǫa (ęste hǫmem; o męu irmão)?

Do you know Lisbon (this man; my brother)?

(*b*) Certain verbs, however, that have a direct object in English take a prepositional object in Portuguese. Common verbs of this type are:

abeirar-se de	to approach	**fiar-se de** (*or* **em**)	to trust
abusar de	to abuse, misuse	**gostar de**	to like
apoderar-se de	to seize	**gozar de**	to enjoy
apossar-se de	to seize	**inteirar-se de**	to discover, find out
aproximar-se de	to approach	**lembrar-se de**	to remember
carecęr de	to lack	**mudar de**	to change
desconfiar de	to distrust	**partir de**	to leave (*a place*)
desfrutar de	to enjoy	**passar de**	to exceed, go beyond
duvidar de	to doubt, question	**prescindir de**	to omit, leave aside
esquęcęr-se de	to forget	**puxar de**	to pull, tug
		servir-se de	to use
		zombar de	to deride, ridicule
assistir a	to attend (be present at)	**fąltar a**	not to fulfil, to break
chegar a	to reach (*a place*)	**ǫbedecęr a**	to obey

opọr-se a	to oppose	sọbreviver a	to survive
renunciar a	to renounce	subir a	to mount, board
resistir a	to resist		

casar(-se) com	to marry (take in marriage)	encontrar-se com	to meet, come across
dar com	to meet, come across	parecer-se com	to resemble

confiar(-se) em	to trust	ingressar em	to enter
entrar em	to enter	pegar em	to seize
influir em	to influence	penetrar em	to penetrate
		reparar em	to notice

dar pạra ⎫ to overlook,
deitar sọbre ⎰ look out on to

dar por   to notice

A notícia carẹce de fundamento.   The report is unfounded.

Ẹu não me fiava dẹle.   I didn't trust him.

Resistiu à tentação de ir.   He resisted the temptation to go.

Não há prazẹr de que não desfrutem.   There's no pleasure they don't enjoy.

Ọpõe-se a que entrem em casa.   He objects to their going into the house.

NOTES.   1. **Mudar** takes a direct object when it means *to make changes in*; a prepositional object when it means *to make a change of*.

Mudei os mẹus projẹctos.	I've changed my plans.
Mudou o tom da sua vọz.	He changed the tone of his voice.
Mudei de propósito.	I've changed my mind.
Mudou de tom.	He changed his tone.
Vamos mudar de casa.	We're going to move house.

2. When used with a direct object, **casar** means *to join or give in marriage*; when used reflexively it means *to get married* (but also **casar com**, *to get married to*).

Casou a filha com um lojista abastado. He married his daughter to a wealthy shopkeeper.

Casou(-se) com a filha do capitão. He married the captain's daughter.

Contou-me que queria casar-se. He told me he wanted to get married.

3. **Jogar**, *to play* (*games*), is occasionally followed by **a** (*at*), but, like English, usually omits it. The definite article may be included.

Jogar (ao *or* **o) futebọl.** To play (at) football.

But **jogar às cartas,** *to play* (*at*) *cards*, is more normal.

4. The verbs **ensinar,** *to teach*, and **chamar,** *to call*, take a direct or indirect object, depending on circumstances which are best illustrated by the following examples.

Ensinava apẹnas três alunos. He was teaching only three pupils.

Ensinava os alunos a lẹr. He was teaching the pupils to read.

Ensinava aos alunos a geografia. He was teaching the pupils geography.

Chamei um táxi. I hailed a taxi.

Chamei mẹu pai. I called (to) my father.

Chamei-lhe idiọta. I called him a fool.

The Brazilian construction for this last expression (**Chamei-o de idiọta**) is gaining increasing currency in European Portuguese nowadays.

5. The two verbs *to need*, **precisar** and **necessitar,** are optionally followed by **de.**

(*c*) Conversely to (*b*), certain verbs that have a direct object in Portuguese take a prepositional object in English. Common verbs of this type are:

agradecẹr	to be grateful for	**aproveitar**	to profit from, by
aguentar	to put up with	**buscar**	to look for
aprovar	to approve of	**comentar**	to comment on

considerar	to look upon	presentear	to present with
escutar	to listen to	procurar	to look for
esperar	to wait for	ruminar	to ponder over
lamentar	to be sorry about	sentir	to be sorry about
meditar	to think over	suportar	to put up with
pagar	to pay for	vestir	to put on

Agradeci-lhe a sua bondade.   I thanked him for his kindness.

Agradecęr-lhe-ia que me trouxęsse o pacǫte.   I would be grateful to you if you brought me the parcel.

Comentámos as notícias.   We commented on the news.

Com que o pagaste?   What did you pay for it with?

NOTES.   1. An English direct object with one of these verbs becomes the indirect object in Portuguese: *i.e.*, *I paid him for it* becomes **Paguei-lho** (*lit.*, *I paid it to him*). See also the last example above.

2. **Esperar** has an alternative construction with **por**:

Esperarei pelo fiscal.   I'll wait for the inspector.

The continuous tenses of **esperar** are best rendered by **estar à espęra de**:

Ęu estava à espęra do combǫio das sęte hǫras.   I was waiting for the seven o'clock train.

3. **Presentear** has an alternative construction with **com**:

Presenteei-$\begin{Bmatrix} \text{o com} \\ \text{lhe} \end{Bmatrix}$** o chapéu.**   I presented him with the hat.

230. VERBS THAT TAKE AN INDIRECT OBJECT IN ENGLISH OR PORTUGUESE.   (*a*) An indirect object in English is translated by an indirect object in Portuguese, and vice versa.

À minha mãe dei uma pulseira e ao męu pai uma garrafa de conhaque.

I have given a bracelet to my mother and a bottle of brandy to my father.

REMEMBER: 1. In English the preposition *to* introducing the indirect object is frequently omitted.   This is not possible in Portuguese, nor is it possible for preposition and indirect object to be separated as occurs frequently with English interrogatives and relatives.

Entregou o sẹu exercício ao professọr.
He handed the teacher his exercise.

A tọdos infundia confiança.
He used to give everyone confidence.

A quem dẹste o recado?
Who(m) did you give the message to?

É o mẹsmo a quem dẹvo o dinheiro.
It's the same man I owe the money to.

2. The preposition **a** is not expressed with a weak pronoun object.

Mandámos-lhe um presente. We sent him a present.
Cạusou-nos uma desilusão. It caused us a disappointment.
Proporcionava-lhes grandes vantagens. It afforded them great advantages.

(b) The indirect object forms are used in Portuguese also in the following special cases:

(1) To indicate a person directly interested in or related to the action of the verb. The English equivalent is usually: (i) as in Portuguese, the ethic dative or dative of interest (*Make them a cup of tea*), or (ii) the preposition *for* followed by the person interested (*We are house-hunting for him. Would you do this for me?*).

Não me perdọa as minhas faltas. He doesn't forgive me my mistakes.
Quẹres preparar-lhe uma chávena de chá? Would you make him a cup of tea?
Tem cạusado muita infelicidade aos sẹus pais. He has caused his parents much unhappiness.
Conseguiu-mo um amigo. A friend got it for me.
Consẹrtas-me isto? Can you fix this for me?

(2) (Closely related with (1).) To indicate the owner of parts
of the body, clothing, and certain personal belongings and mental
faculties to which action is being done. The English possessive
adjective is then translated by the Portuguese definite article.
Unlike Spanish, the weak object pronoun is not used if the action
is performed upon oneself [see § 138 (a) NOTE].

Lavou-lhes a cara. She washed their faces.
Lavou a cara aos filhos. She washed her children's faces.
Quebrei-lhe o braço direito. I broke his right arm.
Encheram-se-lhe os olhos de lágrimas. Her eyes filled with
tears.
Pintaram-nos os braços a nós. They painted *our* arms.
Queres atar-me os atacadores? Will you fasten my (shoe)-
laces?
Salvaram-lhe a vida. They saved his life.
Chamou-lhe a atenção. He attracted your attention.

but **Lavei a cara.** I washed my face.
    Quebrou o braço direito. He broke his (own) right arm.
    Pusemos o chapéu. We put our hats on.
    Tiraram a jaqueta. They took their jackets off.

NOTE: The part of the body is usually named in the singular if the
action is concerned with only one per person:

Lavámos a cara.	We washed our faces.
but **Lavámos as mãos.**	We washed our hands.
Tiraram o chapéu.	They took their hats off.
but **Tiraram as luvas.**	They took their gloves off.
Atei-lhes a mão direita.	I tied their right hands.
but **Atei-lhes as duas mãos.**	I tied their two hands.

(3) To indicate the person *from* (or *of*) whom something is
concealed, requested or acquired.

A quem comprou V. Exa. este carro? Who(m) did you buy
this car from, sir?
Furtaram-lhe todas as suas riquezas. They robbed him of all
his wealth.

385

Ęsta guęrra arrebatou à Espanha as suas últimas colónias.
This war snatched from Spain her last colonies.

Exigia demais aos sęus ministros. He demanded too much
of his ministers.

Ọcultou a verdade a sęu pai. He concealed the truth from
his father.

231. VERBS THAT TAKE A PREPOSITIONAL OBJECT IN ENGLISH AND
PORTUGUESE. (*a*) Where an English verb and its Portuguese
equivalent take a preposition, the preposition generally corresponds in the two languages or can be explained by reference to
certain broad tendencies (*e.g.*, **de** translates English *with* after
verbs that imply filling, loading, covering, etc.).

Está a brincar com o filho. He's playing with his son.

Enchęram o caminhão de pranchas. They filled the lorry
with planks.

O imperadọr cumulou-o de honras. The emperor loaded
him with honours.

(*b*) With certain verbs, however, the prepositions do not correspond and broad generalizations offer no help:

acabar com	to put an end to, finish with	**cuidar de**	to look after, care for
alimentar-se de (*or* **com**)	to feed on	**dar com**	to come across (meet)
cheirar a	to smell of	**dar pạra**	to look on to
compade-cẹr-se de	to be sorry for, take pity on	**deitar sọbre** (*or* **pạra**)	to look on to
congratular por	to congratulate on	**dependẹr de**	to depend on
consentir em	to consent to	**despedir-se de**	to say good-bye to
contar com	to count on, to rely on	**destacar-se sọbre** (*or* **em**)	to stand out against
convir em	to agree to	**divertir-se com**	to be amused by

encontrar-se com	to come across (meet)	prescindir de	to do without
encostar-se a	to lean against	presidir a	to preside over
falar com (*or* a)	to speak to	puxar de	to pull (at *or* on)
falar em (*or* de)	to talk about	reparar em	to take note of
felicitar por	to congratulate on	rir-se com	to laugh at (=be amused by)
interessar-se por	to be interested in, take an interest in	rir-se de	to laugh at (=make fun of)
maravilhar-se de	to wonder at	sabẹr a	to taste of, smack of
namorar-se de	to fall in love with	sonhar com	to dream of
ọcupar-se de (*or* em)	to attend to, look after	sorrir-se com(*or*de)	to smile at
ọlhar pạra	to look at	tratar-se de	to be about, deal with
pegar em	to get hold of	triunfar de	to triumph over
pensar em	to think of *or* about	tropeçar com	to run into (=come across)
portar-se com	to behave towards	vingar-se de	to take revenge for (*or* on)
		vivẹr de	to live on

Divertiu-se muito com ẹsta história. He was very amused by this story.

Felicitei-o pelo sẹu grande êxito. I congratulated him on his great success.

Consente (em) que o façamos assim. He consents to our doing it this way.

NOTES. 1. **Falar a** suggests that the subject does the talking; **falar com** that there is discussion (*i.e.*, almost *to have a talk with*).

2. **Ọlhar** is occasionally found with a direct object, especially when used reflexively.

Ọlharam-se furiọsos. They looked at each other furiously.

3. **Pensar de** means *to think of* (= *to have an opinion on*).

O que é que o Sr. pensa dęle? What do you think of him?
but Em que é que vǫcê está a pensar? What are you thinking of?

4. **Presidir** is sometimes found with a direct object.

VOCABULARY

apǫiar-se em	to lean on	**nęgro**	black
apostar	to bet	**nomear**	to appoint,
arrimar-se a	to lean on		nominate
assegurar[1]	to assure	**notar**	to note, notice
constar (de)	to consist (of)	**paralisar**	to paralyse; to
o curso	course		bring to a
o desejo	desire		standstill; to
diferente	different		grind to a halt
a doença	illness	**passar sem**	to do without
a edição	edition	**passear**	to walk, stroll;
elegante	elegant		to ride
a esperança	hope	**o perdão**	pardon, forgive-
o estudo	study		ness
fiar	to spin	**preguiçǫso**	idle, lazy
formar	to form	**próximo**	last, just
o gǫsto	taste; pleasure	**passado**	finished
o grito	shout, cry,	**puro**	pure
	scream	**quatro**	four; a few
inocente	innocent		(*colloquial*)
justamente	just, exactly	**querido**	dear, beloved,
longínquo	distant		well loved
a meditação	meditation	**ralhar com**	to scold, tell
modęrno	modern	*or* **a**	off
o motivo	reason, motive;	**a razão**	reason (*usually*
	cause		power of)
o mundo	world	**repreendęr**	to reprehend
a naturęza	nature	**por**	for

[1] With indirect object of the person addressed.

reprovar por	to reprove for	**o sorriso**	smile
responder		**o tecido**	textile
por	to answer for	**a terra**	earth; land;
roubar (a)	to steal (from)		ground;
o sacrifício	sacrifice		homeland,
ser aprovado			district
(em)	to pass (*exams.*)	**o texto**	text
ser reprovado		**tremer** [1]	to tremble
(em)	to fail (*exams.*)	**trocar**	to exchange

breve
em breve
dentro em breve } soon
dentro em pouco
logo

logo de princípio	right from the outset
com efeito	indeed
de baixo	from below, from downstairs
de cima	from above, from upstairs
para baixo	downwards, downstairs
para cima	upwards, upstairs
fazer um exame	to take, sit an exam.
tirar um curso	to take a course

Study also the verbs listed in §§ 229–31.

EXERCISES

I. (*a*) *Study and translate:* Faltou à sua palavra.   Os que sobre-
viveram à guerra.   Ela opôs-se ao novo projecto.   Escu-
tem!   Prescindindo duma tal possibilidade.   Presenteei-o
com um relógio.   Asseguro-lhe que tudo isto é verdade.
Não aguento mais.   Encostou-se à parede.   Não respondo
por mim.   As montanhas destacavam-se negras sobre o céu.
Encontrei-me com que já se haviam ido embora.   Ali dei
com um turista norte-americano.   Tenho de lhe falar
imediatamente.   Triunfou dos seus inimigos.   Não pôde
resistir ao frio.   Falou-nos no novo curso de literatura.

[1] The gerund of this verb is usually avoided because of confusion with
tremendo (*tremendous*).

(b) *Translate:* He won't remember me. I drew near to the window. It depends on what my father says. They put on their overcoats. His uncle got it for him. He scolded his children for being lazy. His hands were trembling. Have you noticed this wall? They had been waiting for him for more than twenty minutes. It was then that I found out the truth. He's very like his elder brother. Those who have come don't exceed twenty. We can't do without his help. Listen to all he says. The room smelt of cats. Will you get my luggage down, please?

II. (a) *Study and translate:* 1. Não espera ninguém nem está para ninguém. 2. Nunca pude compreender a necessidade que tem certa gente de conhecer a natureza da doença que lhes ameaça roubar uma pessoa querida. 3. Ao entrarem no quarto ouviram vir de baixo um grito forte. 4. Há quatro dias vejo todas as tardes, quando chego à janela, o meu vizinho a passear em frente da casa, arrimado ao braço da netinha. 5. Agradecer-lhes-ia muito, cavalheiros, que tivessem a bondade de dizer quatro palavras a meu filho antes de se irem embora. 6. Já sei que não têm deixado nem um único dia de te pedirem perdão pelo mal que se portaram contigo. 7. Não encontrávamos motivo nenhum para duvidar da sua sinceridade. 8. Não consigo compreender por que motivo não cessara um momento de pensar em vocês. 9. — Já não gostamos do cão que nos compraram no mês próximo passado. — Pois então que o troquem por outro! 10. Se forem aprovados nos exames poderão tirar um curso suplementar no estudo da moderna poesia europeia.

(b) *Translate:* 1. I bet they'll resolve not to let him enter the house again, however innocent his reasons are. 2. He will never succeed in realizing his greatest hopes and desires unless he learns to do without such false friends and to make certain sacrifices. 3. Indeed she assured him that she had been advised to renounce the world and its pleasures; she had decided to devote herself to a life of pure meditation. 4. The headmaster congratulated him on his excellent work and presented him with an elegant de luxe (**de luxo**) edition of the complete works of Machado de Assis. 5. In studying this matter it is very important that we leave aside our own feelings. 6. She washes her own hair on Fridays, and she washes her children's on Saturday. 7. It has been said that the young of today are lazy and spend their (= the) time dreaming of the impossible. 8. She asked her father but the latter did not wish a daughter of his to get married to a student who lived on nothing but his illusions. 9. The other day I came across an old friend who was about to leave for Brazil on the following morning. 10. I had my car stolen the day before yesterday and it still hasn't been found.

III. (a) *Study and translate:* Uma noite, Gomes trouxe-nos a notícia de que na vila cada vez chegavam mais polícias vindos[1] da capital. Os homens que se reuniam em casa de Costa Araújo ouviram aquilo e não estranharam, porque se recordavam de que tinha sido quase sempre assim. Mas logo as suas caras se abriram num sorriso de gosto e esperança, ao saberem, por Nemésio, que na cidade se formara um terceiro grupo. Dizia-se, também, que todos os operários da terra, até os das longínquas margens do rio São Francisco iam dar a sua solidariedade aos dali. Fiassem quer lã quer algodão, todas as fábricas de tecidos do país paralisariam em breve. Miguel ouviu Nemésio exclamar:

— O que nos faltava era justamente a solidariedade de todos os operários. Se a tivéssemos tido logo de princípio, tudo isto já tinha acabado!

(b) *Translate:* Peter sat down at the (**à**) table which showed his number, and picked up the paper, which was already lying there. At the outset he did not want to look at it, because he was afraid that he would find it too difficult. So he spent a few minutes looking round him at the other

[1] Note that **vindo** may be used adjectivally to mean *having come, who had come*; similar constructions are common with **chegado** and **caído**.

students before examining the paper. "Let's see," he said to
(**com**) himself. It was worse than he had imagined. "I
don't know why they give us so much to do in three hours,"
he thought. "They seem to think that in eight months,
more or less, we can learn enough Portuguese to be able not
only to understand these stupid Portuguese texts, but to
write the language as well. And they do not even allow us to
bring dictionaries with us! It is as if they had never been
students themselves, and had not the least (**menor**) idea of
how many different things one has to learn at the same time.
Every teacher thinks that his course is the most important,
and is not interested in what is done in other classes. I'd
like to see some of them take all these exams!"

LESSON XXXVIII

232. RELATIVE PRONOUNS: (*a*) These are the following:

que	who, whom, which, that
quem	who, whom
o qual, a qual, os quais, as quais	who, whom, which, that
o que (*neuter*)	which

(*b*) *Preliminary Distinctions*

(1) A relative pronoun may refer to persons or things, and, within its own clause, it may be the subject, the direct object, or the prepositional object of the verb. There are thus six principal functions to be taken into account when deciding which relative pronoun to use in a given case in Portuguese:

SUBJECT

$\begin{cases}\text{(It is the boy) } who \text{ came yesterday.} \\ \text{(I have a car) } that \text{ goes very fast.}\end{cases}$

DIRECT OBJECT

$\begin{cases}\text{(It is the boy) } whom \text{ we saw yesterday.} \\ \text{(I have a car) } that \text{ I want to sell.}\end{cases}$

PREPOSITIONAL OBJECT

$\begin{cases}\text{(It is the boy) to } whom \text{ we talked yesterday.} \\ \text{(I have a car) in } which \text{ I travel a lot.}\end{cases}$

REMEMBER: These different functions may at times be confused in English by the omission of the relative pronoun (*e.g., It is the boy we saw yesterday*) or by the placing of the preposition after the subordinate verb (*e.g., I have a car that I travel a lot in*) or by both these things together (*e.g., It is the boy we talked to yesterday*). None of this is possible in Portuguese.

(2) A relative clause may be restrictive or non-restrictive:

Restrictive	*Non-Restrictive*
The boys who speak Portuguese are going to Portugal.	The boys, who speak Portuguese, are going to Portugal.
There is a lady coming whom you already know.	His wife is coming, whom you already know.

In its restrictive use *who speak Portuguese* serves to limit the antecedent *boys*, telling us *which* boys are going to Portugal; in the non-restrictive use the antecedent is already limited in the speaker's mind (*these boys*, *those boys*), and *who speak Portuguese* serves merely to give an additional fact about them. Similarly, in the other case, the restrictive *whom you already know* helps to indicate *which* lady is coming, whereas the non-restrictive use simply adds a new fact about a lady who is already sufficiently defined. The omission of a restrictive takes away something essential from the principal idea it is desired to express; the omission of a non-restrictive clause merely suppresses a subordinate—and independent—idea.

(c) *The Relative Pronoun as Subject or Direct Object*

(1) This is usually **que** for both persons and things.

É o rapaz que veio ontem. It's the boy who came yesterday.
É o rapaz que vimos ontem. It's the boy we saw yesterday.
Tenho um carro que anda muito depressa. I have a car that goes very fast.
Tenho um carro que desejo vender. I have a car I want to sell.

(2) In a non-restrictive clause, however, **o qual, a qual,** *etc.*, indicating number and gender, may also be used, especially in literary style with persons when **que** might lead to confusion; **a quem** (*whom*) is also used.

Assustou-se com a volta de Pedro, $\left\{ \begin{array}{l} \text{o qual} \\ \text{que} \end{array} \right\}$ **estava gravemente ferido.** She was frightened at the return of Peter who was badly wounded.

Assustou-se com a vọlta de Pẹdro, $\left\{\begin{array}{l}\textbf{o qual}\\ \textbf{a quem}\end{array}\right\}$ **acreditava mọrto.** She was frightened at the return of Peter whom she believed dead.

Fọmos despedir-nos da mãe do João, $\left\{\begin{array}{l}\textbf{a qual}\\ \textbf{que}\end{array}\right\}$ **vọltava pạra casa.** We went to see John's mother off, who was returning home.

Fọmos despedir-nos da mãe do João, $\left\{\begin{array}{l}\textbf{a qual}\\ \textbf{a quem}\end{array}\right\}$ **o mẹu amigo já conhẹce.** We went to see John's mother off, whom you already know.

(3) The neuter **o que** must be used when the antecedent is not a specific noun.

Fọi-se embọra, o que me surpreendẹu. He went away, which surprised me.

Oferecẹu-se cọmo guia, o que lhe agradecẹmos muito. He offered himself as a guide, for which we were very grateful to him.

(4) In clauses introduced by words such as *it is I who, it was they whom, it has been these books which,* the relative pronoun is usually **que.** For persons this may be replaced by **quem.** When **quem** is the subject of the relative clause, its verb *must always go in the third person singular,* regardless of the person and number of the antecedent.

Sọmos nós $\left\{\begin{array}{l}\textbf{que tẹmos}\\ \textbf{quem tem}\end{array}\right\}$ **de ir.**
It is we who have to go.   We are the ones who have to go.

És tu $\left\{\begin{array}{l}\textbf{que tens}\\ \textbf{quem tem}\end{array}\right\}$ **de fazê-lo.**
It is you who have to do it.

Ẹra Portugal que estava isolado.
It was Portugal that was isolated.

É vọcê $\left\{\begin{array}{l}\textbf{que}\\ \textbf{a quem}\end{array}\right\}$ **vimos ontem.**
It's you we saw yesterday.

(d) The Prepositional-Object Relative Pronoun

The form of the relative pronoun is influenced by the preposition that precedes it. Thus **a, de, em, com, por** and **sọbre** most frequently take **que** (sometimes **o qual**) with things and **quem** (sometimes **o qual**) with persons. The remaining prepositions (including all compound prepositions) usually take only **o qual**. However, when the antecedent is not a specific noun, the neuter **o que** must be used in *all* cases; the construction *preposition*+**o que** may also be used absolutely.

É o rapaz com $\left\{\begin{array}{l}\textbf{quem}\\ \textbf{o qual}\end{array}\right\}$ **falámos ontem.**

It's the boy we talked to yesterday.

Tenho um carro $\left\{\begin{array}{l}\textbf{em que}\\ \textbf{no qual}\end{array}\right\}$ **viajo muito.**

I've got a car in which I travel a lot.

Fale vọcê com a senhọra junto à qual me colocar.

Talk to the lady beside whom I place myself.

Havia uma janẹla do alto da qual se via tọda a cidade.

There was a window from which could be seen the whole city.

Parei à nọva estação de serviço defronte da qual há um vẹlho casal.

I stopped at the new filling station opposite which there is an old farmhouse.

Houve então uma pausa durante a qual não se ouviu nada.

There was then a pause during which nothing could be heard.

Brigámos muito tempo, no que fizẹmos uma sandice cọmo nunca se fẹz outra.

We quarrelled for a long time, whereby we committed an act of unequalled stupidity.

Após o que saí a tomar o ar.

After that (=which) I went out to take the air.

233. OTHER USES OF **quem.** Besides its above uses **quem** may be used in certain cases without an antecedent:

(i) in place of **alguém que** (*someone who*) and **ninguém que** (*no one who*).

Procuro $\begin{cases} \textbf{quem} \\ \textbf{alguém que} \end{cases}$ **me ajude.** I'm looking for someone to help me.

Não há $\begin{cases} \textbf{quem} \\ \textbf{ninguém que} \end{cases}$ **o compreenda.** There's no one who understands it.

(ii) in place of **o que** (*or* **aquêle que**) to translate *he who, she who*, etc., used in a generalizing sense.

$\left. \begin{matrix} \textbf{O que} \\ \textbf{Aquêle que} \\ \textbf{Quem} \end{matrix} \right\}$ **trabalhar mais, ganhará mais.**

$\left. \begin{matrix} \text{He who} \\ \text{Whoever} \end{matrix} \right\}$ works more will earn more.

NOTE: In a similar generalizing sense **quanto(s)** may replace **tôdo o que, tôdos os que,** etc.

Tirei-lhe $\begin{cases} \textbf{tôdo o dinheiro que} \\ \textbf{quanto dinheiro} \\ (\textit{even } \textbf{tôdo o dinheiro quanto}) \end{cases}$ **tinha.**

I took from him all the money he had.

Enganam-se $\begin{cases} \textbf{tôdos os que} \\ \textbf{quantos} \end{cases}$ **pensam assim.**

All who think like that are deceiving themselves.

Perdeu $\begin{cases} \textbf{tudo o que} \\ \textbf{quanto} \\ \textbf{tudo quanto} \end{cases}$ **possui.**

He has lost all he possesses.

234. OTHER RELATIVES.

(*a*) **cujo (-a, -os, -as)**   whose, of whom, of which

This is a relative adjective and agrees in number and gender with the thing possessed.

397

Vimos uma casa cujas janẹlas estavam partidas.
We saw a house the windows of which were broken.

NOTES: 1. It is a grave mistake to render the above sentence as follows: **Vimos uma casa as janẹlas da qual estavam partidas.**
2. When the principal function of the subordinate clause is to indicate the ownership (and not to say something further about the object owned) **cujo** is avoided by the use of **pertencẹr a** (*to belong to*).

Conheço a rapariga $\begin{cases} \textbf{a quem} \\ \textbf{à qual} \end{cases}$ **pertence ẹste livro.**
I know the girl whose book this is.

(b) **onde**   where, in which
aonde, pạra onde   where, to which
donde   from where, from which
cọmo   that, in which (=how)

É a povoação $\begin{cases} \textbf{a que} \\ \textbf{à qual} \\ \textbf{aonde} \end{cases}$ **vamos agọra.**
It is the town we are going to now.

Ọcorrẹu na casa $\begin{cases} \textbf{em que} \\ \textbf{na qual} \\ \textbf{onde} \end{cases}$ **morava.**
It happened in the house where he lived.

O que me desagrada é a maneira cọmo o diz.
What annoys me is the way (in which) he says it.

NOTE: **Quando** is best not used as a relative.

o dia em que sucedẹr isto   the day when this happens

Fọi o ano em que morrẹu sẹu pai.   It was the year (when) his father died.

Fọi então que notei que ẹra cẹgo.   It was then that I noticed he was blind.

235. RELATIVE WITH INFINITIVE. A relative may be followed by an infinitive in cases such as the following, where part of the verbs **devẹr** or **podẹr** is understood.

Tinha muito que fazẹr.   I had a lot to do.

Não tenho mais nada $\left\{\begin{array}{l}\textbf{que}\\\textbf{pạra}\\\textbf{a}\end{array}\right\}$ **dizẹr.**   I've nothing more to say.

Isso não tem nada $\left(\left\{\begin{array}{l}\textbf{que}\\\textbf{a}\end{array}\right\}\textbf{vẹr}\right)$ **comigo.**   That's got nothing to do with me.

Não tinha (a) quem visitar.   He had no one to visit.

Não tinham amigos com quem falarem.   They had no friends to talk to.

Não encontrava janẹla pela qual escapar.   I couldn't find a window through which to escape.

Procurei um ponto de vantagem, do alto do qual vẹr a procissão.   I looked for a vantage-point from which to see the procession.

Note the alternative **a** after **nada** in the second and third examples, and the alternative **pạra** in the second example.

236. INTERROGATIVES. (a) Portuguese interrogative adjectives, pronouns and adverbs are:

onde	where	**quanto -a**	how much; *pl.*
aonde	where (to)	**-os -as**	how many
pạra onde	where (to)	**(o) que** *pron.*	what
donde	where . . . from	**que** *adj.*	what, which
porque	why	**qual** (*pl.*	
cọmo	how	**quais)**	which, what
quando	when	**quem**	who, whom
		de quem	whose

Aonde vai vọcê?   Where are you going?
Perguntou-me aonde ia.   He asked me where I was going.
Cọmo vão fazê-lo?   How are they going to do it?

Não quis dizer como iam fazê-lo. He wouldn't say how they were going to do it.

Quanto gastaram? How much did they spend?

Nem sabia quantos escudos tinham gasto. He didn't even know how many escudos they had spent.

De quem são estes livros? Whose books are these?

Quando foi descoberta esta ilha? When was this island discovered?

Porque é que é tão preguiçoso? Why is he so idle?

Donde é que é o Sr.? Where do you come from?

Quais destas cores prefere? Which of these colours does she prefer?

Quem lhe disse isso? Who told you that?

NOTES. 1. Interrogative words are used in direct and indirect questions.

2. The pronoun **o que** is a variant of **que**. It is particularly used in conversational Portuguese where the interrogative pronoun **que** is less common. It is also the form which *must* be used in indirect questions:

Não sabíamos o que dissera. We didn't know what he had said.

3. An interrogative pronoun, adjective or adverb may be followed by an infinitive.

Não sabia (por) onde começar. He didn't know where to begin.

Nem sabiam que livro escolher. They didn't even know which book to choose.

Como explicar-lhe o que sucedeu? How [are we] to explain to him what happened?

4. **Como** means *how* (= *in what way*). Thus the English *how do you* (*did he*, etc.) *like* . . ., when it asks for an opinion rather than a choice, is not translated by **como + preferir,** but by **que + parecer.**

Como prefere o seu café? How do you like your coffee? (*i.e.*, black or white, with or without sugar, etc.)

Que lhe parece o café? How do you like the coffee? (*i.e.*, what do you think of it?)

237. EXCLAMATIVES. The most common of the Portuguese exclamatives are:

cọmo	what
quanto (-a, -os, -as)	how much, what a lot
que	what (a); how
qual, quais	how great
qual, quais	. . ., indeed
quem + *synthetic plupf.*	would that I, if only I

Cọmo! Ousas dizẹr-me tal! What, you dare to say such a thing to me!

Quanto trabalha ẹste họmem! How hard (*or* What a lot) this man works!

Que falta de inteligência! What (a) lack of intelligence!

Que bọa idẹia (que) tem! What a good idea he's got!

Que plano excelente! What an excellent plan!

Que alẹgre (que) está vọcê! How cheerful you are!

Que bem (que) cantam! How well they sing!

Qual fọi a nọssa alegria! How great our joy was!

Qual poẹta $\left(\left\{\begin{matrix}\text{e}\\\text{nem}\end{matrix}\right\}\text{qual carapuça}\right)$**!** Poet, indeed!

Qual história! What rubbish! Nonsense!

Qual o quê! Nonsense!

Quais sọldados $\left\{\begin{matrix}\text{e}\\\text{nem}\end{matrix}\right\}$ **qual carapuça!** Come off it—soldiers, indeed!

Quem pudẹra dormir um mês! If only I could sleep for a month!

NOTES. 1. **Que** followed by a noun translates the English *what a!* A qualifying adjective may be placed before or, more usually, after the noun. When there is a verb present a second **que** is often placed before the verb for euphony or cadence, as in the fourth, sixth and seventh examples above.

2. Followed by an adjective or adverb alone, **que** translates the English *how!* (see sixth and seventh examples). With adjectives and the verb *to be* four constructions are in fact possible.

Que
Quão } terrível é a vingança de Dẹus!

Cọmo
Quanto } é terrívẹl a vingança de Dẹus!

How terrible the vengeance of God is!

3. The expression { e / nem } qual carapuça is untranslatable and merely intensifies the note of incredulity.

VOCABULARY

o acento	accent	a máquina	machine
ajoelhar(-se)	to kneel (down)	a música	music
amigo de	friendly with	o nada	nothingness
o caso	case	outros	
o conselho	advice; council	muitos	many other(s)
a cortesia	courtesy, polite-	para com	towards (of
	ness		attitudes, be-
o devaneio	daydream,		haviour, etc.)
	reverie	pendurar	to hang (up)
devẹras	really, truly	o podẹr	power
o engenheiro	engineer[1]	preocupar-se	
esbaforido	out of breath	(de)	to worry (about)
a estrada	(main) road	prosseguir	to continue
a gratidão	gratitude	o rouxinọl	nightingale
o ideal	ideal	o sotaque	accent (= drawl,
inventar	to invent		twang)
o lado	side	sugerir	to suggest
a matéria	subject	a tradução	translation
	(academic)		

ẹssa é bọa
ọra ẹssa[2] }!   really, come now!

metẹr-se a caminho   to set out (on one's way)

sẹr bem { lido / versado } (em)   to be well { read / versed } (in)

Study also the relatives, interrogatives and exclamatives listed in §§ 232–7.

[1] Or, usually, anyone with a degree in natural sciences.
[2] This expression also renders *Don't mention it.*

EXERCISES

I. (*a*) *Study and translate:* Este é o ideal que perseguimos.
Houve um momento em que nos perdemos. Há sempre
alguém que deseja sugerir outro curso de acção. Foram
eles quem inventou esta máquina. O professor a cujo lado
andava. Depois do que me ajoelhei diante dela. É o amigo
com quem cheguei ontem. Não há quem o entenda. Nem
sabia a quem pedir ajuda. Como é estúpida aquela rapariga!
Porque não escrever-lhe já, já? Qual escrever! Logo se
meteram a caminho. Ouça, que bem que canta aquele
rouxinol! Qual música nem qual carapuça! Quantas vezes
parece perderem-se no nada dos seus devaneios! Que lhe
parece esta tradução? Não havia mais nada a discutir.
Quanto tenho a pagar? Não tínhamos tempo a perder.

(*b*) *Translate:* The man we saw yesterday. The reason why
I did it. The lady for whom we bought it. The case we
were discussing. The subject in which he is well read.
The door behind which I hung my coat. The accent with
which he speaks. Whose ideas are these? What is the
reason? What do you think of the new road? Which
brother do you really prefer? What a lovely view! What a
lot of people! I had no one to go with. He didn't know
where to begin. What rubbish. If only I were a soldier.
Come off it—soldier indeed!

II. (*a*) *Study and translate:* 1. Mas que ridículo que estás!
Que não te vejam assim! 2. Somos nós que temos de pensar
na dificuldade do problema. 3. Fui procurar quem me
ajudasse a resolver estas e outras muitas dificuldades. 4.
Essa é boa, José; não parece bem que você zombe assim
dum homem com quem penso casar dentro em muito pouco.
5. Desprezam-me por acreditarem que faltei à minha palavra. 6. Entramos agora numa época de dificuldades, da
qual não sei como vamos sair. 7. Além do que, o dizê-lo
ele ter-me-ia estranhado muitíssimo, a não ser por alguma
coisa que me escreveu no ano passado. 8. Achavam-se

reunidas muitas pessoas de importância, dentre as quais se destacava o senhor Pereira, presidente do Conselho. 9. O ministro viu-se obrigado a confessar aos jornalistas que não tinha mais nada a dizer-lhes. 10. Parecia que o senhor engenheiro Martins, por ser tão rico e tão amigo do ministro, não tinha podido encontrar quem se interessasse pelo seu novo projecto.

(*b*) *Translate:* 1. He assured them that that was the only reason for his parents' not having come as well. 2. It appears that they have nothing of importance to tell us. 3. Had I known it, I should have written straight away asking them for help. 4. Which are the most important cities in Brazil, where are they situated, and to what do they owe their importance? 5. Up till now it has always been they who have helped me; now it is I who can do something for them. 6. It is not we who must change [our] opinion. 7. This is one of the problems that is still to be studied. 8. They took us to an old house the windows of which were all broken. 9. There's no one understands him when he starts talking about politics. 10. We should be interested (= It would interest us) to know for what reason you refuse to accept the remedy that has been prepared.

III. (*a*) *Study and translate:* O pobre velhote ficou surpreendido porque naquela época o engenheiro era conhecido de todos e uma pessoa de suma importância, e pôs-se a tremer. Mas o secretário disse-lhe que não se preocupasse, de modo que saíram ambos da pequena loja e encaminharam-se para a fábrica, que não ficava muito longe. Mal se apresentara o velho, disse-lhe o engenheiro com grande cortesia: — Meu amigo, vou começar por abraçá-lo como prova da minha gratidão e depois restituir-lhe-ei o dinheiro que lhe devo desde há tantos anos. O operário não sabia o que dizer nem fazer, e mal pôde crer o que ouvira. — Nunca se perde o fazer bem — prosseguiu o engenheiro. Prometi não esquecer nunca a sua bondade para comigo. Peça-me o que quiser, e se estiver no meu poder, eu lho outorgarei.

(*b*) *Translate:* One evening I was sitting in front of the fire (**à lareira**). Although I had a book in my hand, I was not reading, through being tired and because the story was not very interesting. My sister with whom I lived was already in (**na**) bed and the dog was fast asleep. The clock struck eleven and I was just about to go to bed when somebody knocked at the door. Having opened it I was surprised to find a policeman there, evidently out of breath. I led him into the lounge and made him sit down. After a while he was able to speak and tell me all that had happened. A small black car had passed him on the road but he had noticed nothing unusual and had walked on. A few minutes later, however, he saw the same car which had stopped and the driver of which looked very ill. Only with difficulty had he been able to get him out of the car. He had been told I was a doctor and had run as fast as he could to where I lived.

LESSON XXXIX

238. WORD ORDER: NOUN AND ADJECTIVE. Adjectives, except those which indicate or limit rather than describe, usually follow the noun in Portuguese [§ 34 and § 38]. However, describing adjectives, too, are placed before the noun when they are used in a less literal or more emotive sense, and when they do not therefore serve primarily to characterize or select.

a **casa branca,** the white house (*the adjective helps to identify the house*)

but a **branca nęve,** the white snow (*the adjective is logically unnecessary*)

um **cavalo nęgro,** a black horse (*literal sense of* black)

but um **nęgro pensamento,** a black thought (*figurative sense of* black)

Similarly, common descriptive adjectives such as **pequęno** and **lindo,** which are used frequently before the noun, nevertheless follow when they have full selective force. Thus, to the question *who did this?* one might reply o **nǫvo colęga;** to the question *which colleague did this?*, on the other hand, the reply o **colęga nǫvo** would be more appropriate.

An adjective modified by an adverb tends to become more selective, more analytical, and therefore follows the noun [§ 34 NOTE].

É um amigo muito bom. He is a very good (type of) friend.
o irmão mais alto, the tallest brother

In a few cases, however, this analytical function is not present and the *adverb + adjective* precede.

É muito bom amigo. He's a very good friend.
É muito męu amigo. He's a very good friend of mine.
a mais profunda escuridão, darkest night (*lit.,* the deepest darkness)

In the earlier cases the friend and the brother are individualized by the adjectives; in the latter ones the group *adverb + adjective + noun* is presented synthetically, as almost the equivalent of an absolute superlative [§ 201 (*c*)].

NOTES. 1. **Algum,** *some,* placed after the noun, may have the negative sense of **nenhum: sem dúvida nenhuma/alguma,** *without any doubt;* **não fêz dano nenhum/algum,** *it didn't do any damage.*

2. A following **mesmo** may intensify not only the noun [§ 38 (3)] but also a pronoun or adverb: **o pai mesmo,** *the father himself;* **eles mesmos,** *they themselves;* **aqui mesmo,** *on this very spot;* **ontem mesmo,** *only yesterday;* **agora mesmo,** *this very instant, just now.* Compare also the position of **não** in similar cases: **hoje não,** *not today;* **aqui não,** *not here;* etc.

239. WORD ORDER: MAIN ELEMENTS OF THE SENTENCE. The order of the main elements of the sentence in Portuguese is far less rigid than in English and is largely a matter of style. However, the following indications should prove useful:

(*a*) *The Verb*

The verb can be considered as the nucleus of the sentence. If we disregard conjunctions, negative adverbs and weak pronoun objects, we can say that it almost always occupies the first or second position after a pause (*i.e.*, usually, though not always, the first or second position in its own clause). Here, then, lies the first important difference between English and Portuguese: the verb in Portuguese, in all types of sentence, appears frequently in the initial position. This is often because the subject is unexpressed apart from the verb ending, but also because the subject in Portuguese may be used after the verb, particularly when it is composed of several words or when it is in a subordinate clause, or for reasons of emphasis. The order *verb-subject* is compulsory when the verb is used parenthetically (*i.e.*, after words quoted) and virtually compulsory when the verb is an infinitive or past participle.

De mais a mais,[1] **Paulo não quẹr ir.** Besides, Paul doesn't want to go.

Dormiram tọda a nọite. They slept all night.

Irẹmos lọgo que chegar mẹu irmão. We shall go as soon as my brother arrives.

Mẹu pai trabalha muito.⎫
Trabalha muito mẹu pai.⎭ My father works hard.

Vem um senhọr que vọcê não conhẹce. There's a gentleman coming whom you don't know.

E assim chegámos tọdos. And so we all arrived.

— Vem ạmanhã — respondẹu o irmão. "Come tomorrow," the brother replied.

Fọi-se embọra ao chegar o dọno. He went away when the owner arrived.

Terminada a lição, partimos tọdos. When the lesson was over we all left.

NOTES. 1. To say that the verb occupies the first or second position does not mean that it is the first or second word, but rather the first or second grammatical unit. In **E assim chegámos tọdos** there is an example of inversion to prevent the verb's moving beyond the second position. The tendency to such inversion is not really so marked as in German, but it is none the less quite strong.

2. With the inverted order in the third example compare the popular English *He works hard, my father*. The stress is then alike in the two languages, though inversion in Portuguese is by no means limited to popular usage. In English the addition of *there* before the verb may help to keep the Portuguese order of words (*cf.* example 5, above).

Lọgo se apresentou outra dificuldade. Then there appeared another difficulty.

(b) The Pre-Verbal Element

One main element may precede the verb. Usually, as in English, this element is the subject or an adverb or adverbial

---

[1] Also written **demais a mais.**

phrase; but occasionally, too, it is the direct or indirect object, placed before the verb for emphasis, and especially in more literary style it may be a noun or adjective complement.

Sęu filho chegou ontem à nǫite.   Your son got here last night.
Em seguida vǫltou pạra casa.   Then he went off home.
À paz sęgue-se a guęrra.   Peace is followed by war.
Lǫgo se cǫrtam as árvores.   Then the trees are cut.
Mạs isso não o encontra o Sr. aqui.   But you don't find *that* here.
A mim não me dissęram nada.   They haven't said anything to *me*.
Filho és; pai serás.   You are a son; you will be(come) a father.
Muito difícil seria contar tudo.   It would be very difficult to relate it all.

(c) Post-Verbal Elements

The normal order of elements used after the verb is the following: (1) adverb (or short adverbial phase), (2) noun or adjectival complement, (3) subject, (4) direct object, (5) indirect object, (6) prepositional phrase.

Fia-se demais (1) **do męu irmão** (6).   He trusts my brother too much.
Tinha vindo ạlguma vęz (1) **sęu pai** (3).   Your father had come on the odd occasion.
Pǫis não é má (2) **a solução** (3).   Well, the solution isn't bad.
É muito grande (2) **a casa de vǫcês** (3)?   Is your house very big?
Tinha chamado ladrão (2) **ao sęu filho** (4).   He had called your son a thief.
Parecęu-me lǫgo de princípio (1) **muito bǫa** (2) **ęsta idęia** (3).   This idea seemed very good to me from the very beginning.
Enviei uma saudação (4) **à minha nǫiva** (5) **de Madrid** (6).   I sent my fiancée a greeting from Madrid.

This order, however, is far from absolute. Much depends on the length of the different elements, for there is a strong tendency for short elements to be placed near the verb and for longer ones to be separated from it.

> **Não o fęz nunca** (1) **męu pai** (3). My father has never done it.
>
> but **Não o fiz ęu** (3), **nunca** (1). I have never done it.
>
> **É portuguęsa** (2), **sua mãe** (3)? Is your mother Portuguese?
>
> but **Vǫcê** (3) **é portuguęsa** (2)? Are you Portuguese?
>
> **Não chegava tarde** (1) **nenhum** (3). None of them used to arrive late.
>
> but **Não chegava nenhum** (3) **tão tarde cǫmo ęle.** None of them used to arrive as late as he did.

This same tendency, as well as the desire for elements belonging together to be placed together, frequently causes the attraction of a noun by a following adjectival clause [see above, (a), example 5].

> **Enviei uma saudação** (4) **à minha nǫiva** (5). I sent my fiancée a greeting.
>
> but **Enviei à minha nǫiva** (5) **uma saudação** (4) **que não esperava.** I sent my fiancée a greeting she wasn't expecting.

240. ARCHAISMS. (a) **Mui** [muĩ]. In very elevated, literary Portuguese, **muito** (when=*very*) may occasionally be replaced by the archaic **mui.**

A sua proveniência histórica é mui ǫbscura. Its historical origin is very obscure.

(b) **Mǫr.** This is an archaic variant of **maiǫr.** It is used mainly as the second element of double-barrel nouns and means *in-chief, e.g.,* **o capitão-mǫr,** *captain-in-chief*; **o cronista-mǫr,** *head chronicler;* **o ąltar-mǫr,** *high altar*; **o guarda-mǫr,** *chief customs officer*; it also exists in the noun **o mǫrdǫmo,** *majordomo,* the adverb **mǫrmente,** *mainly, in the main,* and the preposition **por mọr de**, *in addition to, because of, for the sake of*.[1]

(c) **Grão** (*fem.* **grã**). This former variant of **grande** is now confined to use as the first element of double-barrel nouns: **o grão-duque**, *Grand Duke*; **a Grã-Bretanha**, *Great Britain*.

(d) **Bẹl**. This former variant of **bẹlo** is now confined to the expression **a (sẹu) bẹl-prazẹr**, *as (he) thinks fit*.

VOCABULARY

a ạlgibeira	pocket	movẹr-se	to move
o alimento	food	o pensa-	
apṛessar-se	to hurry (up)	mento	thought
atrás	ago, before, earlier	pensativo	pensive, thoughtful
aviar-se	to hurry (up)	percorrẹr	to go all over
o bairro	quarter, district	pitorẹsco	picturesque
brilhar	to shine	presente	present (*not absent*)
a comida	food		
o convidado	guest	a saúde	health
definitivo	definitive, final	servir	to serve
a destruição	destruction	o talhẹr	cover (*at table*)
diário	daily	tomar a	to take
a entrada	entrance, entry	sério	seriously
o họrrọr	horror	trabalhadọr	hard-working
imóvẹl	motionless	o vale	valley
incapaz	incapable	ventar	to blow, be windy
lọiro	fair, blond		

de bọa vontade
com muito gọsto } willingly, with pleasure
com muito prazẹr

de facto — in fact, indeed

corrẹr }
tomar } riscos — to { run / take } risks

dar vontade de — to make (someone) want to
não faz mal — it doesn't matter, no harm done

Study also the words listed in § 240.

---

[1] **Por mọr de** is mainly regional and dialectal; the two latter meanings are a corruption of **por amọr de**.

I. (a) *Study and translate:* Estive umas semanas em Nova Iorque. Começavam a chegar outros operários. Conheço a Pedro melhor que João. Conheço a Pedro melhor que a João. À guerra segue-se a paz. Que trabalhadoras são estas mulheres! Ocorreu-me um negro pensamento. Não me restava mais nada a dizer. Sem eu explicar-lho primeiro. Sem explicar-lho primeiro seu pai. A mim não me importa nada que digam coisas assim. Tinha-o visto anos atrás. Logo entrou o guarda-mor. O general de Gaulle falou contra a entrada da Grã-Bretanha no Mercado Comum. A seu bel-prazer.

(b) *Translate:* She is a charming girl. The valley of Santarém is very picturesque. I like [it] very much. Through my not knowing anything. Then his brother appeared. She had fair hair. We all refused to take it seriously. The elder son is not in good (**bem de**) health. On Saturdays the two sisters usually arrive together. Shall we wait until he arrives? In fact it was almost impossible to move. But what does it matter to *you*? We heard the door open. Huge pictures were hanging on the walls. What *were* we to do? What were *we* to do?

II. (a) *Study and translate:* 1. Eu, quando pequeno, ouvia contar muitas vezes que estava doente um amigo ou um vizinho. 2. Logo, imediatamente, a pessoa que contava ou a que ouvia ficava um momento pensativa. 3. Foi em 1901 que se publicou a edição definitiva da sua obra. 4. Pedem para falar consigo dois senhores que acabam de chegar de Londres. 5. Claro está que não faz mal que sigam tomando tais riscos, mas eu não gosto, francamente. 6. Pareciam muito difíceis as explicações que nos dera. 7. Este jovem não sabe tantas línguas como seu irmão, mas nem por isso deixa de me parecer mais inteligente. 8. Ver uma paisagem pitoresca, ouvir cantar uma mulher encantadora não me dá vontade de me dedicar à retórica, mas antes de me calar.

9. Lá fora estava ventando, embora brilhasse um sol alegre.
10. O exército percorreu a cidade toda procurando comida.

(b) *Translate:* 1. Even if what you tell me is true I shall none the less have complete confidence in any idea that that gentleman proposes to me. 2. It seems very unlikely to us that such a solution will be accepted, so we have decided to talk no more about the matter. 3. The soldiers all requested that the general should grant them more food. 4. He told them that he would do so willingly, but they would have to wait until they reached Évora. 5. She told the children that if they were good she would buy them all a present when she went into town. 6. He is a very hard-working boy and he has a very good memory for the things that interest him. 7. I assured them that my memory did not deceive me so much that I was incapable of remembering which was my own brother. 8. I was writing my daily letter when Philip came into the room and asked me for my sister's address. 9. His parents were present when the guests arrived. 10. He stood motionless on seeing the horror of so much destruction.

III. (a) *Study and translate:* Estavam abertas as janelas quando Pedro entrou no quarto de dormir, mas foi fechá-las imediatamente porque já caíra a noite. Depois de colocar sob a cama as malas, desceu à sala de jantar e tomou assento a uma mesa pequena com talheres para duas pessoas. Logo se lhe apresentou um criado.

— V. Ex.ª janta só? — perguntou. — Estou à espera dum amigo — respondeu. Vem ver-me às oito e meia. Pode servir-nos dentro dum quarto de hora. Vai chegar em breve e estará com fome.

Pedro tirou o bilhete postal que lhe enviara Luís e voltou a lê-lo. Perguntou a si próprio se deveras viria esta noite. Porque escolhera Luís este hotel que ficava tão longe da cidade? Pois enquanto guardava o bilhete na algibeira, abriu-se a porta e o seu amigo entrou, todo sujo e esbaforido.

(*b*) *Translate:* Last Sunday the Fernandes family, who live in the poorest quarter of Curitiba, had closed the shop and were finishing their meal. As it was fine, Senhor Fernandes decided to go for a walk. Soon afterwards Senhora Fernandes, who was looking through the window, saw a young man stop in front of the door. He wished her good evening and explained to her that her sister was very ill and had asked him to tell her to come at once. Senhora Fernandes told him she was very grateful. "I must hurry," she said to her son. "Take this money and give it to your father when he comes back." Then she ran to catch the bus at the corner. Fortunately when she reached her sister's she found that it wasn't too serious (**grave**). She had been eating too much, as usual (**como sempre**).

LESSON XL

241. THE PREPOSITIONS em AND a. In expressions involving (*a*) *place*, (*b*) *time*, there exists some difficulty in distinguishing between these two prepositions. The following rules, though not exhaustive, hold good for the vast majority of cases.

(*a*) *Place*

(1) In general, **em** indicates *rest at* a place, whereas **a** (or **para**) indicates *motion to* a place.

Estou em casa.	**Moro em Lisboa.**
I'm at home.	I live in Lisbon.
Morava em Mafra.	**Vou à esquina.**
He lived at Mafra.	I'm going to the corner.
Chegou a casa.	**Chegaram ao hotel.**
She arrived home.	They arrived at the hotel.

O comboio chegou à estação.
The train arrived in the station.

Foi ver Pedro a Paris.
He went to see Peter in Paris.

Fomos visitar meu tio ao Estoril.
We went to visit my uncle at Estoril.

Foram tomar uma pinga a um bar.
They went to a bar for a drink.

Vão jantar ao novo restaurante grego.
They're going for dinner at the new Greek restaurant.

Vamos para a cidade (*or* **ao centro**).
We're going into town.

Já foi para a cama.
He's already gone to bed.

(2) Usually **a** translates English *in*, *into*, *on*, *on to*, when there is motion but little suggestion of complete enclosure.

Caiu ao poço. He fell into the well.

Atiraram-se $\left\{\begin{array}{l}\text{à água}\\\text{ao mar}\end{array}\right\}$. They flung themselves into the $\left\{\begin{array}{l}\text{water}\\\text{sea}\end{array}\right\}$.

Deitou-o ao chão (*or* **por terra**). She threw it on the ground.

Caiu ao chão (*or* **por terra**). He fell (on) to the ground (*from a height*).

Saiu à (*or* **para a**) **rua.** He went out into the street.

Subimos ao (*or* **para o**) **terraço.** We went up on to the terrace.

NOTE: **Caiu no chão** implies falling to the ground from a sitting or standing position. **Caiu no rio** implies total immersion.

(3) **Em** translates *into* when there is motion and complete enclosure and also in cases of change or division.

Entrei no quarto.
I went into the room.

Mergulhei no rio.
I dived into the river.

Convertemo-lo em casa de hóspedes. We changed it into a guest house.

Partiu-o em dois.
He divided it into two (*or* in half).

NOTE: **Andar em** renders *to attend* or *frequent* a place of learning.

> **Ando na escola técnica.** I go to the technical college.

Observe also: **Andava em Lisboa.** He used to knock about Lisbon.

(4) **A** indicates *rest at* a place in the following circumstances:

(i) as an alternative to **em** after **morar**, *to live* (or its synonyms

viver, residir), when reference is made to a particular address or locality of a town or city.

Mora $\left\{ \begin{array}{l} \textbf{ao} \\ \textbf{no} \end{array} \right\}$ **Chiado.** He lives in the Chiado (*a district of Lisbon*).

Desejam morar $\left\{ \begin{array}{l} \textbf{à} \\ \textbf{na} \end{array} \right\}$ **Rua dos Combatentes.** They want to live in the Rua dos Combatentes.

but: **Morámos no número 2, Travessa de São Paulo.** We lived at number 2, Travessa de São Paulo.

(ii) in a number of stock adverbial or prepositional expressions:

à mesa	at (the) table	**a (mão)**	
à porta	at the door	**esquerda**	on the left
à janela	at the window	**à borda de**	on the edge of
à sombra	in the shade	**à margem**	
ao sol	in the sunshine	**de**	on the edge of
ao ar livre	in the fresh air	**ao lado de**	at the side of
a bordo	on board	**ao pé de**	near to; at the
ao norte	in the north		foot of
ao sul	in the south	**aos pés de**	at the foot (feet)
a oeste	in the west		of
a $\left\{ \begin{array}{l} \textbf{este} \\ \textbf{leste} \end{array} \right\}$	in the east	**ao sopé de**	at the foot of (*a hill or mountain*)
ao luar	in the moonlight	**à luz de**	in (*or* by) the light of
à (mão)		**ao longo de**	along(side)
direita	on the right	**a** + *quantity*	
		+ de	(away) from

Bata você à porta. Knock at the door.

Todos estavam sentados à mesa. They were all sitting at the table.

Estoril está a uns trinta quilómetros de Lisboa. Estoril is about thirty kilometres from Lisbon.

A nossa casa fica a uma milha de distância. Our house is a mile away.

NOTE: In most cases position *at rest* is translated into Portuguese by **em**. In certain of the above cases **em** would give a different meaning. **Gibrạltar está ao sul da Espanha** (*to the south of*); **Estoril está a oẹste de Lisbọa** (*to the west of*); but **Portugal está no oẹste da Eurọpa** (*in the west of*). Note also **nas margens de** (*on the banks of*).

(iii) in a number of expressions where it is interchangeable with **em**:

ao **no** }	**meio**	in the middle, in the midst	**ao** **no** }	**canto**	in the corner
ao **no** }	**centro**	at in } the centre	**à** **na** }	**esquina**	at on } the corner
ao **no** }	**fundo**	at the bottom, at the end	**à** **na** }	**página**	on page
ao **no** }	**alto**	at the top, on top			

Ao fundo do corredọr achava-se uma pọrta. At the end of the corridor there was a door.
À página vinte lẹmos que ... On page twenty we read that ...

(b) *Time*

(1) In general, **em** translates English *on, in*, whereas **a** renders *at*.

nos dias úteis on workdays	**no Verão** in summer	**às cinco họras** at five o'clock
no dia seguinte[1] on the following day	**naquẹle ano** in that year	**a ẹsse tempo** at that time
noutra ọcasião on another occasion	**no século passado** in the last century	**ao amanhecẹr** at daybreak

---

[1] But usually *ao* **outro dia**, *on the following day.*

em data errada on the wrong date	na hora da nossa morte in the hour of our death	ao fim do mês at the end of the month
na manhã ante- rior on the morning before	naqueles tempos in those days	a(o) princípio at the outset

(2) Before the nouns **instante** and **momento** *at* is translated by **em**, except when they are introduced by **qualquer, todo** or **cada,** in which case the relevant preposition is **a.**

naquele momento at that moment	nesse instante at that instant	a todo o momento at every moment

Note also : **num instante,** *in an instant, instantly.*

(3) Portuguese often uses **em** where in English there is no preposition or where a preposition has been omitted.

na próxima semana   **no dia seguinte**
next week   (on) the following day

Não o vi em todo o dia/ano.

I haven't seen him all day /year.

(n)a semana passada   **(n)o ano que vem**
last week   (in) the coming year

(4) For days of the week, dates and periods of the day see §§ 69–71, 81.

242. FURTHER USES OF THE PREPOSITION **de.** Apart from its normal functions (=*of, from, about*) this preposition is also used in the following cases:

(1) to indicate the cause of a given action or reaction (English *with, at, for,* etc.).

Alegro-me muito do seu êxito. I'm very pleased at your success.

Pôs-se a saltar de alegria. He started to jump for joy.

Estavam a tremer de frio. They were shivering with cold.

(2) to translate *with*, *in* and *by*, when they introduce the means or instrument of a given action.

Este campo está semeado de trigo. This field is sown with wheat.

Vestiu-se de pręto. She dressed in black.

Pintaram as pǫrtas de vęrde. They painted the doors (in) green.

A cidade está rodeada de muralhas. The city is surrounded by walls.

NOTE: In the last case the function of **de** comes close to that of **por** when it introduces an agent [§ 220]. **De** may in fact introduce the agent after the passive of a verb of feeling, but **por** is more usual in modern Portuguese.[1]

Ęra aborrecido por (*also* **de**) **tǫdos.** He was detested by all.

É querido de tǫdos. He is loved by everybody.

(3) to indicate in what capacity or with what status someone does something (English *as* + indefinite article).

Trabalhou de enfermeira num hǫspital. She worked as a nurse in a hospital.

Sęrve-nos de guia. He acts as our guide.

Quem cantou de tenǫr? Who sang (as) tenor?

NOTE: **Cǫmo** may often be used rather than **de**:

> **Trabalhou cǫmo enfermeira.** She worked as a nurse.
> **Alistou-se cǫmo praça.** He joined up as a private.

(4) to translate *in* in the sense of *as to*, *with regard to*, *as far as—is* (*are*) *concerned*.

Encontro-me muito melhǫr de saúde. I feel much better in health.

Ęra muito pequęno de cǫrpo. He was very small in body.

---

[1] Note also **acompanhado de** (*accompanied by*) and **seguido de** (*followed by*).

(5) to give adjectival function to a verb, noun, adverb or adverbial phrase.

a máquina de escrever	the typewriter
papęl de fumar	cigarette-paper
o campo de batalha	the battlefield
uma męsa de carvalho	an oak table
a menina dos ǫlhos vęrdes	the green-eyed girl
os dias doutrǫra	bygone days
as províncias de além-mar	the overseas provinces
os anos de antes da guęrra	the pre-war years
but o lugar em frente	the seat opposite
a fotografia abaixo	the photograph below
etc.	

NOTE: Pąra is similarly used to indicate function in cases where **de** might suggest content or composition.

um cǫpo pąra vinho	a wineglass
uma escǫva pąra o cabęlo	a hairbrush

But **uma escǫva de dentes** (*a toothbrush*), because no confusion is likely.

(6) to indicate means of transport.

Hǫje vim de carro.	Today I came by car.
Viajo sempre de $\left\{\begin{array}{l}\textbf{combǫio}\\ \textbf{avião}\end{array}\right\}$.	I always travel by $\left\{\begin{array}{l}\text{train}\\ \text{air}\end{array}\right\}$.

But note: **a cavalo** (*on horseback*), **a pé** (*on foot*), **por avião** (*by* .*air*mail); **de pé** (*on foot*; *standing*) is also found.

(7) to indicate positions or attitudes of parts of the body, clothing, etc.

Entrou de bengala na mão.	He came in (with his) stick in (his) hand.
de joelhos	on his knees
de mãos dadas	hand in hand
de chapéu na mão	hat in hand

(8) occasionally, to render *in* before names of seasons.

na
de } **Primavẹra**   in spring

243. CAUSAL CONJUNCTIONS.   (*a*) When a causal clause precedes the main clause it is not normally good style to use the conjunction **porque** (*because*); preferable are **cọmo** (*as*), **visto que** (*seeing that*), **já que** (*seeing that*) and **porquanto** (*since*).

Porquanto é muito inteligente, sai sempre aprovado nos exames.   It's because he's very clever that he always passes examinations.

(*b*) If the causal clause follows the main clause the conjunctions available include the foregoing and also **porque** (*because*), **pọis (que)** (*for, because*) and **que** (*for, because*).

Vamos andando que não vale a pẹna (o) ficarmos aqui.   Let's be off for there's no point in our staying here.

VOCABULARY

a fim de	in order to	fazẹr uma	
à mão	at hand, to hand	excursão	to go for a trip
o ar	air; appearance	o lago	lake
a atenção	attention	a milha	mile
atirar	to throw, fling	o prado	meadow
banhar-se	to bathe	o público	
o bọsque	wood (*place*)	ledọr	reading public
o carvalho	oak, oak tree	(em) quanto	as for, with
convertẹr	to convert	a	regard to
deixar cair	to drop	a variẹdade	variety
estar interes-sado em	to be interested in	vizinho	neighbouring, nearby

ao
no } princípio
aos
nos } princípios } do mês   at the beginning of the month

ao no} em meados no meado } meio } de Junho	in the middle of June
ao no} fim aos nos} fins } do século XIX	at the end of the nineteenth century
na tua idade	at your age
noutras idades	in other ages
de viagem	on a journey
de volta	back
à idade de aos } quinze anos	at the age of fifteen
em férias	on holiday
no ao} mesmo tempo	at the same time

Study also the expressions listed in §§ 241–3.

EXERCISES

I. (a) *Study and translate:* Nas margens do Douro. Está de viagem. Quando estiver de volta. Partiu em férias. Naquele dia. Ao mesmo tempo. No meado do século XV. Aos fins de Março. De mãos escondidas nas algibeiras. Vim de carro eléctrico. Rodeado de amigos. Seguido do seu cão. Em data errada. Está ao canto do quarto. No alto da colina. Na sua idade. Aos quinze anos. Ao ar livre. Ao sopé da montanha. À mão esquerda.

(b) *Translate:* The stone fell into the sea. She flung herself into the water. He dropped it on the ground. We have converted them into one house. He used to knock about Luanda. Who's at the door? They came on board. He ran alongside the quay. Sintra is situated to the north of Estoril. Angola is in the south-west of Africa. At the beginning of June. On page fifteen. At the bottom of the well. In the centre of the room. By airmail. He arrived on horseback and left on foot. We're not interested in this.

II. (a) *Study and translate:* 1. Asseguro-lhes que poucos países haverá na Europa em que se possa gozar de uma maior variedade de paisagens do que na Espanha. 2. Conquanto fosse amado de toda a gente, mal pôde achar quem o ajudasse a cumprir a tarefa. 3. Porquanto tem feito um tempo tão terrível, estou com medo de que este ano não produzam muito os campos e prados. 4. Ao ouvirem as felizes notícias, puseram-se a saltar de alegria. 5. Santa Maria, reza por nós agora e na hora da nossa morte. 6. Logo que te tiveres vestido, desejo que vás comigo ao centro. 7. Saltou ao mar e tudo ficou acabado num instante. 8. Se você viesse a Coimbra, servir-lhe-ia de guia com muito gosto. 9. Contou-me que acabara de comprar uma mesa de carvalho para a sala de jantar. 10. Caiu de joelhos suplicando-lhes que não matassem o marido.

(b) *Translate:* 1. There is an enormous difference between working through illusion and working out of necessity. 2. It was only then that it was learnt he was leaving for Angola in the middle of January. 3. Because of the threat of a revolution the prime minister always had a revolver at hand. 4. I am very grateful to him for the interest he shows in everything I do. 5. On the following morning the weather was perfect and the mountains, still covered with snow, stood out enormous against the blue sky. 6. At the beginning of the twentieth century there appeared one day, in one of the least important papers of the capital, a piece of news of great interest to (=for) the reading public. 7. Mr Martins told me to ask my brother for the books we had lent him the previous week. 8. He wants someone to explain to him what one must do in order to go as a guide with foreign tourists. 9. He warned them that by not accepting the solution proposed to them by the manager, they were making every kind of agreement practically impossible. 10. He explained to them that he always kept his revolver ready to be used (=in order to use it) at any moment.

III. (*a*) *Study and translate:* Na semana passada João e Miguel fizeram uma excursão ao campo. Levantaram-se muito cedo, a fim de chegarem à estação às oito horas. Quando o João saiu de casa para a rua o ar estava fresquinho e o céu estava carregado de nuvens. O Miguel, que morava pertinho, à Rua dos Ingleses, já estava à espera à esquina. Correram à estação tão rápido como puderam. No comboio encontraram-se com vários amigos e cantaram canções com eles. Desceram do comboio numa pequena vila e caminharam até chegar a um grande prado; aqui se sentaram à sombra dum grande carvalho para almoçar. O sol rompeu por entre as nuvens e brilhou alegremente nos campos e bosques. À tarde banharam-se num lago vizinho; a água estava bastante morna e ambos os rapazes sabiam nadar bem.

(*b*) *Translate:* It suddenly seemed probable that the bridge would collapse when the next train crossed it. As soon as Johnny had convinced himself of this, he realized that he must try to get to the station before they let another train leave. One was about to depart, he knew, at twenty to one, and it was twenty past twelve already. The station was almost three miles away. He started to run. He ran as if his life depended on his arriving on time. Twice he nearly fell, but he managed not to. If only it weren't so hot or he weren't wearing so many clothes! Without stopping he took off his jacket and dropped it on the ground. But four minutes later, on arriving at the top of the hill from where he could see the station, he saw the train approaching him. Was it possible he was mistaken with regard to the time? And now, would he be able to attract anyone's attention?

SUPPLEMENTARY EXERCISES

The following exercises are provided for the benefit of students who may feel the need of extra practice at various stages of progress through the Grammar. They are grouped in five-lesson sequences. Any new words will be found in the vocabularies at the end of the book.

I. LESSONS I–V

(*a*) *Study and translate:* 1. Mas não é possível ler o livro em três horas. 2. Aonde vão as senhoras? 3. Quem vai enviar a carta à mãe de Pedro? 4. O senhor Gonçalves é muito inteligente e trabalha na universidade. 5. Quantos irmãos tem você? 6. Na página dezasseis na lição dois lemos que Lisboa é em Portugal. 7. Há grande confusão porque há cinco hospitais na pequena cidade onde moramos. 8. O cura é o último bastião da religião cristã. 9. Há muitos volumes grandes e interessantes na biblioteca da Universidade de Coimbra. 10. Os pais de Miguel não lêem jornal algum. 11. Vamos vender o rádio porque não gostamos dos programas. 12. Os dois órfãos vão ter de ir morar com os avós. 13. Coimbra é uma cidade beiroa. 14. Quando vamos estudar o Sol e os planetas? 15. Na terceira lição o professor vai falar das muitas nações e tribos que há na grande família europeia. 16. Aprendemos a língua portuguesa e temos um livro português. 17. Vão fazer alguma mudança na loja? 18. A casa dos tios de Miguel é mais alta do que a loja do velho senhor alemão. 19. Na mesa há muitos e belos copos, pratos, chávenas e pires. 20. O velho lojista com quem moramos vai partir para Londres.

(*b*) *Translate:* 1. The third lesson is not as simple as the second one. 2. We don't like the furniture of the old house. 3. How many apples have you got? 4. John's father is writing a guidebook of the streets of Lisbon. 5. The Pope himself is not the driving force of the Christian religion. 6. The two women are reading an interesting book on the ideas of Bergson. 7. Why aren't they going to like the wines of Portugal? 8. The old priest hasn't got any objection to the boy's ideas. 9. I'm going to send a telegram to John's parents. 10. I buy a lot of potatoes and tomatoes at Mary's uncle's shop. 11. There are two stations at Coimbra and one has four platforms. 12. The two Catalan ladies are very impolite. 13. In one of John's brother's factories they manufacture barrels for the wine that they send to Lisbon. 14. Who do you study with in the library? 15. I have various friends who sell papers in the street. 16. The poor shopkeeper's got too much bread but he hasn't enough potatoes! 17. The bookseller's children are studying a map of Portugal. 18. Some of the dramas of Shakespeare have too many characters. 19. The old Andalusian's daughter is very pretty but she isn't very polite. 20. Michael's grandparents don't read many magazines.

2. LESSONS VI–X

(a) *Study and translate:* 1. Vou partir para Londres a dez de Junho. 2. De quem é aquela caneta vermelha? 3. Este carro é muito pequeno para os meus avós. 4. Qual é o mais novo dos dois? 5. O pobre livreiro não está contente porque tem demasiados livros na loja. 6. Quem era aquele senhor velho? 7. Os rapazes portugueses estavam a vender mexilhões no cais. 8. A minha mãe sentia vontade de estudar a língua alemã. 9. Sendo velhos trabalhavam muito menos do que a minha irmã. 10. Tínhamos de levar em conta que não chegava a tempo. 11. Quando vamos explorar Lisboa? 12. Partiam antes do meio-dia e meia hora. 13. Este homem e esta mulher moravam naquela casa. 14. Não gostávamos dos móveis desse hotel. 15. A quem pertencia este carro? 16. Donde é Miguel? 17. Estava um pouco triste porque as peras não estavam maduras. 18. Quando ia para casa dos meus tios, quase sempre descansava durante a viagem. 19. Eu vou para a cidade mas tu tens de trabalhar aqui. 20. Nós não gostamos deste peixe.

(b) *Translate:* 1. It was a quarter past eight. 2. We used to leave on the 9.45 p.m. train. 3. The inn is made of stone. 4. Being ill he had to go to (the) hospital. 5. They used to leave the boxes at the factory. 6. His children always go hungry when he hasn't got enough money. 7. How old is she? 8. It was very bad weather and very windy. 9. It was always dark when I arrived at my parents'. 10. We're going to the pictures on Saturday night. 11. New Year's Day is the first day of the year. 12. My father was working in the vineyard. 13. It's her birthday on Tuesday. 14. According to Philip she was still working yesterday. 15. We have an examination tomorrow at 2.30 sharp. 16. Both his children were very tired and very hungry. 17. What is a boa constrictor? 18. What are his objections to the previous census? 19. It was a summer's day in the month of May. 20. But *we* are going to have a lot to do tomorrow.

3. LESSONS XI–XV

(a) *Study and translate:* 1. O avião estava para chegar. 2. Nunca lia nem livros nem revistas nem sequer jornais. 3. Vamos dar um passeio pelo parque. 4. Mas isso é muito interessante! Quem lho disse? 5. Quando era que chegava a casa o filho do professor? 6. Onde é que ficam os seus papéis? 7. É certo que está um tanto abafado lá fora. 8. Todos o viram mas ninguém o procurava. 9. Ambos tomámos assento em cima. 10. Foi quando te vi que tive vontade de to dizer. 11. Era quando te via que tinha vontade de to dizer. 12. De todos os modos vamos ter com Filipe amanhã à tarde, às duas horas. 13. Deu-lhe uma moeda de vinte e cinco tostões. 14. A senhora D. Maria estava mal quando chegou. 15. O que é que puseram na mesa? 16. Onde esteve Pedro tanto tempo? 17. Para onde foram elas quando chegaram os seus amigos? 18. Estes são os livros que me deram ontem à noite. 19. As raparigas com quem eu vim falam bem o francês. 20. As pessoas que dizem que o português é fácil não o estudaram.

(b) *Translate:* 1. I was about to give him the letter when he got off the bus. 2. She was having tea with your mother. 3. I'm going to tell them that my daughter is not at home. 4. The man who told me so was his father-in-law. 5. Where did you leave those bricks? 6. Somebody's waiting for you downstairs. 7. The boy who came this morning is here now. 8. I went to the new market and bought fish, coffee, potatoes and apples for my mother. 9. She's bought two new hats. 10. Dona Maria is a trifle lazy and the plates are not always clean. 11. It was raining when we arrived. 12. Yesterday she received a letter from her husband. 13. Tonight I'm going to spend the evening at home. 14. She was writing a letter when her mother came in. 15. It was one o'clock in the morning when they left.   16. One day it rained, and I didn't give them their exercises.   17. Further on there was a very high building.   18. As for me, I haven't the slightest (**menọr**) idea.   19. We both saw him at about twenty past twelve.   20. The family used to have breakfast at half past seven every morning.

4. LESSONS XVI–XX

(a) *Study and translate:* 1. Quando foi que grelhaste estes tomates? 2. Pescávamos sempre naquele rio.   3. Não podes emprestar-me nem cinco cruzeiros?   4. Levaram-lhes três taças de champanhe. 5. O Papa Leão XIII desejava excomungar o rei mas não pôde. 6. Pode recomendar-nos uma boa casa de hóspedes, pertinho? 7. Foi só então que o avistámos.   8. Quando lhe disse isso a rapariga corou.   9. Mal termináramos a lição de geografia quando o professor morreu.   10. Não posso compreender porque o fez. 11. O padeiro faliu no ano de 1946 por não poder vender bastante pão.   12. Não vês os meus pais? Porquê?   13. A mãe trabalhava na cozinha a preparar o primeiro almoço.   14. Depois da refeição Martinho levantou a mesa.   15. O general havia descoberto a verdade antes da nossa partida.   16. Tendo arrumado os cinco pacotes foi buscar a empregada catalã.   17. Sempre que o vejo, conta-me a mesma velha anedota.   18. Quem nos dera esquecer o que ela nos disse!   19. Todos fôramos para a Covilhã havia três semanas.   20. Disse-nos que lhe sobravam quase dois mil cruzeiros.

(b) *Translate:* 1. As soon as he had received the telegram he went straight home.   2. You must close the door before leaving.   3. We have sold them at thirty pounds a dozen.   4. First of all he explained to them why he had left so early.   5. The important thing is to finish it now before going home because we shan't have time in the morning.   6. The mother wished her children good morning on entering the room.   7. Children are always hungry. 8. They jumped out of bed because it was already half past seven. 9. What did he do after winding up his watch?   10. The girl had a very beautiful voice.   11. What had he got in his left hand? 12. At what time did you return home?   13. Where had they got to after lunch?   14. The boy told them he hadn't had anything to eat or drink.   15. The girls with whom I spoke speak French and Spanish very well.   16. I'm going into town to do some shopping. 17. Every time he arrives before eight he has a meal with his parents. 18. She came into the dining-room while I was laying the table. 19. It is necessary for you to get to know such people. 20. First of all you must fry the potatoes slowly.

5. LESSONS XXI–XXV

(a) *Study and translate:* 1. Há meia hora que te espero aqui. Onde tens estado? 2. Tinham escrito o telegrama. 3. Deixaram escrita a carta. 4. Vivi três anos em Santos. 5. Tu tens de prepará-los todos. 6. Quando despertei, já não sabia o que sucedera na noite anterior. 7. Procurámo-la em toda a parte mas em vão. 8. Ao receber o convite tal foi a sua surpresa que se afundou numa poltrona. 9. É inútil comprar tantos legumes e fruta que já não sentimos fome. 10. Tudo o mais é ilusão. 11. Estavam todos sentados no salão a escutar o rádio. 12. Vou vestir-me antes de mais nada. 13. O que se faz agora? 14. Como se chamava a esposa do senhor Basto? 15. Eu escrevê-lo-ei no salão. 16. Sem ela tudo isto seria totalmente impossível. 17. Disse-nos que faria todo o possível para terminar o livro a tempo. 18. Não sei como no-la traria senão assim. 19. Não podes esperar um momentinho? Seguramente não tens tanta pressa! 20. Todo o bom professor sabe que certos estudantes são muito mais inteligentes do que ele.

(b) *Translate:* 1. My mother has been going to that shop for a long time; we all go to it. 2. This maid has been serving in this house for many years. 3. We have been washing clothes in the bathtub because we haven't got a better place in which to do it. 4. He used to get up very early in the morning and go to bed very late at night. 5. I must send his wife some flowers. 6. Everybody else thinks this is ridiculous but frankly I'm very fond of the idea. 7. He put his jacket on. 8. You have broken his left arm! 9. I can't grasp why they detest each other so much. 10. He always seems to arrive when we're having tea on the lawn. 11. Finally he told us he didn't believe in God either. 12. He asked me for the hundred escudos which I had owed him so long. 13. It seems to me you're wrong, but who knows? 14. We all intend to leave on the afternoon train. 15. It would be ridiculous to continue like this. 16. The dustman will tell him so on Monday. 17. All three of them came into the bedroom one after another. 18. Those inside had worked since one o'clock. 19. The policeman told me that he is to measure the corpse and that nobody else must touch it.

20. According to the canons of the Christian religion she can now do nothing but pray.

6. LESSONS XXVI–XXX

(a) *Study and translate:* 1. Implorei-lhe que respondesse imediatamente. 2. Pediu-nos licença para escrever à sua filha. 3. Vimo-la a correr através da Praça da República. 4. Ordenou-lhe que ficasse onde estava mas não quis fazê-lo. 5. Talvez fosse melhor esperar cá até que venha um polícia. 6. Por muito que tentasse, acharia quase impossível abrir esta porta. 7. Não acreditava que a fizesse para si. 8. Não me dei conta de que morresse durante a guerra civil. 9. Julgou que tivesses chegado antes de nós. 10. Fá-lo-íamos todos sob condição que não dissesses nada a minha prima. 11. Esqueceu-me explicar-lhe que necessitávamos de falar consigo imediatamente. 12. Depois contou-me que perderam a ocasião de o matar. 13. É uma vergonha que ele não saiba ler nem escrever. 14. Ei-la aqui a dormir neste maple. 15. Aqui jaz o cadáver de um grande herói português. 16. Certo soldado insistia que nos convinha fazê-lo. 17. Outro insistia em que o não fizéssemos. 18. Estranhei que me tivessem compreendido. 19. É possível que o tenhas visto? 20. É muito improvável que o fizessem a tempo.

(b) *Translate:* 1. Let's all wait here in case he leaves before we do. 2. The general told the soldier to kill the poor old woman. 3. So long as you go and visit my parents, I shall say nothing more about this matter. 4. Who is teaching Michael to dance? 5. She told me he was only the second baker in (de) Oporto to attempt to do this. 6. She wrote to us saying she was sorry she couldn't come on Friday. 7. It is necessary for us to hear what he has to say. 8. Wherever he goes he will always find friends. 9. It is impossible for her to come this morning. 10. I want to buy a jacket that I like. 11. I don't think he'll lose his watch this (desta) time. 12. She did it in order that we should admire her. 13. I ordered the waiter to bring me a beer. 14. However good it may be, I know one even better. 15. He promised to give a pound to the boy who wrote the best poem. 16. He ran into the room. 17. But he said he was in no hurry to leave. 18. He was in the garden busy doing nothing. 19. I must finish this exercise before he comes back. 20. It is curious that so many people like this sort of play.

7. LESSONS XXXI–XXXV

(a) *Study and translate:* 1. Quando suceder isso, não terei mais confiança no mundo em que vivemos. 2. Ao examinarem-no os ministros, acharam inútil prosseguir com os seus projectos. 3. Onde estiveres, nunca deixes de trazer esta rosa. 4. Queira dizer-nos onde fica a Rua da Prata. 5. Fazia favor, sabe onde mora a Sra. D. Maria Tavares? 6. Ao saírem da fábrica deram com um grupo de operários. 7. Oxalá não estivera tão cansada! 8. Se não tivesse andado de farda teria passado despercebido. 9. Irei embora a não ser que me entregues a chave. 10. Embora andassem nos sessenta, parecia sempre estarem muito bem de saúde. 11. Que esperem lá fora todas! 12. Quando voltarem, perguntem por mim em pessoa. 13. Sigam para a frente, faz favor! 14. Todo o passageiro que cuspir terá que pagar cinquenta escudos. 15. — Foge, foge, meu pai, disse o filho mais novo. 16. Estão mortas ambas há cinco anos. 17. Mataram os três soldados. 18. Foi-lhe entregue um telegrama vindo de Paris. 19. Estava deitada na cama, imóvel. 20. O motorista ficou atónito ao ver o que sucedera.

(b) *Translate:* 1. She says that if you'll believe that you'll believe anything. 2. Whatever he does next, he won't be able to solve the problem. 3. I can't carry on like this, cost what it may. 4. I ascertained what he had done next. 5. If he falls now he'll break his neck. 6. There were several fine pictures hanging on the walls of the lounge. 7. As soon as I get home, I'll phone my father. 8. I'll talk to her as soon as I can, but I don't believe I've got time to today. 9. I eat steak, rice and beans every day. 10. If you're going shopping, I want you to bring me some lettuce. 11. I shall have to tell her so when next I see her. 12. It's no use your talking like that if you're not going to do anything about it yourself. 13. Whatever happens, I'm going round to his house this evening so we can finish what we began. 14. I can't write English, but I'll do the best I can. 15. If we go into town tomorrow perhaps we'd better leave the house straight (**logo**) after breakfast, don't you think? 16. Far be it from me to presume such a thing! 17. The (**Da**) last time I saw them, they looked as though they were dying of thirst. 18. If you arrive before me you will have to wait so that I can open the door for you. 19. Don't tell me he's done it again! 20. Would you mind telling me when we get there?

8. LESSONS XXXVI–XL

(a) *Study and translate:* 1. Apesar da sua má conduta, toda a gente a tratou como a uma senhora. 2. Faço-o por tua causa e não para ela. 3. Para que vieste cá? 4. O cura presidiu à reunião. 5. Assegurou-se que não havia motivo para se preocuparem. 6. Não é minha culpa que chegassem em data errada. 7. Vamos subir para o terraço. 8. Ao ver-me deitou a correr ao meu encontro. 9. Qual o quê! É incrível que haja quem diga coisas tão estúpidas. 10. Ao verem-me os seus pais, perguntaram-me porque nunca os visitara o meu avô. 11. Expliquei-lhes que não era que não quisesse, mas que já não estava em condições de o fazer. 12. Quem teria acreditado que fossem possíveis tais coisas! 13. Saiu zangada, de olhos no chão. 14. É assim como a gente se porta em geral. 15. Congratularam-no pelo seu grande êxito. 16. Mas quanto a nós, o que havíamos de dizer-lhe? 17. Os heróis vão sempre triunfando da lei da morte. 18. A mim não me disseram nada. 19. Ora essa! É insuportável, isso! 20. A gente nem sempre goza de tão boa sorte.

(b) *Translate:* 1. She reproved him for his stupidity. 2. If only I could sleep for a week! 3. It was only then that she concluded that the plan was impossible. 4. Only yesterday I was talking to the boy whose mother has done so much for our church. 5. I understand they got married last Tuesday. 6. In the middle of the field there stood an enormous oak. 7. They're always dreaming of liberty, but it will always be denied them. 8. If I've told you once, I've told you a hundred times, it's a question of courage and nothing else. 9. Let's go and see him off at the station. 10. A strange face suddenly appeared at the window, reflected in the moonlight. 11. Apparently he no longer lives in the Chiado. 12. She used to live at number three, Avenida Rio Branco. 13. Further on and to the north, there was a large country house. 14. It's strange that she always used to dress in black, especially in that climate. 15. The old man was walking slowly along the road, stick in hand, followed by his little dog. 16. I shall be glad when we've finished with this book. 17. At first they decided to hail a taxi, but then they changed their minds. 18. What an unusual accent he possesses! 19. How great our surprise was when she brought us the good news! 20. How beautifully that nightingale is singing!

APPENDIX I
REGULAR VERB TABLES

REGULAR VERBS

There are three classes or conjugations of verbs in Portuguese, known from their infinitive endings as **-ar** (or first-conjugation), **-er** (or second-conjugation) and **-ir** (or third-conjugation) verbs.

I. -ar	II. -er	III. -ir
e.g., comprar	*e.g.*, vender	*e.g.*, partir

INFINITIVES

(a) Impersonal

PRESENT

comprar, *to buy*	vender, *to sell*	partir, *to depart*

PERFECT

ter comprado, *to have bought*	ter vendido, *to have sold*	ter partido, *to have departed*

(b) Personal or Inflected

PRESENT

comprar	vender	partir
comprares	venderes	partires
comprar	vender	partir
comprarmos	vendermos	partirmos
comprardes	venderdes	partirdes
comprarem	venderem	partirem

PERFECT

ter comprado	ter vendido	ter partido
teres comprado	teres vendido	teres partido
ter comprado	ter vendido	ter partido
termos comprado	termos vendido	termos partido
terdes comprado	terdes vendido	terdes partido
terem comprado	terem vendido	terem partido

434

GERUNDS

PRESENT

comprando, *buying*	vendendo, *selling*	partindo, *departing*

PERFECT

tendo comprado, *having bought*	tendo vendido, *having sold*	tendo partido, *having departed*

PAST PARTICIPLE

comprado, *bought*	vendido, *sold*	partido, *departed*

INDICATIVE MOOD

PRESENT

I buy, do buy, am buying, etc.	*I sell, do sell, am selling*, etc.	*I depart, do depart, am departing*, etc.
compro	vendo	parto
compras	vendes	partes
compra	vende	parte
compramos	vendemos	partimos
comprais	vendeis	partis
compram	vendem	partem

IMPERFECT

I bought, was buying, used to buy, etc.	*I sold, was selling, used to sell*, etc.	*I departed, was departing, used to depart*, etc.
comprava	vendia	partia
compravas	vendias	partias
comprava	vendia	partia
comprávamos	vendíamos	partíamos
compráveis	vendíeis	partíeis
compravam	vendiam	partiam

PRETERITE

I bought, did buy, have bought, etc.	*I sold, did sell, have sold*, etc.	*I departed, did depart, have departed*, etc.
comprei	vendi	parti
compraste	vendeste	partiste
comprou	vendeu	partiu
comprámos	vendemos	partimos
comprastes	vendestes	partistes
compraram	venderam	partiram

435

FUTURE

I shall buy, etc.	*I shall sell*, etc.	*I shall depart*, etc.
comprarei	venderei	partirei
comprarás	venderás	partirás
comprará	venderá	partirá
compraremos	venderemos	partiremos
comprareis	vendereis	partireis
comprarão	venderão	partirão

CONDITIONAL

I should buy, etc.	*I should sell*, etc.	*I should depart*, etc.
compraria	venderia	partiria
comprarias	venderias	partirias
compraria	venderia	partiria
compraríamos	venderíamos	partiríamos
compraríeis	venderíeis	partiríeis
comprariam	venderiam	partiriam

PERFECT CONTINUOUS

I have been buying, etc.	*I have been selling*, etc.	*I have been departing*, etc.
tenho comprado	tenho vendido	tenho partido
tens comprado	tens vendido	tens partido
tem comprado	tem vendido	tem partido
temos comprado	temos vendido	temos partido
tendes comprado	tendes vendido	tendes partido
têm comprado	têm vendido	têm partido

COMPOUND PLUPERFECT

I had bought, etc.	*I had sold*, etc.	*I had departed*, etc.
tinha comprado	tinha vendido	tinha partido
tinhas comprado	tinhas vendido	tinhas partido
tinha comprado	tinha vendido	tinha partido
tínhamos comprado	tínhamos vendido	tínhamos partido
tínheis comprado	tínheis vendido	tínheis partido
tinham comprado	tinham vendido	tinham partido

SYNTHETIC PLUPERFECT

I had bought, etc.	*I had sold*, etc.	*I had departed*, etc.
comprara	vendera	partira
compraras	venderas	partiras
comprara	vendera	partira
compráramos	vendêramos	partíramos
compráreis	vendêreis	partíreis
compraram	venderam	partiram

I shall have bought, etc.	*I shall have sold,* etc.	*I shall have departed,* etc.
terei comprado	terei vendido	terei partido
terás comprado	terás vendido	terás partido
terá comprado	terá vendido	terá partido
teremos comprado	teremos vendido	teremos partido
tereis comprado	tereis vendido	tereis partido
terão comprado	terão vendido	terão partido

CONDITIONAL PERFECT

I should have bought, etc.	*I should have sold,* etc.	*I should have departed,* etc.
teria comprado	teria vendido	teria partido
terias comprado	terias vendido	terias partido
teria comprado	teria vendido	teria partido
teríamos comprado	teríamos vendido	teríamos partido
teríeis comprado	teríeis vendido	teríeis partido
teriam comprado	teriam vendido	teriam partido

IMPERATIVE MOOD

buy	*sell*	*depart*
compra	vende	parte
comprai	vendei	parti

SUBJUNCTIVE MOOD

PRESENT

(that) I (may, should) buy, etc.	*(that) I (may, should) sell,* etc.	*(that) I (may, should) depart,* etc.
compre	venda	parta
compres	vendas	partas
compre	venda	parta
compremos	vendamos	partamos
compreis	vendais	partais
comprem	vendam	partam

IMPERFECT

(that) I bought, might *(should)* buy, etc.	*(that)* I sold, might *(should)* sell, etc.	*(that)* I departed, might *(should)* depart, etc.
comprasse	vendesse	partisse
comprasses	vendesses	partisses
comprasse	vendesse	partisse
comprássemos	vendêssemos	partíssemos
comprásseis	vendêsseis	partísseis
comprassem	vendessem	partissem

FUTURE

(if, when, etc.) I buy, etc.	*(if, when,* etc.) I sell, etc.	*(if, when,* etc.) I depart, etc.
comprar	vender	partir
comprares	venderes	partires
comprar	vender	partir
comprarmos	vendermos	partirmos
comprardes	venderes	partirdes
comprarem	venderem	partirem

PERFECT

(that) I *(may, should)* have bought, etc.	*(that)* I *(may, should)* have sold, etc.	*(that)* I *(may, should)* have departed, etc.
tenha comprado	tenha vendido	tenha partido
tenhas comprado	tenhas vendido	tenhas partido
tenha comprado	tenha vendido	tenha partido
tenhamos comprado	tenhamos vendido	tenhamos partido
tenhais comprado	tenhais vendido	tenhais partido
tenham comprado	tenham vendido	tenham partido

PLUPERFECT

(that) I had bought, might *(should)* have bought, etc.	*(that)* I had sold, might *(should)* have sold, etc.	*(that)* I had departed, might *(should)* have departed, etc.
tivesse comprado	tivesse vendido	tivesse partido
tivesses comprado	tivesses vendido	tivesses partido
tivesse comprado	tivesse vendido	tivesse partido
tivéssemos comprado	tivéssemos vendido	tivéssemos partido
tivésseis comprado	tivésseis vendido	tivésseis partido
tivessem comprado	tivessem vendido	tivessem partido

FUTURE PERFECT

(*if, when,* etc.) *I have bought,* etc.	(*if, when,* etc.) *I have sold,* etc.	(*if, when,* etc.) *I have departed,* etc.
tiver comprado	tiver vendido	tiver partido
tiveres comprado	tiveres vendido	tiveres partido
tiver comprado	tiver vendido	tiver partido
tivermos comprado	tivermos vendido	tivermos partido
tiverdes comprado	tiverdes vendido	tiverdes partido
tiverem comprado	tiverem vendido	tiverem partido

APPENDIX II

THE PORTUGUESE OF BRAZIL

Brazilian Portuguese (*BP*) differs from European Portuguese (*EP*) roughly to the same extent that American English differs from "Standard" English. Regrettably, there is much disagreement on the part of authorities as to the exact nature of *BP*, and this situation is aggravated by often widely differing usage. The present study limits itself to an account of the differences in educated usage between *EP* and *BP*.

PRONUNCIATION

ORAL VOWELS

a.

(i) cąda, mąs *often pron.* [majs], pąra;

(ii) always closed before a nasal consonant: ąmanhã, comprąmos (*pret.*).

(iii) unstressed **a** is usually open [a].

e. *Stressed*, as in *EP* except:

(i) always [e] before a palatal where *EP* [ɐ]: vẹjo, tẹnho;

(ii) always closed before a nasal consonant: rẹma.

Unstressed, as in *EP* except:

(i) where *EP* has [ə], *BP* usually has [e], but has [i] in the final position;

(ii) always closed before a nasal consonant: condẹnar.

o. *Stressed*, as in *EP* except always closed before a nasal consonant: **fome, toma.**

Unstressed, usually closed, but [u] in final position; it is always closed before a nasal consonant: **comigo.**

ORAL DIPHTHONGS. These are all as in *EP* with the exception of **ei**, which, where [ɐj] in *EP*, is pronounced [ej] in *BP*; **primeiro** [pri'mejru].

NASAL VOWELS AND DIPHTHONGS. These are all as in *EP* with the exception of **-em, -ens** (*EP* [ɐj̃], [ɐj̃ʃ]) which are pronounced [ej̃(s)] in *BP*: **vendem** ['vẽndej̃].

CONSONANTS. (*a*) **d** never has the fricative value [đ]; (*b*) **s, x** and **z** which in Rio are pronounced as in *EP* are elsewhere pronounced [s] before an unvoiced consonant and in the final position, and [z] before a voiced consonant.

NOTES. 1. Even among the well educated some speakers vacillate in the pronunciation of **qu**, *i.e.*, between [k] and [kw], in the words **adquirir, questão** and a few more.

2. Although the practice is considered slovenly by purists and is resisted in most of the Northeast, there is a marked tendency even among well educated speakers for **d** and **t** to suffer palatalization when followed by **i**, unstressed **e** (when=[i]) or a consonant:

　　disse ['dʒisi];
　　descrente [dʒis'krẽntʃi]
　　ritmo ['ɹɹitʃimu].

3. [ɹɹ] is standard in Brazil where EP has [rr] or [ɹɹ]; it also represents final **-r**. With many speakers it resembles English **h**.

ORTHOGRAPHY AND THE WRITTEN ACCENT

Despite the *Acordo Ortográfico* of 1945 which standardized spelling and the use of the written accent for both Portugal and Brazil, Brazilians have in practice regarded it as an imposition to be resisted. Examination of educated modern usage reveals the following norms which differ from *EP* usage.

ORTHOGRAPHY

(i) *EP* **c** and **p** where not uttered are also not written in *BP*: **ação** (*EP* **acção**), **batismo** (*EP* **baptismo**).[1]

(ii) *EP* **mm** and **nn** are simplified in *BP*: **comumente** (*EP* **comummente**), **conosco** (*EP* **connosco**).

(iii) *BP* nearly always prefers **ou** to **oi** where in *EP* there exists a choice (see § 148).

(iv) *EP* **porque** (when=*why*) is written **por que** in *BP*.

(v) **Catorze** has a variant **quatorze** [kwaᶦtorzi]; 16, 17 and 19 are written **dezesseis, dezessete, dezenove** and are pronounced accordingly; 18 is pronounced **dezoito**.

(vi) Vacillation exists in the spelling of the following: **se/si** (*if*); **quase/quási; tribo/tríbu.**

WRITTEN ACCENT

(i) Since in *BP* **a, e** and **o** are always closed before a nasal consonant, such *EP* words as **comprámos, helénico, cómico** are written **compramos, helênico, cômico;** by the same token the circumflex accent of *EP* **dêmos** (*pres. subj.* of **dar**) is dropped in *BP* as there is no difference between its pronunciation and that of the preterite **demos** (*EP* **demos**).

(ii) *BP* retains the acute accent on words which in *EP* end in **-eia, -eico: idéia, onomatopéico.**

(iii) When the **u** of **gu** and **qu** is pronounced before **e** or **i**, *BP* uses a diaeresis: **cinqüenta** (or **cincoenta**), **argüir.**

(iv) Until April 1971 stressed *closed* **e** and **o** of the penult took a circumflex in *BP*, if there were other words spelled alike that had *open* **e** and **o**: **rêgo** (*furrow*), **rego** (*I water*); **a côrte** (*court*), **o corte** (*cut*).

---

[1] In *BP* etymological **c** tends not to be uttered in even more words of this type than in *EP* and is consequently omitted from the orthography; noteworthy in this respect are **o fato** (*fact*) and **o jato** (*jet*); vacillation is often found, *e.g.*, **a se(c)ção**, *section*.

ACCIDENCE AND SYNTAX

PRONOUNS

(i) The pronouns **tu** and **vós** (and all associated forms and verb-endings) are used in *BP* only in poetry, prayers and in the remoter parts of Rio Grande do Sul; their functions are taken over by **vǫcê** and **vǫcês** (with *their* associated forms and verb-endings).

(ii) The collocation of the weak object pronoun is very flexible in *BP*. In practice, despite constant attempts to regularize the situation, the only firm rule is that the pronoun ought not to be the first word of a sentence, although even this tends to be waived by many speakers and writers.

(iii) In colloquial usage there is a marked tendency to replace the weak object pronouns **o, a, os, as** with the strong object pronouns **ęle (êle), ęla, ęles (êles), ęlas,** which naturally always follow the verb: **Vi ęla** (*I saw her*).

(iv) There is a strong tendency in *BP* (found also in colloquial *EP*) for such contractions as **mo, lho, no-lo,** etc. to be avoided by the use of disjunctive pronouns. This is standard practice in everyday speech. Thus **dęu-mo** becomes **dęu-o a mim** (or, more simply, **dęu-me**).

VERBS

(i) In the written language the formation of the compound pluperfect (indicative and subjunctive) is very commonly made with **havęr.**

(ii) In the spoken language (and occasionally in the written language) there is a growing tendency for **tęr** to replace **havęr** to render *there is, there were,* etc.

(iii) The gerund is more common in *BP* than in *EP*; in general it takes over the functions of **a**+infinitive where in *EP* there exists a choice, and is particularly used after verbs of perception, a construction which purists tend to avoid in *EP*.

Vi-o atravessando a rua. I saw him cross(ing) the street.

MISCELLANEOUS

(i) The possessive adjectives are quite frequently used without the definite article: **Onde está meu chapéu?**

(ii) The definite article is usually omitted after **todo** (=*every*): *BP* **todo homem**, *EP* **todo o homem.**

(iii) *So . . . as* and *as . . . as* are usually rendered by **tão . . . quanto** (*EP* **tão . . . como**).

(iv) **Algo** is used in *BP* to translate *something*, as a perfectly normal alternative to **alguma coisa.**

(v) There is a tendency in spoken *BP* to resist inversion after an interrogative; this is effected by using the order *interrogative+subject+verb*, *e.g.*, **Onde João está?** or by liberal use of **é que**, *e.g.*, **O que é que você estava fazendo quando eu o vi?**

LEXICAL AND SEMANTIC DIFFERENCES

This is a vast subject which lies basically beyond the scope of this work. Listed here are the *BP* lexical variants of words in the everyday vocabulary of Portuguese. It should not, however, be assumed that the alternatives are mutually exclusive, though this is true in some instances.

EP	*BP*	*Meaning*
tu	**você**	you ([*very*] *familiar*)
a senhora	{ **a senhorinha** / **a senhorita** }	miss; you (*to unmarried lady*)
a rapariga	**môça**	girl
o criado	**o garção, garçon**	waiter
toda a gente	**todo (o) mundo**	everybody
o caminho de ferro	**a estrada de ferro**	railway
o comboio	**o trem**	train
o cais	**a plataforma**	platform

EP	BP	Meaning
a bilheteira	a bilheteria, o guichê	booking-office
o autocarro	{ o ônibus / a lotação }	bus
o (carro) eléctrico	o bonde	tram
a paragem	a parada	bus-stop, tramstop
a algibeira	o bôlso	pocket
o cordel	o barbante	string
o corvo	o urubu (*nearest equivalent*)	crow
o desporto	o esporte	sport
a erva	o capim	grass
a esquadra de polícia	a delegacia	police station
o fato	o terno	suit
o fato de banho	a roupa de banho, o maiô	swimming-costume
o fumo	a fumaça	smoke
o pequeno/primeiro almoço	o café da manhã	breakfast
o polícia	o policial	policeman
o tabaco	o fumo	tobacco
novo	môço	young
tão ... como	tão ... quanto	as ... as
apanhar	pegar	to catch, seize
apear-se	saltar	to alight
chegar a	chegar em	to arrive at, in
deitar	botar	to throw
mobilar	mobiliar[1]	to furnish
pôr	botar	to put
registar	registrar	to register

[1] The present indicative is **mobílio, mobílias**, etc.

445

VOCABULARY

The vocabulary aims to be complete for the purposes of this course. It does not, however, include articles [§§ 12–13], demonstratives [§ 45], possessives [§ 51], numerals [§§ 29, 67–68], days of the week [§ 70], months [§ 71], seasons [§ 72], personal pronouns [§§ 167–171] or any contractions [see *Index*]. Adverbs in **-mente** are included only in special cases. Numbers refer to paragraphs: *via* indicates that a change of construction is necessary; N. = Note.

PORTUGUESE–ENGLISH

a, to, at [a *and* **para**, 28; "*personal*" **a**, 227; *conditional* **a**, 228 (i); **a** *and* **em**, 241]

a **aba**, skirt; brim

abafado, sultry

abaular, to camber

o **abdómen**, abdomen

abeirar-se (de), to approach, draw near (to)

abotoar, to button (up)

abraçar, to embrace, hug

abrir, to open

abster-se, to abstain

abstracto, abstract

abusar de, to abuse, misuse

acabar, to finish; **acabar com**, to put an end to; **acabar de**, to have just; **acabar por**, to finish by

a **acção**, action

aceitar, to accept

acender, to light, switch on

o **acento**, accent

acerca de, concerning

achar, to find; to think; **não acha?** isn't it?, don't you agree?

aclarar, to clarify

o **aço**, steel

acolá, there, over yonder

acompanhar, to accompany, go with, come with

aconselhar, to advise [174 (1) (iv)]

acontecer, to happen

acordar, to wake (up), awake, awaken (*transitive or intransitive*); **acordar-se**, to wake up, awake

o **acordo**, agreement; **de acordo**, agreed, in agreement

os **Açores**, the Azores

acostumar, to accustom; **acostumar-se a**, to get used to

acreditar, to believe [163]

acrescentar, to add

activo, active

446

o **acto,** act

o **açúcar,** sugar

o **açude,** dam, weir

acudir, to (run to) help, rush up

acusar, to accuse

a **adaptação,** adaptation

adaptar, to adapt

adeus, good-bye

adeusinho, cheerio

adiar, to postpone, put off

o **adjectivo,** adjective

admirar, to admire

admirável, admirable, re-markable

a **adopção,** adoption

adoptar, to adopt

adoptivo, adoptive

adorável, adorable

adormecer, to go to sleep

adquirir, to acquire, get

o **adro,** church square

advertir, to notice; to warn

aéreo, air (*adj.*)

o **aeroporto,** airport

o **afã,** urge, bustle, enthusiasm

afastar-se, to go away, move away

afazer, to accustom, inure

o **afecto,** affection

afeiçoado (a), fond (of)

afinal, at last, after all

afligir, to grieve, afflict

afoito, daring, bold

África, Africa

afundar-se, to collapse, slump

agir, to act, operate

agitar a mão, to wave

agora, now

agradar, to please

agradável, pleasant

agradecer, to thank; to be grateful for

agradecido, grateful

agredir, to attack

a **água,** water

aguentar, to stand, put up with

aí, there

ainda, still, yet; even; **ainda não,** not yet; **ainda quando,** even if; **ainda que,** although; even though; even if; **ainda se,** even if

airado, airy

ajaular, to cage up

ajoelhar(-se), to kneel(down)

a **ajuda,** help

ajudar, to help

o **álcool,** alcohol

a **aldeia,** village

alegrar, to gladden; **alegrar-se,** to be glad

alegre, cheerful, gay

a **alegria,** joy, cheerfulness

além (de), beyond; **além disso,** besides, further-more; **além do que,** be-sides, furthermore

a **Alemanha,** Germany

alemão, German

alentejano, of the Alentejo

o **Alentejo,** the Alentejo

o **alerta,** alarm, alert

alertar, to alert

Alexandre, Alexander

o **Algarve,** the Algarve

algarvio, of the Algarve

a **álgebra,** algebra

a **algibeira,** pocket

o **algodão,** cotton

algo, somewhat, rather; something

alguém, someone, some-body

algum, some; **algum tanto,** somewhat

algures, somewhere

o **alho,** garlic
alhures, elsewhere
ali, there
aliás, besides, furthermore; otherwise, or else
alimentar-se, to feed (oneself)
o **alimento,** food
a **alma,** soul
o **almíscar,** musk
almoçar, to (have) lunch
o **almoço,** lunch; o **pequeno** (*or* **primeiro**) **almoço,** breakfast; **tomar o pequeno** (*or* **primeiro**) **almoço,** to have breakfast
o **alojamento,** lodging
o **altar-mor,** high altar
alto, high, tall; **ao** (*or* **no**) **alto de,** on top of
a **altura,** height, tallness; time, period
alugar, to hire, rent; to let
aluir-se, to collapse
amanhã, tomorrow
amanhecer, to dawn; **ao amanhecer,** at daybreak
amar, to love
amarelo, yellow
a **ambiguidade,** ambiguity
ambíguo, ambiguous
ambos, both
a **ameaça,** menace, threat
ameaçar, to threaten
amém, amen (*colloquial*)
ámen, amen
a **América,** America; a **América do Norte,** North America; a **América do Sul,** South America
americano, (Latin) American
a **amiga,** friend
o **amigo,** friend
amigo de, friendly with

amiudar, to redouble
amiúde, often
a **amizade,** friendship
anabaptista, anabaptist
ancho, wide, broad
andaluz, Andalusian
a **Andaluzia,** Andalusia
andar, to walk, go, run; to be [205]; **andar de farda,** to be in uniform, wear uniform
o **andar,** floor, storey
a **anedota,** anecdote
anelar, to long (for)
anglo-saxão, Anglo-Saxon
o **animal,** animal
animar, to encourage, urge; to brighten, liven, cheer (up)
o **ano,** year; *via* **fazer anos,** to be one's birthday; **ter ... anos,** to be ... (years old); **aos ... anos,** at the age of ...; **ano lectivo,** academic year; **ano escolar,** school year
ao anoitecer, at nightfall
ansiar, to long (for), yearn (for)
ante, before, at [145 (*c*) (1)]
anteontem, the day before yesterday
anterior, previous
antes, before(hand); rather [198 (*b*) N. 3]; **antes de,** before [145 (*c*) (1)]; **antes (de) que,** before; **quanto antes,** as soon as possible
antigamente, formerly, previously
antigo, old, ancient; former
antipático, unlikeable
antiquar, to antiquate
António, Ant(h)ony

anunciar, to announce; to advertise

apagar, to put out, extinguish, quench

apanhar, to pick up, catch, seize, get

aparecer, to appear, come into view

o **apartamento,** flat, apartment

o **aparte,** aside

apaular, to make marshy

apear-se, to get down, get off, alight

apenas, only; no sooner, hardly, scarcely

apertado, tight

apesar de, in spite of

apetecer, to please, attract; *via* to fancy, feel like

aplacar, to placate, appease

aplicado, hard-working

apoderar-se (de), to take possession (of), seize

apoiar, to support; **apoiarse em,** to lean on

após, after [145 (c) (4)]

apossar-se (de), to take possession (of), seize

apostar, to bet

aprazer, to please

apreciar, to appreciate

aprender, to learn

apresentar, to introduce, present; **apresentar-se,** to appear

apressar-se, to hasten, hurry (*not a verb of motion*)

aprovar, to approve; **ser aprovado (num exame),** to pass (an exam)

aproveitar, to profit (by)

aproximar-se (de), to approach, draw near (to)

apto, apt

aquecer, to warm, heat

aquém (de), short (of), on this side (of)

aqui, here; **por aqui,** this way

o **ar,** air; manner, appearance

árabe, Arab, Arabic

Aragão (*m.*), Aragon

o **arenque,** herring

a **Argentina,** Argentina, the Argentine

argentino, Argentinian

arguir, to censure; to imply, infer

armar, to arm

o **armário,** cupboard

o **armazém,** large store; warehouse

o **arrais,** boatswain, bosun, mate

arranjar, to arrange, fix, put right

arrebatar, to snatch

arrefecer, to cool (off)

arrepender-se, to repent

arrimar-se a, to lean against

o **arroz,** rice

arruinar, to ruin

arrumar, to put away, stack away; to pack (*a suitcase*, etc.)

a **arte,** art

a **árvore,** tree

a **asa,** wing

o **asbesto,** asbestos

o **asfalto,** asphalt

a **Ásia,** Asia

o **asno,** ass

o **aspecto,** appearance, aspect

aspergir, to sprinkle

aspirar, to aspire

assar, to roast

assegurar, to assure

assentar, to settle, set (down)

o **assento,** seat; **tomar assento,** to take a seat

assim, so, thus, like this (*or* that); **assim como,** just as; **assim que,** as soon as

assistir (a), to attend, be present (at)

assumir, to assume, take on

o **assunto,** matter, subject

atar, to tie, fasten, attach

até, until, as far as, (up) to; even; **até amanhã,** see you tomorrow; **até à vista,** see you, be seeing you; **até que,** until, till

a **atenção,** attention

atento, attentive

ateu, atheistic

atirar, to throw, fling, hurl

a **atitude,** attitude

a **atracção,** attraction

atrair, to attract

atrás, behind; ago, earlier before; **atrás de,** after [145 (c) (4)]; behind

através de, through, across

atravessar, to cross

atrever-se, to dare

atrevido, bold, daring

a **audição,** audition

a **aula,** class; classroom; **a sala de aula,** classroom

aumentar, to increase

a **Áustria,** Austria

austríaco, Austrian

o **autocarro,** bus

o **autor,** author

autorizar, to authorize

auxiliar, auxiliary; to help

avançar, to advance

avante, onward

ave, hail (*religious*)

averiguar, to ascertain, find out

o **avião,** aeroplane

aviar-se, to hurry up

avisar, to inform, warn, let know

o **avô,** grandfather

a **avó,** grandmother

os **avós,** grandparents; ancestors, forebears

azul, blue

o **bacalhau,** cod(fish)

a **bacia,** basin

a **baciada,** basinful

a **bactéria,** bacterium

a **bacteriologia,** bacteriology

a **bagagem,** luggage, baggage

o **bago,** berry

bailar, to dance

a **bainha,** scabbard, sheath

o **bairro,** quarter, district

baixinho, softly, in a low voice

baixo, low; **cá em baixo,** downstairs; down here; **lá em baixo,** downstairs; down there; **de baixo,** from downstairs; from below; **para baixo** (*motion*), downstairs; below; downwards; **por baixo de,** underneath

o **balcão,** (shop) counter

o **balde,** bucket, pail

baloiçar, to swing

banal, banal

a **bandeja,** tray

o **bando,** band, gang

banhar-se, to bathe

a **banheira,** bath(tub)

o **banho,** bath; **a casa de banho,** bathroom; **o quarto de banho,** bathroom; **tomar banho,** to have a bath; **tomar banhos de sol,** to sun-bathe

baptismal, baptismal

o **baptismo,** baptism
o **baptista,** baptist
o **baptistério,** baptist(e)ry
baptizar, to baptize
o **bar,** bar (*for drinks*)
barato, cheap; cheaply
barbear-se, to (have a) shave
a **barca,** barge, ferry
o **barril,** barrel
bastante, rather, fairly,
   pretty, quite, enough
bastar, to suffice, be enough
o **bastião,** bastion
a **batata,** potato; **batatas fritas,** chips; **batatinhas fritas,** crisps
bater, to strike, hit; **bater à
   porta,** to knock; **bater
   (com),** to bang
o **baú,** trunk (*luggage*)
beber, to drink
beirão, of Beira
a **seu bel-prazer,** as he thinks
   fit
a **beleza,** beauty
belo, beautiful, lovely
bem, well; **andar bem,** to
   go well, prosper, thrive; **ir
   bem a,** to suit; **estar bem,**
   to be well; **está bem,** all
   right, O.K.; **o bem,** good
   [103 (*a*)]
a **bengala,** (walking) stick
a **bênção,** blessing
a **biblioteca,** library
bicolor, two-tone
o **bife,** steak; 'limey' (*i.e.*,
   Englishman)
o **bilhete,** ticket; o (**bilhete)
   postal,** postcard
bimotor, twin-engine(d)
a **boca,** month
um **bocado,** a bit, a little; a piece,
   a morsel

o **boi,** ox
a **boiada,** drove of oxen
boiar, to float
a **bola,** ball
o **bolo,** cake
bom, good; **andar bom,** to
   be well; **estar bom,** to be
   well; **está bom,** all right.
   O.K.
o **bombom,** sweet, bonbon
a **bondade,** goodness, kindness; **ter a bondade de,** to
   be so good as to, *via* please
bonito, nice, pretty
à **borda de,** on the edge of
a **bordo,** on board
o **bosque,** wood (*area of trees*)
o **braço,** arm
bramir, to roar
branco, white
o **Brasil,** Brazil
brasileiro, Brazilian
Brasília, Brasilia
o **brejeiro,** urchin, loafer, rascal, layabout
breve, brief; soon; (**dentro)
   em breve,** soon
brilhante, brilliant
brilhar, to shine, sparkle
brincalhão, playful
bulir, to move, stir, budge
buscar, to seek (to), look for;
   ir buscar, to go and get,
   fetch; **vir buscar,** to come
   and get; **mandar buscar,**
   to send for

cá, here [99 (*a*)]
a **cabeça,** head
o **cabelo,** hair
o **cabo,** end; cape, promon-
   tory; o **Cabo da Boa Esperança,** the Cape of
   Good Hope

a **cabra montês,** mountain goat
o **cabrito,** kid
caçar, to hunt
o **cacau,** cocoa
cada, each [Lesson XXXII, Vocab. N.]; **cada vez mais,** more and more; **cada vez menos,** less and less
o **cadáver,** corpse,(dead) body
a **cadeira,** chair
o **café,** coffee; café; **tomar café,** to have coffee; **tomar o café,** to have breakfast
o **cafezal,** coffee-plantation
a **cãibra,** cramp
cair, to fall
o **Cairo,** Cairo
o **cais,** quay, wharf; (railway) platform
a **caixa,** box
o **caixão,** coffin
calar(-se), to be silent
as **calças,** trousers
o **cálice,** calix; chalice; wineglass; calyx
o **cálix,** calix; chalice; calyx
a **calma,** calm; heat
o **calor,** heat; **fazer calor,** to be hot (*weather*); **ter calor, estar com calor,** to be hot (*people*); **sentir calor,** to feel hot (*people*)
a **cama,** bed; **na cama,** in bed; **ir para a cama,** to go to bed
o **caminho,** lorry, truck
caminhar, to walk
o **caminho,** road, way; **no caminho, pelo caminho,** on the way; **meter-se a caminho,** to set out (on one's way)

a **camioneta,** motor-coach; lorry, truck
Camões, Camoens
camoniano, pertaining to Camoens
o **campo,** country(side); field
o **Canadá,** Canada
canadense, Canadian (*this form is Brazilian*)
canadiano, Canadian
a **canalha,** rabble
a **canção,** song
a **caneca,** beermug, tankard
a **caneta,** pen
canhoto, left-handed; awkward, gauche
o **cânon,** canon, rule
cansado, tired
cansar-se, to get tired, grow tired
cansativo, tiresome
cantar, to sing
o **canto,** corner
o **cão,** dog
capaz, able, capable
capcioso, captious
o **capim,** grass (*Brazilian*)
a **capital,** capital (*city*)
o **capital,** capital (*money*)
o **capitão,** captain; **o capitão-mor,** captain-in-chief, captain of the guard
o **capítulo,** chapter
a **cara,** face
o **carácter,** character
a **característica,** characteristic
característico, characteristic
a **caracterização,** characterization
caracterizar, to characterize
o **cárcere,** prison
cardar, to card
carecer de, to lack
a **meu cargo,** in my charge

a **carne,** flesh; meat; **carne
de vaca,** beef
caro, dear, expensive
carregado, overcast; loaded
o **carro,** car; o **(carro) eléctrico,** tram(car); o **carro
de aluguel (aluguer),**
taxi; hackney carriage
a **carta,** letter
Cartago (*f*), Carthage
o **cartão,** cardboard; card
o **cartaz,** poster
o **carteiro,** postman
o **carvalho,** oak, oak tree
o **carvão,** coal
a **casa,** house; **em casa,** at
home; **para casa,** (to)
home; **a casa de banho,**
bathroom; **a casa de
hóspedes,** guest-house; **a
casa de pasto,** restaurant,
eating-house; **a casa vizinha,** next door; **andar
(** *or* **estar) na casa dos
trinta,** to be thirtyish
casar, to marry, join in marriage; **casar(-se) com,** to
get married to
o **casaco,** coat, jacket
a **casinha,** cottage
o **caso,** case
Castela (*f.*), Castile
castigar, to punish
catalão, Catalan
por minha causa, for my sake,
because of me
causar, to cause
causativo, causative
ter cautela, estar com cautela,
to be careful
o **cavalheiro,** gentleman
o **cavalo,** horse
cavaquear, to chat
a **caveira,** skull
cear, to have supper

cedo, early (*adv.*)
cego, blind
a **ceia,** supper
célebre, famous
o **censo,** census
o **centro,** centre
o **ceptro,** sceptre
com certeza, certainly
certo, (a) certain; sure; true
a **cerveja,** beer
César, Caesar
cessar, to cease
o **céu,** sky; heaven
o **chá,** tea
chamar, to call; **chamar-
se,** to be called
o **champanhe,** champagne
o **chão,** ground, floor
o **chapéu,** hat
a **charrua,** plough
a **chave,** key
a **chávena,** (tea)cup
a **Checoslováquia,** Czechoslo-
vakia
checoslovaco, Czechoslovakian
o **chefe,** chief, boss, head
a **chegada,** arrival
chegar, to arrive; to suffice,
be enough; **chegar a,** to
reach, arrive at, come to;
chegar tarde, to be late,
arrive late; **chegar-se,** to
draw close
cheio, full; fed up
cheirar, to smell
chinês, Chinese
o **chocalho,** cow-bell
choco, broody; addled;
stagnant
o **chocolate,** chocolate
choramingar, to whimper
chorar, to cry, weep
chover, to rain

453

o **chumbo,** lead

a **chuva,** rain

a **cidade,** city, town; **ir para a cidade,** to go into town

o **cientista,** scientist

a **cima,** summit, top; **cá em cima,** upstairs; up here; **lá em cima,** upstairs, up there; **de cima,** from upstairs, from above; **para cima** (*motion*), upstairs, above; upwards; **em cima (de),** on (top) (of); **por cima (de),** above

o **cinema,** cinema, pictures

cinzento, grey

cioso, jealous

a **cistectomia,** cystectomy

o **ciúme,** jealousy

cível, civil (*law*)

civil, civil

a **civilização,** civilization

civilizar, to civilize

a **clarabóia,** skylight

claro, clear; clearly, of course

o **clima,** climate

o **clímax,** climax

coar, to filter

o **cobertor,** blanket

cobrir, to cover

o **códex,** codex

o **códice,** codex

coibir, to curb

a **coisa,** thing; **alguma coisa,** something

o **colégio,** college (*private*)

a **colher,** spoon

a **colherada,** spoonful

a **colina,** hill

colocar, to put, place, set

coloidal, colloidal

com, with; **com efeito,** indeed; [*concessive* **com,** 228 (ii)]

combinado, agreed, settled

o **comboio,** train

a **combustão,** combustion

começar, to commence, begin, start

a **comédia,** comedy

comentar, to comment on

comer, to eat, have a meal

comerciar, to trade

o **cometa,** comet

a **comida,** food

como, as, like, how

o **cômoro,** hillock, mound

compacto, compact

compadecer-se (de), to sympathize (with), take pity (on), feel sorry (for)

compelir, to compel

competir, to compete; to behove

completo, complete; **por completo,** completely

compor, to compose

comportar-se, to behave (oneself)

a **compra,** purchase; **ir às compras, ir fazer compras,** to go shopping

comprar, to buy

comprazer-se, to take pleasure

compreender, to understand, grasp

a **compreensão,** understanding, grasp, comprehension

comprido, long

comprometer-se, to undertake

conceder, to concede, grant

conciso, concise

concluir, to conclude

a **conclusão,** conclusion

concordar, to agree
condenar, to condemn
a **condição,** condition; **com a condição que, sob condição que,** on condition (that)
condizer, to match, tally
a **conduta,** behaviour, conduct
o **condutor,** conductor
conduzir, to lead, drive, conduct
confessar, to confess
a **confiança,** confidence
confiar (em), to confide (in); to trust; to hope
confinar (com), to border (on)
o **conflito,** conflict
conformar-se, to agree; to be satisfied
conforme, according to; depending on whether; **é conforme,** it all depends
confundir, to confuse
a **confusão,** confusion
a **congestão,** congestion
congratular, to congratulate
conhecer, to know, be acquainted with
conquanto, although
por **conseguinte,** consequently
conseguir, to manage, succeed; to obtain, get, achieve
o **conselho,** advice, counsel; council
consentir, to consent
por **consequência,** consequently
consertar, to mend, put right, fix
conservar, to conserve, preserve, keep
considerar, to consider
consistir, to consist
consolar, to console
constante, constant

constar, to consist; **do que me consta,** apparently, as far as I know, as I see it
construir, to construct, build
o **cônsul,** consul
o **consulado,** consulate
consumir, to consume
a **conta,** account; bill; **dar-se conta,** to realize; **levar em conta,** to bear in mind, take into account
contactar (com), to get in touch (with), contact
contanto que, provided (that), so long as
contar, to count, relate, tell
contemporâneo, contemporary
contentar-se, to content oneself
contente, pleased, content, happy
conter, to contain
continuar, to continue
contra, against
a **contracção,** contraction
contradizer, to contradict
contrariar, to go against
ao **contrário, pelo contrário,** on the contrary
contravir, to contravene
contudo, however, nevertheless
a **convecção,** convection
convencer, to convince
convencionado, agreed
converter, to convert
a **convexão,** convection
a **convicção,** conviction
o **convicto,** convict
o **convidado,** guest
convidar, to invite
convir, to agree; to be fitting, be appropriate
o **convite,** invitation

o **copo,** glass (*the container*)

a **cor,** colour

o **coração,** heart

a **coragem,** courage; **perder a coragem,** to lose courage

corar, to blush

coroar, to crown

o **corpo,** body

o **correio,** post, post-office; **a estação do correio,** post-office

correr, to run; **correr riscos,** to run risks

corrigir, to correct

cortar, to cut

cortês, polite

a **cortesia,** politeness, courtesy

a **costa,** coast

costumar, to be wont to; *via* usually

o **costume,** custom, habit

cotidiano, daily

a **cousa,** thing (*archaic*)

o **coveiro,** gravedigger

o **covil,** den, lair

a **Covilhã,** Covilhã

a **covinha,** dimple

a **cozinha,** kitchen; cuisine, cooking

cozinhar, to cook

o **credor,** creditor

crer, to believe, think [163]

crescer, to grow

a **criada,** maid; waitress

o **criado,** servant; waiter

a **criança,** child

cristão, Christian

o **cronista-mor,** head chronicler

cru, raw

cruel, cruel

cruzar, to cross, go through

o **cruzeiro,** cruzeiro (*Brazilian monetary unit*)

Cuba (*f.*), Cuba

ter cuidado, estar com cuidado, to be careful

cuidar, to think; **cuidar de,** to look after, care for

cumprimentar, to greet, pay one's respects to

cumprir, to fulfil, accomplish; **cumprir (com) o seu dever,** to do one's duty; **cumprir uma tarefa,** to complete a task

o **cura,** priest

curioso, curious, odd, inquisitive

o **curso,** course; **tirar um curso,** to take a course (*of study*)

curto, short

cuspir, to spit

custar, to cost; **custar (trabalho) a alguém (a) fazer,** *via* to find very difficult to do

a **custo,** with difficulty

dançar, to dance

dar, to give [74 (*d*)]; **dar a,** to begin to, set off; **dar graças (a),** to thank, give thanks; **dar ordem (para),** to order, give orders; **dar um passo,** to take a step; **dar-se conta (de),** to realize

a **data,** date

de, of, from, about [242]; **de per si,** on his own, of his own accord

debaixo (de), under(neath) [145 (*c*) (7)]

decerto, certainly, for certain

decidir(-se), to decide

declarar, to declare

dedicar, to devote, dedicate

o **dedo,** finger

o **defeito,** fault, defect

defender, to defend

a **defesa,** defence

definitivo, definitive, final

defronte de, facing, in front of

o **degrau,** step

deitar, to throw, hurl, fling; to pour; **deitar a,** to begin to, set off; **deitar para, deitar sobre,** to overlook, look out on to; **deitar-se,** to lie down; to go to bed

deixar, to leave; to let, allow, permit; **deixar cair,** to drop; **deixar de,** to leave off, stop; **não deixar de,** not to fail to, to be sure to

delgado, thin, slender

demais, too; too much; **o(s) demais,** the rest, the others; **demais (a mais),** besides

demasiado, too much

denegrir. to denigrate

dentro (de), inside, within

depender, to depend

depois, after(wards); **depois de,** after [145 (c)]; **depois que,** after

depor, to depose; to put down; to state (*in evidence*)

depressa, quickly, fast

derradeiro, last (of all)

a **derrota,** defeat, rout

derrotar, to defeat, rout

desabrido, insolent, disagreeable

desagradar, to displease

desaparecer, to disappear

desatar, to untie, unfasten; **desatar a,** to burst out

descansar, to rest

descer, to go (come, take, bring) down, lower

descobrir, to discover; to learn, find out

desconfiar de, to distrust, mistrust

descorar, to discolour; to bleach

descortês, impolite, rude, discourteous

descrever, to describe

a **descrição,** description

desculpar, to excuse

desde, since, from [145 (c) (5)]; **desde já,** at once; **desde que,** since

desejar, to desire, wish

o **desejo,** desire

desenhar, to design, draw

desesperar, to despair

desfazer, to undo, ruin

desfrutar de, to enjoy

o **desgosto,** displeasure

desiludido, disappointed

despedir, to dismiss; **despedir-se de,** to take leave of, say good-bye to, see off

despender, to spend (*money*)

despercebido, unobserved

despertar, to awake; to wake up; **despertar-se,** to awake, wake up

despir, to undress; **despir-se,** to get undressed

o **desporto,** sport

desprazer, to displease

desprezar, to despise

desprovido, destitute

destacar-se, to stand out

a **destruição,** destruction

destruir, to destroy

deter, to detain; **deter-se,** to stop

detrás (de), (from) behind

Deus, God

a **deusa,** goddess
devagar, slowly
o **devaneio,** daydream, reverie
dever, to have to, must; o
dever, duty
deveras, truly, really
devolver, to give back
devoto, devout, fond
o **dia,** day; **bom dia** (*or* **bons
dias**), good morning; **dias
feriados,** Sundays and
public holidays; **dias
úteis,** weekdays
o **diabo,** devil
diante (de), in front (of)
[145 (c) (1)]
diário, daily
a **dicção,** diction
o **dicionário,** dictionary
a **dieta,** diet
a **diferença,** difference
diferente, different
difícil, difficult, hard
a **dificuldade,** difficulty
digno, worthy
o **dinheiro,** money
dinamarquês, Danish; Dane
a **direcção,** direction
directamente, straight
o **director,** manager; director;
headmaster
direito, right; straight (*adv.*)
dirigir-se, to make one's
way
a **discussão,** discussion
discutir, to discuss
dispor, to arrange, dispose
disposto, disposed, inclined
disputar, to dispute, argue
(about)
dissolver, to dissolve
dissuadir, to dissuade
a **distância,** distance
distinguir, to distinguish
distinto, distinct

distraído, distraught, ab-
sent-minded
distribuir, to distribute
dito, said; **está dito,** right
you are; **tenho dito!** so
there!
diversos, divers(e), various
divertir, to amuse
a **dívida,** debt
dividir, to divide
a **divisão,** division; room
dizer, to say, tell
doce, sweet
a **doença,** illness
doente, ill
doido, mad
Dom, [105 (6)]
domar, to tame
Domingos, Dominic
dona, [105 (6)]; a **dona,**
owner (*f.*)
a **doninha,** weasel
o **dono,** owner
do que, than
doravante, henceforth, from
now on
dormir, to sleep
a **dose,** portion, dose
o **doutor,** doctor
o **duelista,** duellist
a **duquesa,** duchess
durante, during, for
a **dúvida,** doubt
duvidar, to doubt; to question

e, and
o **ectoplasma,** ectoplasm
a **edição,** edition
o **edifício,** building
efectuar, to bring about
eficaz, effective
eis, behold; here is (are) [177]
elástico, elastic

458

a **electricidade,** electricity
a **elegância,** elegance
elegante, elegant
eleger, to choose, pick; to elect
em, in, at, on [94 (c) (2)]; [em *and* a, 241]; **em frente de,** facing, opposite; in front of; **em linha recta,** in a straight line; **em seguida,** next, then
emaranhar, to entangle
embainhar, to sheathe
embarcar, to embark
embora, although; away
o **embrulho,** parcel
a **ementa,** menu
a **empada,** pie
empecer, to prevent, hinder, impede
empenhar-se, to insist
empestar, to infect, contaminate
a **empregada,** maid; employee
o **empregado,** employee; clerk
empregar, to employ, use
o **emprego,** job
emprestar, to lend
encaminhar-se, to make one's way
encantador, charming, enchanting
encarregar, to entrust, give to do; **encarregar-se,** to undertake, take charge, ensure
encharcado, soaked
encher, to fill
encobrir, to hide
encomendar, to (place on) order
encontrar, to find; to meet; **encontrar-se,** to find oneself, be; **encontrar-se com,** to meet, find (out), come across

o **encontro,** meeting, encounter; **ir (vir) ao encontro de,** to go (come) to meet
encostar-se a, to lean against
o **endereço,** address
endoidecer, to madden
enérgico, energetic
enfiar, to slip on; to slip along
enfim, finally; in short
enganado, wrong
enganar, to deceive; **enganar-se,** to be mistaken
o **engano,** deception
engelhar, to wrinkle
o **engenheiro,** engineer; science graduate
engomar, to starch
engraçado, funny; quaint, cute, delightful
engraixar, to clean, polish (*footwear*)
enjaular, to cage (up)
enquanto, while
enraizar, to take root
ensaiar, to try out
o **ensaio,** essay
ensanguentado, bloody, gory
ensinar, to teach
então, then
ao **entardecer,** at fall of evening, in the evening
entender, to understand
a **entrada,** entrance, entry, way in
entrar, to enter, go in, come in; **entrar a,** to begin to
entre, between, among(st)
entreaberto, half open, ajar
entregar, to hand (in, over); to deliver

entreter, to entertain
entrever, to glimpse
entupir, to block (up)
envelhecer, to grow old
envergonhar-se, to be a-shamed
enviar, to send
envolver, to wrap; to involve
enxugar, to wipe, wipe dry
eoceno, eocene
a **época,** period, time, age
erguer, to raise, lift
erigir, to erect
errar, to err; to wander
o **erro,** mistake, error
erróneo, erroneous, wrong
o **ervanário,** herbalist
ervar, to poison (*arrows*)
a **ervilha,** pea
esbaforido, out of breath, panting
esbeltar, to make slender
o **escabeche,** pickle
escapar, to escape
a **escola,** school
escolar: o ano escolar, school year
escolher, to choose, pick, select
esconder, to hide
a **escova,** brush
escrever, to write
o **escritor,** writer
o **escritório,** office
o **escudo,** escudo (*Portuguese monetary unit*)
o **escultor,** sculptor
escuro, dark
escusar, to excuse
escutar, to listen (to)
esferoidal, spheroidal
o **esfíncter,** sphincter
esforçar-se, to strive, try hard

o **esforço,** effort
esgotar, to drain, exhaust
esmiuçar, to (express in) detail
a **Espanha,** Spain
espanhol, Spanish; Spaniard
a **espécie,** kind, sort
o **espelho,** mirror
a **esperança,** hope
esperar, to hope; to expect; to wait (for); **esperar por,** to wait for
a **espontaneidade,** spontaneity
a **esposa,** wife
o **esposo,** husband
esquecer, to forget; to escape, not to occur; **esquecer-se,** to forget
esquerdo, left
a **esquina,** corner (*convex*)
estabelecer, to establish, set up
a **estação,** station; season; **estação de (*or* do) caminho de ferro,** railway-station; **estação de (*or* do) correio,** post-office
a **estada,** stay
os **Estados Unidos,** United States
a **estalagem,** inn
estar, to be [48–50, 74 (*b*), 79, 220–221]; to be in, at home; **estar com**+*noun,* to be [61]
o **este,** east
estéril, sterile, barren
Estêvão, Stephen
estimar, to esteem
os **estofos,** upholstery
o **Estoril,** Estoril
a **estrada,** (main) road
estrangeiro, foreign

o **estrangeiro,** foreigner
estranhar, to surprise; to be surprised (at)
estranho, strange, odd
estreito, narrow
estruir, to destroy (*obsolescent*)
o **estudante,** student
estudar, to study
o **estudo,** study
a **estupidez,** stupidity
estúpido, stupid
eterno, eternal
a **eufonia,** euphony
a **Europa,** Europe
europeizar, to europeanize
europeu, European
o **evangelho,** gospel
evidente, evident
evitar, to avoid
exacto, exact
o **exame,** exam(ination); **fazer um exame,** to take (sit) an exam; **ser aprovado (reprovado) num exame,** to pass (fail) an exam
examinar, to examine, look at
a **excelência,** excellence
excelente, excellent
a **excepção,** exception
excepcional, exceptional
excepto, except
exceptuar, to except
excessivo, excessive
exclamar, to exclaim
exclusive (*adv.*), exclusive, excluding
excomungar, to excommunicate
o **exemplar,** copy
o **exemplo,** example; **por exemplo,** for example

o **exercício,** exercise
o **exército,** army
exigir, to demand
existir, to exist
o **êxito,** success; **ter êxito,** to be successful
o **ex-ministro,** ex-minister
expedir, to send, dispatch
explicar, to explain
a **exploração,** exploration; exploitation
explorar, to explore; to exploit
expor, to expose
a **expulsão,** expulsion
o **êxtase,** ecstasy, rapture
exterior, exterior, outer
extorquir, to extort
extraordinário, extraordinary, unusual
a **extremidade,** end, extremity
extremo, extreme

a **fábrica,** factory
fabricar, to manufacture
a **faca,** knife
a **facção,** faction
faccioso, factious
fácil, easy
o **facto,** fact; **de facto,** in fact, as a matter of fact
o **factótum,** factotum
falador, talkative
falar, to talk, speak
falso, false
a **falta,** lack
faltar, to be missing; *via* to be short of, lack [127]; **faltar a,** to break (*word, promise,* etc.)
a **fama,** fame
a **família,** family
famoso, famous
fartar-se, to grow tired

461

a **fartura,** plenty

o **fato,** suit

a **fava,** bean (broad *or* kidney)

o **favor,** favour; **fazer (o) favor de,** *via* please, kindly [196]

fazer, to do, make [62]; **fazer anos,** *via* to be one's birthday; **fazer a barba,** to shave; **fazer compras,** to do the shopping; **fazer uma excursão,** to go on a trip, outing, excursion; **fazer (o) favor de,** *via* please, kindly; **fazer uma mala,** to pack a suitcase; **fazer uma pergunta,** to ask a question; **fazer uma viagem,** to go on a journey, take a trip; **fazer uma visita,** to pay a visit; **fazer bem em,** to be right in (*or* to); **fazer mal em,** to be wrong in (*or* to)

fechar, to close, shut

a **federação,** federation

o **feijão,** bean (haricot, string, French *or* runner)

desta feita, this time, on this occasion

feito, done, made; **está feito!** really!; **ser feito de,** to have become of

felicitar, to congratulate

Félix, Felix

feliz, happy

felpudo, shaggy

a **fénix,** phoenix

as **férias,** holiday(s); **em férias,** on holiday

a **festa,** party

fiar, to spin.

fiar-se de, to trust

ficar, to stay; to remain; to be left; to wait; to continue to be; to become; to be; to be situated; [80, 127, 222]; **ficar noivo,** to get engaged

a **ficção,** fiction

fictício, fictitious

a **Figueira da Foz,** Figueira da Foz

Filipe, Philip

a **filha,** daughter

o **filho,** son; **os filhos,** children, sons and daughters

a **filosofia,** philosophy

o **fim,** end, aim; **a fim de,** in order to; **a fim (de) que,** in order that; **por fim,** finally, at last

final, final, last

fingir, to pretend, feign

fitar, to stare (at)

fixar, to fix

Flandres (*f.*), Flanders

a **flor,** flower

florescer, to flourish

o **flux,** flux

o **fogo,** fire

folgar, to be glad, rejoice; to relax

a **fome,** hunger; **ter fome,** to be hungry; **estar com fome,** to be hungry; **sentir fome,** to feel hungry; **passar fome,** to go hungry

fora (de), outside; **cá fora,** out here; **lá fora,** out there

a **força,** force; **força motriz,** driving force; **as forças,** strength

forçar, to force

formar, to form

formoso, beautiful, lovely

formular, to form, formulate

a **fornada,** batch

o **forno,** oven, cooker

forte, strong; loud

o **fósforo,** match

o **fóssil,** fossil
a **foto,** photo, snap
fraccionário, fragmentary
a **França,** France
francamente, frankly
francês, French, Frenchman
franco-prussiano, Franco-Prussian
franzir, to wrinkle
a **frase,** sentence; phrase
o **freguês,** customer
Frei, Brother (*religious*)
a **frente,** front; **em frente (de),** facing, opposite; in front (of); straight on; **para (a) frente,** forwards; **à frente (de),** at the front (of)
a **frequência,** frequency; **com frequência,** frequently
frequente, frequent
fresco, cool; fresh
fresquinho, chilled, nice and cold (*of drinks*)
a **fricção,** friction
frigir, to fry
frio, cold; **estar frio,** to be cold (*weather*)
fritar, fry
a **frouxidão,** flabbiness, floppiness
frouxo, flabby, slack, loose, feeble
a **fruta,** fruit
fugir, to flee
fumar, to smoke
o **fundo,** bottom, back(ground), end
furtar, to steal

a **Gália,** Gaul
a **galinha,** hen; chicken (*served at table*)
a **ganga,** nankeen
ganhar, to earn, win, gain

ganir, to yelp
o **garfo,** fork
a **garrafa,** bottle
gastar, to spend (*money*)
o **gato,** cat; **o gato montês,** mountain cat
a **gazua,** picklock
gelar, to freeze
a **gelha,** wrinkle
o **gelo,** ice
o **general,** general
o **genro,** son-in-law
a **gente,** people; **toda a gente,** everybody
gentio, heathen
genuíno, genuine
a **geografia,** geography
a **geração,** generation
geral, general
gerar, to generate
o **gerente,** manager
o **gigante,** giant
a **gorjeta,** tip, gratuity
gostar (de), to like; **gostar imenso de,** to be very fond of, enjoy very much
o **gosto,** pleasure; **com muito gosto,** willingly
o **governo,** government
gozar de, to enjoy
a **Grã-Bretanha,** Great Britain
grande, big, great
grão, great [240 (*c*)]
o **grão,** grain
o **grão-duque,** Grand Duke
a **gratidão,** gratitude
o **grau,** degree
grego, Greek
a **grelha,** grill
grelhar, to grill
o **grito,** shout, cry, scream
grosso, thick, bulky
o **grupo,** group
o **guarda,** guard, keeper
o **guarda-chuva,** umbrella

o **guarda-mor,** chief customs officer

guardar, to keep; to put away (*in cupboard, pocket,* etc.); **guardar-se de,** to take care not to

a **guerra,** war

o **guia,** guide; guide-book

Guilhermina, Wilhelmina

a **Guiné,** Guinea

hábil, able, capable, skilful

habilitar, to enable

o **habitante,** inhabitant

o **hábito,** habit, custom

habituar, to accustom

a **Haia,** the Hague

a **harpa,** harp

o **harpejo,** harping

a **Havana,** Havana

haver, to have; *via* there is, etc. [118, 126]; **haver de,** to be to [126 (vi)]

o **Havre,** Le Havre

o **hectolitro,** hectolitre

Heitor, Hector

Henrique, Henry

o **heptágono,** heptagon

herbívoro, herbivorous, herbivore

herdar, inherit

hesitar, to hesitate

o **hífen,** hyphen

hindu, Hindu

a **história,** history; story

hiulco, gaping, yawning

hoje, today

a **Holanda,** Holland, the Netherlands

holandês, Dutch

o **homem,** man

o **homenzarrão,** lout

a **hora,** hour; que **horas são?** what time is it?; **são horas de,** it is time to; **às três horas,** at three o'clock

o **horror,** horror

hospedar-se, to put up, lodge, stay

o **hóspede,** guest; **a casa de hóspedes,** guest-house

o **hospital,** hospital

hospitaleiro, hospitable

o **hotel,** hotel

o **hotelzinho,** guest house

humilde, humble

ibérico, Iberian

a **ictiologia,** ichthyology

o **ideal,** ideal

a **ideia,** idea

idêntico, identical

a **igreja,** church

igual, equal

a **ilha,** island

a **ilusão,** illusion

o **imã,** magnet (*colloquial*)

imaginar, to imagine

o **íman,** magnet

imediatamente, immediately, at once

imediato, immediate; **no dia imediato,** the day after

a **imitação,** imitation

imitar, to imitate

imóvel, motionless, still

impedir, to prevent, hinder, impede

implorar, to implore

impor, to impose

a **importância,** importance

importante, important

importar, to matter; to import

impossível, impossible

impregnar, to impregnate

a **impressão,** impression

impressionante, impressive

imprimir, to print

improvável, improbable, unlikely

inaguentável, unbearable
incapaz, incapable, unable
incendiar, to set fire to
incitar, to incite
inclinado, inclined
inclusive (*adv.*), inclusive, included
incolor, colourless
o **inconveniente,** snag
incrível, incredible, unbelievable
incumbir, to be incumbent, behove
o **índex,** index
indicar, to indicate, point out
o **índice,** index
indolor, painless
induzir, to induce
inelástico, inelastic
a **infecção,** infection
infecto, infected
infelizmente, unfortunately
inferior, inferior, lower
influir em, to influence
as **informações,** information; **pedir informações,** to make enquiries
a **infracção,** infringement
infundir, to infuse
inglês, English; Englishman
a **Inglaterra,** England
ingressar, to enter
o **inimigo,** enemy
inimitável, inimitable
injectar, to inject
inobservado, unobserved, unheeded, unnoticed
inocente, innocent
inospitaleiro, inhospitable
insignificante, insignificant
insistir, to insist
o **instante,** instant
instruir, to instruct
insubstituível, irreplaceable

inteirar-se, to discover, learn, find out
inteiro, whole, entire
inteligente, intelligent, clever
intenso, intense
intentar, to intend
interessante, interesting
interessar, to interest; **interessar-se (por),** to be interested (in), take an interest (in)
o **interesse,** interest
interior, interior, inner
o **intérprete,** interpreter
a **intersecção,** intersection
intervir, to intervene, interfere
íntimo, intimate
inútil, useless
a **invasão,** invasion
o **invasor,** invader
a **inveja,** envy
invejar, to envy
invejoso, envious
a **invenção,** invention
inventar, to invent
ir, to go [24,74]; **ir ao encontro de,** to go and (*or* to) meet; **ir às compras,** to go shopping; **ir bem a,** to suit; **ir buscar,** to go and get; **ir ter com,** to go and meet, go and see; **ir (-se) embora,** to go away; **ir nas onze,** to be getting on for eleven o'clock; **ir nos trinta,** to be going on thirty
a **irmã,** sister
o **irmão,** brother
Isabel, Isabella, Isobel, Elizabeth
isentar, to exempt, let off
Isidoro, Isidore

a Itália, Italy
italiano, Italian

já, already; now; at once; ever, at any time
a jactância, boastfulness
jactar-se, to boast
o jacto, jet
jamais, never; ever (*after superlative*)
a janela, window
jantar, to dine, have dinner
o jantar, dinner; **a sala de jantar,** dining-room
o Japão, Japan
a jaqueta, short rustic jacket *or* tunic
o jardim, garden
jazer, to lie, be situated
o jeito, knack, skill; **deste jeito,** (in) this way, like this
o jesuíta, Jesuit
a jibóia, boa constrictor
João, John
jogar, to play; to gamble
o jogo, game
o jornal, (news)paper
o jornalista, newspaperman, journalist
jovem, young
o jovem, young man, youth
judaizar, to make Jewish
judeu, Jewish; Jew
jugoslavo, Jugoslav(ian)
o juiz, judge
o juízo, sense, judgment
julgar, to judge; to think
júnior, junior
juntar, to join, amass, gather together
junto, together
justamente, just, exactly
justificar, to justify
a juventude, youth

lá, there
a lã, wool
o lábio, lip
lacerado, lacerated
a lactose, lactose
o lado, side; **de lado a lado,** from side to side; **ao lado de,** beside, next to; **de ambos os lados,** on both sides; **do lado de,** on the side of
o lago, lake
a lágrima, tear
lamber, to lick
lamentar, to lament, bewail
o lápis, pencil
a laranja, orange
largar, to begin
largo, wide, broad
a largura, width, breadth
lavar, to wash
o lavrador, farmer
a legião, legion
o legume, vegetable
a lei, law
o leite, milk
o leitor, reader
lembrar, to remember; to remind; to come to mind; **lembrar-se (de),** to remember
o lençol, sheet
o lente, lecturer (*at Coimbra*)
ler, to read
o leste, east
o letreiro, notice
levantar, to raise; **levantar-se,** to get up, rise, stand up
levar, to take (away), fetch, bring, carry; **levar a,** to cause to; **levar em conta,** to take into account, bear in mind

a **liberdade**, freedom, liberty
a **libra**, pound (*weight or sterling*)
a **lição**, lesson
a **licença**, permission; **com licença**, excuse me
o **liceu**, grammar school
a **ligadura**, bandage
ligeiro, light
o **limiar**, threshold, doorway
limpo, clean
lindo, beautiful, pretty, nice
a **língua**, tongue, language
linguístico, linguistic
o **líquen**, lichen
a **liquidação**, liquidation
liquidar, to liquidate
líquido, liquid
Lisboa, Lisbon
lisboeta, (of) Lisbon
a **lista**, list; menu
a **literatura**, literature
a **livraria**, bookshop
livre, free; unoccupied, vacant
o **livreiro**, bookseller
o **livro**, book
o **lixeiro**, dustman
o **lobo**, wolf
lógico, logical
logo, presently; next, then; soon; at once; therefore; **até logo**, see you, be seeing you; **logo depois**, soon after
lograr, to succeed (in), manage (to)
a **loja**, shop, store
o **lojista**, shopkeeper
Londres, London
longe, far away; **ao longe**, in the distance; **longe de**, far from
longínquo, distant

longo, long
louvar, to praise
a **Lua**, moon
o **luar**, moonlight
o **lugar**, place
Luís, Lewis, Louis
luso-brasileiro, Luso-Brazilian
lustroso, shiny
lutar, to struggle
a **luva**, glove
o **luxo**, luxury; **de luxo**, de luxe
luxuoso, luxurious
a **luz**, light
luzir, to shine

a **maçã**, apple
a **maçada**, bore, nuisance, washout
maçar, to irk, bore, irritate
o **maciço**, clump
a **madeira**, wood (*substance*)
a **madeixa**, hank, skein
a **madrepérola**, mother-of-pearl
a **madressilva**, honeysuckle
a **madrugada**, dawn, early morning
maduro, mature; ripe
a **mãe**, mother
magro, thin
maior, bigger, biggest; greater, greatest; main, principal
a **maioria**, majority
mais, more; most
mal, ill; hardly; badly; scarcely, no sooner; **mal-humorado**, ill-tempered; **mal-passado**, underdone, rare
o **mal**, evil
a **mala**, (suit)case

mal-humorado, bad-tempered

maluco, mad

a **malva,** mallow

mandar, to send; to order, tell; **mandar buscar, mandar chamar,** to send for

a **maneira,** manner, way; **desta maneira,** (in) this way, like this

a **manhã,** morning

manifesto, obvious

a **manteiga,** butter

manter, to maintain

a **mão,** hand; **à mão,** at hand, to hand

o **mapa,** map

o **maple,** armchair

a **máquina,** machine

o **mar,** sea

maravilhar-se, to marvel, wonder

a **maré,** tide

a **margem,** margin, edge, bank

Maria, Mary, Marie, Maria

o **marido,** husband

Marrocos (*m.*), Morocco

Martinho, Martin

mas, but

matar, to kill

a **matéria,** matter; subject (*academic*)

o **matiz,** hue; nuance

mau, bad

a **máxima,** maxim

a **màzona,** slut

mediar, to mediate

medíocre, mediocre

medir, to measure

a **meditação,** meditation

meditar, to meditate, ponder

o **medo,** fear; **ter medo, estar com medo,** to be afraid; **sentir medo,** to feel afraid

a **meia-noite,** midnight

meio, half (a); **ao meio, no meio,** in the middle, in the midst

o **meio-dia,** midday, noon

o **mel,** honey

melancólico, melancholy

melhor, better; best

melhorar, to improve

o **melro,** blackbird

a **memória,** memory; memoir

a **menina,** girl; you

o **menino,** boy; you

menor, less, lesser, least; smaller, smallest

menos, less, least; **ao menos, pelo menos,** at least

mentir, to lie, tell lies

a **mentira,** lie; **ser mentira,** to be untrue

o **mercado,** market

merecer, to deserve

meridional, southern

o **mês,** month

a **mesa,** table; **a toalha de mesa,** table-cloth; **pôr a mesa,** to lay the table; **levantar a mesa,** to clear the table

mesmo, same, very; self; even (*adv.*)

o **mestre(-escola),** (school)-master

meter, to put (in); **meter-se a,** to set about; **meter-se a caminho,** to set out; **meter-se em,** to meddle in

mexer, to stir, move, budge, fidget

o **México,** Mexico
o **mexilhão,** mussel
a **mezinha,** potion
Miguel, Michael
o **milionário,** millionaire
militar, military
o **mínimo,** minimum
o **ministro,** minister; o **pri-meiro ministro,** Prime Minister
o **minuto,** minute
o **miolo,** core, brain
miúdo, petty
Moçambique (*m.*), Mozambique
moderno, modern
o **modo,** way, means; **deste modo,** (in) this way, like this
a **moeda,** coin
moer, to grind
mofar(-se) (de), to mock (at), deride
o **moinho,** mill
moiro, Moor(ish)
a **moita,** clump
o **molde,** mould
molhado, wet
o **molho,** sauce
o **momento,** moment
monótono, monotonous
a **montanha,** mountain
montês, mountain (*adj.*)
o **monumento,** monument
mor, chief, head [240]; **por mor de,** in addition to [240]
morar, to live, dwell, reside
morder, to bite
o **mordomo,** majordomo
moreno, brown, dark, swarthy
mormente, mainly, in the main
morno, warm

morrer, to die
a **morte,** death
morto, dead; killed
a **mostarda,** mustard
mostrar, to show
o **motivo,** motive, reason
o **motorista,** driver; motorist
o **móvel,** piece of furniture; **os móveis,** furniture
mover(-se), to move
a **mudança,** change
mudar, to change
mui, very [240]
muito, very; too; much, a lot of; *pl.* many, a lot of; (*of time*) long; very much [46]
a **mulher,** woman; wife
o **mulherão,** hefty woman, virago
a **mulherona,** hefty woman, virago
multicolor, many-coloured, multicoloured
multicor, many-coloured, multicoloured
o **mundo,** world
a **música,** music
mùtuamente, mutually, each other, one another

a **nação,** nation
nacional, national
nada, nothing
o **nada,** nothingness
nadar, to swim
namorar-se, to fall in love
não, no; not; **ainda não,** not yet; **já não,** no more, no longer; **pois não,** of course; isn't it?; **não ... mais que, não ... senão,** only; **não obstante,** notwithstanding; in spite of; nevertheless
nascer, to be born

a **nata**, cream
natural, natural
a **natureza**, nature
o **navio**, ship
necessário, necessary
a **necessidade**, necessity, need
necessitar, to need
negar, to deny; **negar-se**, to refuse
negociar, to negociate
negro, black
nem, neither; nor; **nem (sequer)**, not even
nenhum, none, not one, (not) any, no
nervoso, nervous
a **neta**, granddaughter
o **neto**, grandson, grandchild
ninguém, nobody, no one
o **ninho**, nest
nocturno, nocturnal
a **noite**, night
à **noitinha**, at dusk
a **noiva**, fianceé; bride
o **noivo**, fiancé; bridegroom; **ficar noivo**, to get engaged
o **nome**, name
nomear, to appoint
o **nordeste**, north-east
normal, normal
normalizar, to normalize
o **noroeste**, north-west
o **norte**, north
norte-americano, American
notar, to note
a **notícia**, (piece of) news, information; *pl.* news
a **noute**, night (*archaic*)
a **nova**, (piece of) news, information; *pl.* news
Nova Iorque, New York
novamente, again, once more

novo, new; young; **de novo**, again
nu, naked, nude, bare
nublado, cloudy, clouded
o **número**, number
nunca, never
a **nuvem**, cloud

ó, *interjection used before a vocative*
o **oásis**, oasis
obedecer, to obey
a **objecção**, objection
o **objectivo**, object(ive)
oblíquo, oblique
a **obra**, work
a **obra-prima**, masterpiece
obrar, to work
a **obrigação**, obligation
obrigado, -a, thanks, thank you
obrigar, to oblige
obsequiar, to favour
o **obséquio**, favour; **faz obséquio**, please
a **observação**, observation; remark
observar, to observe; to remark
o **obstáculo**, obstacle
obstar, to hinder, prevent
obstruir, to obstruct
obter, to obtain, get
óbvio, obvious
a **ocasião**, opportunity
ocorrer, to occur
octogenário, octogenarian
octogonal, octagonal
o **oculista**, oculist
ocultar, to hide
ocupar, to occupy; **ocupar-se**, to busy oneself
odiar, to hate
o **oeste**, west
oferecer, to offer

o **oficial**, officer; official
olhar, to look, watch
o **olho**, eye
o **ombro**, shoulder
onde, where; in which
o **ónix**, onyx
onomatopeico, onomatopoeic
ontem, yesterday
o **oólito**, oolite
a **opção**, option
o **ópera**, opera
a **operação**, operation
o **operário**, workman, worker
a **opinião**, opinion
opor, to set against; **opor-se
(a)**, to oppose, object (to)
a **oportunidade**, opportunity
oportuno, opportune
optar, to opt
a **óptica**, optics
óptico, optical
o **optimismo**, optimism
optimista, optimistic; optimist
óptimo, best; excellent
o **que**, what
orar, to pray
orçar, to estimate
a **ordem**, order
ordenar, to order; to ordain
o **orfão**, orphan
o **órgão**, organ
a **origem**, origin
originário, native
ornar, to adorn, decorate
a **ortografia**, orthography,
spelling
o **osso**, bone
ou, either; or
o **ouro**, gold
ousar, to dare
o **outeiro**, hill
outorgar, to grant
outrem, other people, others

outro, (an)other
outrora, formerly, (of) yore,
yesteryear
o **ouvido**, ear; hearing
ouvir, to hear; to listen to;
ouvir dizer que, to hear
that; **ouvir falar de**, to
hear of
o **ovo**, egg
oxalá (que), would (that), if
only
o **oxigénio**, oxygen

a **pá**, spade; shovel
o **pacote**, package, packet
o **pacto**, pact
a **padaria**, bakery; confectioner's
o **padeiro**, baker; confectioner
pagar, to pay (for)
a **página**, page
o **pai**, father
pairar, to hover
os **pais**, parents
o **país**, country
a **paisagem**, scenery, landscape
a **palavra**, word
a **palha**, straw
pálido, pale, pallid, wan
o **pântano**, marsh
o **pão**, bread; loaf
o **pãozinho**, roll
o **papa**, Pope
o **papel**, paper
o **papelão**, pasteboard
para, for; by; (in order) to;
towards; [**para** *and* **a**, 28;
para *and* **por**, 226]; **para
que**, in order that; **para
com**, towards (*of beha-
viour, attitudes*, etc.)
a **paragem**, (bus, tram) stop
paralisar, to paralyse; to
grind to a halt

471

parar, to stop
parecer, to seem, appear; *via* to think (of) [127]; **parecer-se com**, to resemble
parecido, similar
a **parede**, wall
o **parente**, relative, relation
o **parque**, park
a **parte**, part, -where
a **partida**, departure
partido, broken
partir (de), to depart, leave; to break
passado, past, last
o **passado**, past
passar, to pass; to spend (*time*); **passar bem**, to keep well; **passar de**, to exceed; **passar sem**, to go (*or* do) without; **passar-se**, to happen; **passar fome**, to go hungry; **passar sede**, to experience thirst
passear, to walk, stroll
o **passeio**, walk; pavement, sideset, sidewalk; **dar um passeio**, to go for a walk
o **passo**, step, pace; **dar um passo**, to take a step
o **pastor**, shepherd
a **pata**, paw
o **patim**, skate
a **patrulha**, patrol
a **pátria**, homeland, (native) country
o **pau**, stick
o **paul**, marsh
a **pausa**, pause
a **paz**, peace
a **pazada**, shovelful, spadeful
o **pé**, foot; **a pé**, on foot; **de pé**, on foot; standing; **em pé**, standing

o **pedal**, pedal; **pedal da embraiagem**, clutch-pedal
pedir, to ask (for), request; **pedir para**, to ask (permission) to; **pedir licença para**, to ask permission to; **pedir emprestado**, to borrow
a **pedra**, stone
pedrês, piebald
a **pedrinha**, pebble
Pedro, Peter
pegado, stuck
pegar em, to get hold of, pick up, seize
o **peitilho**, shirtfront
o **peito**, breast, bosom, chest
o **peixe**, fish
pelar, to peel
pelejar, to fight
a **pena**, grief, pain, trouble; **ser pena**, to be a shame, pity; **valer a pena**, to be worth it, worth the trouble
pendurar, to hang (up)
penetrar, to penetrate
a **península**, peninsula
o **pensamento**, thought
a **pensão**, boarding-house
pensar, to think, consider, ponder over; to intend
pensativo, pensive, thoughtful
pequeno, small, little
de per si, by oneself, of one's own accord
a **pêra**, pear
Pêra, Petra, Peta
perante, before, at [145 (c) (1)]
perceber, to perceive; to understand
percorrer, to travel over, wander about, go all over

o **perdão,** pardon, forgiveness
perder, to lose; to waste (*time*); to miss (*transport*)
perdoar, to pardon, forgive
perfectível, perfectible
perfeito, perfect
a **pergunta,** question; **fazer uma pergunta,** to ask (*or* put) a question
perguntar, to ask, inquire; **perguntar a si mesmo,** to wonder
o **perigo,** danger, peril
perigoso, dangerous
o **período,** period
permitir, to let, allow, permit
a **perna,** leg
pernoitar, to spend the night
Pêro, Peter
persa, Persian
perseguir, to pursue, to persecute
perseverar, to persevere
a **personagem,** character
persuadir, to persuade
pertencer, to belong
pertinho (de), nearby, close by (to)
perto (de), near (to)
pesado, heavy
pescar, to fish
o **pescoço,** neck
o **pêssego,** peach
o **pessimismo,** pessimism
pessimista, pessimistic, pessimist
péssimo, extremely bad
a **pessoa,** person
pezudo, big-footed, lumbering
a **pia,** sink; font
o **pichel,** tankard, beermug
pictórico, pictorial

a **pimenta,** pepper
pintar, to paint
a **pirâmide,** pyramid
o **pires,** saucer
pitoresco, picturesque
o **planeta,** planet
a **pletora,** plethora
pobre, poor
o **poço,** well
poder, to be able, can; **não poder deixar de,** not to be able to help (doing)
o **poder,** power
o **poema,** poem
a **poesia,** poem; poetry
o **poeta,** poet
a **poetisa,** poetess
pois, for; then, next; so; yes; **pois não,** of course; isn't it?; **pois que,** since, as, because
polir, to polish
a **polícia,** police
o **polícia,** policeman
a **política,** policy, politics
político, political
a **poltrona,** armchair, easy chair
o **pombal,** dovecot
pombalino, Pombaline
o **pombo,** dove, pigeon
ponderoso, ponderous
a **ponte,** bridge
o **ponto,** point; **estar a(o) ponto de,** to be on the point of; **em ponto,** exactly (*of time*)
a **população,** population
por, through, by, for [105 (8), 145, 220; **por** *and* **para,** 226]; **por ... que,** however; **por agora,** for the time being
pôr, to put, place; **pôr-se,** to set (*sun*); **pôr-se a,** to set

about, burst out; **pôr a mesa,** to lay the table

porco, filthy

o **porco,** pig

porém, however, nevertheless, but

porfiar, to persist

porquanto, since, because

porque, why; because

porquê, why

a **porta,** door

portar-se, to behave, act

o **porto,** port, harbour

o **Porto,** Oporto

portuense, (of) Oporto

português, Portuguese

a **possibilidade,** possibility

possível, possible

possuir, to possess

o **postal,** postcard

posterior, posterior, hind

posto que, although

pouco, little, not much; *pl.* few, not many; **pouco a pouco,** gradually; **pouco depois,** soon after; **por pouco,** almost, nearly

poupar, to save, spare

o **povo,** people

a **praça,** (public) square

o **prado,** meadow

a **praia,** beach

a **prática,** practice

prático, practical

o **prato,** plate

precisar, to need; to be necessary

preciso, necessary; precise

o **preço,** price

o **prédio,** building

predizer, to predict, foretell, forecast

preencher, to fill up (*forms*, etc.)

preferir, to prefer; *via* would rather

pregar, to preach

preguiçoso, lazy, idle

premiar, to reward

prender, to catch, capture; to attach, fasten

preocupar, to worry, harass; **preocupar-se,** to worry, be worried

preparar, to prepare

prescindir de, to leave aside, omit, do without

a **presença,** presence

presenciar, to witness, be present at

presente, present

o **presente,** present, gift

presentear, to present, bequeath

o **presidente,** president

presidir (a), to preside (at), preside (over)

a **pressa,** haste; **ter pressa, estar com pressa,** to be in a hurry; **à pressa,** in haste

prestes, ready

presumir, to presume

pretender, to claim; to intend

o **pretexto,** pretext

preto, black

prevenir, to anticipate, forestall, prevent, forewarn

prever, to foresee

a **prima,** cousin

primeiro, first; **primeiro que,** before; **primeiro que tudo,** first of all; **pela primeira vez,** for the first time; **em primeiro lugar,** in the first place

o **primo,** cousin

principal, main, principal

principiar, to begin

o **princípio**, principle, beginning

o **problema**, problem

procurar, to seek, look (for); to try

a **produção**, production

produzir, to produce

o **professor**, teacher

profundo, deep, profound, sound

o **programa**, programme

progredir, to progress

proibir, to forbid, prohibit

o **projecto**, plan, project

prometer, to promise

pronto, ready; prompt

pronunciar, to pronounce, utter

propor, to propose; **propor-se**, to propose (to)

proporcionar, to offer, make available

próprio, own

prosseguir, to continue, carry on

proteger, to protect

a **prova**, proof

provar, to prove; to try out, test

provável, probable, likely

prover, to provide, purvey

a **província**, province

provir, to originate

próximo, next, near; **próximo passado**, just past, just elapsed

prudente, prudent

publicar, to publish

o **público**, public; audience; o **público ledor**, reading public

o **pulso**, pulse, wrist

puro, pure

puxar (de), to pull (at, on), tug (at, on)

o **quadro**, picture

qual, which, what [57, 232, 236, 237]

qualquer, any (one), whichever, what(so)ever

quando, when; whenever; **vai senão quando**, all of a sudden; **quando muito**, at the most

quanto, all that; how much; *pl.* how many; **quanto antes**, as soon as possible; **(em) quanto a**, as for, with regard to

quão, how [103, N., 237, N. 2]

o **quarto**, room; quarter

quase, almost, nearly; **quase nada**, hardly anything

quatro, four; a few (*colloquial*)

que, who, whom, which; that; than, as; for; what, which; how, what (a)

quê, what

o **queijo**, cheese

queimar, to burn (*transitive*)

queixar-se, to complain

quem, who, whom; **de quem**, whose; **a quem**, whom

quente, hot

querer, to want, like, love

querido, dear, beloved

a **questão**, question

o **questionário**, questionnaire

o **quilo(grama)**, kilo(gramme)

o **quilómetro**, kilometre

a **quinta**, country estate, farm

quinze dias, fortnight

quotidiano, daily

a **rádio**, radio, wireless (*in general*)

o **rádio**, radio, wireless (*set*)

a **radiotelefonia,** wireless telephony

a **radiotelegrafia,** wireless telegraphy

a **rainha,** queen

ralhar, to scold, reproach

a **rapariga,** girl

o **rapaz,** boy

a **rapaziada,** prank; (bunch of) lads

rápido, quick; fast; quickly

rasgar, to tear (up)

a **ratazana,** rat

o **ratinho,** mouse

o **rato,** rat

a **razão,** reason; **ter razão, estar com razão,** to be right

reaccionário, reactionary

reagir, to react

o **real,** real (*old Portuguese coin*)

na **realidade,** in fact, really, actually

realizar, to bring about, carry out

recair, to relapse, fall back

recear, to fear

receber, to receive

a **recepção,** reception

reclinado, reclining

recomendar, to recommend

reconhecer, to recognize, acknowledge

recordar(-se), to remember

redarguir, to retort

ao **redor (de), em redor (de),** around

a **refeição,** meal

reflectir, to reflect

o **reflexo,** reflex

refractário, refractory

reger, to rule, be in force

a **regra,** rule

regressar, to return

let; regulated, put right

o **rei,** king

a **relação,** relation(ship)

relacionado, related

reler, to re-read

reles, worthless

a **religião,** religion

o **relógio,** watch, clock

a **relva,** lawn, sward, grass

o **relvado,** lawn, sward, grass

relvoso, grassy, sward-like, turf-like

remar, to row

remediar, to remedy

o **remédio,** remedy

renunciar (a), to renounce

reparar (em), to notice

de **repente,** suddenly

repetir, to repeat

repreender, to reprehend

o **representante,** representative

reprovar, to reprove; (*in exam*) to fail, "plough" (*transitive*)

requerer, to require, request

resignar-se, to resign oneself

resistir (a), to resist

resolver, to solve; to resolve; **resolver-se,** to resolve

o **respeito,** respect

responder (de), to answer (for), reply

a **resposta,** answer, reply

restar, to remain, be left (over); to subtract

o **restaurante,** restaurant

restituir, to give back

o **resultado,** result

resumir, to summarize, abridge, resume

reter, to retain

retirar(-se), to retire, withdraw

a **retórica,** rhetoric

retorquir, to retort

retrógrado, retrograde

a **retrospecção,** retrospection

a **reunião,** meeting

reunir, to gather together

revelar, to reveal

rever, to see again

a **revista,** magazine

a **revolução,** revolution

revolver, to revolve

o **revólver,** revolver

rezar, to pray

rico, rich; excellent

ridículo, ridiculous

rio, river; o **Rio de Janeiro,** Rio de Janeiro

rir, to laugh; **rir(-se) de,** to laugh at

o **rival,** rival

a **roda,** wheel; à **roda (de),** around, about

rodear, to surround; to go round

roer, to gnaw, nibble

rogar, to ask, request

o **romance,** novel

romano, Roman

romper, to tear, burst, break asunder

a **rosa,** rose

roto, torn

roubar, to steal

a **roupa,** clothes

o **rouxinol,** nightingale

a **rua,** street, road

o **ruído,** noise

ruim, bad, evil

ruivo, reddish, auburn

ruminar, to ponder (over)

a **Rússia,** Russia

russo, Russian

sabichão, priggish, know-all

o **saco,** sack, bag

o **sacrifício,** sacrifice

sacudir, to shake

sadio, healthy, healthful, wholesome

a **saia,** skirt

a **saída,** exit, way out

sair, to go (come) out, leave; to depart

o **sal,** salt

a **sala,** room; **sala de jantar,** dining-room; **sala de estar,** living room; **sala de visitas,** lounge

a **salada,** salad

o **salão,** sitting-room

o **salário,** wages

saltar, to jump

salvar, to save, rescue

salve, hail (*religious*)

sandeu, stupid

o **sangue,** blood

santo, holy; saint

São, Saint

são, sound

o **sapato,** shoe

o **sapo,** toad

o **sarau,** evening party, soirée

a **sardinha,** sardine

satisfatório, satisfactory

satisfazer, to satisfy

a **saudade,** nostalgia, yearning; homesickness; **ter saudade(s) de, estar com saudade(s) de,** to yearn for, long for, miss

saudar, to pay one's respects to

a **saúde,** health

saxão, Saxon

Saxónia, Saxony

saxóni(c)o, Saxon

se, if; whether; **como se,** as if; **se bem que,** although

477

a sé, cathedral

a secção, section
seccional, sectional
seco, dry

o secretário, secretary

o sector, sector

o século, century

a seda, silk

a sede, thirst; ter sede, estar com sede, to be thirsty

a sege, chaise

o segeiro, coach-maker

o segredo, secret
seguinte, following
seguir, to follow; to carry on, keep on; seguir-se, to come next
segundo, according to (what); depending on whether
seguro, sure, certain
selvagem, wild, savage
sem, without; sem que, without

a semana, week
semelhante, such (a); similar
semiusto, parched
sempre, always, ever; para sempre, for ever; para todo (o) sempre, for ever and ever; sempre que, whenever, every time that; provided (that)

o senhor, gentleman; you

a senhora, lady; you

Vossa Senhoria, you
sensabor, insipid, boorish
sensaborão, insipid, boorish

o senso, sense
sentar, to seat; sentar-se, to sit down

o sentimento, feeling
sentir, to feel, sense, hear; to be sorry (about), regret; sentir-se, to feel (of one-self); sentir calor, fome, frio, medo, saudades (de), sede, sono, vontade de, to feel hot, hungry, cold, afraid, nostalgic, thirsty, sleepy, inclined; sentir falta de, to miss

ser, to be [48–50, 74, 79, 220–221]; ser feito de, to have become of; ser mentira, to be untrue; ser verdade, to be true; a não ser que, unless

o serão, evening; passar o serão em família, to spend the evening at home

sério, serious; a sério, seriously

a serra, saw; (mountain-) range

servir, to serve; servir de, to serve as, act as; servir para, to serve to; servir-se de, to use, make use of

severo, severe

Sevilha, Seville

sexual, sexual

o silêncio, silence

sim, yes

simpático, nice, likeable

simples, simple, single

a sinceridade, sincerity

a sintaxe, syntax

a situação, situation, position
situar, to situate

só, alone; only; a sós, all alone, on one's own

soar, to sound

sob, under(neath) [145 (c)]

sobrar, to be more than enough; via to have more than enough [127]

sobre, on, upon, about [145 (c)]

sobrecarregar, to overload

a **sobremesa**, dessert
sobretudo, especially, in particular
o **sobretudo**, (over)coat
sobreviver (a), to survive
soer, to be wont to; *via* usually
soerguer, to raise slightly
o **Sol**, sun
o **sol**, sunlight, sunshine, heat of the sun
o **soldado**, soldier
a **solidariedade**, solidarity
soltar, to (set) loose, loosen
a **solução**, solution
somar, to add up
a **sombra**, shade, shadow
somenos, scant, of little worth
sonhar (com), to dream (of)
o **sono**, sleep; **ter sono, estar com sono**, to be sleepy; **sentir sono**, to feel sleepy; **pegar no sono**, to get off to sleep
a **sopa**, soup
ao **sopé de**, at the foot of (*hill*, etc.)
Sor, Sister (*religious*)
Sóror, Sister (*religious*)
sorrir, to smile; **sorrir(-se) com**, to smile at
a **sorte**, luck, fate
sossegar, to relieve, quieten, calm down
o **sotaque**, accent, drawl, twang
o **sotavento**, leeward
sotopor, to place underneath
sózinho, alone
subentendido, taken for granted
subir, to go (come) up; to take (bring, fetch) up
(de) **súbito**, suddenly

sub-reptício, surreptitious
substituir, to substitute, replace
a **sucção**, suction
suceder, to happen
o **sudoeste**, south-west
sueco, Swedish
o **sueste**, south-east; **sou'wester (hat)**
suficiente, sufficient, enough
sugar, to suck
sugerir, to suggest
sugestivo, suggestive
a **Suíça**, Switzerland
suíço, Swiss
sujeitar, to subject; to pin down
sujo, dirty
o **sul**, south
sul-americano, South American
sumir, to hide; **sumir-se**, to vanish, disappear
sumo, extreme
a **superfície**, surface
superior, superior; upper
suplementar, additional, supplementary
suplicar, to beseech, entreat
supor, to suppose
suportar, to put up with; to undergo; to bear, tolerate
surgir, to arise
surpreender, to surprise
a **surpresa**, surprise
suspender, to hang (up), suspend
suspirar, to sigh; to yearn
o **suspiro**, sigh
suster, to sustain

a **taça**, champagne glass
o **taful**, gambler
tal, such (a); **um tal**, a certain, such a

o **talher**, cover (*at table*)
talvez, perhaps, maybe
também, also, too, as well;
   também não, neither, not
   ... either
o **Tamisa**, the Thames
tanto, so much; *pl.* so many
tão, so, such, as
tão-pouco, neither, not ...
   either
tardar, to take (a long time)
tarde, late; **chegar tarde**,
   to be late
a **tarde**, afternoon, evening
à **tardinha**, at fall of evening
a **tarefa**, task
a **tarifa**, tariff
o **táxi**, taxi
o **teatro**, theatre
o **tecido**, textile
   teimar, to persist, insist,
   keep on
o **Tejo**, the Tagus
telefonar, to telephone
o **telegrama**, telegram
a **televisão**, television
   temer, to fear, be afraid
a **temperatura**, temperature
o **templo**, temple
o **tempo**, weather; time; **a** (*or*
   em) **tempo**, in time, on
   time
a **temporada**, spell, while,
   season
tencionar, to intend
a **tendência**, tendency
tenro, tender
tentar, to tempt; to try, attempt
ter, to have [30, 61, 118, 129,
   130]; **ter empenho em**, to
   insist on; **ter gosto em, ter
   prazer em**, to have (take)
   pleasure in; **ter forças
   para**, to have the strength

to; **ter motivo para**, to
have cause (*or* good reason)
to; **ter tempo de** (*or*
para), to have (the) time
to; **ter lume** (*or* **fogo**), to
have a light; **ter as horas**,
to have the (right) time
terminar, to finish
a **terra**, earth, land; homeland
terrível, terrible
a **testemunha**, witness
o **têxtil**, textile
o **texto**, text
a **tia**, aunt
o **tijolo**, brick
tilintar, to jingle
a **tinta**, ink
tinto, red (*of wine*)
o **tio**, uncle; **os tios**, uncles;
   aunt and uncle
o **tipo**, type
tirar, to pull, tug; to take off;
   to take out; to take (away)
   from
a **toalha**, towel; **toalha de
mesa**, table-cloth
todavia, however, still, yet,
even so
todo, all, every [161]; **toda a
gente**, everybody
o **toiro**, bull
tomar, to take; **tomar
banho, café, chá, o pe-
queno** (*or* **primeiro**) **almoço**, to have a bath,
coffee, tea, breakfast;
**tomar assento, riscos, a
sério**, to take a seat, risks,
seriously, **tomar emprestado**, to borrow; **tomar o
sol** (*or* **banhos de sol**), to
sun-bathe; **tomar o café**,
to have breakfast
o **tomate**, tomato
a **tômbola**, tombola

o **tórax,** thorax
torcer, to twist
tornar, to give back; **tornar a**
to do again; **tornar-se,** to
become
a **torre,** tower
o **tostão,** tostão (*old Portuguese coin*)
total, total, utter
o **touro,** bull
trabalhador, hard-working
trabalhar, to work
o **trabalho,** work
o **tractor,** tractor
a **tradução,** translation
traduzir, to translate
a **tranquilidade,** tranquillity
tranquilo, calm, tranquil
o **transeunte,** passer-by
transgredir, to transgress
o **trânsito,** transit; traffic
transpor, to cross
o **transporte,** transporte
transverso, transverse
tratar, to treat; **tratar-se de,**
to be a question of, be
about
trazer, to bring, fetch; to
wear
tremendo, tremendous
tremer, to tremble
tricolor, three-tone, in three
colours
triste, sad, gloomy
a **tristeza,** sadness
triunfar, to triumph
o **triunfo,** triumph
trocar, to change, exchange
o **troco,** change
tropeçar, to stumble
tudo, all, everything [161]
o **tumulto,** tumult
turco, Turk, Turkish
o **turista,** tourist

ultimamente, recently
último, last; recent
unicamente, recently
único, only, sole
uns, some, a few
usar, to use
útil, useful
utilizar, to use, utilize
a **uva,** grape

a **vaca,** cow
vacilar, to vacillate
a **vadiice,** vagrancy
o **vadio,** vagrant
vago, vague, unoccupied
o **vale,** valley
valer, to be worth
o **valor,** value
vão, vain
o **varapau,** stick, cudgel
a **variedade,** variety
vários, several
veemente, vehement
vegetal, vegetable
a **velhice,** old age
velhinho, dear old
velho, old
o **velho,** old man
a **velhota,** (dear) old lady
o **velhote,** (dear) old man
vencer, to overcome
vender, to sell
ventar, to blow, be windy
vento, wind; **fazer vento,**
to blow, be windy
ver, to see; **a meu ver,** in
my opinion; **ter (que ver)
com,** to have to do with
a **verdade,** truth; **ser verdade,** to be true
verde, green; immature (*of
wine*)
a **vergonha,** shame; **ser uma
vergonha,** to be a disgrace

481

verificar-se, to happen, take place

vermelho, red

verter, to translate

o **vestido,** dress

vestir, to dress; to wear; to put on; **vestir-se,** to get dressed

a **vez,** time, occasion; **às vezes, por vezes, algumas vezes, alguma vez, de vez em quando,** sometimes; **alguma vez,** ever (at any time); **muitas vezes,** often; **raras vezes,** seldom; **desta vez,** this time; **cada vez mais,** more and more; **cada vez menos,** less and less; **outra vez,** again; **em vez de,** instead of

a **Via Láctea,** Milky Way

a **viagem,** journey

viajar, to travel

a **vida,** life

vigilante, vigilant

a **vila,** village, hamlet

a **vindima,** vine- (wine-, grape-) harvest

vindo, having come, who came

vingar, to avenge, revenge

o **vinhedo,** vineyard

o **vinho,** wine

vir, to come; **vir ao encontro de,** to come and (or to) meet; **vir buscar,** to come and (or to) get; **vir ter com,** to come and (or to) meet; **que vem,** next

a **virgem,** virgin, maiden

a **virtude,** virtue

o **vírus,** germ, virus

a **visita,** visit; visitor

visitar, to visit

a **vista,** sight, view

visto que, seeing that

a **viúva,** widow

o **viúvo,** widower

viver, to live

vizinho, neighbouring, nearby, near

o **vizinho,** neighbour

voar, to fly

você, you

a **volta,** walk (or run) round, spin; **dar uma volta,** to go for a walk round (or a spin); to turn, twist; **à, em, por volta de,** around, about

voltar, to return, come (go) back; **voltar a,** to do again; **voltar para casa,** to go (back) home; **voltar-se,** to turn (round); **voltar-se para,** to turn to(wards), wheel on

a **vontade,** will; **ter vontade de, estar com vontade de,** to want to, feel like, have a good mind to; **dar vontade de,** to make (someone) feel like; **de boa vontade,** willingly

a **voz,** voice

a **xícara,** (coffee) cup

o **xilofone,** xylophone

zangar-se, to get angry

o **zelo,** zeal

zombar (de), to make fun (of), deride, ridicule

a **zona,** zone, belt

able, capaz; hábil; **to be able,** poder [112]

about, (*concerning*) de, sobre, acerca de; (*around*) ao redor de, em redor de, à roda de; **at about,** à volta de, por volta de, por; **to be about,** tratar(-se) de; **to be about to,** estar para

above, em cima (de); por cima (de); por sobre; para cima; **from above,** de cima; **above all,** sobretudo

to abridge, resumir

abroad, estrangeiro (*m.*)

to abstain, abster-se [102]

to abuse, abusar de

academic year, ano (*m.*) lectivo

accent, acento (*m.*); sotaque (*m.*)

to accept, aceitar

accommodation, alojamento (*m.*)

to accompany, acompanhar

to accomplish, cumprir

according as, segundo, conforme

according to (what), segundo, conforme

account, conta (*f.*); **to take into account,** levar em conta

to accuse, acusar

to accustom, acostumar, afazer, habituar

to acknowledge, reconhecer

acquaintance, conhecido (*m.*)

to acquire, adquirir

across, através de; **to come across** (*meet, find*), dar com, encontrar-se com

to act, agir

action, acção (*f.*)

active, activo

to adapt, adaptar

to add, acrescentar; **add up,** somar

in addition, além disso, além do que, aliás, demais (a mais); **in addition to,** além de, por mor de

additional, suplementar

addled, choco

address, endereço (*m.*)

adjective, adjectivo (*m.*)

admirable, admirável

to admire, admirar

to adopt, adoptar

adoption, adopção (*f.*)

adoptive, adoptivo

adorable, adorável

to adorn, adornar, ornar

to advance, avançar

to advertise, anunciar; pôr anúncios

advice, conselho(s) (*m.*)

to advise, aconselhar [174 (1) (iv)]

aeroplane, avião (*m.*)

affection, afecto (*m.*)

to afflict, afligir

to afford (*offer*), proporcionar

afraid: to be afraid, ter medo, estar com medo

Africa, África (*f.*)

after, depois; depois de, após [145 (c)]; ao fim de; depois que

afternoon, tarde (*f.*); **good afternoon,** boa(s) tarde(s)

afterwards, depois

again, de novo, novamente, outra vez, mais uma vez; *via* voltar a, tornar a [p. 277]

against, contra

age, idade (*f*); (*period*) época (*f.*)

ago, há, faz [126 (*b*) (iv)], atrás

to **agree,** concordar, convir, estar de acordo; **it is agreed,** está combinado; está convencionado

agreement, acordo (*m.*); **in agreement,** de acordo

aim, fim (*m.*)

air, ar (*m.*)

aircraft, avião (*m.*)

airport, aeroporto (*m.*)

airy, airado

ajar, entreaberto

alcohol, álcool (*m.*)

alert, alerta (*m.*); **to alert,** alertar

Algarve (*adj.*), algarvio

algebra, álgebra (*f.*)

to **alight,** apear-se

all, todo; tudo [161]

to **allow,** deixar, permitir [174 (1)]

almost, quase; por pouco

alone, só, sozinho; **all alone,** a sós

along, ao longo de, por

already, já

also, também

altar, altar (*m.*); **high altar,** altar-mor

although, ainda que, se bem que, posto que, embora, conquanto [p. 304]

always, sempre

to **amass,** juntar

amen, ámen; amém (*colloquial*)

America, América (*f.*)

american, americano; norte-americano

among(st), entre

to **amuse,** divertir; **to be amused,** divertir-se

amusing, engraçado, divertido

anabaptist, anabaptista

ancient, antigo; **extremely ancient,** antiquíssimo

and, e; mais

Andalusia, Andaluzia (*f.*)

Andalusian, andaluz

anecdote, anedota (*f.*)

anglo-saxon, anglo-saxão, anglo-saxónico

angry, zangado; **to get angry,** zangar-se

animal, animal (*m.*)

to **announce,** anunciar

another, outro

answer, resposta (*f.*)

to **answer,** responder

Anthony, Antony, António

to **anticipate,** antecipar, prevenir

to **antiquate,** antiquar

any, algum, qualquer; *after neg.* nenhum

anybody (anyone), alguém; *after neg.* ninguém

anything, alguma coisa, qualquer coisa, algo; *after neg.* nada

anywhere, nalguma parte, em qualquer parte; *after neg.* em nenhuma parte

apartment, apartamento (*m.*)

apparently, ao que (me) parece, do que me consta

to **appeal,** apetecer [174 (1) (i)]

to **appear,** parecer; aparecer, apresentar-se

appearance, ar (*m.*), aspecto (*m.*)

to **appease,** aplacar

apple, maçã (*f.*)

to **appoint,** nomear

to appreciate, apreciar

to approach, aproximar-se (de), abeirar-se (de), avizinhar-se (de)

to approve, aprovar [229 (c)]

apt, apto

Arab, árabe

Aragon, Aragão (m.)

Argentina, Argentina (f.)

Argentinian, argentino

to argue, disputar; (*infer*) arguir

arm, braço (m.)

armchair, poltrona (f.), maple (m.); cadeira (f.) de braços

army, exército (m.)

around, ao redor de, em redor de, à roda de; (*about*) uns

to arrange, arranjar, dispor [102]

arrival, chegada (f.)

to arrive, chegar

as, como; tal como; quando, ao; (*while*) enquanto; (**such**) **as,** tal como; **as . . . as,** tão . . . como; **as far as,** (*up to*) até (a); **as much, as many,** tanto(s); **as soon as,** assim que, logo que; mal, apenas, não bem; *via* em + *gerund*; **as soon as possible,** quanto antes; **as for,** (em) quanto a; **as well,** (*also*) também

to ascertain, averiguar

ashamed: to be ashamed of, envergonhar-se de

Asia, Ásia (f.)

aside, aparte (m.); **to leave aside,** prescindir de

to ask, (*enquire*) perguntar; (*request*) pedir, rogar; **ask for,** pedir; **ask a question,** fazer uma pergunta

aspect, aspecto (m.)

to aspire, aspirar

to assure, assegurar

at, em, a, ante, perante [145 (c) and 241]; **at once,** imediatamente, (*now*) desde já, já (já), num instante

atheistic, ateu

to attack, atacar, agredir [111 (d)]

to attempt, tentar

to attend, assistir a; andar em; **attend to,** atender a, ocupar-se de *or* em

attention, atenção (f.)

attentive, atento

attitude, atitude (f.)

to attract, atrair [213]

audition, audição (f.)

aunt, tia (f.)

Austria, Áustria (f.)

Austrian, austríaco

author, autor (m.)

to authorize, autorizar

auxiliary, auxiliar

to avenge, vingar

to avoid, evitar

to awake, acordar, despertar; acordar(-se), despertar(-se)

away: to go away, ir(-se) embora

awkward, canhoto

Azores, Açores (m./pl.)

back, costas (f./pl); **to be back,** estar de volta

bacteriology, bacteriologia (f.)

bacterium, bactéria (f.)

bad, mau, ruim

badly, mal

bad-tempered, mal-humorado

bag (= *case*), mala (f.)

baggage, bagagem (f.)

baker, padeiro (m.)

bakery, padaria (f.)

banal, banal

to bang, bater (com)

bank, banco (m.)

baptism, baptismo (*m.*)
baptismal, baptismal
baptist, baptista (*m.*)
baptist(e)ry, baptistério (*m.*)
to baptize, baptizar
bar, (*for drinks*) bar (*m.*)
bare, nu [32 (3)]
barely, mal; apenas
barrel, barril (*m.*)
basin, bacia (*f.*)
basinful, baciada (*f.*)
bastion, bastião (*m.*)
batch, fornada (*f.*)
bath: to have a bath, tomar banho, banhar-se
bathroom, casa (*f.*) de banho, quarto (*m.*) de banho
bath, bathtub, banheira (*f.*), tina (*f.*)
to bathe, banhar-se
to be, ser, estar [48–50, 74, 79, 220, 221]; ficar [80, 222]; ter, estar com [61]; fazer [62]; haver [126]; encontrar-se, achar-se; **be (destined, intending) to,** haver de
beach, praia (*f.*)
bean, (*haricot, runner, French*) feijão (*m.*); (*broad, kidney*) fava (*f.*)
to bear, (*carry*) levar, carregar; (*put up with*) aguentar, suportar; **bear in mind,** levar em conta, ter presente
to beat, bater
beautiful, lindo, belo, formoso
beauty, beleza (*f.*)
because, porque [243]
to become, tornar-se, ficar
bed, cama (*f.*); **to go to bed,** ir para a cama, (ir) deitar-se; **in bed,** na cama
to bedeck, marchetar
bedroom, quarto (*m.*) de dormir
beef, carne (*f.*) de vaca

beer, cerveja (*f.*)
beermug, pichel (*m.*), caneca (*f.*)
before, havia, fazia, atrás [126, 131]; antes (de), diante (de), ante, perante [145 (*c*) and (*e*)]; antes que, primeiro que
beforehand, antes, dantes
to begin, começar, principiar [174 (2) (iv)]
beginning, princípio (*m.*), começo (*m.*)
to behave, portar-se, comportar-se
behaviour, conduta (*f.*)
behind, atrás (de); por trás (de)
to behove, competir, incumbir, cumprir, caber [174 (1) (i)]
to believe, acreditar, crer [163]
to belong (to), ser (de), pertencer (a)
beloved, querido
below, sob, debaixo de; por baixo de; em baixo, abaixo; para baixo; **from below,** de baixo
to bend, torcer
beneath, *see* **below**
beside, ao lado de, junto a, junto de
besides, além de; além disso, demais (a mais), além do que, aliás
best, melhor
to bet, apostar
better, melhor
between, entre
beyond, além (de)
big, grande
big-footed, pezudo
bigger, maior
biggest, maior
bill, conta (*f.*)
birthday, aniversário (*m.*), *via* fazer anos

bit, pouco; **a bit,** um pouco, um bocado
to **bite,** morder
black, preto, negro
blanket, cobertor (*m.*)
blighter, malandro (*m.*)
blind, cego
to **block (up),** entupir [111 (*e*)]
blond, louro, loiro
blue, azul
to **blush,** corar
boa constrictor, jibóia (*f.*)
to **board,** entrar (em), subir (a)
on **board,** a bordo
boarding-house, pensão (*f.*), casa (*f.*) de hóspedes
to **boast,** jactar-se
boastfulness, jactância (*f.*)
body, corpo (*m.*); (*corpse*) cadáver (*m.*)
bold, afoito, atrevido
boldness, afoiteza (*f.*)
bone, osso (*m.*)
book, livro (*m.*)
bookseller, livreiro (*m.*)
bookshop, livraria (*f.*)
to **border (on),** confinar (com)
bore, maçada (*f.*); maçador (*m.*)
to **bore,** maçar
born: to be born, nascer
to **borrow,** pedir emprestado; tomar emprestado
boss, chefe (*m.*)
bosun, arrais (*m.*)
both, ambos, os dois [162]
bottle, garrafa (*f.*)
bottom, fundo (*m.*)
boy, rapaz (*m.*), menino (*m.*)
box, caixa (*f.*)
Brasilia, Brasília (*f.*)
Brazil, Brasil (*m.*)
Brazilian, brasileiro
bread, pão (*m.*)
to **break,** partir, quebrar

breakfast, pequeno almoço (*m.*), primeiro almoço (*m.*); **to (have) breakfast,** tomar o pequeno (*or* primeiro) almoço, tomar o café
breath: out of breath, esbaforido
brick, tijolo (*m.*)
bride, noiva (*f.*)
bridegroom, noivo (*m.*)
bridge, ponte (*f.*)
brief, breve, curto
to **bring,** trazer; levar; **bring about,** efectuar, realizar; **bring together,** juntar, reunir; **bring to a standstill,** paralisar; **bring up(stairs),** subir; **bring down(stairs),** descer
broken, partido, quebrado
broody, choco
brother, irmão (*m.*); Frei (*religious*)
to **budge,** bulir [111 (*e*)], mexer
to **build,** construir [215]
building, edifício (*m.*), prédio (*m.*)
bulky, grosso
bull, touro (*m.*), toiro (*m.*)
to **burn,** queimar
bus, autocarro (*m.*)
busy, ocupado; **to busy oneself,** ocupar-se, entreter-se
but, mas, porém; senão [133]
butter, manteiga (*f.*)
to **button (up),** abotoar
to **buy,** comprar
by, por; (*time*) para [226]

Caesar, César (*m.*)
café, café (*m.*)
to **cage (up),** ajaular
cake (=*bun*), bolo (*m.*)
calix, calyx, cálix (*m.*), cálice (*m.*)

to call, chamar; [229 (b) N.4] **call on,** visitar; **be called,** chamar-se

to calm, sossegar

to camber, abaular

Camoens, Camões

Camonean, camoniano

Can, poder [112]; saber [112]

Canada, Canadá (m.)

Canadian, canadiano; canadense (*Brazilian form*)

canon, cânon (m.)

capable, capaz

Cape of Good Hope, Cabo (m.) da Boa Esperança

capital, capital (m.) (*money*); capital (f.) (*city*)

captain, capitão (m.); **captain-in-chief,** capitão-mor (m.)

captious, capcioso

to capture, prender

car, carro (m.)

card, cartão (m.); **postcard,** (bilhete) postal (m.)

cardboard, cartão (m.)

to care for, cuidar de

careful: **to be careful,** ter cuidado (*or* cautela), estar com cuidado (*or* cautela)

to carry, levar, carregar; **carry on,** seguir; **carry out,** fazer, realizar, efectuar, cumprir (com)

Carthage, Cartago (f.)

case, caso (m.); (*suitcase*) mala (f.); **in case,** caso [181 (g) (3)]

Castile, Castela (f.)

cat, gato (m.); **mountain cat,** gato (m.) montês

Catalan, catalão

to catch, prender; apanhar; dar com (=meet)

cathedral, sé (f.)

to cause, causar; **cause to,** levar a

cautious: **to be cautious,** ter

cautela (*or* cuidado), estar com cautela (*or* cuidado)

to cease, cessar

to censure, arguir

census, censo (m.)

centre, centro (m.)

century, século (m.)

certain, certo; (*sure*) seguro, certo; **a certain,** certo; um tal; **certainly,** com certeza, decerto, por certo

chair, cadeira (f.)

chaise, sege (f.)

chalice, cálix (m.), cálice (m.)

champagne, champanhe (m.); **champagne glass,** taça (f.)

change, mudança (f.); (money) troco (m.)

to change, mudar; trocar

chapter, capítulo (m.)

character, carácter (m.); personagem (m. or f.)

characteristic, (*adj.*) característico; (*noun*) característica (f.)

characterization, caracterização (f.)

to characterize, caracterizar

charge: **in my charge,** a meu cargo

charming, encantador

to chat, cavaquear

cheap, barato

cheerful, alegre

cheerfulness, alegria (f.)

cheerio, adeusinho

cheese, queijo (m.)

chicken, galinha (f.)

chief, chefe (m.)

child, criança (f.)

children, crianças (f./pl.); filhos (m./pl.)

Chinese, chinês

chips, batatas fritas (f./pl.)

chocolate, chocolate (m.)

to **choose**, escolher, eleger
Christian, cristão
chronicler, cronista (*m.*); **head chronicler**, cronista-mor (*m.*)
cinema, cinema (*m.*)
civil, civil
to **civilize**, civilizar
to **clarify**, aclarar
class, aula (*f.*); classe (*f.*)
classroom, aula (*f.*), sala (*f.*) de aula
clean, limpo
to **clean (shoes)**, engraixar (sapatos)
clear, claro
clerk, empregado (*m.*)
clever, inteligente
climate, clima (*m.*)
climax, clímax (*m.*)
clock, relógio (*m.*)
to **close**, fechar
close-fitting, apertado
clothes, roupa (*f.*)
cloud, nuvem (*f.*)
cloudy, nublado
clump, maciço (*m.*)
clumsy, canhoto
clutch-pedal, pedal (*m.*) da embraiagem
coach-maker, segeiro (*m.*)
coal, carvão (*m.*)
coast, costa (*f.*)
coat, casaco (*m.*); (*overcoat*) sobretudo (*m.*)
cocoa, cacau (*m.*)
cod(fish), bacalhau (*m.*)
codex, códex (*m.*), códice (*m.*)
coffee, café (*m.*); **to have coffee**, tomar café
coffee-cup, xícara (*f.*)
coffee-plantation, cafezal (*m.*)
coffin, caixão (*m.*)
coin, moeda (*f.*)
cold, frio (*noun and adj.*); **to be cold**, fazer frio, estar frio

(*weather*); ter frio, estar com frio (*persons*); **nice and cold**, fresquinho (*drinks*); **to go cold**, arrefecer
to **collapse**, aluir-se, afundar-se
college, colégio (*m.*) (*private*); liceu (*m.*)
colour, cor (*f.*)
colourless, incolor
combustion, combustão (*f.*)
to **come**, vir; ir; **come now!** ora essa, essa é boa; **come on!** vamos embora; **come to**, chegar a, vir a; **come across** (*meet, find*), dar com, encontrar-se com; **come back**, voltar, regressar; **come from**, ser de, provir de; **come down**, descer; **come up**, subir; **come in(to)**, entrar (em); **come out**, sair; **come with**, acompanhar
comedy, comédia (*f.*)
comet, cometa (*m.*)
to **command**, mandar, ordenar, dar ordem, dizer [174]
to **commence**, começar [174 (2) (iv)]
to **comment (on)**, comentar
common, comum
compact, compacto
to **compel**, compelir
to **complain**, queixar-se
complete, completo
completely, completamente, por completo
to **compose**, compor [102]
comprehension, compreensão (*f.*)
to **concede**, conceder, outorgar
concise, conciso
to **conclude**, concluir
conclusion, conclusão (*f.*)
to **condemn**, condenar
condition, condição (*f.*); **on**

condition (that), com a condição que, sob condição que
conductor, condutor (*m.*)
to **confess,** confessar
confidence, confiança (*f.*)
to **confuse,** confundir
confusion, confusão (*f.*)
congestion, congestão (*f.*)
to **congratulate,** congratular, felicitar
to **consent,** consentir
consequently, por conseguinte, por consequência
to **conserve,** conservar
to **consider,** considerar, pensar
to **consist (of),** consistir (em), constar (de)
to **console,** consolar
constant, constante
to **construct,** construir [215]
consul, cônsul (*m.*)
to **consume,** consumir [111 (*e*)]
to **contact,** contactar com
to **contain,** conter [102]
to **contaminate,** contaminar, empestar
content, contente
to **content,** contentar
to **continue,** continuar, prosseguir
to **contradict,** contradizer [102]
contrary: on the contrary, ao contrário, pelo contrário
to **contravene,** contravir [102]
convict, convicto (*m.*)
conviction, convicção (*f.*)
to **convince,** convencer
to **cook,** cozinhar
cool, fresco, fresquinho
to **cool off,** arrefecer
copy, exemplar (*m.*)
corner, canto (*m.*) (*concave*) esquina (*f.*) (*convex*)
corpse, cadáver (*m.*)
to **correct,** corrigir

to **cost,** custar
cottage, casinha (*f.*)
cotton, algodão (*m.*)
council, conselho (*m.*)
counsel, conselho (*m.*)
to **count,** contar; **count on,** contar com
counter, balcão (*m.*)
country, (*rural*) campo (*m.*); (*state*) país (*m.*); (*native*) pátria (*f.*); (*region*) terra (*f.*)
countryside, campo (*m.*); paisagem (*f.*)
courage, coragem (*f.*)
course, curso (*m.*); **to take (attend) a course,** tirar um curso
courteous, cortês
courtesy, cortesia (*f.*)
cousin, primo (*m.*); prima (*f.*)
cover, talher (*m.*) (*at table*)
to **cover,** cobrir [110]
cow, vaca (*f.*)
creditor, credor (*m.*)
cross, mal-humorado
to **cross,** cruzar, atravessar, transpor
cruel, cruel
cruzeiro, cruzeiro (*m.*)
cry (*shout*), grito (*m.*)
to **cry** (*weep*), chorar
cudgel, varapau (*m.*)
cup, chávena (*f.*)
to **curb,** coibir [217]
curious, curioso
custom, costume (*m.*)
customer, freguês (*m.*)
customs, alfândega (*f.*); **chief customs officer,** guarda-mor (*m.*)
to **cut,** cortar
cute, engraçado
cystectomy, cistectomia (*f.*)
Czechoslovak(ian), checoslovaco

daily, diário, cotidiano, quotidiano
to dance, dançar, bailar
Dane, dinamarquês (*m.*)
danger, perigo (*m.*)
dangerous, perigoso
Danish, dinamarquês
to dare, atrever-se, ousar
daring, atrevido, afoito, ousado; (*noun*) afoiteza (*f.*)
dark, escuro; moreno
date, data (*f.*)
daughter, filha (*f.*)
to dawn, amanhecer
day, dia (*m.*)
daybreak, amanhecer (*m.*)
daydream, devaneio (*m.*)
dead, morto, falecido
to deal with, lidar com, tratar de
dear, caro, querido
death, morte (*f.*)
to deceive, enganar
deception, engano (*m.*)
to decide, decidir(-se)
to decorate, decorar, adornar
to dedicate, dedicar
deep, profundo
defeat, derrota (*f.*)
to defeat, derrotar
defect, defeito (*m.*)
to defend, defender
definitive, definitivo
to deliver, entregar
to demand, exigir
den, covil (*m.*)
to denigrate, denegrir [111 (*d*)]
to deny, negar
to depart, partir
departure, partida (*f.*)
to depend, depender; **it (all) depends,** é conforme
to depose, depor [102]
to deride, zombar de
to descend, descer
to describe, descrever

description, descrição (*f.*)
to deserve, merecer
to design, desenhar
desire, desejo (*m.*)
to desire, desejar
to despair, desesperar
to despise, desprezar
dessert, sobremesa (*f.*)
to destroy, destruir [215]
destruction, destruição (*f.*)
detail: to (express in) detail, esmiuçar, pormenorizar, detalhar
to detain, deter [102]
to devote, dedicar
devout, devoto
diction, dicção (*f.*)
dictionary, dicionário (*m.*)
to die, morrer
difference, diferença (*f.*)
different, diferente
difficult, difícil
difficulty, dificuldade (*f.*); **with difficulty,** a custo
dimple, covinha (*f.*)
to dine, jantar
dining-room, sala (*f.*) de jantar
direction, direcção (*f.*)
director, director (*m.*)
dirty, sujo
to disappear, desaparecer, sumir-se [111 (*e*)]
disappointed, desiludido
to discolour, descorar
discourteous, descortês
to discover, descobrir, aprender, saber, inteirar-se
to discuss, discutir
discussion, discussão (*f.*)
disgrace: it's a disgrace, é uma vergonha
to dismiss, despedir [142]
to displease, desagradar, desprazer
displeasure, desgosto (*m.*); desprazer (*m.*)

to dispose, dispor [102], arranjar
to dispute, disputar
to dissolve, dissolver
to dissuade, dissuadir
    distance, distância (*f.*); **in the distance,** ao longe
    distant, longínquo, distante
    distinct, distinto
to distinguish, distinguir
to distribute, distribuir
    district, distrito (*m.*); terra (*f.*), região (*f.*); bairro (*m.*)
to distrust, desconfiar de
to divide, dividir
    division, divisão (*f.*)
to do, fazer; **do without,** passar sem, prescindir de; **do one's duty,** fazer o seu dever, cumprir (com) o seu dever; **have to do with,** ter (que ver) com
    doctor, médico (*m.*), doutor (*m.*) [p. 170]
    dog, cão (*m.*)
    Dominic, Domingos
    door, porta (*f.*)
    dose, dose (*f.*)
    doubt, dúvida (*f.*)
to doubt, duvidar
    dovecot, pombal (*m.*)
    down: down here, cá em baixo; **down there,** lá em baixo
    downstairs, lá em baixo, cá em baixo; para baixo; **from downstairs,** de baixo
to drain, esgotar
to draw, desenhar, traçar
    drawing-room, salão (*m.*), sala (*f.*) de estar, sala (*f.*) de visitas
to dream, sonhar
    dress, vestido (*m.*)
to dress, vestir
    dressed: to get dressed, vestir-se

to drink, beber
to drive, conduzir, guiar
    driver, motorista (*m.*)
    driving force, força (*f.*) motriz
to drop, deixar cair
    dry, seco, enxuto
to dry, enxugar
    dueller, duellist, duelista (*m.*)
    during, durante
    dustman, lixeiro (*m.*)
    Dutch, holandês
    duty, dever (*m.*); **to do one's duty,** fazer o seu dever, cumprir (com) o seu dever
to dwell, morar, residir

    each, cada; cada um, cada qual; **each other,** se, um ao outro, *etc.* [139]
    ear, ouvido (*m.*)
    earlier, mais cedo; havia (*or* fazia)[126 (*b*) (iv)], atrás
    early, cedo (*adv.*)
    earn, ganhar
    earth, terra (*f.*)
    easily, facilmente; asinha (*archaic*)
    east, este (*m.*), leste (*m.*)
    easy, fácil
to eat, comer
    eating-house, casa (*f.*) de pasto
    ecstasy, êxtase (*m.*)
    ectoplasm, ectoplasma (*m.*)
    edge, borda (*f.*), margem (*f.*)
    edition, edição (*f.*)
    effective, eficaz
    efficacious, eficaz
    efficient, eficaz
    effort, esforço (*m.*); **to make an effort,** esforçar-se; **to be a great effort,** *via* custar trabalho a
    egg, ovo (*m.*)
    either, ou; quer [194 (*e*)]
    elastic, elástico

to elect, eleger
  electricity, electricidade (*f.*)
  elegance, elegância (*f.*)
  elegant, elegante
  Elizabeth, Isabel
  else, mais; demais; [133, 141]
to embrace, abraçar
to employ, empregar
  employee, empregado (*m.*)
  empty, vazio; (*vacant*) livre,
    vago
to enable, habilitar
to encourage, animar
  end, fim (*m.*), cabo (*m.*);
    extremidade (*f.*), fundo (*m.*)
to end, terminar; **end up,** acabar
  enemy, inimigo (*m.*)
  energetic, enérgico
  engaged: to get engaged,
    ficar noivo
  England, Inglaterra (*f.*)
  English, inglês
  Englishman, inglês (*m.*)
to enjoy, gozar de, desfrutar de;
    (*like*) gostar de; **enjoy one-
    self,** divertir-se
  enormous, enorme
  enough, bastante; **to be
    enough,** chegar, bastar
to entangle, emaranhar
to enter, entrar; ingressar; in-
    ternar-se
to entertain, entreter [102],
    divertir
  entire, inteiro
  entrance, entrada (*f.*)
to entreat, suplicar
to entrust, encarregar
  entry, entrada (*f.*)
  envious, invejoso
  envy, inveja (*f.*)
to envy, invejar
to erect, erigir
to err, errar
  erroneous, erróneo

  error, erro (*m.*)
to escape, escapər
  escudo, escudo (*m.*)
  especially, sobretudo
  essay, ensaio (*m.*)
to establish, estabelecer
to esteem, estimar
to estimate, orçar
  eternal, eterno
  Europe, Europa (*f.*)
  European, europeu
to europeanize, europeizar
  even, ainda, mesmo, até; **even
    if,** ainda que; **even though,**
    ainda que; **not even,** nem
    (sequer)
  evening, tarde (*f.*) [81]; **good
    evening,** boa(s) tarde(s)
  ever, (*at any time, on any
    occasion*) já, alguma vez;
    (*after superlative*) jamais;
    (*after negative*) nunca, jamais;
    for ever, para sempre; **for
    ever and ever,** para todo (o)
    sempre
  every, todo [161], cada; **every
    day,** todos os dias, cada dia;
    every time (that), sempre
    que
  everybody (everyone), toda
    a gente, todos
  everything, tudo [161]
  everywhere, em toda a parte,
    por toda a parte
  evident, evidente
  evil, mal (*m.*); mau, ruim
  ex-, ex-
  exact, exacto
  exam., exame (*m.*)
to examine, examinar
  examination, exame (*m.*); **to
    take (sit) an examination,**
    fazer um exame; **to pass
    (fail) an examination,** ser

493

aprovado (reprovado) num exame

example: for example, por exemplo

to exceed, passar de

excellent, óptimo, excelente

except, excepto

to except, exceptuar

exception, excepção (f.)

exceptional, excepcional

excessive, excessivo, sobejo

to exchange, trocar

to exclaim, exclamar

exclusive, exclusive (adv.)

to excuse, desculpar, excusar

to exempt, isentar

exercise, exercício (m.)

to exhaust, esgotar

to exist, existir

exit, saída (f.)

expensive, caro

to explain, explicar

to exploit, explorar

to explore, explorar

to expose, expor [102]

exterior, exterior

to extinguish, apagar

to extort, extorquir

extraordinary, extraordinário

extreme, extremidade (f.); (adj.) sumo, extremo

eye, olho (m.)

face, cara (f.), rosto (m.), face (f.)

facing, em frente (de), defronte (de)

fact, facto (m.); in fact, as a matter of fact, de facto

faction, facção (f.)

factious, faccioso

factotum, factótum (m.)

to fail, fracassar; (exam) reprovar (transitive), ser reprovado; not to fail to, não deixar de

fair, loiro, louro

to fall, cair [213]

false, falso

fame, fama (f.)

family, família (f.)

famous, famoso, célebre

far (away), longe

farm, quinta (f.)

farmer, lavrador (m.)

fast, rápido, depressa

to fasten, atar, prender

father, pai (m.); padre (m.) (religious)

favour, favor (m.), obséquio (m.)

to favour, obsequiar

fear, medo (m.)

to fear, ter medo de, recear, temer

fed up, farto, cheio

Federation of British Industries, Federação (f.) das Indústrias Britânicas

to feed, dar de (or a) comer a; feed on, alimentar-se de (or com)

to feel, sentir [110]; (of oneself) sentir-se; feel afraid, cold, hot, thirsty, hungry, sleepy, nostalgic, like, sentir medo, frio, calor, sede, fome, sono, saudades (de), vontade (de)

Felix, Félix

to fetch, levar, trazer, ir buscar, vir buscar

few, poucos; a few, alguns, uns, quatro

fiancé, noivo (m.)

fiancée, noiva (f.)

fictitious, fictício

fiction, ficção (f.)

to fidget, mexer

to fight, pelejar

to fill, encher; fill in (or up), preencher (forms, etc.)

to filter, filtrar, coar [218]

filthy, porco
final, final, definitivo
finally, finalmente, por fim, por último
to **find,** encontrar, achar, dar com
fine, bom, bonito, lindo
finger, dedo (*m.*)
to **finish,** terminar, acabar
fire, fogo (*m.*); to **set fire to,** incendiar, deitar fogo a
first, primeiro; **at first,** a(o) princípio
fish, peixe (*m.*)
to **fish,** pescar
to **fit,** caber [134]
fit: as he thinks fit, a seu bel-prazer
fitting: to be fitting, convir [102]
to **fix,** fixar; consertar
flair: to have a flair for, dar para, ter jeito para
Flanders, Flandres (*f.*)
flat, apartamento (*m.*)
to **flee,** fugir [111 (*e*)]
flesh, carne (*f.*)
to **fling,** deitar, lançar, atirar
to **float,** boiar
floor, chão (*m.*), soalho (*m.*); (*storey*) andar (*m.*)
to **flourish,** florescer
flower, flor (*f.*)
flux, flux (*m.*)
to **follow,** seguir
following, seguinte
fond: to be (very) fond of, gostar (imenso) de, ser (muito) afeiçoado a
food, comida (*f.*), alimento (*m.*)
foot, pé (*m.*); **on foot,** a pé
footstep, passo (*m.*); (*footprint*) pegada (*f.*)
for, para, por, durante [226 (b)]; que, pois, pois que [243]

to **forbid,** proibir [174·(3) (ii)]
to **force,** forçar
to **forecast,** predizer [102]
foreign, estrangeiro
foreigner, estrangeiro (*m.*)
to **foresee,** prever [102]
to **foretell,** predizer [102]
to **forget,** esquecer(-se); *via* esquecer *used impersonally* [174 (1) (i)]
to **forgive,** perdoar [204 (*c*)]
forgiveness, perdão (*m.*)
fork, garfo (*m.*)
to **form,** formar, formular
former, anterior; antigo; aquele
formerly, anteriormente; antigamente, (d)antes; outrora
to **formulate,** formular
fortnight, quinze dias
fossil, fóssil (*m.*)
fractional, fraccionário
France, França (*f.*)
Franco-Prussian, franco-prussiano
frankly, francamente
free, livre
freedom, liberdade (*f.*)
to **freeze,** gelar
French, francês
Frenchman, francês (*m.*)
frequency, frequência (*f.*)
frequent, frequente
friction, fricção (*f.*)
friend, amigo (*m.*), amiga (*f.*)
friendly with, amigo de
friendship, amizade (*f.*)
from, de, desde [145 (*c*)]
front: in front of, diante de; em frente de
fruit, fruta (*f.*)
to **fry,** frigir, fritar
to **fulfil,** cumprir (com); **not to fulfil,** faltar a
full, cheio
funny, engraçado

furniture, móveis (*m./pl.*), mobiliário (*m.*)

to gain, ganhar
gambler, taful (*m.*)
game, jogo (*m.*)
garden, jardim (*m.*)
to gather together, reunir, juntar
general, general (*m.*); (*adj.*) geral
generally, geralmente, em geral
to generate, gerar
generation, geração (*f.*)
gentleman, senhor (*m.*), cavalheiro (*m.*)
genuine, autêntico, genuíno
geography, geografia (*f.*)
germ, vírus (*m*).
German, alemão
Germany, Alemanha (*f.*)
to get, obter [102], conseguir, adquirir; persuadir; (*become, grow*) tornar-se; (*to a place*) chegar; **get to,** chegar a; **get to know,** (chegar a) conhecer; **get to sleep,** adormecer, pegar no sono; **get angry,** zangar-se; **get dressed,** vestir-se; **get undressed,** despir-se; **get lost,** perder-se; **get old,** envelhecer; **get down,** apear-se; **get up,** levantar-se; **get in,** entrar; **get out,** sair [213]; **get hold of,** pegar em; **to come** (go) **and get,** vir (*or* ir) buscar; **to have got (to),** ter (que *or* de)
giant, gigante (*m.*)
girl, rapariga (*f.*), menina (*f.*)
to give, dar; **give back,** devolver, restituir, tornar; **give up,** renunciar a
glad, alegre; **to be glad,** alegrar-se

glass, copo (*m.*); (*substance*) vidro (*m.*)
to glimpse, entrever [102]
gloomy, triste, melancólico
glove, luva (*f.*)
to go, ir; (*mech.*) andar; (*become*) tornar-se; **go against,** contrariar; **go all over,** percorrer; **go away, off,** ir(-se) embora; afastar-se; **go back,** voltar; **go beyond,** passar de; **go down,** descer; **go in,** entrar; **go on,** seguir; **go out,** sair; **go round,** dar a volta (a); **go up,** subir; **go with,** acompanhar, ir com; **go to bed,** ir para a cama, (ir) deitar-se; **go to sleep,** adormecer, pegar no sono; **go from bad to worse,** andar (*or* ir) de mal a pior
goat, cabra (*f.*); **mountain goat,** cabra (*f.*) montês
good, bom; **to be so good as to,** ter a bondade de; **for good,** para sempre, definitivamente
good-bye, adeus; **to say good-bye,** despedir-se
goodness, bondade (*f.*)
gospel, evangelho (*m.*)
to govern, governar, reger
government, governo (*m.*)
gradually, pouco a pouco
grain, grão (*m.*)
grammar school, liceu (*m.*)
granddaughter, neta (*f.*)
Grand Duke, grão-duque (*m.*)
grandfather, avô (*m.*)
grandmother, avó (*f.*)
grandparents, avós (*m./pl.*)
grandson, neto (*m.*)
to grant, outorgar, conceder
grape, uva (*f.*)
grape-harvest, vindima (*f.*)

to **grasp,** (*understand*) compreender

grass, erva (*f.*), relva (*f.*)

grassy, relvoso

grateful, agradecido;' **to be grateful for,** agradecer

gratitude, gratidão (*f.*)

gratuity, gorjeta (*f.*)

gravedigger, coveiro (*m.*)

gravy, molho (*m.*)

great, grande

greatest, sumo, maior

Greek, grego

green, verde

to **greet,** cumprimentar, saudar [217]

grey, cinzento

to **grieve,** afligir

grill, grelha (*f.*)

to **grill,** grelhar

to **grind,** moer; **grind to a halt,** paralisar

ground, chão (*m.*), terra (*f.*)

group, grupo (*m.*)

to **grow,** crescer

guard, guarda (*m.*)

to **guard,** guardar

guest, convidado (*m.*), hóspede (*m.*)

guest-house, casa (*f.*) de hóspedes, hotelzinho (*m.*), pensão (*f.*)

guide, guia (*m.*)

guide-book, guia (*m.*)

Guinea, Guiné (*f.*)

habit, hábito (*m.*)

Hague, the, Haia (*f.*)

hail, ave, salve (*religious only*)

hair, cabelo (*m.*)

half, meio (*adj.*); **half past,** e meia; **half-open,** entreaberto

hand, mão (*f.*); **at hand, to hand,** à mão; **on the one hand,** por um lado; **on the other hand,** por outro lado

to **hand** (**in, over**), entregar

to **hang** (**up**), pendurar

to **happen,** acontecer, suceder, ocorrer, verificar-se, passar-se

happy, feliz, contente

hardly, mal; apenas

hard-working, aplicado, trabalhador

harp, harpa (*f.*)

in **haste,** à pressa

hat, chapéu (*m.*)

to **hate,** odiar [100 (*e*)]

to **have, have got,** ter [30, 61, 118, 129, 130]; haver [118] **have** (**got**) **to,** ter que, ter de, dever; **have just,** acabar de [132]; **have ... done,** mandar fazer, fazer fazer

head, cabeça (*f.*); chefe (*m.*); *via* mor [240]

headmaster, director (*m.*)

health, saúde (*f.*)

healthful, sadio

healthy, são, sadio

to **hear,** ouvir; **hear of,** ouvir falar de; **hear that,** ouvir dizer que

hearing, ouvido (*m.*)

heart, coração (*m.*)

heat, calor (*m.*)

to **heat,** aquecer, esquentar

heaven, céu (*m.*)

heavy, pesado

hectolitre, hectolitro (*m.*)

Hector, Heitor

help, ajuda (*f.*)

to **help,** ajudar; **to go** (**come, rush**) **to help,** acudir a; **not to help** (**doing**), não poder deixar de

hen, galinha (*f.*)

Henry, Henrique

heptagon, heptágono (*m.*)

herbalist, ervanário (*m.*)
herbivore, herbívoro (*m.*)
here, aqui, cá [98 (*a*)]
to **hesitate,** hesitar, vacilar
to **hide,** esconder, ocultar, encobrir
high, alto
hill, colina (*f.*)
to **hinder,** impedir, empecer,
  tolher [174 (3) (ii)]
Hindu, hindu [32 (3)]
to **hire,** alugar
history, história (*f.*)
hold: to get hold of, pegar em
to **hold fast,** sujeitar, segurar
holiday, dia (*m.*) feriado; *pl.*
  férias (*f.*/*pl.*); **on holiday,**
  em férias
Holland, Holanda (*f.*)
hollow, oco
holy, santo
home, casa (*f.*), lar (*m.*); **at
  home,** em casa; **(to) home,**
  para casa; **to return home,**
  voltar para casa; **to arrive
  home,** chegar a casa
homeland, pátria (*f.*), terra (*f.*)
**homesick: to be homesick
  (for),** ter (*or* estar com)
  saudades de
honeysuckle, madressilva (*f.*)
hope, esperança (*f.*)
to **hope,** esperar
horror, horror (*m.*)
horse, cavalo (*m.*)
hospital, hospital (*m.*)
hot, quente; **to be hot,** fazer
  calor (*weather*); ter calor,
  estar com calor (*persons*)
hour, hora (*f.*)
house, casa (*f.*); **at the house
  of,** em casa de; **to the house
  of,** para casa de
to **hover,** pairar
  how, como; o [103]; quão
  [103]; **how!** que [237];

how much, how many,
  quanto(s); **how great!** qual
  [237]; **how long,** quanto
  tempo
however, contudo, porém,
  todavia; por ... que
to **hug,** abraçar
hunger, fome (*f.*)
hungry: to be hungry, ter
  fome, estar com fome
to **hunt,** caçar
hurry: to be in a hurry, ter
  pressa, estar com pressa
to **hurry (up),** aviar-se, apressar-se
husband, marido (*m.*), esposo
  (*m.*)
hyphen, traço (*m.*) de união,
  hífen (*m.*)

Iberian, ibérico
ice, gelo (*m.*)
idea, ideia (*f.*)
ideal, ideal (*m.*)
identical, idêntico
idle, preguiçoso
if, se; **as if,** como se; como que;
  even if, ainda que
ill, doente, mal
illness, doença (*f.*)
ill-tempered, mal-humorado
illusion, ilusão (*f.*)
to **imagine,** imaginar
to **imitate,** imitar
immediate, imediato
to **impede,** impedir, empecer,
  tolher [174 (3) (ii)]
to **implore,** implorar [181 (*a*) N.5]
to **imply,** arguir
impolite, descortês
to **import,** importar
importance, importância (*f.*)
important, importante
to **impose,** impor [102]
impossible, impossível
to **impregnate,** impregnar

to **impress,** impressionar
impressive, impressionante
improbable, improvável
to **improve,** melhorar
in, em
incapable, incapaz
to **incite,** incitar
inclined (to), disposto (a)
inclusive, inclusive (*adv.*)
to **increase,** aumentar
incredible, incrível
incumbent: to be incumbent, incumbir, competir, cumprir, caber
indeed, com efeito, de facto, na verdade, na realidade
index, índex (*m.*), índice (*m.*)
to **indicate,** indicar
to **induce,** induzir
inelastic, inelástico
infected, infecto
infection, infecção (*f.*)
to **infer,** arguir
inferior, inferior
to **infest,** empestar
to **influence,** influir em
to **inform,** avisar
information, informações (*f.*/ *pl.*)
to **infuse,** infundir
inhabitant, habitante (*m.*)
to **inherit,** herdar
inimitable, inimitável
to **inject,** injectar
ink, tinta (*f.*)
inn, estalagem (*f.*)
inner, interior
innocent, inocente
to **inquire,** perguntar
inquisitive, curioso
inside, dentro (de)
insignificant, insignificante
insipid, sensaborão
to **insist,** empenhar-se, ter empenho, insistir, porfiar, teimar

instant, instante (*m.*)
instead of, em vez de, em lugar de
to **instruct,** instruir
intelligent, inteligente
to **intend,** tencionar, pensar, pretender, intentar
intense, intenso, intensivo
interest, interesse (*m.*)
to **interest,** interessar
interested: to be interested in, interessar-se por, estar interessado em
interesting, interessante
to **interfere,** intervir [102]
interior, interior
interpreter, intérprete (*m.*)
intersection, intersecção (*f.*)
to **intervene,** intervir [102]
intimate, íntimo
into, a, em [241]
to **introduce,** apresentar
invasion, invasão (*f.*)
to **invent,** inventar
invention, invenção (*f.*)
invitation, convite (*m.*)
to **invite,** convidar
to **irk,** maçar, ralar
irreplaceable, insubstituível
Isabella, Isabel
Isidore, Isidoro
Isobel, Isabel
Italian, italiano
Italy, Itália (*f.*)

jacket, casaco (*m.*)
Japan, Japão (*m.*)
jealous, cioso, ciumento
Jew, judeu (*m.*)
Jewess, judia (*f.*)
Jewish, judeu
job, tarefa (*f.*) (*task*); emprego (*m.*) (*post*)
John, João

to **join,** juntar
journalist, jornalista (*m.*)
journey, viagem (*f.*)
joy, alegria (*f.*)
to **judge,** julgar
to **jump,** saltar
junior, júnior
just, em ponto; mesmo; justamente; **just as,** assim como; **to have just,** acabar de [132]
to **justify,** justificar

to **keep,** guardar, conservar; **keep well,** passar bem; **keep (on) -ing,** seguir + *gerund*; teimar em, persistir em
key, chave (*f.*)
to **kill,** matar
kilo(gramme), quilo(grama) (*m.*)
kilometre, quilómetro (*m.*)
kind, espécie (*f.*), tipo (*m.*); (*adj.*) bom, amável
kindness, bondade (*f.*)
king, rei (*m.*)
kitchen, cozinha (*f.*)
knack, jeito (*m.*)
to **kneel (down),** ajoelhar(-se)
knife, faca (*f.*)
to **knock (at the door),** bater (à porta)
to **know,** saber; conhecer; [135 (*a*) (1)] **know how to,** saber; **get to know,** conhecer
know-all, sabichão
known: well known, conhecido

lacerated, lacerado
lack, falta (*f.*)
to **lack,** carecer de; *via* faltar [127]
lacking: to be lacking, faltar
lactose, lactose (*f.*)
lady, senhora (*f.*), dama (*f.*)
lair, covil (*m.*)

lake, lago (*m.*)
land, terra (*f.*)
landscape, paisagem (*f.*)
language, língua (*f.*)
last, último, derradeiro, final, definitivo; passado, próximo passado; **at last,** por fim
late, tarde (*adv.*); **to be late,** chegar tarde
latest, último
latter, este
to **laugh,** rir; **laugh at,** rir-se de, mofar-se de, zombar de; rir-se com (*be amused by*)
law, lei (*f.*)
lawn, relva (*f.*)
to **lay waste,** ermar, devastar
lazy, preguiçoso
to **lead,** conduzir
leaf, folha (*f.*)
to **lean (on),** apoiar-se (em), arrimar-se (a); **lean against,** encostar-se a
to **learn,** aprender; saber, descobrir, inteirar-se (de)
least, menos; **at least,** ao menos, pelo menos
to **leave,** partir, ir(-se) embora; deixar; (*a place*) partir de, sair de; **leave aside,** prescindir de; **leave off,** deixar de
lecture, aula (*f.*), conferência (*f.*)
lecture-room, (sala de) aula (*f.*)
leeward, sotavento (*m.*)
left, esquerdo; **to be left,** sobrar, restar, ficar
left-handed, canhoto
leg, perna (*f.*)
legion, legião (*f.*)
to **lend,** emprestar
lengthy, comprido, longo

less, menos; **less and less,** cada vez menos
lesser, menor
lesson, lição (*f.*)
to let, deixar, permitir; (*lease*) alugar
lest, com medo (de) que
letter, carta (*f.*)
Lewis, Luís
liberty, liberdade (*f.*)
library, biblioteca (*f.*)
to lick, lamber
lie, mentira (*f.*); **to be a lie,** ser mentira
to lie, jazer; (*tell lies*) mentir
life, vida (*f.*)
to lift, levantar, erguer; **lift slightly,** soerguer
light, luz (*f.*); (*adj.*) ligeiro; claro
to light, acender
like, como; **like this (that),** assim; **to feel like,** sentir ganas (de)
to like, gostar de
likeable, simpático
lip, lábio (*m.*)
liquid, líquido
Lisbon, Lisboa (*f.*)
list, lista (*f.*)
to listen (to), escutar
literature, literatura (*f.*)
little, (*amount*) pouco; (*size*) pequeno; **a little,** um pouco (de), um bocado (de); **little boy,** rapazinho (*m.*); **little girl,** rapariguinha (*f.*)
to live, morar; viver
living: to earn one's living, ganhar a vida
to load, carregar
loaf, pão (*m.*), fogaça (*f.*)
to lodge, hospedar-se
lodging, alojamento (*m.*)
logical, lógico
London, Londres (*m.*)

long, longo, comprido
to long, anelar, ansiar, suspirar
to look, olhar; **look at,** olhar (para); examinar; **look after,** cuidar de; ocupar-se de (*or* em); **look for,** procurar, buscar; **look upon,** considerar; **look like,** parecer-se com; **look out on to,** dar para, deitar para, deitar sobre
lorry, caminhão (*m.*), camioneta (*f.*)
to lose, perder [173]
lot: a lot (of), *via* muito
loud, forte, alto
Louis, Luís
lounge, sala (*f.*) de visitas, sala (*f.*) de estar, salão (*m.*)
lout, homenzarrão (*m.*)
to love, amar
lovely, formoso, belo
low, baixo; **in a low voice,** baixinho (*adv.*)
lower, inferior, mais baixo
luck, sorte (*f.*)
lucky: to be lucky, ter sorte, estar com sorte
luggage, bagagem (*f.*)
lunch, almoço (*m.*)
to (have) lunch, almoçar
Luso-Brazilian, luso-brasileiro
luxe: de luxe, de luxo
luxury, luxo (*m.*)

machine, máquina (*f.*)
mad, maluco, doido, louco
madam, minha senhora
made: to be made of, ser de
magazine, revista (*f.*)
magnet, íman (*m.*), imã (*m.*)
maid, criada (*f.*), empregada (*f.*)
main, principal
mainly, mormente
to maintain, manter [102]

majordomo, mordomo (*m.*)
majority, maioria (*f.*)
man, homem (*m.*)
to **manage (to),** conseguir, lograr,
  poder, chegar (a)
manager, director (*m.*), gerente
  (*m.*)
to **manufacture,** fabricar
many, muitos; **how many,**
  quantos; **not many,** poucos;
  as (*or* **so**) **many,** tantos; **too
  many,** demasiados
many-coloured, multicor,
  multicolor
map, mapa (*m.*)
margin, margem (*f.*)
to **mark,** corrigir
market, mercado (*m.*)
to **marry,** casar(-se) [229]
marsh, paul (*m.*)
marshy: to make marshy,
  apaular
Martin, Martinho
to **marvel,** maravilhar-se
Mary, Maria
masterpiece, obra-prima (*f.*)
to **match,** condizer (com) [102]
matter, assunto (*m.*)
to **matter,** importar; **it doesn't
  matter,** não faz mal
maxim, máxima (*f.*)
meadow, prado (*m.*)
meal, refeição (*f.*); **to have a
  meal,** comer
to **measure,** medir [142]
meat, carne (*f.*) (de vaca)
to **mediate,** mediar
meditation, meditação (*f.*)
to **meet,** encontrar, encontrar-se
  com; **to go (come) to meet,**
  ir (vir) ao encontro de, ir
  (vir) ter com
meeting, reunião (*f.*)
melancholy, melancólico
memoir, memória (*f.*)

memory, memória (*f.*)
menace, ameaça (*f.*)
menu, ementa (*f.*), lista (*f.*)
Mexico, México (*m.*)
Michael, Miguel
midday, meio-dia (*m.*)
middle, meio (*m.*); meado (*m.*)
midnight, meia-noite (*f.*)
mile, milha (*f.*)
military, militar
milk, leite (*m.*)
Milky Way, Via (*f.*) Láctea
to **mind,** *via* não importar-se de
minister, ministro (*m.*)
minute, minuto (*m.*)
mirror, espelho (*m.*)
miscellaneous, diversos
to **miss,** perder (*transport*); (*long
  for*) sentir (a) falta de, ter
  saudades de
mistake, erro (*m.*)
mistaken: to be mistaken,
  enganar-se, estar enganado
to **misuse,** abusar de
to **mock,** mofar (-se de), zombar
  (de)
modern, moderno
moment, momento (*m.*)
money, dinheiro (*m.*)
monotonous, monótono
month, mês (*m.*)
monument, monumento (*m.*)
moon, Lua (*f.*)
moonlight, luar (*m.*), lua (*f.*)
Moor, Moiro (*m.*), Mouro
  (*m.*)
Moorish, moiro, mouro,
  moirisco, mourisco
more, mais; **more and more,**
  cada vez mais
morning, manhã (*f.*); (*early*)
  madrugada (*f.*); **good morning,** bom dia, bons dias
Morocco, Marrocos (*m.*)

most, mais; -íssimo [201 (*c*)]; a maioria (de), a maior parte (de)

mother, mãe (*f.*); madre (*religious*)

motionless, imóvel

motive, motivo (*m.*)

motor-coach, camioneta (*f.*)

motorist, motorista (*m.*)

to **mount,** subir a

mountain, montanha (*f.*)

mouse, ratinho (*m.*)

mouth, boca (*f.*)

to **move,** mover, bulir, mexer

Mozambique, Moçambique (*m.*)

much, muito; **very much,** muitíssimo

multicoloured, multicor, multicolor

music, música (*f.*)

mussel, mexilhão (*m.*)

must, *via* dever, ter que, ter de; **must not,** *via* não dever

mustard, mostarda (*f.*)

naked, nu [32 (3)]

name, nome (*m.*)

napkin, guardanapo (*m.*)

narrow, estreito

nation, nação (*f.*)

national, nacional

natural, natural

nature, natureza (*f.*)

near, perto (de); vizinho, próximo

nearby, pertinho (de)

nearly, quase; por pouco

necessary, necessário, preciso; **to be necessary,** ser preciso, ser necessário, precisar, *via* há que, *etc.* [126 (6) (v)]

necessity, necessidade (*f.*)

to **need,** precisar (de), necessitar (de)

to **negotiate,** negociar, comerciar

neighbour, vizinho (*m.*)

neighbouring, vizinho

neither, nem; também não, tão-pouco [76]

nervous, nervoso

never, nunca, jamais [76]

nevertheless, mas, porém, contudo, todavia, ainda assim, não obstante

new, novo

news, notícias (*f.*/*pl.*), novas (*f.*/*pl.*)

newspaper, jornal (*m.*)

newspaperman, jornalista (*m.*)

New York, Nova Iorque (*f.*)

next, (*adj.*) próximo; que vem; seguinte; imediato; (*adv.*) logo, pois, depois, em seguida, após o que, então; **next to,** ao lado de, junto a, junto de, ao pé de; **next door,** a casa (*f.*) vizinha

nice, bonito, lindo, bom; simpático (*likeable*)

night, noite (*f.*); **good night,** boa(s) noite(s); **last night,** ontem à noite

nightfall, anoitecer (*m.*)

nightingale, rouxinol (*m.*)

no, não; nenhum [76]; **no one,** ninguém [76]; **no more, no longer,** já não, não . . . mais

nobody, ninguém [76]

noise, ruído (*m.*), barulho (*m.*)

to **nominate,** nomear

noon, meio-dia (*m.*)

nor, nem [76]

normal, normal

north, norte (*m.*); **North America,** América (*f.*) do Norte; **North Africa,** África (*f.*) do Norte

North-American, norte-americano

north-east, nordeste (*m.*)
north-west, noroeste (*m.*)
not, não; **not even,** nem (sequer); **not yet,** ainda não; [76]
to **note,** notar
nothing, nada [76]
nothingness, nada (*m.*)
notice, letreiro (*m.*), aviso (*m.*)
to **notice,** advertir, dar por, reparar em, notar, observar
notwithstanding, não obstante
novel, romance (*m.*)
now, agora, já
nowhere, em nenhuma parte; nenhures (*literary*)
nuance, matiz (*m.*)
number, número (*m.*); **a number of,** uns (quantos)
nude, nu [32 (3)]

oak (tree), carvalho (*m.*)
oasis, oásis (*m.*)
to **obey,** obedecer [229 (*c*)]
object, objecto (*m.*)
to **object,** opor-se [102]
objection, objecção (*f.*)
obligation, obrigação (*f.*)
to **oblige,** obrigar
oblique, oblíquo
to **observe,** observar
obstacle, obstáculo (*m.*)
to **obstruct,** obstruir
to **obtain,** obter [102], adquirir, conseguir **obvious,** evidente, manifesto, óbvio
occasion: on this occasion, desta feita, desta vez
to **occupy,** ocupar
to **occur,** ocorrer
octagonal, octogonal
octogenarian, octogenário (*m.*)
odd, curioso, estranho
of, de
off, de

to **offer,** oferecer; deparar, proporcionar
office, escritório (*m.*)
officer, oficial (*m.*)
official, oficial (*m.*)
often, muitas vezes, amiúde, a miúdo, com frequência
old, velho, antigo; **old age,** velhice (*f.*); **old man,** velho (*m.*), velhote (*m.*); **old woman,** velha (*f.*), velhota (*f.*); **dear old,** velhinho; **to grow old,** envelhecer; **to be. .. years old,** ter ... anos (de idade)
on, em, sobre, em cima de [145 (*c*)]; **on foot,** a pé
once, uma vez; **once more,** outra vez, mais uma vez
only, (*adj.*) só, sozinho, único; (*adv.*) apenas, só, somente, tão somente, unicamente; *via* não ... mais que, não ... senão
onomatopoeic, onomatopeico
onward, avante
onyx, ónix (*m.*)
open, aberto
to **open,** abrir
opera, ópera (*f.*)
operation, operação (*f.*)
opinion, opinião (*f.*); **in my opinion,** a meu ver
Oporto, o Porto (*m.*)
opportune, oportuno
opportunity, ocasião (*f.*), oportunidade (*f.*)
to **oppose,** opor-se a [102]
opposite, em frente (de), defronte (de)
to **opt,** optar
optical, óptico
optics, óptica (*f.*)
optimism, optimismo (*m.*)
optimist, optimista (*m.*)
optimistic, optimista

optimum, óptimo
option, opção (*f.*)
or, ou; quer [194 (*e*)]
oracle, oráculo (*m.*)
orange, laranja (*f.*)
order, ordem (*f.*); **in order to,** para, a fim de; **in order that,** para que, a fim (de) que
to **order,** ordenar, mandar, dar ordem, dizer, encomendar, pedir
organization, organização (*f.*)
origin, origem (*f.*)
to **originate,** provir [102]
orphan, órfão (*m.*), órfã (*f.*)
orthography, ortografia (*f.*)
other, outro; **others,** outros, outrem; **other people,** outrem; **each other,** [139]
otherwise, aliás, doutra maneira, doutro modo
ought, dever [156 (*c*)]
out, fora (de); **out of** (*because of*), por; **out and out,** de todo em todo
outer, exterior
outside, (cá) fora, (lá) fora
oven, forno (*m.*)
over, por cima de, por sobre
overcast, carregado
overcoat, sobretudo (*m.*)
to **overcome,** vencer
to **overload,** sobrecarregar
to **overlook,** dar para, deitar para, deitar sobre
own, próprio
owner, dono (*m.*), proprietário (*m.*)
ox, boi (*m.*)
oxygen, oxigénio (*m.*)

to **pacify,** aplacar
to **pack,** fazer (uma mala, as malas), arrumar (uma mala, as malas)

package, pacote (*m.*)
packet, pacote (*m.*)
pact, pacto (*m.*)
page, página (*f.*)
painless, indolor
to **paint,** pintar
pale, pálido
pallid, pálido
paper, papel (*m.*); (*newspaper*) jornal (*m.*)
to **paralyse,** paralisar, entrevar
parcel, embrulho (*m.*), encomenda (*f.*)
pardon, perdão (*m.*)
to **pardon,** perdoar [204 (*c*)]
parents, pais (*m./pl.*)
park, parque (*m.*)
part, parte (*f.*)
in particular, sobretudo
party, festa (*f.*)
to **pass,** passar; entregar; **pass an exam,** ser aprovado num exame
passerby, transeunte (*m.*)
past, passado (*m.*); passado (*adj.*)
pasteboard, papelão (*m.*)
path, senda (*f.*), caminho (*m.*)
to **pay (for),** pagar; **pay one's respects (to),** cumprimentar, saudar [217]
pea, ervilha (*f.*)
peace, paz (*f.*)
peach, pêssego (*m.*)
pear, pêra (*f.*)
pebble, pedrinha (*f.*)
to **peel,** pelar [218]
pen, caneta (*f.*)
pencil, lápis (*m.*)
to **penetrate,** penetrar (em)
peninsula, península (*f.*)
pensive, pensativo
people, gente (*f.*); povo (*m.*)
pepper, pimenta (*f.*)

to **perceive,** perceber
perfect, perfeito
perfectible, perfectível
perhaps, talvez
peril, perigo (*m.*)
period, período (*m.*), época (*f.*)
permission, licença (*f.*)
to **permit,** permitir [p. 274]
to **persecute,** perseguir
to **persevere,** perseverar
Persian, persa
to **persist,** persistir, teimar
person, pessoa (*f.*)
to **persuade,** persuadir
pessimist, pessimista (*m.*)
pessimistic, pessimista
Peter, Pedro, Pêro
Philip, Filipe
phoenix, fénix (*f.*)
photo, foto (*f.*)
phrase, frase (*f.*)
to **pick,** escolher, eleger; **pick up,**
apanhar, pegar em
pickle, escabeche (*m.*)
pictorial, pictórico
picture, quadro (*m.*), gravura
(*f.*)
picturesque, pitoresco
pie, empada (*f.*)
piebald, pedrês
pig, porco
pity: it's a pity, é pena
to **placate,** aplacar
place, lugar (*m.*); **in place of**
me, em meu lugar; **in the**
first place, em primeiro
lugar
to **place,** pôr, meter, colocar;
place underneath, sotopor
[102]
plan, projecto (*m.*)
planet, planeta (*m.*)
plate, prato (*m.*)
platform, cais (*m.*)

to **play,** jogar (*games*), brincar
playful, brincalhão
pleasant, agradável
please, faz favor [196]
to **please,** agradar, alegrar,
aprazer, comprazer
pleased: to be pleased,
alegrar-se
pleasure, prazer (*m.*), gosto
(*m.*); **to take pleasure in,**
comprazer-se em, ter gosto
(*or* prazer) em
plenty, muitos; *via* sobrar
[127]; (*noun*) fartura (*f.*)
plethora, pletora (*f.*)
pocket, algibeira (*f.*)
poem, (*epic*) poema (*m.*), (*lyric*)
poesia (*f.*)
poet, poeta (*m.*)
poetess, poetisa (*f.*)
poetry, poesia (*f.*)
point: to be on the point
of, estar para, estar a ponto
de
to **point out,** indicar
police, polícia (*f.*)
policeman, polícia (*m.*)
policy, política (*f.*)
to **polish,** polir, engraixar
polite, cortês, polido
politeness, cortesia (*f.*)
political, político
politics, política (*f.*)
to **ponder (over),** pensar, ruminar
ponderous, ponderoso
poor, pobre
pope, papa (*m.*)
population, população (*f.*)
port, porto (*m.*)
portion, dose (*f.*)
Portugal, Portugal
Portuguese, português
Port wine, vinho (*m.*) do Porto
position, situação (*f.*)

to possess, possuir [214]
possibility, possibilidade (*f.*)
possible, possível
postcard, (bilhete) postal (*m.*)
posterior, posteriór
postman, carteiro (*m.*)
post-office, correio (*m.*),
   estação (*f.*) de (*or* do) correio
to postpone, adiar
potato, batata (*f.*)
potion, mezinha (*f.*)
power, poder (*m.*)
practical, prático
practice, prática (*f.*)
to praise, louvar
to pray, rezar, orar
prayer, oração (*f.*), reza (*f.*)
to preach, pregar
precise, preciso
to predict, predizer [102]
to prefer, preferir [110]
to prepare, preparar; preparar-se
   (para)
present, presente, actual (*adj.*);
   presente (*m.*)
to present, apresentar; presentear
   [229 (*c*)]
presently, logo
to preside, presidir [231 (*b*)]
president, presidente (*m.*)
to presume, presumir
to pretend, fingir
pretext, pretexto (*m.*)
pretty, bonito, lindo (*adj.*);
   bastante (*adv.*)
to prevent, impedir, empecer,
   tolher [174 (3) (ii)]
previously, antes, dantes,
   anteriormente
price, preço (*m.*)
priest, cura (*m.*)
priggish, sabichão
principal, principal
prison, cárcere (*m.*)
probable, provável

problem, problema (*m.*),
   questão (*f.*)
to produce, produzir
production, produção (*f.*)
to profit (by, from), aproveitar;
   aproveitar-se (de)
profitable: to be profitable,
   aproveitar
profound, profundo
programme, programa (*m.*)
to progress, progredir [111 (*d*)]
to prohibit, proibir [174 (3) (ii)]
project, projecto (*m.*)
to promise, prometer
prompt, pronto
to pronounce, pronunciar
proof, prova (*f.*)
to propose, propor [102]; **propose
   to,** propor-se
to protect, proteger
to prove (*turn out*), tornar-se
to provide, prover [193], abas-
   tecer, fornecer
provided (that), contanto que,
   sempre que
province, província (*f.*)
prudent, prudente
public, público (*m.*); **reading
   public,** público ledor
to publish, publicar
to pull, puxar, tirar; **pull at** (*or*
   on), puxar de, tirar de
to punish, castigar, punir
pure, puro
to pursue, perseguir
to purvey, prover [193]
to put, pôr, meter, colocar; **put an
   end to,** acabar com; **put
   away,** guardar, arrumar; **put
   down,** pousar, assentar,
   depor; **put on,** pôr, vestir;
   put out, apagar; **put right,**
   consertar, arranjar, regular;
   put up, hospedar-se; **put up
   with,** aguentar, suportar

quaint, engraçado
to quarrel, brigar
quarter, quarto (m.); bairro (m.)
quay, cais (m.)
queen, rainha (f.)
question, pergunta (f.); to ask (or put) a question, fazer uma pergunta
to question, duvidar (de); interrogar
questionnaire, questionário (m.)
quick, rápido
quickly, depressa, rápido, rapidamente, à pressa
quiet, tranquilo

radio, rádio (f.); (set) rádio (m.)
rain, chuva (f.)
to rain, chover
to raise, erguer, levantar; raise slightly, soerguer
range (of mountains), serra (f.)
rare, raro; (underdone) mal-passado
rascal, brejeiro (m.)
rat, ratazana (f.)
rather, algo, um tanto, algum tanto; (preferably) antes; via preferir
raw, cru [32 (3)]
to reach, chegar a
to react, reagir
to read, ler [24]
read: well read (in), bem lido (em)
reader, leitor (m.)
reading public, público (m.) ledor
real, real (m.); (adj.) verdadeiro
to realize, dar-se conta
really, deveras; está feito!
reason, motivo (m.); razão (f.)
to receive, receber
recent, último, recente

recently, ultimamente
reclining, reclinado
to recognize, reconhecer
to recommend, recomendar
red, vermelho, encarnado; (of wine) tinto
to redouble, amiudar
to reflect, reflectir [193]
reflex, reflexo (m.)
to refuse, negar-se, recusar
regard: with regard to, (em) quanto a
region, região (f.)
to regret, sentir, arrepender-se (de)
to rejoice, alegrar-se, folgar
to relate, contar
relation, relação (f.); parente (m.)
relative, parente (m.)
to relieve, sossegar
religion, religião (f.)
to rely on, contar com
to remain, ficar, permanecer, restar, sobrar
to remark, observar
remedy, remédio (m.)
to remember, lembrar(-se), recordar(-se); via lembrar used impersonally [174 (1) (i)]
to renounce, renunciar (a)
to rent, alugar
to repeat, repetir [110]
to repent, arrepender-se
reply, resposta (f.)
to reply, responder
to reprehend, repreender
representative, representante (m.)
to reproach, ralhar
to reprove, reprovar
to request, pedir, rogar; requerer
to require, necessitar (de), precisar (de), requerer [193]
to re-read, reler [102]

to resemble, parecer-se (com)

to reside, morar, residir

to resign oneself, resignar-se, contentar-se

to resist, resistir (a)

to resolve, resolver(-se)

respect, respeito (*m.*); **to pay one's respects (to),** saudar, cumprimentar

to rest, descansar

restaurant, restaurante (*m.*), casa (*f.*) de pasto

result, resultado (*m.*)

to resume (*summarize*), resumir

to retain, reter [102]

to retire, retirar-se; (*from working*) reformar-se

to retort, retorquir, redarguir

retrospection, retrospecção (*f.*)

to return, voltar, regressar; (*give back*) devolver, restituir, tornar

to reveal, revelar

reverie, devaneio (*m.*)

revolution, revolução (*f.*)

revolver, revólver (*m.*)

to reward, premiar

rhetoric, retórica (*f.*)

rice, arroz (*m.*)

rich, rico

to ride, passear (a cavalo, de carro, etc.)

to ridicule, zombar de

ridiculous, ridículo

right, direito; **right you are,** está dito; **right from the start,** logo de princípio; **to be right,** ter (*or* estar com) razão; **to be right to,** fazer bem em

ripe, maduro

risk, risco (*m.*)

rival, rival (*m.*)

river, rio (*m.*)

road, caminho (*m.*); rua (*f.*); (*main road*) estrada (*f.*)

to roar, bramir, rugir

to roast, assar

to rob, roubar, furtar

roll, pãozinho (*m.*)

room, sala (*f.*), quarto (*m.*), divisão (*f.*)

round, ao redor de, em redor de, à roda de; (*through*) por; **to walk round,** dar a volta a

to row, remar

to ruin, arruinar

rule, regra (*f.*), cânon (*m.*); **as a rule,** como regra geral; de costume

to rule, reger, governar

to run, correr; **run away,** fugir, abalar; **run to help,** acudir a; **run into,** dar com, encontrar-se com, tropeçar com; **run risks,** correr riscos

Russia, Rússia (*f.*)

Russian, russo

sacrifice, sacrifício (*m.*)

sad, triste

sadness, tristeza (*f.*)

Saint, Santo, São, Santa [105 (6)]

sake, *via* por; **for my sake,** por minha causa

salad, salada (*f.*)

salt, sal (*m.*)

same, mesmo [38 (3)]

sardine, sardinha (*f.*)

to satisfy, satisfazer [102]

sauce, molho (*m.*)

saucer, pires (*m.*)

savage, selvagem

to save, poupar; (*rescue*) salvar

saw, serra (*f.*)

Saxon, saxão, saxónio, saxónico

to say, dizer; **say to oneself,** dizer (de si) para si, dizer consigo, dizer entre si

scarcely, mal; apenas

scenery, paisagem (f.)

sceptre, ceptro (m.)

school, escola (f.)

schoolmaster, mestre-escola (m.), professor (m.)

scientist, cientista (m.)

to scold, ralhar

to scorn, desprezar

scoundrel, brejeiro (m.), malandro (m.)

scream, grito (m.)

sculptor, escultor (m.)

sea, mar (m.)

seat, assento (m.); **to take a seat,** tomar assento; **to seat,** sentar

secret, segredo (m.)

secretary, secretário (m.)

section, secção (f.)

sectional, seccional

sector, sector (m.)

to see, ver; **see off,** despedir-se de; **see you (later),** até à vista; **seeing that,** visto que, já que

to seek, procurar, buscar

to seem, parecer

to seize, apanhar, pegar em, apoderar-se de, apossar-se de, prender

self, mesmo [38 (3)]

to sell, vender

to send, mandar, enviar, expedir; **send for,** mandar chamar, mandar buscar; **send away,** mandar embora

senior, sénior

to sense, sentir [110]

sentence, frase (f.)

sergeant, sargento (m.)

serious, sério

seriously, a sério

servant, criado (m.), criada (f.)

to serve, servir

to set, pôr, meter, colocar; (of sun) pôr-se; **set alight,** acender; **set down,** pousar, assentar; **set loose,** soltar; **set out,** dispor; meter-se a caminho; **set up,** estabelecer

to settle, assentar

settled, combinado, ajustado

several, vários

severe, severo

Seville, Sevilha (f.)

sexual, sexual

shade, sombra (f.)

shaggy, felpudo

to shake, sacudir

shame: it's a shame, é pena

to shatter, esmiuçar

to (have a) shave, fazer a barba, barbear-se

to sheathe, embainhar

sheet, lençol (m.)

shelf, estante (f.), prateleira (f.)

shepherd, pastor (m.)

to shine, luzir, brilhar; engraixar (shoes)

shiny, lustroso

shirt, camisa (f.)

shirtfront, peitilho (m.)

shoe, sapato (m.)

shop, loja (f.)

shopkeeper, lojista (m.)

shopping: to do the shopping, (ir) fazer compras, ir às compras

short, curto, breve

shortly afterwards, pouco depois, logo depois

shoulder, ombro (m.)

shout, grito (m.)

shovel, pá (f.)

shovelful, pazada (f.)

to show, mostrar

to shut, fechar
  side, lado (*m.*); **at the side of,** ao lado de; **on the side of,** do lado de; **on this side of,** deste lado; aquém de; **on both sides,** de ambos os lados; **from side to side,** de lado a lado
to sigh, suspirar
  sight, vista (*f.*)
  silence, silêncio (*m.*)
  simple, simples, singelo
  since, desde; desde que (*temporal*); pois que, porquanto (*causal*)
  sincerity, sinceridade (*f.*)
to sing, cantar
  sir, senhor (*m.*), *via* Vossa Excelência
  sister, irmã (*f.*); Sor, Sóror (*religious*)
to sit (down), sentar-se; **to be sitting (seated),** estar sentado
  sitting-room, sala (*f.*) de estar
to situate, situar
  situation, situação (*f.*)
  skilful, hábil
  skill, jeito (*m.*)
  skirt, saia (*f.*); aba (*f.*)
  skull, caveira (*f.*)
  sky, céu (*m.*)
  skylight, clarabóia (*f.*)
  slack, frouxo
  sleep, sono (*m.*); **to go to sleep,** adormecer, pegar no sono
to sleep, dormir
  sleepy: to be sleepy, ter (*or* estar com) sono; **to feel sleepy,** sentir sono
  slender, esguio, esbelto, delgado, franzino; **to make slender,** esbeltar
  slim, esbelto, franzino

slowly, devagar
to slump, afundar-se
  slut, mazona (*f.*), mulherzinha (*f.*)
to smack (of), saber (a)
  small, pequeno
  smaller, menor; mais pequeno
  smallest, menor; mais pequeno
to smell (of), cheirar (a)
  smile, sorriso (*m.*)
to smile, sorrir; **smile at,** sorrir-se com
to smoke, fumar
  snag, inconveniente (*m.*)
  snap, foto (*f.*)
to snatch, arrebatar
  so, assim, assim pois, por isso, porisso, portanto, pois; tão; **who said so?** quem o disse?; **so long,** até logo; **so much,** tanto; **so many,** tantos
  soaked, encharcado
  softly (*of voice*), baixinho
  soldier, soldado (*m.*)
  solidarity, solidariedade (*f.*)
  solution, solução (*f.*)
to solve, resolver
  some, algum; alguns; uns
  somebody, alguém
  someone, alguém
  something, alguma coisa, algo
  sometimes, às vezes, por vezes, algumas vezes, alguma vez, de vez em quando
  somewhat, algo, um tanto, algum tanto
  somewhere, nalguma parte, algures
  son, filho (*m.*)
  song, canção (*f.*)
  soon, (em) breve, dentro em breve, dentro em pouco, logo; **soon after,** logo depois, pouco depois

sorry: to be sorry, arrepender-se, sentir (muito); **to be sorry about,** sentir, lamentar; **to be sorry for,** compadecer-se de; **sorry!** desculpe, perdão, perdoe-me

sort, espécie (*f.*), tipo (*m.*), género (*m.*)

soul, alma (*f.*)

sound, são; sadio; profundo

to sound, soar

soup, sopa (*f.*)

south, sul (*m.*); **South Africa,** África (*f.*) do Sul; **South America,** América (*f.*) do Sul

South-American, americano, sul-americano

south-east, sueste (*m.*)

southern, meridional

south-west, sudoeste (*m.*)

Spain, Espanha (*f.*)

Spaniard, espanhol (*m.*)

Spanish, espanhol

to speak, falar

species, espécie (*f.*)

spell, temporada (*f.*)

spelling, ortografia (*f.*)

to spend, passar, levar (*time*); gastar, despender (*money*); **spend the night,** pernoitar

spheroidal, esferoidal

spin: to go for a spin, dar uma volta

to spin, fiar, dobar

to spit, cuspir

spite: in spite of, apesar de, não obstante

spontaneity, espontaneidade (*f.*)

spoon, colher (*f.*)

spoonful, colherada (*f.*)

sport, desporto (*m.*)

to sprinkle, aspergir

square, praça (*f.*), largo (*m.*)

to stack away, arrumar

stagnant, choco

to stand, estar, ficar de pé; aguentar, suportar; **stand out,** destacar-se

standing, em pé, de pé

to starch, engomar

to stare (at), fitar

to start, *see* **to begin**

station, estação (*f.*)

stay, estada (*f.*), permanência (*f.*)

to stay, ficar, permanecer; estar

steak, bife (*m.*)

to steal, furtar, roubar

step, passo (*m.*); **to take a step,** dar um passo

Stephen, Estêvão

sterile, estéril

stick, bengala (*f.*)

still, ainda (*temporal*); todavia, ainda assim (*concessive*)

to stir, mexer, bulir, mover(-se)

stone, pedra (*f.*)

to stop, parar [218], deter-se [102]; ficar

storey, andar (*m.*)

story, história (*f.*)

straight, direito, directamente

strange, estranho, curioso

street, rua (*f.*)

strength, forças (*f./pl.*)

to strike, dar (as horas) [74 (*d*)]

to strive, esforçar-se

to stroll, passear

strong, forte

to struggle, lutar

student, estudante (*m.*)

study, estudo (*m.*)

to study, estudar

to stumble, tropeçar

stupid, estúpido

stupidity, estupidez (*f.*)

subject, assunto (*m.*); matéria (*f.*) (*academic*)

to subject, sujeitar

to substitute, substituir
to succeed, ter êxito; **succeed in,** conseguir, lograr
success, êxito (*m.*)
successful: to be successful, ter êxito
such, tal, semelhante; tão
suction, sucção (*f.*)
suddenly, de repente, (de) súbito, (vai) senão quando
to suffice, chegar, bastar
sufficient, suficiente
sugar, açúcar (*m.*)
to suggest, sugerir
suit, fato (*m.*)
to suit, ficar bem a
suitable, oportuno
sultry, abafado
to summarize, resumir
sun, Sol (*m.*)
to sun-bathe, tomar o sol (*or* banhos de sol)
sunlight, sol (*m.*)
sunny: to be sunny, fazer sol
sunshine, sol (*m.*)
superior, superior
supper, ceia (*f.*); **to have supper,** cear
supplementary, suplementar
to support, apoiar
to suppose, supor [102]
surface, superfície (*f.*)
surprise, surpresa (*f.*)
to surprise, surpreender
surprised: to be surprised (at), estranhar
to surround, rodear
to survive, sobreviver
to sustain, suster [102]
sward, relva (*f.*), relvado (*m.*)
sward-like, relvoso
sweet, doce
to swim, nadar
Swiss, suíço

to switch off, apagar (*light*); desligar (*radio*); **switch on,** acender (*light*); ligar (*radio*)
Switzerland, Suíça (*f.*)
syntax, sintaxe (*f.*)

table, mesa (*f.*); **to lay (set) the table,** pôr a mesa; **to clear the table,** levantar a mesa
tablecloth, toalha (*f.*) de mesa
Tagus, Tejo (*m.*)
to take, levar; tomar; tirar; **take a course,** tirar um curso; **take an exam.,** fazer um exame; **take an interest in,** interessar-se por; **take a seat,** tomar assento; **take a step,** dar um passo; **take a trip,** fazer uma viagem; fazer uma excursão; **take away,** tirar, levar embora; **take good care not to,** guardar-se de; **take into account,** levar em conta; **take note of,** reparar em; **take off,** tirar, despir; **take out,** tirar (de), puxar (de); **take pity on,** compadecer-se de; **take place,** suceder, verificar-se, passar-se, realizar-se; **take revenge for** (*or* **on**), vingar-se de; **take risks,** tomar riscos; **take root,** enraizar; **take seriously,** tomar a sério; **take time,** levar tempo; tardar a
taken for granted, subentendido
to talk, falar; **talk about,** falar de, em, sobre, acerca de; **talk to,** falar a, falar com
talkative, falador
tall, alto
to tally, condizer [102]

to tame, domar

tankard, pichel (*m.*), caneca (*f.*)

task, tarefa (*f.*)

taste, gosto (*m.*)

to taste (of), saber (a)

taxi, táxi (*m.*), carro (*m.*) de aluguel, carro (*m.*) de aluguer

tea, chá (*m.*); **to have tea,** tomar chá; **cup of tea,** chavena (*f.*) de chá

to teach, ensinar

teacher, professor (*m.*)

teacup, chávena (*f.*)

tear, lágrima (*f.*)

to tear (up), rasgar; **tear asunder, apart,** romper

telegram, telegrama (*m.*)

to telephone, telefonar

television, televisão (*f.*)

to tell, dizer, contar

temperature, temperatura (*f.*)

temple, templo (*m.*)

to tempt, tentar

tendency, tendência (*f.*)

terrible, terrível

text, texto (*m.*)

textile, tecido (*m.*), têxtil (*m.*)

Thames, Tamisa (*m.*)

than, [199] do que; que; de; a; senão; quando

to thank, dar graças a, agradecer

thank you, thanks, obrigado, -a

that: that's that, tenho dito, e lá se arranjam; **like that,** assim

theatre, teatro (*m.*)

then, então, nessa altura; logo, pois, depois, em seguida, então

there, aí, ali, acolá, lá [98]; **there is,** *etc.*, *via* haver

thick, espesso; grosso

thin, delgado, magro

thing, coisa (*f.*)

to think, pensar, julgar, cuidar, *via* parecer [127]

three-tone, tricolor

this: like this, assim

thorax, tórax (*m.*)

though, ainda que, embora, posto que, conquanto, se bem que [p. 304]

thought, pensamento (*m.*)

thoughtful, pensativo

threat, ameaça (*f.*)

to threaten, ameaçar

threshold, limiar (*m.*)

through, por, através de

to throw, deitar, lançar, atirar

thus, assim

to tie, atar

tight, apertado

till, até; até que

time, tempo (*m.*); vez (*f.*); horas (*f./pl.*); época (*f.*); temporada (*f.*)

tip, gorjeta (*f.*)

to tire, cansar

tired, cansado; **to get tired of,** cansar-se de, fartar-se de

tiresome, cansativo, maçador

to, a, para

today, hoje

together, junto(s)

tomato, tomate (*m.*)

tomorrow, amanhã

tongue, língua (*f.*)

tonight, esta noite (*f.*)

too, demais; muito; também; **too much,** demasiado; (*adv.*) demais; **too many,** demasiados

toothbrush, escova (*f.*) de (*or* dos) dentes

top, alto (*m.*); **on top of,** em cima de, ao alto de, no alto de

total, total

tourist, turista (*m.*)

towards, para, em direcção a, na direcção de; para com (*of behaviour, attitude*)

tower, torre (*f.*)

town, cidade (*f.*); (*small township*) vila (*f.*); **to go into town,** ir para a cidade, ir ao centro

to trade, comerciar

train, comboio (*m.*)

tram, (carro) (*m.*) eléctrico

tranquil, tranquilo

to transgress, transgredir

to translate, traduzir, verter

translation, tradução (*f.*), versão (*f.*)

to travel, viajar

tray, bandeja (*f.*)

to treat, tratar

tree, árvore (*f.*)

to tremble, tremer

tremendous, tremendo

tribe, tribo (*f.*)

trip: to take a trip, fazer uma viagem; **to go on a trip,** fazer uma excursão

to triumph, triunfar

trousers, calças (*f./pl.*)

true, certo, seguro, verdadeiro; **to be true,** ser verdade

truly, deveras

trunk, baú (*m.*)

trust, confiança (*f.*)

to trust, fiar-se de (*or* em), confiar (-se) em

truth, verdade (*f.*)

to try, tentar, procurar

to tug, puxar (de), tirar (de)

tumult, tumulto (*m.*)

turf-like, relvoso

to turn, voltar-se; **turn round,** voltar-se; **turn towards (to, on),** voltar-se para

twice, duas vezes

twin-engined, bimotor

to twist, torcer

twisted, torto

two-tone, bicolor

type, tipo (*m.*)

ulterior, ulterior

umbrella, guarda-chuva (*m.*)

unbelievable, incrível, inacreditável

uncle, tio (*m.*)

to uncover, descobrir

under, sob, debaixo de; por baixo de

underdone, mal passado

underneath, sob, debaixo de; por baixo de

to understand, compreender, entender, perceber

understanding, compreensão (*f.*)

to undertake, encarregar-se, comprometer-se

to undo, desfazer [102]; desatar

to undress, despir [110]

undressed: to get undressed, despir-se

unfortunately, infelizmente

unheeded, inobservado

to unite, unir

United States of America, Estados (*m./pl.*) Unidos da América

university, universidade (*f.*)

unless, a não ser que, a menos que

unlikeable, antipático

unlikely, improvável

unobserved, inobservado; despercebido

unoccupied, livre, vago

until, até; até que

untrue: to be untrue, ser mentira

unusual, extraordinário

515

up: up here, cá em cima; **up there,** lá em cima; **to get up,** levantar-se; **to wake up,** acordar, despertar; **up to,** até (a)

upholstery, estofos (*m.*/*pl.*)

upon, sobre

upper, superior, de cima

upstairs, cá em cima, lá em cima; para cima; **from upstairs,** de cima

urchin, brejeiro (*m.*)

to urge, animar

use: to be of no use, não prestar

to use, usar, utilizar, empregar, servir-se de, valer-se de

useful, útil

useless, inútil

usually, *via* costumar

utter, total

to utilize, utilizar

to vacillate, vacilar

vagrant, vadio (*m.*)

vague, vago

vain, vão

valley, vale (*m.*)

value, valor (*m.*)

to value, orçar

variety, variedade (*f.*)

various, diversos; vários (*after noun*)

vegetable, legume (*m.*); vegetal (*adj.*)

vehement, veemente

very, muito; mui [240]; mesmo, próprio; verdadeiro

view, vista (*f.*)

village, aldeia (*f.*), vila (*f.*)

vine-harvest, vindima (*f.*)

vineyard, vinhedo (*m.*)

virtue, virtude (*f.*)

virus, vírus (*m.*)

visit, visita (*f.*); **to pay a visit,** fazer uma visita

to visit, visitar

visitor, visita (*f.*), visitante (*m.*)

voice, voz (*f.*)

wage(s), salário (*m.*)

to wait, esperar; ficar

waiter, criado (*m.*)

waitress, criada (*f.*)

to wake up, despertar, acordar

walk: to go for a walk, dar um passeio

to walk, andar, passear, caminhar

wall, parede (*f.*)

to wander, errar, vagar, vaguear

to want, querer, desejar, ter vontade de

war, guerra (*f.*)

warm, morno

to warm, aquecer, esquentar

to warn, advertir, avisar, prevenir

to wash, lavar

washout, maçada (*f.*); fracasso (*m.*)

to waste, malgastar, desperdiçar; gastar, despender (*not money*); perder (*time*)

watch, relógio (*m.*)

to watch, olhar (para), ver, contemplar

water, água (*f.*)

to wave, agitar a mão

way, caminho (*m.*); maneira (*f.*), modo (*m.*), jeito (*m.*); **(in) this way,** desta maneira; **this way,** por aqui; **way out,** saída (*f.*); **to make one's way,** dirigir-se, encaminhar-se

to wear, trazer, vestir, usar

weasel, doninha (*f.*)

week, semana (*f.*)

to weep, chorar

well, poço (*m.*); (*adv.*) bem; (*interjection*) pois; **well known,** conhecido; **well read,** bem lido; **well versed,** bem versado; **as well** (*also*), também

west, oeste (*m.*)

wet, molhado

what, que, o que; qual [57]; **what for,** porque; porquê; para que

when, quando

whence, donde

whenever, quando, sempre que; quando quer que

where, onde; **where from,** donde; **where to,** aonde, para onde

wherever, onde quer que; onde

whether, se; quer [194 (*e*)]

which, que; qual [57]

while, temporado (*f.*); enquanto

whimsical, esdrúxulo

white, branco

whole, inteiro, todo

wholesome, sadio

who, quem, que, o qual [232]

whom, (a) quem, que, o qual [232]

whose, (*relative*) cujo; (*interrogative*) de quem

why, porque, porquê

wide, largo

width, largura (*f.*)

wife, esposa (*f.*), senhora (*f.*), mulher (*f.*)

wild, selvagem, bravo

Wilhelmina, Guilhermina

will, vontade (*f.*)

willingly, de boa vontade, com muito gosto

to win, ganhar

wind, vento (*m.*)

to wind up, dar corda a

window, janela (*f.*)

windy: to be windy, fazer vento, ventar

wine, vinho (*m.*)

wineglass, cálice (*m.*) (*for Port wine*); taça (*f.*) (*for champagne*); *otherwise* copo (*m.*)

wine-harvest, vindima (*f.*)

wing, asa (*f.*)

to wipe (dry), enxugar

wireless, rádio (*f.*); (*set*) rádio (*m.*)

wireless telegraphy, radiotelegrafia (*f.*)

wise, prudente, sábio

to wish, desejar

with, com

to withdraw, retirar-se

within, dentro (de)

without, sem; sem que [181 (*g*) (2)]

witness, testemunha (*f.*)

to witness, presenciar

woman, mulher (*f.*)

to wonder, maravilhar-se; perguntar a si mesmo (*or* próprio)

wont: to be wont to, costumar

wood, madeira (*f.*); bosque (*m.*)

wool, lã (*f.*)

word, palavra (*f.*)

work, trabalho (*m.*); obra (*f.*)

to work, trabalhar

worker, operário (*m.*)

workman, operário (*m.*)

world, mundo (*m.*)

to worry, preocupar; preocuparse

worse, pior

worst, pior

worth: to be worth, valer; **not to be worth it** (*or* **the trouble**), não valer a pena

worthless, reles

to wrap (up), envolver

wrinkle, gelha (*f.*)
to **wrinkle,** franzir, engelhar
to **write,** escrever
  writer, escritor (*m.*)
  wrong, erróneo, incorrecto; falso; **to be wrong,** não ter razão, não estar com razão, enganar-se, estar enganado; **to be wrong in** (*or* **to**), fazer mal em

xylophone, xilofone (*m.*)

year, ano (*m.*); **in the year . . .,** no ano de . . .
yellow, amarelo
to **yelp,** ganir
yes, sim; pois; [206]
yesterday, ontem
yet, ainda; contudo, todavia, porém
young, novo, jovem
younger, mais novo
youth, juventude (*f.*); (*young man*) jovem (*m.*)

INDEX

The references are to paragraphs and their sub-sections (N. = Note).   The treatment of peculiarities pertaining to individual words is mainly referred to in the preceding Vocabularies.

521